Software for The Complete Investment Book: All the programs on disk and ready to go.

The Complete Investment Book • Box 205 • Short Hills, NJ 07078

Please send me:

PROGRAMS ON DISK

All the programs from *The Complete Investment Book,* including a set of sample runs.

☐ IBM PC ☐ Apple II (80 Column Board required) $67.50

THE COMPLETE INTEGRATED PROGRAM PACKAGE $90

A disk containing a Master Menu Program, File Access
(for data storage and management), and Graphics.

☐ IBM PC ☐ Apple II (80 Column Board required)

☐ My check is enclosed (with this card)

Charge to my account: ☐ Master Card   ☐ Visa   ☐ American Express

Card No. _____
          (include interbank number for Master Card)

Expiration Date _____

Signature _____
          (required for credit card purchase)

Name_____

Address_____

City _____ State_____ Zip_____

Price includes postage and handling and applicable sales tax. Offer subject to change or cancellation without notice.

The Complete Investment Book

Trading Stocks, Bonds, and Options with Computer Applications

Richard Bookstaber

Scott, Foresman and Company
Glenview, Illinois • London

ISBN 0-673-15952-3

Library of Congress Cataloging in Publication Data

Bookstaber, Richard M., 1950-
   The complete investment book.

   Bibliography: p.
   Includes index.
   1. Investments—Handbooks, manuals, etc.
2. Investment analysis—Handbooks, manuals, etc.
3. Investments—Data processing—Handbooks, manuals,
etc. I. Title.
HG4527.B62 1984   332.63'22   84-20267

1 2 3 4 5 6 – KPF – 89 88 87 86 85 84

IBM is a registered trademark of International Business Machines, Inc.

Figure 8-2 adapted from Sarkis J. Khoury: *Investment Management*. Copyright © by Macmillan Publishing Company. With permission.

Figure 13-1 adapted from Farrell: *Guide to Portfolio Management*, p. 137. New York, McGraw Hill, 1983. With permission.

Table 21-1 reprinted by permission of The Wall Street Journal. © Dow Jones & Company, Inc., 1984. All Rights Reserved.

Figure 22-1 adapted from Bookstaber, R.: *Option Pricing and Strategies in Investing*, Fig. 4-1. © 1981, Addison-Wesley, Reading, MA. With permission.

Figure 22-2 adapted from Bookstaber, R.: *Option Pricing and Strategies in Investing*, Figs. A-1 and A-3. © 1981, Addison-Wesley, Reading, MA. With permission.

Figure 22-3 adapted from Bookstaber, R. and Clarke, R.: *Option Strategies for Institutional Investment Management*, Fig. 2-2. © 1983, Addison-Wesley, Reading, MA. With permission.

Notice of Liability
The information in this book is distributed on an "AS IS" basis, without warranty. Neither the author nor Scott, Foresman and Company shall have any liability to customer or any other person or entity with respect to any liability, loss, or damage caused or alleged to be caused directly or indirectly by the programs contained herein. This includes, but is not limited to, interruption of service, loss of data, loss of business or anticipatory profits, or consequential damages from the use of the programs.

To Pam

Preface

The merging of computer technology and quantitative methods gives rise to powerful yet practical methods for investment analysis. This book is intended as a resource for making these methods available to the sophisticated individual investor. The book covers the most valuable tools for investment analysis in the areas of bonds and bond futures, stocks, technical systems, and options. Each chapter in the book is written to be self-contained, so the reader can extract those ideas and trading methods which are of interest without wading through preliminary material. The book is application oriented. All the ideas and concepts are developed directly into trading strategies.

The computer programs at the ends of the chapters serve as an indication of the immediate applicability of the methods in the book. These programs will convert past prices and other data into clear-cut trading strategies. The book also stands on its own as a guide to investments. It is not intended in any way simply to be a manual for the use of the computer programs. The programs are a tool both to illustrate and to facilitate the strategies.

There is no end to new investment strategies. Investment books in the last few years have proposed strategies that range from alpha to omega. As far as popular books on investments go, this book is one of the more difficult. This is an unavoidable result of my intention to provide trading techniques used by professional traders and by major investment institutions, and to provide these techniques in a form the individual investor can understand and use. To this end I have tried to present only the essentials, and I have tried to present them in as clear a manner as possible. However, common sense alone would suggest that these trading methods are not always easy to grasp.

I am indebted to many colleagues, in both the professional investment and academic communities, for assisting me in the writing of this book. Roger Clarke, Robert Hagin, and Randy Johnson have read through the entire manuscript, adding new insights and eliminating many of my errors. The development of the computer programs in the book has proven to be a difficult and time-consuming task, and has been possible only through the help of a number of computer programmers and research assistants. I am especially indebted to Michael Boren for his programming assistance in all phases of the development of the book. Robert Harliss provided both advice and programming assistance for the basis and bond arbitrage programs. Kenneth Isle and Rod Jackson provided assistance for the technical programs and several of the option programs. Mark Enzenberger provided assistance for programming the dividend capitalization model, and Rory Terry helped in writing several of the options programs. Roger Clarke provided the original code for the program on options in portfolio analysis. Don Adolphson provided the linear and quadratic programming methods that have been used in the immunization and portfolio diversification programs. I would like to express appreciation to the Graduate School of Business at Brigham Young University for providing me with the resources and the environment for writing this book, and to Richard Staron of Scott, Foresman for approaching me with the suggestion of doing this book.

The concepts and trading methods in this book are not of my own invention. While some of the strategies have never been published before, all of these are methods that have been used successfully in the investment community. My role has been to synthesize, evaluate, and explain. The references at the ends of the sections give an indication of the origin of many of the trading ideas, and will serve to lead the reader to more a detailed discussion of the concepts underlying the strategies.

Richard Bookstaber

Contents

1
Introduction

It was a cold overcast day in the middle of a busy week, hardly the time to run off to an investment seminar. But this seminar was taking place nearby, was free of charge, and featured one of the most prominent, popular investment advisors in the country.

I arrived ten minutes early. People were already flowing into the atrium of the building. To avoid the crowd on the main floor, I headed right up to the balcony. As I came to the entrance, I found myself looking into a wall of people, people jammed into the aisles and wedged back into the entrance of the 2,500-seat hall. Some were taking seats on the steps.

A man on the stage said over the loud speaker, "The fire marshall has informed us that only those with seats may remain in the hall. There can be no standing in the aisles or sitting on the steps." No one seemed to believe him; everyone stood their ground.

I managed to squeeze my way over to the edge of a row, and right in the middle of it saw what must have been the only vacant seat left in the hall. A coat was draped over the seat. I tripped my way past twenty sets of knees, returned the coat to its owner in the adjacent seat, and sat down.

The man on the stage made another appeal, "Ladies and Gentlemen, we cannot begin the seminar until all aisles are emptied, and the steps have been vacated. We have arranged for an overflow area in the Madsen Recital Hall. The seminar will be relayed into there."

The aisles were finally cleared at 10:15. The speaker's daughter, in her early twenties, came up to make the introduction. Finally, at 10:30, the investment speaker stepped up to the podium. This seminar was taking place in the winter of 1980. Since September 1979, gold had increased from $400 an ounce to a peak of over $800 an ounce. Silver was being pushed to the $50 mark from the more common $10 to $20 levels.

The speaker warmed up by recounting the dangers facing the economy: the power of the Federal Reserve, the follies of deficit spending, and the inevitability of hyperinflation. Then came the forecasts. Gold would shortly double in price, breaking the $1,500-an-ounce mark. Such a prediction did not seem all that ludicrous at the time, given what had already happened to the price of gold. And silver was only getting started at its current price of nearly $50 an ounce. He urged those in the audience to stock up on silver; just three rolls of silver dimes would soon be enough to finance a year of college education.

Of course, things didn't work out that way. It wasn't long before gold was back down to the $400 range, and three rolls of silver dimes were not worth much more than three rolls of any other sort of dimes.

A year later, this same advisor was quoted in the Wall Street Journal as saying, "I am thrilled to death that gold has been going down. I've been predicting that gold might go as low as $400 an ounce. Right now I'm cheering for lower, lower, lower." No mention was made of how many of his followers were cheering with him.

Such was the demand for investment advice in a town as small and unambitious as Provo, Utah. And such was the quality of the advice given.

No endeavor seems to occupy so many people, with so little success, as trying to win at the investment game. No other area so coddles those who are thought to have the answers. No field contains so many prescriptions for success as there are for ways to beat the market. Any reasonable person contemplating reading an investment book—and any reasonable person contemplating writing an investment book—must ask at the outset why its advice distinguishes it from all the advice that has been given in the thousands of seminars, newsletters, and books.

This book is different because it is not giving investment advice. It is giving tools for individual investment analysis.

This book contains over a score of professional trading strategies and methods of proven profitability. It details what they are and how they work, and provides the computer programs to implement them. The strategies in the book distinguish it both in terms of the sophistication of the strategies, and in terms of the breadth of the approaches to trading. The strategies are state-of-the-art approaches to investment trading and management that are highly respected in the investment profession. They are not a compilation of one person's pet theories.

This book's objective is not just to lay out these strategies, but to make them usable. The book is not meant to be purely descriptive—the information is meant to be implemented. Therefore, the strategies are described in practical, simple terms. But, it must be emphasized that they are never simplified at the risk of losing their power or profit potential. For example, the strategies and programs for bond arbitrage and basis trading are separated out into Treasury bills, notes, and bonds, because each type of instrument has features that must be considered separately and explicitly for arbitrage trading. The convertible bond pricing takes the possibility for early call and the effect of dividend payments into account, because these are realities that affect the successful implementation of convertible bond trading. Few books or articles take these details into account. We do here because they are important details from a trading standpoint.

THE TRADING STRATEGIES

The trading strategies in this book are intended to represent a wide range of profitable investment approaches, extending from technical systems to valuation models; from arbitrage trading strategies to the more conservative methods of risk management. Two principle criteria have been used in selecting the strategies. First, each strategy and trading method must be suitable for computer-based analysis. Second, each must be based on a sound, intelligent approach to investments.

The orientation toward computer-based analysis not only means the methods are quantitative rather than qualitative. It also means the methods lead to clear-cut recommendations. These trading strategies are not highly subjective or judgmental. They will give the same signals to any two investors; they will lead any two investors using the same information and techniques to the same conclusions. This is a natural result of designing computer-based systems. Computers cannot handle the ambiguities and judgment calls that are common in many qualitative investment methods. Trading strategies and profit opportunities must be rigorously spelled out.

Another aspect of the emphasis on computer suitability is the requirement that the methods actually be usable by the individual investor. This means the strategies we consider, although computer-intensive, are not data-intensive. They do not rely on large data banks, or on data that are difficult to obtain. Indeed, for the most part, the trading systems in this book depend on no more than past and current prices and interest rates.

Naturally, this restriction excludes a number of attractive systems from consideration. For example, we do not consider technical systems based on short sales or short interest, bond pricing based on macroeconomic models or Federal Reserve data, or fundamental stock analysis methods that require extensive balance sheet data or financial ratio analysis. Still, as a glance through the book will indicate, the breadth and richness of strategies that can be covered without resorting to extensive data requirements is impressive.

While the computer orientation of the book may take some subjectivity out of trading, the determination of just what constitutes a sound and intelligent trading system cannot help but be subject and judgmental.

There are as many trading systems as there are traders. And every system in use is obviously considered to be sound by at least one trader. Furthermore, there are a number of distinct camps in the investment community supporting different trading philosophies—fundamental analysis, technical analysis, modern portfolio theory, efficient market index trading—each viewing the other as irrational mysticism. I have tried to be eclectic in drawing techniques from all these areas.

Evaluating the various trading strategies can be problematic, since the investment philosophy one starts with will dictate the type of strategy that will be acceptable. An efficient market adherent will discard technical systems out of hand, since the first premise of efficient markets is that past prices convey no information about the course of future prices. A market technician may discount any system that relies on fundamental information, such as earnings and dividend forecasts, since one of the premises of technical analysis is that the security prices, properly interpreted, already convey the impact such forecasts will have on future prices. It is therefore important to maintain a broad perspective, to be aware of the premises that underlie each system. If it is to be properly understood and effectively used, each trading system must be placed in the proper market context. To maintain a well-balanced approach, each trading system is evaluated and discussed using the philosophical standard within which the strategy originated.

THE COMPUTER PROGRAMS

The computer programs in the book, if purchased from software vendors, would cost thousands of dollars. The programs for implementing the trading strategies have been written in IBM BASIC on the IBM Personal Computer. Every effort has been made to use as generic a BASIC as possible, so that adaptation of the programs to other versions of BASIC will require little if any alteration in the code. The programs do not use specialized commands or functions, and there are no Disk Operating System (DOS) commands, such as reading and writing files to and from the disk.

The programs are all self-contained and are menu driven. They are all carefully documented, with introductory descriptions and variable definitions. There is an index at the beginning of each program referencing the line number for each of the main subroutines—the subroutines for inputting the data, doing the computations, and outputting the results. All important equations and program steps, as well as any commands or functions that may differ from one version of BASIC to another, are set apart and described with remark statements.

The programs have been designed for ease of use, simplicity in making adaptation to computers using other versions of BASIC, and transparency so that alterations or expansions can be made. Meeting these three objectives has meant that some detailed and sophisticated programming features have not been used. For example, there are no cursor commands and no graphics. And disk access and files have been avoided. To avoid using the disk, which would require commands that would greatly limit the generality of the programs, all data must be entered from the keyboard. Furthermore, readability has taken precedence over efficiency. There are cases where a more efficient structure would obscure the program logic. In these cases, we have elected to sacrifice elegance for clarity.

The programs are to some extent distinct from the text. The text in each chapter is intended to explain the concepts behind the trading strategy. The text is in no way meant to be merely a user's manual for the programs. Rather, the programs can be thought of as application tools for the methods presented in the text.

The text is well worth reading for those who are interested in state-of-the-art trading methods, even if the programs are never used. For those intending to use the programs, the text gives the background necessary to avoid the "black box syndrome," where programs are used without the user being quite sure of what the programs are doing. Also, it should be kept in mind that the examples and methods described in the text are not necessarily generated from the programs. In some cases, the programs may be too involved, or the output of the programs may be too complex, to be suitable for illustrating the trading methods.

For those who find entering the code by hand too tedious, the programs in the book are available on disk from the author for a small charge. Requests should be addressed to:

> Richard Bookstaber
> The Complete Investment Book
> P.O. Box 205
> Short Hills, NJ 07078

The programs are also available for use on a number of microcomputer systems. These programs are in a more expanded, integrated form, which includes graphics, and which allows data to be entered and saved in files on disk.

I
BOND STRATEGIES

2
Introduction to Bond and Bond Futures Trading

It was not long ago that bond traders were drawn from the same personality group as medieval historians, morticians, and monks. Bond trading was about as exciting and action-packed as watching the drops fall from a melting icicle. A bond's coupon payments dripped in once every six months, the bond finally matured, and that was it. There was little risk and little price variation—bonds were synonymous with low risk, predictable returns.

Starting in the mid-seventies, interest rate volatility made all of this change. With interest rates climbing from their historical levels of four and five percent to double-digit levels, and with sudden swings of a percentage point or more, bond prices started to move around like they were stocks. For example, from the period of September 1981, when interest rates reached a record high, to their low during May 1983, price increases on 30-year Treasury bonds equaled over $400 per $1,000 bond. In fact, during 1981 and 1982, the bond market was actually more volatile than the stock market.

Interest rate uncertainty in the seventies and early eighties dealt an almost fatal blow to the mortgage market as well as many interest rate-sensitive businesses such as insurance companies and savings and loans, and brought to life a new hedging vehicle—the interest rate future contract.

Since their introduction, interest rate futures have grown enormously. There are now futures on Treasury bonds, Treasury notes, and Treasury bills; on bank certificates of deposit, Eurodollars, and on Government National

Mortgage Association (GNMA) issues, called Ginnie Maes. And there are options on some of these as well. The bond futures contract of the Chicago Board of Trade is the most widely traded of all futures contracts. It regularly trades over 100,000 contracts a day, representing an underlying bond value of ten billion dollars per day.

The complex of bonds, bond futures, and options on bonds and bond futures, coupled with the more volatile interest rate environment, has made the bond market one of the most widely followed and highly profitable areas for the trading desks at major brokerage houses and investment banking firms. Many have arbitrage trading desks that do nothing else but basis trading and cash-futures arbitrage. These topics are covered in Chapters 3 and 4.

The increased interest rate volatility has also led many firms to recognize the need to hedge interest rate risk, and the new financial futures have provided the tools for doing so. Firms have focused their expertise on helping large institutional clients use the new interest rate instruments and to implement interest rate hedging strategies such as the immunization strategy, covered in Chapter 8.

Before discussing specific trading and risk management strategies, we now cover some of the elementary aspects of bond pricing and return. We explain how bonds are priced, and the ways in which bond return is measured. A program for doing these calculations can be found at the end of the chapter.

THE BASICS OF BOND PRICES AND BOND YIELDS

BOND VALUATION

The price of a bond is equal to the present value of the future payments accruing to the bondholder. For a zero coupon or pure discount bond, a bond that simply pays its par value at maturity without making any coupon payments before maturity, the bond price is simply the present value of the future payment to be made at maturity. For example, given an interest rate of 10%, a discount bond with a par value of $1000 and with 20 years to maturity will have a price of

$$B = P/(1+r)^T = \$1000/(1.10)^{20} = \$148.64.$$

Here we use B to denote the current bond price, P for the par value of the bond, r for the interest rate, and T for time to maturity.

The pricing of coupon-paying bonds is slightly more involved, since the bond not only pays par value at maturity, it also makes coupon payments of a fixed dollar amount periodically. The amount of these payments, which are generally paid semi-annually, are specified as part of the terms of the bond. For coupon-paying bonds, the present value of the coupons must also be included in determining the bond price. These payments can be looked at as an annuity. The discount rate used in calculating the present value of these payments is based on the general level of interest rates, and on the risk the bond will default. The pricing formula for a coupon-paying bond is

$$B = \sum_{t=1}^{T} \frac{C}{(1+r)^t} + \frac{P}{(1+r)^T}, \tag{1}$$

where r is the per-period interest rate, C is the coupon payment, and T is the number of periods to maturity.

This formula is only correct if the bond is purchased just after a coupon payment is made. Otherwise, the bond purchaser only receives a fraction of the coupon payment equal to the fraction of the time left to the next coupon payment. Essentially, the bond buyer pays the seller the interest that has accrued to the bond from the last coupon payment to the time of purchase. The modifications of the formula to make the adjustments for accrued interest are made in the bond pricing program.

In some cases, it can be useful to think of the bond value as the sum of three component parts. The first is the stream of coupon payments. As just mentioned, this can be looked at as an annuity. The second part is the interest that can be earned by reinvesting these coupon payments for the time remaining until the bond matures. And the third is the present value of the terminal payment, the balloon payment made at the time of maturity.

The second of these, the interest on coupon payments, also called the *interest on interest*, gives a significant portion of the bond value, especially for longer-term bonds, but its impact is often ignored by those who do not follow bonds closely. The effect of compound interest on the reinvested coupon payments is the source of much of the variation in bond prices. This effect is illustrated in Table 2-1. Here, in the first two columns on the left, the coupon interest and the interest on interest accruing to a bond paying $80 a year in semiannual payments of $40 each over a 20-year period is tabulated, assuming the coupon payments received are then reinvested at an 8% rate for the remainder of the 20 years. The two right-hand columns give the total value of coupon payments and the interest on interest for a bond paying $120 in two seminannual payments of $60 each, with a 12% reinvestment rate. In both cases

TABLE 2-1   The Value of Interest on Interest

| | 8% COUPON, 8% REINVESTMENT RATE | | 12% COUPON, 12% REINVESTMENT RATE | |
YEAR	Total Value of Coupon Payments	Total Value of Interest on Coupon Payments	Total Value of Coupon Payments	Total Value of Interest on Coupon Payments
1	80	1.6	120	3.6
2	160	9.86	240	22.48
3	240	25.32	360	58.52
4	320	48.57	480	113.85
5	400	80.24	600	190.85
6	480	121.03	720	292.20
7	560	171.68	840	420.90
8	640	232.98	960	580.35
9	720	305.82	1080	774.34
10	800	391.12	1200	1007.13
11	880	489.92	1320	1283.53
12	960	603.30	1440	1608.93
13	1040	732.47	1560	1989.38
14	1120	878.70	1680	2431.68
15	1200	1043.40	1800	2943.48
16	1280	1228.06	1920	3533.38
17	1360	1434.31	2040	4211.01
18	1440	1663.93	2160	4987.24
19	1520	1918.81	2280	5874.23
20	1600	2201.02	2400	6885.69

the interest on the coupon payments is greater than the total value of the coupon payments themselves by the 20th year. For the 12% bond, the interest on interest is almost three times as great.

Obviously, a higher reinvestment rate would serve to magnify the value of the interest on interest. This point is evident from Table 2-1. If the market interest rate increases above the coupon rate, the coupons can be reinvested at a higher rate, increasing that part of the bond value. Of course, this is counteracted to some degree by the capital loss in the bond price that is necessary to make the coupon rate come in line with the market rate. The interaction of the interest on interest and the capital gain or loss in the bond price are important in both bond swap calculations and in immunization of interest rate risk. This is covered in more detail in Chapters 7 and 8.

BOND PRICE VOLATILITY

Since interest rates are the principle determinant of bond prices, it is useful to look at the impact of market interest rates on bond price changes in more detail.

Bond prices move inversely with interest rates. An increase in the interest rate drops the present value of the coupon payments and the present value of the balloon payment, so the price of the bond—the price paid for the right to receive those payments—must drop to put the bond back in line with the prevailing interest rate. Similarly, a decrease in the market interest rate increases the present value of the future balloon payment, making the return implied by the coupon payments more valuable, and thereby increasing the bond price.

For example, consider a bond selling for its par value of $100 and paying $10 in coupon payments annually. If the current interest rate is 10%, then the price of the bond gives a return consistent with that interest rate. But if the market interest rate rises to 11%, the bond price will need to drop. No one will be willing to buy a bond with a 10% coupon rate in a world of 11% interest rates. The bond price will need to drop to the point that the coupon payment and future capital appreciation gives a return consistent with those higher interest rates.

The percentage change in the bond price induced by a change in the market interest rate will depend on several factors.

First, the volatility of a bond will be higher, the lower the coupon of the bond. That is, the percentage change in the bond price will be greater for a low coupon bond than for a high coupon bond. Figure 2-1 illustrates this by showing the percentage price change of various bonds that results when the interest rate decreases from 10% to 9%. One implication of this is that zero coupon bonds will have the greatest response to interest rate changes. Also, since a lower coupon payment will lead to a lower bond price, bonds that are selling far below par value will be the bonds that are most affected by interest rate changes. On the other hand, bonds selling far above par, those bonds that have very high coupon rates, will be the least affected by interest rate changes.

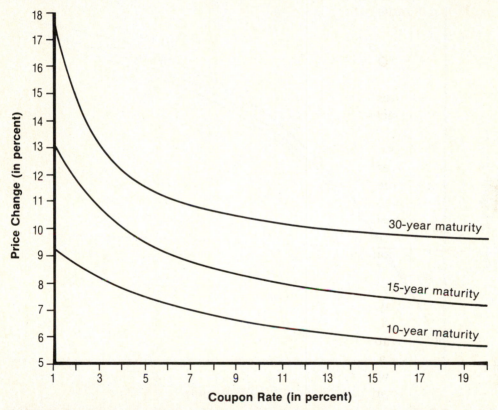

Figure 2-1. The percentage price change induced by a market interest rate decrease from 10% to 9%, plotted as a function of the coupon rate. The price change is plotted for bonds with 10, 15, and 30 years to maturity.

Second, the volatility of a bond will be higher the longer the time remaining to the maturity of a bond. A bond with 30 years remaining to maturity will have a greater percentage price change than a bond with only five years remaining to maturity, other factors equal. This is illustrated in Figure 2-2, which shows the effect of an interest rate decrease from 10% to 9% on bonds as a function of the time remaining to maturity. The bonds are assumed to have 8%, 10%, and 12% coupon rates. This leads to a bond swapping strategy for forecasts of interest rate changes. If interest rates are predicted to go up, it is best to shift from longer maturity to shorter maturity bonds, since the shorter maturity bonds will have less price decline. And if interest rates are

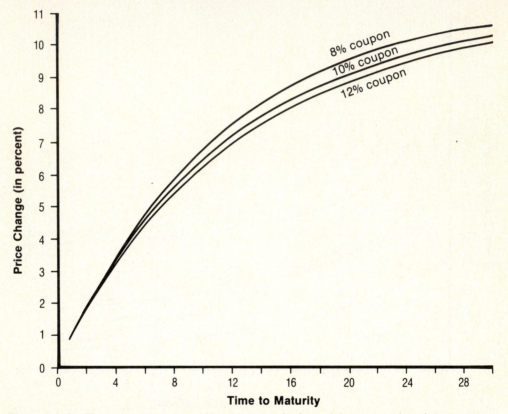

Figure 2-2. The percentage price change induced by a market interest rate decrease from 10% to 9% as a function of time to maturity. The price change is plotted for bonds with 8%, 10%, and 12% coupon rates.

predicted to go down, it is best to move into the longer maturity bonds, since these will realize the greatest price appreciation.

The bond volatility program shows how interest rates will affect bond prices. The program tabulates the bond price for a range of interest rates specified by the user. Figure 2-3 generates the bond price for bonds with various coupon rates as interest rates change. The calculations for this figure were performed using the bond volatility program at the end of this chapter.

One important point to make is that the bond volatility is concerned only with the *instantaneous* changes in bond prices that result from *interest rate changes*. Even if the interest rates do not change, bond prices will change over

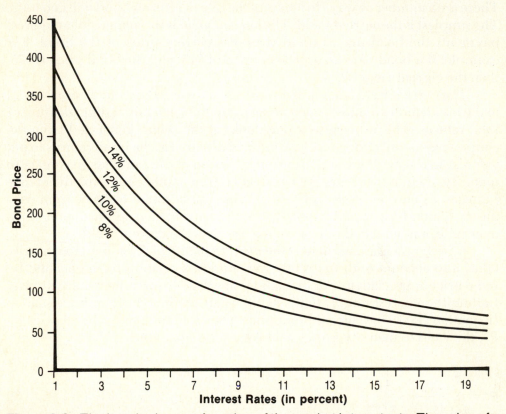

Figure 2-3. The bond price as a function of the market interest rate. The price of a bond with $100 par value is plotted for bonds with 8%, 10%, 12%, and 14% coupon rates.

time, simply because the bond must finally be selling at par at maturity. A bond with a $100 par value will have less of a discount when there is only one year to maturity than when there are twenty years to maturity. And it will finally have no discount at all at the time of maturity. This accretion in bond value, called the accumulation capital gain, is separate and distinct from the bond price changes that result from changes in the market interest rate.

MEASURES OF BOND YIELD

There are a number of ways to measure the rate of return a bond will generate. The simplest is the current yield. The *current yield* is the annual dollar interest payments the bond makes divided by the current price of the bond. For example, if a bond pays an annual coupon of $15, and the bond price is $75, then the current yield is 20%.

The current yield is a popular yield measure; it is the yield measure listed in the bond quotes of most financial sections. But it is a misleading measure of total returns. This is because it only looks at the return generated from the coupon payments, and ignores the return generated as the bond returns to par value at maturity. If a bond is currently priced at $75, and has five years to maturity, then in five years the bond will return another $25—the difference between its current price and its par value—in addition to its coupon payments. Similarly, if a bond is priced above par, it will face capital depreciation over time, and its actual return will be less than the current yield.

A better measure of yield is the *yield to maturity*. The yield to maturity takes into account both the return generated by coupon payments and by bond price appreciation or depreciation. The yield to maturity is computed by finding the interest rate, r, that sets the value of the bond pricing equation (Equation (1)) to the current bond price. Denoting the current bond price by P*, the yield to maturity is the r that solves the equation

$$P^* = \sum_{t=1}^{T} \frac{C_t}{(1+r)^t} + \frac{P}{(1+r)^T} \qquad (2)$$

The yield to maturity can be thought of as the internal rate of return for the set of cashflows generated by a bond, the return that sets the present value of those cashflows equal to the current price of the bond.

The yield-to-maturity calculation, while a better measure of rate of return than current yield, still is not without its limitations. In particular, implicit in the yield to maturity calculation is the assumption that the coupons from the bond can be reinvested at the same interest rate. If the reinvestment rate is not constant throughout the time the bond is outstanding, the true return on the bond will be different than the yield to maturity. A lower reinvestment rate will reduce the total interest on interest earned, and drop the return on the bond, while a higher reinvestment rate will increase the total interest on interest earned, and lead to a higher return.

If the bond is not held to maturity, the yield to maturity is not the relevant return. The *realized yield* is like the yield to maturity, but is adjusted to consider the yield on a bond when the time period the bond is held is less than the time remaining to maturity. The realized yield calculation solves an equation similar to Equation (2), but only for the number of periods specified in the holding period. Unlike the yield to maturity, where the final bond price is constrained to equal par value, there is no such restriction on the end-of-holding-period bond value for the realized yield calculation. This value must be specified in determining realized yield, and this, needless to say, necessitates a forecast by the investor.

BOND PROGRAM OVERVIEW

There are two types of programs in this section of the book covering bond strategies. The first type involves strategies for individual bond trading. They are speculative strategies in the sense that they are short term, with high-return potential. The second type involves methods of bond portfolio strategies and bond portfolio management techniques. They are of more interest to the investor with a portfolio of bonds, who is interested in overall risk management or fine-tuning of the portfolio return.

The next three chapters, Chapters 3, 4, and 5, all revolve around arbitrage trading techniques between spot and futures markets. Chapter 3, on cash-futures arbitrage, lays out the arbitrage trading techniques of what is called the cash-and-carry transaction. While the most popular application of this technique is between spot bonds and bond futures, its principles can be applied to any cash-futures market. The basis trading of Chapter 4 is the next logical step from cash-futures arbitrage. The last of these three chapters, Chapter 5, applies the cash-and-carry technique to another popular arena, the foreign exchange market. It shows how arbitrage strategies can be applied to take advantage of interest rate differentials across currencies.

Chapter 6, covering convertible bonds, presents a pricing formula for determining the correct market price of convertible bonds. Convertible bonds are a combination of a bond and an option that gives the bond holder the right to convert the bond into a prespecified number of shares of stock. The techniques for pricing these bonds thus are an extension of some option pricing methods that are covered in Chapter 22.

Chapters 7 and 8 contain programs for evaluating the profitability of bond swaps and for using a method known as immunization for eliminating the risk that interest rate uncertainty brings to bond portfolio value. The programs given in these two chapters will be particularly useful for the investor involved in larger-scale bond management.

```
10    REM ******************************************************************
20    REM *                BOND PRICING AND ANALYSIS PROGRAM               *
30    REM *                                                                *
40    REM * THIS IS A SERIES OF PROGRAMS TO AID THE INVESTOR IN BOND ANALYSIS. *
50    REM * SELECTION OF DESIRED PROGRAM IS MADE THROUGH A MENU.  EACH PROGRAM *
60    REM * IS PRECEDED BY A BRIEF EXPLANATION OF ITS PURPOSE. AT THE END OF   *
70    REM * EACH PROGRAM THE USER IS RETURNED TO THE MENU.  EACH PROGRAM HAS   *
80    REM * SEVERAL SPECIFIC LOCAL VARIABLES USED IN ITS COMPUTATIONS.     *
90    REM * VARIABLES USED THROUGHOUT THE PROGRAMS ARE AS FOLLOWS:         *
100   REM *                                                                *
110   REM *           P = PAR VALUE OF BOND                                *
120   REM *           C = COUPON RATE                                      *
130   REM *           N = NUMBER OF YEARS TO MATURITY                      *
140   REM *           D = DAYS TO NEXT COUPON PAYMENT                      *
150   REM *           I = MARKET INTEREST RATE                            *
160   REM *          CP = CURRENT MARKET PRICE OF BOND                     *
170   REM *         YLD = CURRENT ANNUAL YIELD                            *
180   REM ******************************************************************
190   REM
200   REM
210   REM ***************************MENU*********************************
220   REM
230    CLS:REM CLEARS SCREEN
240   PRINT TAB(30) "BOND ANALYSIS MENU"
250   PRINT TAB(30) "******************"
260   PRINT TAB(25) "1.  BOND VALUE"
270   PRINT TAB(25) "2.  BOND PRICE VOLATILITY"
280   PRINT TAB(25) "3.  YIELD"
290   PRINT TAB(25) "4.  REALIZED COMPOUND YIELD"
300   PRINT TAB(25) "5.  EXIT TO BASIC"
310   PRINT: INPUT "WHICH COMPUTATION WOULD YOU LIKE TO RUN";CHOICE
320    ON CHOICE GOSUB 370,630,1230,1990,2680
330    GOTO 230
340   REM END OF MENU PROGRAM.
350   REM ******************************************************************
360   REM
370   REM ******************************************************************
380   REM *                     BOND VALUATION                           *
390   REM * THIS PROGRAM WILL COMPUTE THE VALUE OF A BOND, INCLUDING ANY  *
400   REM * INTEREST ACCRUED SINCE LAST COUPON PAYMENT                    *
410   REM ******************************************************************
420    CLS :REM CLEARS SCREEN
430   PRINT "PLEASE ENTER THE FOLLOWING DATA:" :PRINT
440   INPUT "                              PAR VALUE OF BOND: ",P
450   INPUT "                                 COUPON RATE (%): ",C
460   INPUT "                    NUMBER OF YEARS TO MATURITY: ",N
470   INPUT "         NUMBER OF DAYS TO NEXT COUPON PAYMENT: ",D
480   INPUT "                           BOND DISCOUNT RATE (%): ",I
490    YLD = C*P/100 :REM FIND YIELD
500    N = N*2 :REM CHANGE TO SEMIANNUAL FOR COMPUTATIONS
510    D = D/30 :REM CHANGE TO MONTHS FOR COMPUTATIONS
520    I = I/100 :REM CONVERT TO DECIMAL
530    BVAL = ((1-(1+(I/2))^(-N))/I)*2
540    BVAL=(((YLD/2)*BVAL)+(P/(1+I/2)^N)+YLD/2)/(1+I/2)^(D/6)-(YLD/2)*(1-D/6)
```

```
550   PRINT:PRINT:PRINT
560   PRINT USING "THE VALUE OF THE BOND IS: $###,###.##";BVAL
570   PRINT:INPUT "ANALYZE ANOTHER BOND?  (Y/N)",A$
580    IF A$ = "Y" THEN GOTO 420
590   RETURN
600   REM END OF BOND VALUATION PROGRAM--RETURN TO MENU
610   REM ****************************************************************
620   REM
630   REM ****************************************************************
640   REM                    BOND PRICE VOLATILITY                      *
650   REM * THIS PROGRAM COMPUTES BOND PRICE FOR A SELECTED ISSUE  AT TWENTY  *
660   REM * DIFFERENT DISCOUNT RATES.                                    *
670   REM ****************************************************************
680    CLS:REM CLEARS SCREEN
690   REM
700   PRINT "PLEASE ENTER THE FOLLOWING DATA FOR BOND: ":PRINT
710   INPUT "                                        PAR VALUE: ",P
720   INPUT "                                     COUPON RATE (%): ",C
730   INPUT "                                  YEARS TO MATURITY: ",N
740   INPUT "                               CURRENT MARKET PRICE: ",CP
750   INPUT "             LOW DISCOUNT RATE TO ANALYZE (% , >0): ",LR
760   INPUT "            HIGH DISCOUNT RATE TO ANALYZE (% , >0): ",HR
770    RANGE =(HR-LR)/20 :REM COMPUTE RANGE OF INTEREST RATES
780   REM
790   REM COMPUTE YIELD TO MATURITY
800   REM
810    R=((((P-CP)/N)+(P*C/100))/(P+CP))*2
820    GOSUB 940 :REM FIND YIELD TO MATURITY
830    IF ABS(S)<1 THEN GOTO 1010 :REM RESULTS ACCURATE ENOUGH
840    R2 = R :S2 = S
850    R = R+.01 :REM INCREMENT FOR ANOTHER SEARCH POINT
860    GOSUB 940 :REM FIND YIELD TO MATURITY
870    IF ABS(S)<1 THEN GOTO 1010 :REM RESULTS ACCURATE ENOUGH
880    R3 = R :S3 = S
890    R = R+((R2-R)*S)/(S-S2)
900    GOSUB 940 :REM FIND YIELD TO MATURITY
910    IF ABS(S)<1 THEN GOTO 1010 :REM RESULTS ACCURATE ENOUGH
920    R2 =R3 :S2 = S3
930    GOTO 880
940   S=0 :REM SUBROUTINE TO FIND YIELD TO MATURITY
950   FOR I = 1 TO (2*N)
960     S = S+(1+(R/2))^(-I)
970   NEXT I
980    S = (C*P/200*S)+(P/(1+(R/2))^(2*N))
990    S = S-CP
1000  RETURN
1010  YMAT=R*100
1020  PRINT:PRINT USING "THE YIELD TO MATURITY IS ####.## %";YMAT
1030  INPUT "PRESS RETURN TO CONTINUE",B$
1040  REM SET VALUES FOR LOOP COMPUTATIONS
1050   YLD=C*P/100 :REM FIND CURRENT YIELD FOR COMPUTATIONS
1060   N2=N*2 :REM CHANGE TO SEMIANNUAL FOR COMPUTATIONS
1070   CLS:REM CLEARS SCREEN
1080  PRINT "DISCOUNT RATE";TAB(20)"BOND PRICE FOR ";N;" YEARS TO MATURITY"
```

```
1090  PRINT "*************";TAB(20)"****************************************"
1100   FOR I=HR TO LR STEP -RANGE
1110    I1=INT(I*100)/100
1120    I2=I/100 :REM CONVERT TO DECIMAL
1130    BP=((1-(1+(I2/2))^(-N2))/I2)*2
1140    BP=((YLD/2)*BP)+(P/(1+I2/2)^N2)+YLD/2-(YLD/2)
1150   PRINT TAB(1);I1;TAB(34);BP
1160    NEXT I
1170    INPUT "DO YOU WANT TO RUN THIS COMPUTATION FOR ANOTHER BOND? (Y/N)",A$
1180    IF A$="Y" THEN GOTO 680
1190   RETURN
1200  REM END OF BOND VOLATILITY PROGRAM--RETURN TO MENU
1210  REM *****************************************************************
1220  REM
1230  REM *****************************************************************
1240  REM *                    YIELD TO MATURITY                         *
1250  REM * THIS PROGRAM WILL COMPUTE THE CURRENT YIELD, YIELD TO MATURITY, *
1260  REM * AND YIELD TO CALL FOR A GIVEN BOND.                          *
1270  REM *                                                              *
1280  REM *****************************************************************
1290   CLS :REM CLEARS SCREEN
1300  REM
1310  PRINT "PLEASE ENTER THE FOLLOWING DATA FOR BOND":PRINT
1320  INPUT "                         PAR VALUE: ",P
1330  INPUT "                    COUPON RATE (%): ",C
1340  INPUT "                CURRENT MARKET PRICE: ",CP
1350  INPUT "        YEARS TO MATURITY(TO NEAREST HALF YEAR): ",N
1360  INPUT "                IS THIS BOND CALLABLE? (Y/N): ",A$
1370   IF A$ = "N" THEN GOTO 1400
1380  INPUT "YEARS TO FIRST CALL DATE(TO NEAREST HALF-YEAR): ",CALLN
1390  INPUT "                    CALL PRICE: ",CALLP
1400   YIELD = C*P/CP
1410  REM ASSIGN STANDARD COEFFICIENTS FOR YIELD SUBROUTINE
1420   G1=2*N :G2=P
1430   H=1 :H1=1 :H2=1 :L2=G2-CP
1440   GOSUB 1550 :REM FIND YIELD TO MATURITY
1450   YMAT = YLD*200
1460   IF A$="N" THEN GOTO 1510 :REM SKIP CALL COMPUTATION
1470  REM ASSIGN STANDARD COEFFICIENTS FOR YIELD SUBROUTINE
1480   G1=2*CALLN :G2=CALLP
1490   GOSUB 1550 :REM FIND YIELD TO FIRST CALL
1500   YCALL = YLD*200
1510   GOTO 1850 :REM SKIP TO OUTPUT
1520  REM
1530  REM ***********SUBROUTINE TO COMPUTE YIELD TO MATURITY***********
1540  REM
1550   YLD = C*20/(P+CP): REM FIRST APPROXIMATION
1560   GOSUB 1770 :REM PERFORM SEARCH ROUTINE
1570   IF ABS(S)<1 THEN RETURN :REM RESULTS CLOSE ENOUGH
1580   R2=YLD
1590   S2=S
1600   YLD=YLD +.01 :REM INCREASE ACCURACY
1610   GOSUB 1770
1620   IF ABS(S)<1 THEN RETURN
```

```
1630    T1=YLD
1640    T2=S
1650    YLD=YLD +(((R2-YLD)*S)/(S-S2))
1660    IF YLD < 0 THEN YLD = 0 :REM SET LIMITS
1670    IF YLD > 1 THEN YLD = 1
1680    GOSUB 1770 :REM DO ITERATION
1690    IF ABS(S)<1 THEN RETURN
1700    R2=T1
1710    S2=T2
1720    GOTO 1630
1730 RETURN :REM *****************END OF SUBROUTINE****************************
1740 REM
1750 REM *************************ITERATION SUBROUTINE*************************
1760 REM
1770    L1=0
1780    FOR L = 1 TO G1
1790      L1 = L1 +((1+YLD)^(-L))
1800    NEXT L
1810    L1 = (((L1*P)/200)*C)+(2-H2)*G2/((1+YLD)^G1)
1820    S=L1+(H1-1)*((G2-(L2)*.4*T/100)/(1+YLD)^G1)-CP
1830 RETURN :REM *****************END OF SUBROUTINE****************************
1840 REM
1850 REM **************************PRINT RESULTS******************************
1860 REM
1870 PRINT
1880 PRINT USING "         CURRENT YIELD IS ###.##%";YIELD
1890 PRINT USING "  YIELD TO MATURITY IS ###.##%";YMAT
1900    IF A$="N" THEN GOTO 1920
1910 PRINT USING "YIELD TO FIRST CALL IS ###.##%";YCALL
1920 PRINT
1930 INPUT "COMPUTE YIELD FOR ANOTHER BOND? (Y/N)",E$
1940    IF E$="Y" THEN GOTO 1290
1950 RETURN
1960 REM END OF BOND YIELD COMPUTATION PROGRAM--RETURN TO MENU
1970 REM ******************************************************************
1980 REM
1990 REM ******************************************************************
2000 REM *                    REALIZED COMPOUND YIELD                    *
2010 REM * THIS PROGRAM COMPUTES REALIZED COMPOUND YIELD FOR A BOND WITH A *
2020 REM * HOLDING PERIOD WHICH IS LESS THAN THE REMAINING LIFE OF THE BOND. *
2030 REM *                                                              *
2040 REM ******************************************************************
2050    CLS :REM CLEARS SCREEN
2060 REM
2070 PRINT "PLEASE ENTER THE FOLLOWING DATA FOR BOND: " :PRINT
2080 INPUT "                    PAR VALUE: ",P
2090 INPUT "                 COUPON RATE (%): ",C
2100 INPUT "               YEARS TO MATURITY: ",N
2110 INPUT "            CURRENT MARKET PRICE: ",CP
2120 INPUT "          HOLDING PERIOD (YEARS): ",H
2130 INPUT "EXPECTED PRICE AT END OF HOLDING PERIOD: ",PH
2140    IF H<N THEN GOTO 2170
2150 PRINT "THE HOLDING PERIOD MUST BE LESS THAN YEARS TO MATURITY. "
2160    GOTO 2120
```

```
2170   YLD = C/100
2180    GOSUB 2380 :REM FIND YIELD
2190  PRINT:PRINT USING "THE REALIZED YIELD IS ###.##%";YLD*100
2200  INPUT "PRESS RETURN TO CONTINUE",Q$
2210  PRINT "REALIZED YIELD FOR A RANGE OF END-OF-HOLDING-PERIOD PRICES: ":PRINT
2220  PRINT TAB(1);"REALIZED YIELD (%)";TAB(30);"PRICE AT END OF HOLDING PERIOD"
2230    IF H<10 THEN X=INT(.02*P+.1)
2240    IF (H>=10) AND (H<20) THEN X=INT(.04*P+.1)
2250    IF (H>=20) THEN X=INT(.08*P+.1)
2260    IF X<1 THEN X=1
2270    X1=PH-(10*X)
2280    IF X1<0 THEN X1=0
2290    X2=PH+(10*X)
2300    FOR PH=X2 TO X1 STEP -X
2310      GOSUB 2360 :REM FIND YIELD FOR OUTPUT
2320  PRINT USING "     ####.##                        $######.##";YLD*100;PH
2330    NEXT PH
2340    GOTO 2650 :REM SKIP TO END OF PROGRAM
2350  REM
2360  REM ****************SUBROUTINE TO FIND REALIZED YIELD****************
2370  REM
2380    GOSUB 2550 :REM FIND YIELD
2390    IF ABS(S)<1 THEN RETURN :REM RESULTS ACCURATE ENOUGH
2400    R2=YLD
2410    S2=S
2420    YLD=YLD+.01 :REM INCREASE ACCURACY
2430    GOSUB 2550
2440    IF ABS(S)<1 THEN RETURN
2450    T1=YLD
2460    T2=S
2470    YLD=YLD+(R2-YLD)*S/(S-S2)
2480    GOSUB 2550
2490    IF ABS(S)<1 THEN RETURN
2500    R2=T1
2510    S2=T2
2520    GOTO 2450
2530  RETURN :REM ****************END OF SUBROUTINE****************
2540  REM
2550  REM ****************SUBROUTINE TO TEST YIELD VALUES****************
2560  REM
2570    S=0 :B=0
2580    FOR A=1 TO 2*H
2590      B=B+(1+YLD/2)^(-A)
2600    NEXT A
2610    S=CP-(P*C/200*B)-(PH/((1+YLD/2)^(2*H)))
2620  RETURN :REM END OF SUBROUTINE
2630  REM ****************************************************************
2640  REM
2650  INPUT "DO ANALYSIS FOR A DIFFERENT BOND? (Y/N)",A$
2660    IF A$="Y" THEN GOTO 2050
2670  RETURN :REM END OF REALIZED YIELD PROGRAM--RETURN TO MENU
2680    CLS
2690  END
```

3
Cash-Futures Arbitrage: The Cash and Carry Transaction

Suppose you want to take a position in Treasury bonds. There are two markets you can use: the cash bond market, where you can take immediate physical delivery of the bond, and the futures market, where you enter into a contract to take delivery of the bond at a specified future date. The decision of which market to use depends on the answer to one question: Which is cheaper, buying a bond now or using a futures contract to buy it later? Put another way, is it better to make settlement now and carry the actual bond, or to buy a futures contract that allows you to settle later, and that delivers the bond to you later?

To answer this question, let us back away from the bond market for the moment, and consider the decision to buy a less complex asset—gold. As with the Treasury bond market, there is both a cash and a futures market for gold. Suppose you can buy gold on the spot market for $400 an ounce, and can buy gold in the futures market for delivery in one year for $440 an ounce. In either case, you will have physical possession of the gold in one year. If your investment horizon is at least one year, both of these markets give you exactly the same opportunity to gain from an appreciation in the price of gold.

At first glance, the cash market seems far more attractive. If you buy the gold in the cash market, it only costs you $400, while if you do so in the futures market you will need to pay $440 one year from now when the contract comes due.

What may not be so apparent, however, is that if you buy the gold in the cash market, you will incur an interest cost, since you will tie up $400 for the year you are carrying the gold. By contrast, no funds are tied up when entering into a contract for future delivery. (We will ignore any margin costs in the futures contract. Investors can use interest-bearing securities to fulfill the margin requirement. This imposes no costs on investors who have sufficient reserves.)

The decision between the cash and futures market, then, depends on whether the interest-carrying cost in the cash market is larger or smaller than the $40 discount in the cash price. If the interest cost is less than $40, then the cash market will be better, while if the interest cost is greater than $40, then the futures market will be better. Given the $400 price of gold on the cash market, the $40 difference between the cash and the futures price gives an *implied* interest rate for the futures contract of 10%. If the *actual* interest rate in the cash market for the cost of carrying the gold does not equal this implied rate, one of the markets will be preferred to the other. Even more important, if the actual interest rate does not equal this implied rate, it is possible to create a profit by trading between these two markets.

Suppose the interest rate for carrying the gold is just 5%. Then the investor can buy the gold now in the cash market for $400, and at the same time sell the gold in the futures market for $440. In one year, the gold will be delivered for the futures price of $440, while the cost of buying the gold and carrying it for the year is only $420—the $400 cost of the gold plus the $20 interest cost of carry. This transaction will lock in a profit of $20 with zero risk, and, if the gold has been financed through borrowing, with zero net investment. It is an arbitrage profit. If the actual interest rate is higher than the implied rate, the opposite strategy of shorting gold in the cash market and buying in the futures market will yield an arbitrage profit. These strategies are summarized in Table 3-1.

THE CASH AND CARRY TRANSACTION

The transaction just described between the spot and futures market is called a *cash and carry transaction*. It has profit potential in any market with both a cash and a futures instrument when the interest rate implied by the difference between the spot and the futures price does not equal the carrying cost interest rate. But it is most widely used in the interest rate markets.

TABLE 3-1   Cash-Futures Arbitrage in the Gold Market

Assumptions

Cash Market Price = $400
Futures Market Price for One Year Delivery = $440

Case 1:   Interest Rate = 5%

Current Transactions

1. Borrow Funds	400
2. Buy Gold	−400
3. Sell Futures Contract	0
Net Investment	0

Transactions in One Year

1. Deliver Gold at Contracted Price	$440
2. Pay Off Loan	(420)
Net Profit	$ 20

Case 2:   Interest Rate = 15%

Current Transactions

1. Lend Funds	−400
2. Sell (Short) Gold	400
3. Buy Futures Contract	0
Net Investment	0

Transactions in One Year

1. Buy Gold at Contracted Price	$(440)
2. Receive Payment on Loan	$ 460
Net Profit	$ 20

One attraction to using this strategy in the bond market is that a ready market exists in the government bond markets for borrowing or lending bonds. The borrowing and lending rate is called the *repo rate*, which is short for the repurchase rate. A bond dealer, or a well-capitalized investor working through a bond dealer, who wants to execute a cash and carry transaction can finance the cash position at the repo rate. As with the gold example, if this repo rate differs from the implied rate, (called the *implied repo rate*), the cash and carry transaction will lead to a profit.

We now illustrate the cash and carry transaction with two examples. The first example uses Treasury bills, and the second uses Treasury bonds. These two Treasury issues each have their own institutional peculiarities. The Treasury bills are quoted on a banker's discount, and some gymnastics are necessary to convert the Treasury bill quotes into a market price. For Treasury bonds, the complications include coupon payments, and the Treasury bonds, must further be adjusted by a conversion factor in order to make the prices of bonds with differing coupons comparable.

Treasury Bills

Suppose on February 21, a Treasury bill with a maturity date of June 14 is selling at a discount of 9.28%, and the nearest futures contract, the March futures, is selling at 90.80. To translate these discounts into market prices, we multiply the discount by the fraction of the year to maturity, and reduce the face value of the bill by that amount. There are 114 days from February 21 to June 14. The price of the Treasury bill selling at a 9.28% discount, then, given a one million dollar face value, will be

Treasury bill price = Face value ×(1 – discount × fraction of year to maturity) =
$1,000,000 (1 – .0928 × 114/360) = $970,613.

Thus, if on February 21 the Treasury bill is selling at a 9.28% discount, the market price of the bill will be $970,613. An investor buying the bill at that price will receive $1,000,000 at maturity, giving an annualized return of 9.69% over a 365-day year.

Note that the return on the bill is not the same as the discount. The quoted discount is the percent reduction in the price from face value, while the return is the difference between the face value and the purchase price divided by the purchase price.

The price of the futures contract, given a quoted price of 90.80, is computed in a similar manner, but first the discount must be extracted from the quoted price. The discount for the futures contract is the difference between one hundred and the quoted price. For a quoted price of 90.80, the futures discount will be:

Futures discount = 100 – quoted price = 100 – 90.80 = 9.20%.

The market price of the futures is then computed in the same manner as for a Treasury bill. The face value of the futures, which is one million dollars, is reduced by the amount of the discount times the fraction of the year until maturity.

All Treasury bill futures deliver a Treasury bill with approximately 91 days to maturity. The March futures contract expires on March 15 and will deliver the June 14 Treasury bill. The Treasury bill will then be held for 91 days after the futures matures, so the price of the futures contract now will be

Futures Contract Price = 1,000,000(1 – .0920 × 91/360)
                       = $976,744.

Since the Treasury bill is selling for $970,613 on February 21, and the price for selling it in the futures market on March 15 is $976,744, the implied interest rate is

(976,744 – 970,613)/970,613 × 360/23 × 365/360 = 10.02%.

That is, by buying the Treasury bill on February 21 for $970,613, and at the same time selling a March futures contract to deliver the bond on March 15 for 976,744, the investor can net a return of 10.02%.

The two adjustment factors in this calculation require some explanation. The percentage return from the futures and the cash Treasury bill prices are first multiplied by 360/23. Since the transaction spans only 23 days, this factor is used to get an annualized return. The second adjustment is 365/360. This adjustment is made because the Treasury bill is based on a 360-day year, while there are actually 365 days in a year. This means the Treasury bill holder needs only 360 days to get 365 days of interest. To get an actual annualized interest rate, then, the Treasury bill return must be adjusted by the factor of 365/360=1.014. (Obviously, multiplying first by 360/23 and then by 365/360 eliminates the 360-day terms from the calculation of the implied interest rate. We have put both terms in here to bring out explicitly the point that Treasury bills are based on a 360-day year. At the end of the chapter, before the program, we simply use the 365-day adjustment in the computational procedure.)

The 10.02% return from this cash and carry transaction seems easy enough. Just buy a Treasury bill and commit to deliver it in the futures market. The catch, of course, is that money is tied up during the time the Treasury bill is held. If the repo rate, the cost of funds for carrying the Treasury bill from February 23 to March 15, is 10.02%, then there is no profit opportunity. But if the cost of carry differs significantly from this implied interest rate, then the cash and carry transaction will be profitable.

Suppose the actual repo rate over the 23-day period is 9.80%. The cost of carry is twenty-two basis points less than the return from the cash-futures transaction, and there is an arbitrage opportunity. The strategy of buying the Treasury bill and selling the futures, and then unwinding the transaction on March 15 by delivering the Treasury bill will net a .22% arbitrage profit on the original Treasury bill investment. This strategy is outlined in Table 3-2.

If the market repo rate is higher than the implied repo rate, the opposite strategy of selling or shorting the Treasury bill and simultaneously buying a futures will yield a profit.

Treasury Bonds

Treasury bonds are long-term Treasury issues that pay semiannual coupons. The coupon payments differ from one issue to the next, and that makes a direct comparison of the bonds difficult. For example, there is a Treasury bond due in November 2011 that has a 14% coupon, a bond due in August 2013 with a 12% coupon, and a bond due in November 2008 with a 8¾% coupon. For any given market yield, these bonds will all be priced differently. The 14s, with a higher coupon, will be priced higher than the 12s, which in turn will be priced higher than the 8¾s.

In contrast to these various bonds in the cash market, the futures contract for Treasury bonds is based on a bond with 20 years to maturity and with an 8% coupon. This is a *hypothetical* bond. There is no Treasury bond out in the market with this coupon and time to maturity. The immediate problem, then, in dealing between the cash and futures Treasury bond markets is to find some way of smoothing over the differences between the many different bonds. The first task is to devise a way of equilibrating the many bonds, making the bond prices comparable.

TABLE 3-2   Cash-Futures Arbitrage in the Treasury Bill Market

Assumptions

Cash Market Treasury Bill Price = $970,613
Futures Market Price for Delivery in 23 Days = $976,744
Implied Interest Rate = (976,744–970,613)/970,613 × (365/23) = 10.02%

Case 1:   Market Interest Rate = 9.80%

Current Transactions

1. Borrow Funds at 9.80%	$970,613
2. Purchase a Treasury Bill	– 970,613
3. Sell a Futures Contract	0
Net Investment	0

In 23 days:

1. Deliver (sell) Treasury Bill at Contracted Price	$976,744
2. Pay Off Loan	– 976,606
Arbitrage Profit	$ 138

(Net Return = Implied Rate – Market Rate = .22%)

Case 2:   Market Interest Rate = 10.50%

Current Transactions

1. Sell Short a Treasury Bill	$970,613
2. Lend Funds at 10.50%	– 970,613
3. Buy a Futures Contract	0
Net Investment	0

In 23 days:

1. Buy Treasury Bill at Contracted Price	$976,744
2. Receive Payment on Loan	977,035
Arbitrage Profit	$ 291

(Net Return = Market Rate – Implied Rate = .48)

This is done by using a *conversion factor* to relate the prices of different bonds. The conversion factor converts the futures price into the equivalent price of any Treasury bond. The conversion factors are tabulated in a booklet available from the Chicago Board of Trade, and from most investment brokers.

If the 14s of the year 2011 have 26 years to maturity, the conversion factor tables indicate they will have a conversion factor of 1.6056. (The conversion factor is calculated using the time to call, which is five years less than the time to maturity for this bond.) If the futures price for Treasury bonds is $70.00, then the 14s can be delivered against the futures position for a settlement price of 70.00 × 1.6056 = $112.39. An investor with a short position in the futures market can elect to deliver the 14s of 2011 to fulfill the obligation. If the settlement price in the futures market is 70.00 and the investor delivers the 14s, $112,392 will be received for each $100,000 contract covered with these bonds. The investor with a long futures position who receives these Treasury bonds will pay out $112,392 for the delivery of the 14s.

It should be emphasized that the investor who is delivering the bonds, the investor who is on the short side of the futures contract, has the option of selecting which bond to deliver and when to deliver it. Since all the bonds have different market prices and conversion factors, there will generally be one bond that is the cheapest to deliver. This leads to some uncertainty for those on the long side of the contract, and opens up another bond trading game—basis trading. We will get into this in Chapter 4.

Now that we have run through the mechanics of the conversion factor, we can construct an example of a cash and carry transaction for Treasury bonds. Suppose the 14s of 2011 are selling for $112.10 on February 21, and the future price for Treasury bonds is $70.00. (The bond price is quoted in 32nds of a point, so the price of $112.10 is $112.3125 in decimal terms.) The cash and carry transaction involves buying the Treasury bond now, and entering into a futures contract to deliver the bond in 23 days, on March 15, for the futures price times the conversion factor, or $112.39. The return from this transaction is the difference between the cash and futures price, and the accrued interest from the coupon over the 23 days. The cash and futures prices are virtually the same. However, since the holder of the Treasury bond receives a share of the coupon payment for the fraction of the coupon period the bond is held, this transaction will lead to 23 days of the 14% coupon. The bond program for this chapter can be used to show that the overall return from this cash and carry transaction will be 12.34%. That is, the implied repo rate will be 12.34%.

As with the cash and carry transaction for the Treasury bill, if the repo rate for the Treasury bond is less than the implied repo rate from the cash and carry transaction, this will be a profitable strategy. If the actual repo rate for the Treasury bond is greater than the implied repo rate, then the opposite strategy of shorting the bond in cash market and buying it in the futures market will lead to a profit.

TRADING WITH THE CASH AND CARRY TRANSACTION

The implied repo rates for Treasury bonds and Treasury bills can be computed with the programs in this chapter. The programs can also calculate the implied repo rate for Treasury notes, for Eurodollars, and for certificates of deposit. These are all candidates for the cash and carry transaction, since they all have listed futures contracts. Some experience is necessary in dealing with these instruments, however, since they all have their own peculiarities in terms of the form of the price quotes, the accrual of interest, and the delivery mechanism in the futures market. The programs are adjusted to take these into account.

The strategy for cash futures arbitrage is simply stated as follows:

- If the implied repo rate is greater than the market repo rate, buy the cash instrument and sell it forward in the futures market.
- If the implied repo rate is less than the market repo rate, sell short the cash instrument and buy it forward in the futures market.

Implementing the cash and carry transaction requires being closely tied in with the institutional market. The repo rate is generally available to only substantial investors or institutions, and the profit margins for this strategy are expressed in hundredths of a percent, requiring a large amount of capital and very small transactions costs to make worthwhile profits. Also, transactions costs and the bid-asked spread can be a problem, since profits are measured in such small amounts.

In practice, the cash and carry transaction is not completely riskless. Strictly speaking, it is not a pure arbitrage opportunity. One risk arises because it is not always possible to get a term repo rate—a repo rate that will cover the full period of financing. Generally, the repo market is an overnight interest rate market, and the repo rate only applies to overnight positions. Of course, it is always possible to roll over the loan positions from one day to the next. But then there is no guarantee the repo rate will not change against the position. The repo rate now may be attractive, but the overnight rate a week or two later might change enough to lead to a loss for the cash and carry transaction.

A second, and more significant problem, has to do with changes in the basis between the futures and cash prices. The futures price only locks in a guaranteed amount of profit if the futures and the cash markets move exactly in step. It is often the case, however, that the futures prices do not change one for one with the cash prices. This leads to basis risk, a risk that is a central part of any cash-futures strategy. The measurement and effect of basis risk, and strategies for trading on the basis, are the topics of Chapter 4.

CASH-FUTURES ARBITRAGE

Computational Procedure

S = spot price in cash market
F = futures price
T = time to delivery (in number of days)

$$\text{Implied Interest Rate} = \frac{365}{T} \times (F-S)/S.$$

The actual computation may be complicated by the contract terms of the instruments, coupon payments, and other factors. These are treated in the programs for each of the financial instruments.

Trading Strategy

- If the implied interest rate is greater than the market interest rate, buy the cash instrument and sell the futures contract.
- If the implied interest rate is less than the market interest rate, sell short the cash instrument and buy the futures contract.

```
10   REM ************************************************************
20   REM *-            IMPLIED INTEREST RATE (REPO RATE) PROGRAM      *
30   REM *                                                           *
40   REM *   THIS PROGRAM WILL CALCULATE THE IMPLIED REPO RATE FOR T-BONDS,   *
50   REM *   T-BILLS, T-NOTES, EURODOLLAR DEPOSITS, AND CERTIFICATES OF       *
60   REM *   DEPOSIT.   THE PROGRAM IS MENU-DRIVEN.   VARIABLES ARE DIFFERENT *
70   REM *   FOR EACH INSTRUMENT.                                     *
80   REM *                                                           *
90   REM *   VARIABLES:     F = FUTURES PRICE                         *
100  REM *                  P = BOND PURCHASE PRICE                   *
110  REM *                  C = CASH INSTRUMENT YIELD OR DISCOUNT     *
120  REM *                 CO = COUPON                                *
130  REM *                 CF = CONVERSION FACTOR (FOR NOTES AND BONDS)  *
140  REM *                  R = IMPLIED REPO RATE WITHOUT COMPOUNDING *
150  REM *                 RC = IMPLIED REPO RATE WITH COMPOUNDING    *
160  REM *                                                           *
170  REM *                                                           *
180  REM ************************************************************
190    DIM M(6),D(6),Y(6),N(6)
200  CLS
210  REM
220  REM *************************MAIN INPUT SUBROUTINE********************
230  GOTO 370
240  REM
250  REM *************************T-BILL CALCULATIONS********************
260  GOTO 980
270  REM
280  REM **********************EURODOLLAR AND CD CALCULATIONS****************
290  GOTO 1200
300  REM
310  REM ********************TREASURY NOTE AND BOND CALCULATIONS***************
320  GOTO 1410
330  REM
340  REM ***********JULIAN DATE SUBROUTINE FOR CONVERTING CALENDAR DAYS********
350  GOTO 1570
360  REM
370  REM
380  REM ************************************************************
390  REM *-                    MAIN INPUT SUBROUTINE                *
400  REM ************************************************************
410  REM
420  PRINT:PRINT
430  PRINT "                IMPLIED REPO RATE ANALYSIS"
440  PRINT
450  PRINT
460  PRINT " 1. TREASURY BILLS"
470  PRINT " 2. CERTIFICATES OF DEPOSIT"
480  PRINT " 3. EURODOLLAR DEPOSITS"
490  PRINT " 4. TREASURY NOTES"
500  PRINT " 5. TREASURY BONDS"
510  PRINT " 6. EXIT"
520  PRINT: PRINT: INPUT "SPECIFY CHOICE =>",INST
530  IF INST<1 OR INST>6 THEN 370
540   IF INST=1 THEN INST$="BILLS"
```

```
550   IF INST=2 THEN INST$="CD"
560   IF INST=3 THEN INST$="EURO"
570   IF INST=4 THEN INST$="NOTES"
580   IF INST=5 THEN INST$="BONDS"
590   IF INST=6 THEN CLS: GOTO 1950: REM **>END
600   CLS: PRINT"                        IMPLIED REPO RATE ANALYSIS"
610   PRINT "                    ";INST$: PRINT: PRINT: PRINT
620   INPUT "SETTLEMENT DATE (MMDDYY)-- DATE THE FUTURES SETTLES:", DA$
630     M(1)=VAL(LEFT$(DA$,2)):D(1)=VAL(MID$(DA$,3,2)):Y(1)=VAL(RIGHT$(DA$,2))
640     M=M(1):D=D(1):Y=Y(1): GOSUB 1570:N(1)=A
650   INPUT "SALE DATE (MMDDYY)-- DATE TRADE IS ENTERED:",DA$
660     M(2)=VAL(LEFT$(DA$,2)):D(2)=VAL(MID$(DA$,3,2)):Y(2)=VAL(RIGHT$(DA$,2))
670     M=M(2):D=D(2):Y=Y(2): GOSUB 1570:N(2)=A
680   INPUT "MATURITY DATE (MMDDYY)-- DATE CASH INSTRUMENT MATURES:",DA$
690     M(3)=VAL(LEFT$(DA$,2)):D(3)=VAL(MID$(DA$,3,2)):Y(3)=VAL(RIGHT$(DA$,2))
700     M=M(3):D=D(3):Y=Y(3): GOSUB 1570:N(3)=A
710   IF INST=1 THEN 900
720   IF INST<4 THEN 870
730   INPUT "COUPON:"; CO
740   INPUT "PURCHASE PRICE:"; P
750     P= INT(P) + (P-INT(P))/.32:    REM  32NDS **> DECIMAL
760   INPUT "FUTURES PRICE:"; F
770     F= INT(F) + (F-INT(F))/.32:    REM  32NDS **> DECIMAL
780   INPUT "CONVERSION FACTOR:"; CF
790   INPUT "LAST COUPON PRIOR TO SETTLEMENT DATE";DA$
800     M(4)=VAL(LEFT$(DA$,2)):D(4)=VAL(MID$(DA$,3,2)):Y(4)=VAL(RIGHT$(DA$,2))
810     M=M(4):D=D(4):Y=Y(4): GOSUB 1540:N(4)=A
820   INPUT "LAST COUPON DATE PRIOR TO SALE DATE ";DA$
830     M(5)=VAL(LEFT$(DA$,2)):D(5)=VAL(MID$(DA$,3,2)):Y(5)=VAL(RIGHT$(DA$,2))
840     M=M(5):D=D(5):Y=Y(5): GOSUB 1540:N(5)=A
850   INPUT "# OF PAYMENTS DURING HOLDING PERIOD";CN
860     GOTO 900
870   INPUT "ISSUE DATE"; DA$
880     M(6)=VAL(LEFT$(DA$,2)):D(6)=VAL(MID$(DA$,3,2)):Y(6)=VAL(RIGHT$(DA$,2))
890     M=M(6):D=D(6):Y=Y(6): GOSUB 1540:N(6)=A
900     T1= N(3)-N(1)
910     T2= N(3)-N(2)
920     T3= N(3)-N(6)
930   ON INST GOTO 940,1170,1170,1380,1380
940   REM ***********************************************************************
950   REM *                        T - BILLS                                    *
960   REM ***********************************************************************
970   REM
980   REM T-BILL PRICE
990     P= 1 - (C/100)*(T1*.9863)/360
1000  REM PRICE IMPLIED BY FUTURES
1010  INPUT "FUTURES PRICE:"; D
1020    F=1 - (1 - D/100)*(T2*.9863)/360
1030  REM IMPLIED REPO W/ COMPOUNDING
1040    T4= T1 - T2
1050    RC=(((F/P)^(1/(T3*.9863)))-1)*360)*100
1060    R= (F-P)*360/((T3*.9863)*P)*100
1070  PRINT "          CASH T-BILL DISCOUNT:";C
1080  PRINT "                    FUTURES PRICE:";D
```

```
1090 PRINT "          HOLDING PERIOD (DAYS):";T3
1100 PRINT "   IMPLIED REPO W/ COMPOUNDING:";RC
1110 PRINT "  IMPLIED REPO W/O COMPOUNDING:";R
1120 PRINT:PRINT:PRINT
1130 INPUT "DO YOU WISH TO LOOK AT ANOTHER INSTRUMENT (Y/N)";Q$
1140  IF Q$="Y" THEN 200
1150  IF Q$="N" THEN 1950: REM END PROGRAM
1160  GOTO 1130
1170 REM *******************************************************************
1180 REM *                   EURO's and CD's                              *
1190 REM *******************************************************************
1200 PRINT INST$;"CURRENT YIELD (IN PERCENT):";:INPUT C
1210 PRINT INST$;"ORIGINAL YIELD (IN PERCENT):";:INPUT Y
1220  P= ( 1 + (C/100) * (T3*.9863)/360 ) / ( 1 + (Y/100) * (T1*.9863)/360 )
1230 INPUT "FUTURES PRICE:"; D
1240  F= 1 + (1 - D/100) * (T2*.9863)/360
1250  RC=((((F/P)^(1/T1*.9863))-1)*360)*100
1260  R= (((F-P) * 360) / ((T1*.9863) * P)) * 100
1270 PRINT:PRINT:PRINT
1280 PRINT "          CASH ";INST$;" YIELD:";C
1290 PRINT "          ";INST$;" FUTURES PRICE:"; D
1300 PRINT "          HOLDING PERIOD (DAYS):"; T2
1310 PRINT "     IMPLIED REPO RATE W/ COMPOUNDING:"; RC
1320 PRINT "     IMPLIED REPO RATE W/O COMPOUNDING:"; R
1330 PRINT:PRINT:PRINT:
1340 INPUT "DO YOU WISH TO LOOK AT ANOTHER INSTRUMENT (Y/N)";Q$
1350  IF Q$="Y" THEN 200
1360  IF Q$="N" THEN 1950:REM END PROGRAM
1370  GOTO 1340
1380 REM *******************************************************************
1390 REM *                   NOTES and BONDS                              *
1400 REM *******************************************************************
1410  IP= CO * (N(1) - N(4))/360    :REM    INTEREST PURCHASED
1420  IS= CO * (N(2) - N(5))/360    :REM    INTEREST SOLD
1430  PS= F * CF                    :REM    SALE PRICE  (FUT. PRICE x CONV. FAC.)
1440  C= CO * CN/2
1450  XNUM = PS + IS + C - P - IP
1460  DEM1 = (P+IP) * (N(2) - N(1)) / 360  -  C * (N(2) - N(4)) / 360
1470  REPO = (XNUM / DEM1) * 100
1480 PRINT: PRINT: PRINT "          IMPLIED REPO:"; REPO
1490 PRINT: PRINT: PRINT:
1500 INPUT "DO YOU WISH TO LOOK AT ANOTHER INSTRUMENT (Y/N)";Q$
1510  IF Q$="Y" THEN 200
1520  IF Q$="N" THEN 1950:REM END PROGRAM
1530  GOTO 1500
1540 REM *******************************************************************
1550 REM *              JULIAN DATE SUBROUTINE                            *
1560 REM *******************************************************************
1570  ON M GOTO 1600,1630,1600,1720,1600,1720,1600,1600,1720,1600,1720,1600
1580 PRINT CHR$(7);"UNREAL DATE HAS BEEN ENTERED -- RETRY FROM START"
1590  GOTO 620
1600  IF D>31 THEN 1580
1610  GOTO 1750
1620 REM MONTH IS FEB -- LEAP YEAR?
```

```
1630   IF Y/4<>INT(Y/4) THEN 1670
1640   IF Y/400 = INT (Y/400) THEN 1690
1650   IF Y/100 <> INT (Y/100) THEN 1690
1660 REM NO LEAP YEAR -- MO. HAS 28 DAYS
1670   IF D>28 THEN 1580
1680 REM LEAP YEAR -- 29 DAYS
1690   IF D>29 THEN 1050
1700   GOTO 1750
1710 REM MONTH HAS 30 DAYS
1720   IF D>30 THEN 1580
1730 REM TABLE NO OF DAYS FROM FIRST OF YEAR
1740 REM TO FIRST OF EACH MONTH
1750   DATA 0,31,59,90,120,151,181,212
1760   DATA 243,273,304,334
1770   RESTORE
1780   FOR Q=1 TO M
1790     READ A
1800   NEXT Q
1810 REM  GET NUMBER OF DAYS FROM JAN 1 TO
1820 REM  FIRST OF MONTH FROM DATA TABLE
1830 REM COMPUTE # OF DAYS FROM 0/0/0 TO M/D/Y
1840   A= A + Y*365 + INT(Y/4) + D + 1 - INT(Y/100) + INT(Y/400)
1850 REM  POSSIBLY A LEAP YEAR ?
1860   IF INT(Y/4) <> Y/4 THEN 1940
1870 REM  CONTINUE TEST FOR LEAP YEAR
1880   IF Y/400 = INT (Y/400) THEN 1920
1890   IF Y/100 = INT (Y/100) THEN 1930
1900 REM IF MONTH IS JAN OR FEB, ADJUST
1910 REM CALCULATED # OF DAYS
1920   IF M>2 THEN 1940
1930   A=A-1
1940   RETURN
1950 END
```

4
Spreading and Basis Trading in the Bond Market

The price difference between two securities is called the spread or the basis. Trading on the basis involves taking a position in the two securities that will lead to a gain or loss as the basis of the two securities changes. This is a more sophisticated, subtle form of trading than is the outright purchase or sale of a security, for in basis trading, absolute or directional changes do not matter; only relative price changes affect the position value. Among professional futures and options traders, basis trading and spreading are far more popular strategies than taking straight long or short positions. (The terms basis and spread are often distinguished by using basis to refer to the difference between the price of a spot asset and a futures contract on that asset, and using spread to refer to the difference between two futures contracts or between two options.)

Consider a simple strategy of buying a futures contract on corn at a price of $4.00 a bushel, and selling a futures contract on wheat at a price of $5.00 a bushel. The wheat-corn futures spread is then $1.00. Now suppose a drought leads to a rise in both the price of wheat and corn. Suppose the price of the corn future rises to $8.00 a bushel, while the wheat future rises to $9.00 a bushel. A long position in either of these commodities would lead to a substantial profit. But since the spread remains at $1.00, this trade is unaffected by the price rise. The long position in the corn futures leads to a $4 profit, but this is negated by the $4 loss in the short position in the wheat futures. This is illustrated in Figure 4-1, Case 1.

As this example demonstrates, absolute price changes will not affect the basis trader or spreader. What will affect the trader are relative changes in prices, i.e., changes in the spread or basis. To see this, suppose the price of corn remains at $4 a bushel, while the price of wheat moves up a dollar to $6. Since the short side of the position increased in price without a compensating increase in price from the long side, this price shift will result in a loss of $1. This case is illustrated in Figure 4-1, Case 2.

Looking at it another way, shorting the wheat and buying the corn amounts to selling the wheat-corn spread. If the spread drops, the position will increase in value, while if the spread widens, there will be a loss. The dollar increase in the price of wheat widens the spread by $1, leading to a $1 loss.

TYPES OF SPREADS AND BASIS TRADES

In the bond market, the most common strategy is to trade the basis between the cash market and futures market. The cash and carry transaction discussed in the previous chapter is at the core of this basis trade.

Basis trading or spreading can also be done between two futures contracts. The futures contracts may be on the same underlying security or commodity, with the futures having different delivery months. Or, the futures may be on two different but related assets. The wheat-corn spread used in the example above is one common intercommodity spread. Corn and oats are closely related, since they are substitutes in the feeding of livestock and

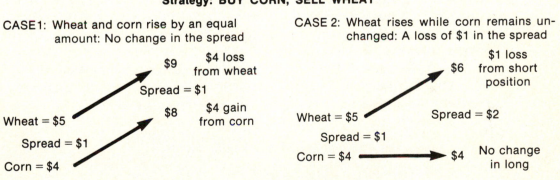

Strategy: BUY CORN, SELL WHEAT

CASE1: Wheat and corn rise by an equal amount: No change in the spread

$9 — $4 loss from wheat
Spread = $1
$8 — $4 gain from corn
Wheat = $5
Spread = $1
Corn = $4

CASE 2: Wheat rises while corn remains unchanged: A loss of $1 in the spread

$6 — $1 loss from short position
Spread = $2
Wheat = $5
Spread = $1
Corn = $4 — $4 No change in long

Figure 4-1. Trading on the wheat-corn futures spread.

poultry. Another popular intercommodity spread is between soybeans and its two products, soybean oil and soybean meal. In the interest rate futures market, interbond spreads may be taken between short- and long-term bonds in order to take advantage of expected shifts in the yield curve. Or spreads may be taken between bonds with different risk characteristics, such as Treasury bills and certificates of deposit.

Every spread and basis trade is motivated by the relationship between securities, and that relationship in turn is driven by different factors from one set of securities to the next. The wheat-corn spread is motivated by the substitutability of the two commodities. The spread between soybeans, soybean oil, and soybean meal, is motivated in part by the processing costs of converting soybeans into these two products. Bond spreads are often motivated by shifts in the yield curve.

In this chapter we will concentrate on one of the most popular, and most complex, basis trades—the trade between the cash and futures in the bond markets. This trade is most commonly done in the Treasury bond market, but can be done with other financial instruments that have traded futures contracts. This basis trade is motivated by inconsistencies between the implied interest rate and market interest rate that lead to the cash and carry transaction, discussed in Chapter 3.

BASIS TRADING AND THE CASH AND CARRY TRANSACTION

In the previous chapter, we described the cash and carry transaction. We showed that if the interest rate implied by the price difference between the cash and the futures instrument was not equal to the market interest rate, an arbitrage profit was possible by taking opposite positions in the cash and the futures. However, we warned that the strategy is not a pure arbitrage strategy, because of basis risk. Here we will discuss that basis risk in more detail.

In the Treasury bond market, the basis is the difference between the cash price and the futures price multiplied by the conversion factor,

Basis = cash price – futures price × conversion factor.

In buying the basis, the investor buys the cash and sells the futures, while in

TABLE 4-1 Basis Trading Strategies

A

Assumptions of Cash and Futures Price Movements

	Cash Price	Futures Price	Conversion Factor	Futures Price × Conversion Factor	Basis (in 32nds)
	12s of 2013				
Today	95–14/32	66–9/32	1.4239	94.38	34/32
In Two Weeks	95–20/32	67–2/32	1.4239	95.49	4/32

B

Profits from Basis Trading Strategies

I. Buy the Basis

Today	Buy ten of the 12s of 2013 954,375	Sell 14 Futures 927,938	Basis=26,437
In Two Weeks	Sell ten of the 12s of 2013 956,250	Buy 14 Futures 938,875	Basis=17,375
Profit	From the Cash Market 1,875	From the Futures Market −10,937	Net Profit −9,062

II. Sell the Basis

Today	Sell ten of the 12s of 2013 954,375	Buy 14 Futures 927,938	Basis=26,437
In Two Weeks	Buy ten of the 12s of 2013 956,250	Sell 14 Futures 938,875	Basis=17,375
Profit	From the Cash Market −1,875	From the Futures Market 10,937	Net Profit 9,062

selling the basis, the investor sells the cash and buys the futures. Money will be made in buying the basis if the cash price increases relative to the futures price; the long position in the cash will profit from a cash price increase more than the short position in the futures will lose. Conversely, money will be made in selling the basis if the futures price increases relative to the cash price.

Table 4-1 presents the results of buying and of selling the basis for a particular price change in Treasury bonds. Section A shows the cash and futures prices for the start of the trade, and the prices two weeks later, when the trade is closed out. The Treasury bond considered in the cash market is the 12% bond maturing in 2013. The conversion factor for this bond (shown in the third column from the left) is 1.4239. As has already been explained, the futures price must be multiplied by this conversion factor to determine the price that will be paid for delivery of the bond. The column on the right in Section A of Table 4-1 is the basis, the difference between the cash bond price and the futures price multiplied by the conversion factor. Following the convention in the bond market, the basis has been converted into thirty-seconds of a point.

The basis dropped by almost a point over the two-week period covered by the table. This occurred because the futures price rose far more than the cash price. This drop in the basis suggests that a strategy of selling the basis would have been profitable, while buying the basis would have led to a loss. Table 4-1, Section B, presents the results of these two strategies, and confirms that this is indeed the case.

In buying the basis, ten of the 12s of 2013 are bought and 14 of the futures contracts are sold. The 14 to 10 ratio comes close to the 1.4239 conversion factor, and thus leads to a nearly equivalent position in the cash and futures market. The initial basis in this transaction is $26,437. Two weeks later the basis shrinks to $17,375, leading to a loss of $9,062. As would be expected, the opposite strategy of selling the basis makes as much money as is lost in buying the basis. This strategy is outlined in Table 4-1, Section B, Part II.

THE EFFECT OF THE CHEAPEST-TO-DELIVER BOND ON THE BASIS

As the example presented in Table 4-1 illustrates, the conversion factor adds a degree of complexity to basis trading with Treasury bonds. The futures price must be multiplied by the conversion factor to determine the price at which the cash bond must be delivered. This means the ratio of futures to cash bonds used in the basis trade must equal the conversion factor.

A second complication for Treasury bond futures arises because the seller of the futures contract has the option to deliver any of a number of Treasury bonds. Generally, there will be one treasury bond that is the cheapest to deliver, and that will be the bond that is delivered. This leads to some uncertainty for the holder of the futures, since it is uncertain just which bond will be delivered against the futures contract. Indeed, the essence of basis risk in Treasury bond trading, besides the financing cost, includes the risk of what bond will be the cheapest to deliver.

The delivery price for a bond is determined by multiplying the futures price by the conversion factor for the particular bond under question. For example, suppose the futures price is 70.00, the conversion factor for the 12s of 2013 is 1.4239, and the conversion factor for the 14s of 2011 is 1.6165. If the 12s are delivered against the futures position, the holder of the futures contract will need to pay $70 \times 1.4239 = 99.67$ for each Treasury bond delivered. If the 14s are delivered, the holder will need to pay $70 \times 1.6165 = 113.16$. Just which Treasury bond will be delivered will depend on which bond has the lowest market price compared to the delivery price. If the 12s are selling in the market for 100.00 while the 14s are selling for 113.16, then the 14s will generally be delivered.

This cheapest-to-deliver feature of the Treasury bond market represents a valuable option for the seller of a futures contract. Since the seller can deliver any eligible bond against the future obligation, the loss from buying the basis is limited. The worst that can happen is for the basis to shrink to zero. On the other hand, there is unlimited potential for gain. Conversely, selling the basis has limited upside potential and unlimited loss. The value of this option will be reflected in the basis, leading the basis to be slightly wider than the cost of carry alone would require. That is, the basis buyer will pay a premium, implicit in the size of the basis, to reflect the downside protection, and the basis seller will gain a premium to compensate for the limited potential gains.

As the time for delivery approaches, the basis between the Treasury bond that will be delivered and the futures price will approach zero. If the basis did not narrow, an arbitrage profit would be possible by shorting the cash and buying the futures contract, thereby earning the basis, and then closing out the position once the futures contract led to delivery of the bond. There can be no expectation that the basis of the nondelivered bonds will narrow, however. This leads to a critical guessing game when trading the basis on Treasury bonds, since the basis for the futures will converge on the cheapest-to-deliver bond as delivery approaches, while the basis for the other bonds might actually widen.

The way in which the conversion factor is calculated leads those bonds with the longest maturity to be the cheapest to deliver. (All it would take to kill the basis trading game for Treasury bonds is for the Treasury to issue a 40-year bond. Under almost all circumstances, such a bond would be the cheapest to deliver.) The 8⅜s of 2008, the 10⅜s of 2009, the 14s of 2011, and the 12s of 2013 are the leading candidates for delivery. Just which of these bonds actually becomes the cheapest to deliver depends on the structure of interest rates. As bond prices fall, the discounted bonds become the cheapest to deliver, and as bond prices rise, the bonds selling at a premium become the cheapest to deliver. The basis risk, then, and the opportunity to profit from basis trading, is greatest in periods of volatile interest rates.

Before leaving the discussion on the conversion factor and the cheapest to deliver, it should be noted that these issues are not unique to the Treasury bond market. The Treasury notes and the Ginnie Maes also use a conversion factor to link the futures market and the delivery of the cash instrument. The same factors will affect basis trading in these markets as affect basis trading for the Treasury bonds.

STRATEGIES FOR BASIS TRADING

The trading rules for basis trading are:

- Buy the basis (buy the cash, sell the futures) if the cash price is expected to rise relative to the futures price (the basis widens).
- Sell the basis (sell the cash, buy the futures) if the cash price is expected to decline relative to the futures price (the basis narrows).

The same trading rules can be extended for trading on the spreads between futures contracts. Obviously, the key issue in successfully trading is finding those factors that affect relative prices, and forecasting the values of those factors.

The computer program for this chapter calculates the futures-cash relationship for a range of basis. The program can be applied to any market where the futures and spot prices are related by a conversion factor. While the most popular market for the basis trading strategies described in this chapter is the Treasury bond market, the program is also designed to do the computations for Treasury notes. The program has two strategic functions. First, while success in basis trading requires accurate forecasts in interest rate and relative bond price movements, the program provides important preliminary calculations for basis trading. Second, the basis program can be used to assess the basis risk inherent in the cash-futures arbitrage strategy discussed in Chapter 3. The program can also show the potential swing in the basis that will arise from shifts in the cash-futures relationship.

BASIS TRADING IN THE BOND MARKET

Computational Procedure

P = cash bond price
F = futures contract price
CF = conversion factor

$$\text{Basis} = P - F \cdot CF$$

Trading Strategy

- Buy the basis (buy the cash bond, sell the futures contract) if the basis is expected to widen.
- Sell the basis (sell the cash bond, buy the futures contract) if the basis is expected to narrow.

```
10    REM ***************************************************************
20    REM *                       BASIS TRADING PROGRAM                 *
30    REM *                                                             *
40    REM * THIS PROGRAM COMPUTES THE BASIS BETWEEN TREASURY BONDS OR   *
50    REM * TREASURY NOTES AND TREASURY BOND OR NOTE FUTURES.  THE PROGRAM *
60    REM * REQUIERS INPUTS OF THE CASH AND FUTURES MARKET DATA, AS WELL *
70    REM * AS THE CONVERSION FACTOR FOR CONVERTING THE FUTURES PRICE INTO *
80    REM * PRICE AT WHICH THE BOND WILL BE DELIVERED.  THE PROGRAM WILL *
90    REM * AUTOMATICALLY CALCULATE THE BOND PRICE FOR A RANGE OF POSSIBLE *
100   REM * PRICES.  THE PROGRAM LISTS PRICES IN 128THS OF A POINT      *
110   REM *                                                             *
120   REM * VARIABLES USED:                                             *
130   REM *                        FP = FUTURES PRICE                   *
140   REM *                        BB = BEGINNING BASIS                 *
150   REM *                        CF = CONVERSION FACTOR               *
160   REM *                    COUPON = COUPON ON BOND                  *
170   REM *                        XP = IMPLIED CASH PRICE              *
180   REM *                                                             *
190   REM ***************************************************************
200   REM
210   REM SET UP ARRAYS AND FUNCTIONS TO BE USED
220   REM
230   DEF FNNV(ZZ)=INT(ZZ/32)+(ZZ-INT(ZZ/32)*32)/100
240   DIM F(32),A(32),B(32),C(32),D(32),E(32),X(32),G(32),H(32),I(32),J(32)
250   DIM K(10)
260   REM
270   REM ***************************************************************
280   REM *                       INPUT SUBROUTINE                      *
290   REM ***************************************************************
300   REM
310   CLS :REM CLEARS SCREEN AND HOMES CURSOR
320   REM GATHER THE INPUT VARIABLES
330   INPUT "   COUPON OF THE CASH ISSUE";COUPON
340   INPUT "   CONVERSION FACTOR    ";CF
350   INPUT "   MATURITY OF THE CASH  (MM,DD,YY)";M1,D1,Y1
360   INPUT "   IS THIS FOR A CBTBOND (1) OR A CBTNOTE (2)";TYPE
370   PRINT "   WHAT IS THE CONTRACT MONTH?"
380   PRINT "              1-MARCH           "
390   PRINT "              2-JUNE            "
400   PRINT "              3-SEPTEMBER       "
410   PRINT "              4-DECEMBER        ";
420   INPUT MONTH
430   IF MONTH=1 THEN MON$="MARCH"
440   IF MONTH=2 THEN MON$="JUNE"
450   IF MONTH=3 THEN MON$="SEPTEMBER"
460   IF MONTH=4 THEN MON$="DECEMBER"
470   INPUT "CONTRACT YEAR";YEAR
480   INPUT "BEGINNING FUTURES PRICE ";FP
490   INPUT "BEGINNING BASIS";BB
500   REM
510   REM ***************************************************************
520   REM *                       BASIS COMPUTATIONS                    *
530   REM ***************************************************************
540   REM
```

```
550 REM DETERMINE THE BASIS VALUES TO BE USED
560 REM
570  M=1
580   IF M>10 THEN GOTO 660
590   K(M)=BB+M-1
600   M=M+1
610   GOTO 580
620   E(L)=YY
630 REM
640 REM DETERMINE THE RANGE OF FUTURES PRICES AND CASH PRICES FOR THE BASIS
650 REM
660   L=0
670 REM FUTURES PRICES
680   XP=INT(FP)*32+((FP-INT(FP))*100)+L
690   L=L+1
700   F(L)=FNNV(XP)
710 REM IMPLIED CASH PRICE (FUTURES PRICE X CONVERSION FACTOR)
720   XP=XP*CF
730 REM CASH PRICES AT THE VARIOUS BASES
740   XX=XP+K(1)
750   YY=FNNV(XX)
760   GOSUB 1550
770   A(L)=YY
780   XX=XP+K(2)
790   YY=FNNV(XX)
800   GOSUB 1550
810   B(L)=YY
820   XX=XP+K(3)
830   YY=FNNV(XX)
840   GOSUB 1550
850   C(L)=YY
860   XX=XP+K(4)
870   YY=FNNV(XX)
880   GOSUB 1550
890   D(L)=YY
900   XX=XP+K(5)
910   YY=FNNV(XX)
920   GOSUB 1550
930   E(L)=YY
940   XX=XP+K(6)
950   YY=FNNV(XX)
960   GOSUB 1550
970   X(L)=YY
980   XX=XP+K(7)
990   YY=FNNV(XX)
1000   GOSUB 1550
1010   G(L)=YY
1020   XX=XP+K(8)
1030   YY=FNNV(XX)
1040   GOSUB 1550
1050   H(L)=YY
1060   XX=XP+K(9)
1070   YY=FNNV(XX)
1080   GOSUB 1550
```

```
1090    I(L)=YY
1100    IF L<17 THEN GOTO 680
1110  REM
1120  REM SUBROUTINE TO DETERMINE THE NUMBER OF 1/128THS
1130  REM
1140  DD=YY*100-INT(YY*100)
1150  IF DD<.25 THEN PL=.1
1160  IF (DD>=.25) AND (DD<.5) THEN PL=.2
1170  IF (DD>=.5) AND (DD<.75) THEN PL=.3
1180  IF DD>=.75 THEN PL=.4
1190  IF PL=.4 THEN GOTO 1630
1200  YY=(INT(YY*100)+PL)/100
1210  GOTO 1670
1220  YY=(INT(YY*100)+1)/100
1230  IF ((YY-INT(YY))>=.32) THEN GOTO 1660
1240  GOTO 1670
1250  YY=INT(YY)+1
1260  RETURN
1270   CLS
1280  REM *********************************************************************
1290  REM *                          OUTPUT SUBROUTINE                        *
1300  REM *********************************************************************
1310  REM
1320   IF TYPE=1 THEN GOTO 1350
1330  PRINT "    CASH FUTURES    << NOTE >>  CONVERSION TABLE FOR ";MON$;YEAR
1340   GOTO 1360
1350  PRINT "    CASH FUTURES    << BOND >>  CONVERSION TABLE FOR ";MON$;YEAR
1360  PRINT "    COUPON:";COUPON," ISSUE:";M1;D1;Y1," CONV. FACTOR";CF
1370  PRINT "    BOND VALUES ARE EXPRESSED IN 128THS OF A POINT"
1380  PRINT "*****************************************************************:
1390  PRINT TAB(11)"BASIS AMOUNTS:"
1400  PRINT  TAB(11)K(1);TAB(19)K(2);TAB(27)K(3);TAB(35)K(4);TAB(43)K(5);TAB(51)K(6);
TAB(59)K(7);TAB(67)K(8)
1410  PRINT "FUTURES:";TAB(37);"BOND PRICE"
1420   I=1
1430   IF I>16 GOTO 1490
1440  REM PRINT OUT THE CASH VALUES
1450  PRINT  USING"####.###";F(I),A(I),B(I),C(I),D(I),E(I),X(I),G(I),H(I)
1460   I=I+1
1470   GOTO 1430
1480  REM REPEAT USING DIFFERENT STARTING FUTURES AND BASIS VALUES
1490  INPUT "  REPEAT USING DIFFERENT FUTURES AND BASIS VALUES (Y/N)";CC$
1500   IF CC$="Y" THEN GOTO 480
1510  END
```

5
Interest Rate Arbitrage Across Currencies

Interest rates vary from one currency to another. It is not unusual for the interest rate for British pounds or German marks to differ significantly from the interest rate for U.S. dollars. This occurs because the capital markets and goods markets of each country as well as savings behavior, monetary control, and inflation levels differ, leading to different demand for the various currencies and, therefore, to different interest rates. It is best to think of the dollar or pound or mark as commodities that are as dissimilar as soybeans are from wheat or corn. While these currencies all provide a similar monetary function, there will be variation in their demand.

Diverging interest rates would at first suggest immediate profit opportunities. For instance, if interest rates are 13% in the United Kingdom and 10% in the United States, it seems sensible simply to borrow dollars and lend pounds, netting a return of 3%, a return equal to the interest rate differential.

The problem with this strategy is that the dollars that have been borrowed are not the same as the pounds that have been lent. The transaction is not completed until the conversion is made back from pounds to dollars, so that the dollar obligation can be paid off. And if the dollar has, in the meantime, strengthened by 3% relative to the pound, the gain in the money market will be exactly offset by the loss in the foreign exchange market. The premium that will need to be paid to convert the pounds back to dollars will offset the interest rate premium made in the pound money market.

But, if the future exchange rate from pounds to dollars can be locked in at a rate below this offsetting premium, then an arbitrage opportunity is available.

STRATEGIES TO PROFIT FROM IMBALANCES BETWEEN THE INTEREST RATE AND EXCHANGE RATE DIFFERENTIALS

Suppose an investor pursues the strategy just suggested. Suppose the investor borrows $2 million for one year at a 10% interest rate and lends it out in pounds sterling at a 13% interest rate. (The funds might be lent out in discount bonds having a one-year maturity.) If the current, spot exchange rate is $2.00/£, in one year the investor will have an obligation to pay back $2.2 million, and will receive £1.13 million from the pound investment.

If the exchange rate remains at $2.00/£ in one year, the investor can convert the £1.13 million to $2.26 million, and net a profit of $60,000 after paying off the loan, giving a return of 3% on the funds borrowed. (The investor does not actually need to borrow the funds to pursue this strategy, he can always use his own capital. We assume the money is borrowed in this example to take the opportunity cost of the money into account explicitly.)

The obvious problem with this strategy is that we do not know what the dollar/pound exchange rate will be in a year when the pounds need to be converted back to dollars. There is therefore some risk to this strategy. At the $2.00/£ exchange rate, the strategy is clearly profitable. But if the exchange rate drops far enough, to $1.50/£, for example, the pounds will come nowhere near covering the dollar obligation, and the strategy will lead to a significant loss.

This uncertainty can be overcome by using the forward market for foreign exchange. In the forward market, we can enter into an obligation to convert pounds into dollars at a future date at a prespecified exchange rate. Let us suppose the forward rate is $1.98/£. At that exchange rate, the 1.13 million pounds will exchange for $2,237,400. After paying off the dollar loan, the investor will be left with $37,400 profit. This profit is riskless and involves no net investment by the investor. The profit is thus a pure arbitrage profit. This strategy is called *covered interest arbitrage*.

The profit from this strategy occurs because the 3% rate of return to the differential interest rates exceeds the implied interest rate in carrying the pounds for a year in the forward market. This is a variation of the cash-futures arbitrage described for the bond market in Chapter 3.

Another way of looking at this transaction is illustrated in Figure 5-1. Future dollars can be converted into future pounds in two different ways. The first method is the money market route: make the conversion by borrowing dollars, converting them to pounds spot, and lending the pounds out. The result is a future obligation to deliver dollars and receive the pounds. The second, less circuitous, method is to enter into a forward contract to deliver a specified amount of dollars for pounds in one year. If the first method is more profitable than the second, the arbitrage strategy involves performing the first conversion while undoing it by reversing the second method of conversion, as illustrated in Figure 5-2.

What relationship between interest rates and exchange rates will equalize these two conversion methods and eliminate profit opportunities? The answer is that the differential between the interest rates must equal the future value of the differential between the spot and forward exchange rates. This relationship is expressed in the following equation:

$$r_d - r_f = (1+r_f) (F - S)/S, \tag{1}$$

where r_d and r_f are the domestic (dollar) and foreign (pound) interest rates, F is the forward rate, and S is the spot exchange rate. The exchange rates are

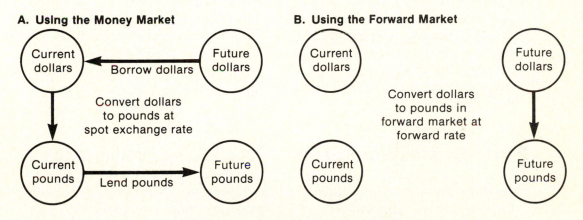

A. Using the Money Market

Current dollars ← Borrow dollars — Future dollars

Convert dollars to pounds at spot exchange rate

Current pounds — Lend pounds → Future pounds

B. Using the Forward Market

Current dollars   Future dollars

Convert dollars to pounds in forward market at forward rate

Current pounds   Future pounds

Figure 5-1. Two methods for converting future dollars into future pounds.

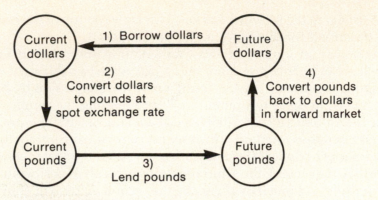

Figure 5-2. A covered interest arbitrage strategy.

expressed in terms of domestic currency per foreign currency (dollars per pound).

To illustrate this equation, let us put in the values for the spot and forward exchange rate, and solve for the interest rate differential that will eliminate the arbitrage opportunity:

$$r_d - r_f = (1+r_f)(F - S)/S = 1.13 \ (1.98-2.00)/2.00 = -.0113. \tag{2}$$

This means the dollar interest rate must be 113 basis points below the pound rate. If, as we have assumed, the pound rate is at 13%, the dollar interest rate would have to be at 11.87% to eliminate the arbitrage opportunity. It is easy to see how this dollar interest rate closes the profit gap. If the two million dollars is borrowed at this interest rate, $2,237,400 will need to be repaid, which is exactly the amount gained through the conversion of the 1.13 million pounds at the $1.98/£ exchange rate.

TRADING STRATEGIES USING COVERED INTEREST ARBITRAGE

Anytime the interest rates and the spot and forward exchange rate fail to meet the conditions of Equation (1), an arbitrage opportunity is possible by applying the strategy just illustrated. The trading rules can be stated as follows:

1. If $r_d - r_f < (1-r_f)(F-S)/S$, borrow the domestic currency at the rate r_d, and convert it into the foreign currency. Lend the money out at the foreign interest rate, r_f. At the same time, cover the conversion of the principal plus interest back into the domestic currency by entering into a forward contract to sell the foreign currency at the rate F.

2. If $r_d - r_f > (1-r_f)(F-S)/S$, borrow the foreign currency at the rate r_f, and convert it into the domestic currency. Lend the money out at the domestic interest rate, r_d. At the same time, cover the conversion of the principal plus interest back into the foreign currency by entering into a forward contract to buy the foreign currency at the rate F.

But don't start counting your profits too soon. Any trading strategy that can be condensed to a one-line relationship, and that involves such prominent and widely traded instruments as foreign exchange and short-term money, is bound to be closely watched. The fact is, the relationship behind covered interest arbitrage is widely known and followed. The forward rate quoted by most banks is even set according to this relationship. So misalignments will be hard to come by.

Another problem with finding profit opportunities is that the bid-offer spread in the foreign exchange market gives some margin for error in this relationship. In the first strategy listed above, where the interest rate differential is too low, the foreign currency must be bought spot and sold forward. In the second strategy, the foreign currency must be sold spot and bought forward. The wider the bid-offer spread, the wider the range where the exchange rate is too high for buying and too low for selling.

For example, suppose it costs $1.99/£ to buy British pounds, and the exchange rate is $1.97/£ to sell British pounds. (The bid-asked spread is then $.02/£.) The interest rate differential must now be less than $(1+r_f)(F-1.99)/1.99$ for the strategy requiring buying pounds to be profitable, or must be greater than $(1+r_f)(F-1.97)/1.97$ for the strategy requiring selling pounds to be profitable. There is thus a wide range of possible movement in the interest differential that will not be exploitable.

The difficulties arising from the bid-asked spread are doubled, for the forward exchange rate will also have a bid-asked spread.

Finally, successful arbitrage requires very favorable borrowing rates.

The competitors in this arena are the major international banks, and few small investors can match their borrowing rates.

In short, while covered interest arbitrage is an appealing strategy, it is not one that can be pursued profitably by most small investors. However, while it does not hold much promise as an active trading strategy, it certainly is worthwhile following as a passive or supplementary strategy. That is, if you are involved in an investment strategy that involves borrowing or lending money in foreign currencies, it is worth shopping around to see which rates give the most desirable interest rate differential, and see whether a hedged investment will lead to a profit.

COVERED INTEREST ARBITRAGE

Computational Procedure

r_d = domestic interest rate
r_f = foreign interest rate
S = spot exchange rate
F = forward exchange rate

The exchange rates are expressed in terms of units of domestic currency per unit of foreign currency.
To eliminate arbitrage:

$$r_d - r_f = (1 + r_f)(F - S)/S.$$

Trading Strategy

- If $r_d - r_f < (1+r_f)(F-S)/S$, borrow the domestic currency at the rate r_d, and convert it into the foreign currency. Lend the money out at the foreign interest rate, r_f. At the same time, cover the conversion of the principal plus interest back into the domestic currency by entering into a forward contract at the rate F.

- If $r_d - r_f > (1+r_f)(F-S)/S$, borrow the foreign currency at the rate r_f, and convert it into the domestic currency. Lend the money out at the domestic interest rate, r_d. At the same time, cover the conversion of the principal plus interest back into the foreign currency by entering into a forward contract at the rate F.

```
10    REM ***********************************************************************
20    REM *                      COVERED INTEREST ARBITRAGE                     *
30    REM *                                                                     *
40    REM * THIS PROGRAM WILL COMPUTE THE INTEREST RATE DIFFERENTIAL IMPLIED    *
50    REM * BY THE FORWARD RATE.  IF THE TWO ARE NOT EQUAL THEN A POTENTIAL     *
60    REM * ARBITRAGE SITUATION EXISTS.                                         *
70    REM *                                                                     *
80    REM *   VARIABLES USED:                                                   *
90    REM *                      RD = THE DOMESTIC INTEREST RATE                *
100   REM *                      RF = THE FOREIGN INTEREST RATE                 *
110   REM *                    SPOT = THE SPOT EXCHANGE RATE                    *
120   REM *                   FORWD = THE FORWARD EXCHANGE RATE                 *
130   REM *                       T = THE NUMBER OF DAYS TO FORWARD DELIVERY    *
140   REM *                   IRDIF = THE INTEREST RATE DIFFERENTIAL            *
150   REM *                  IMPDIF = THE IMPLIED INTEREST RATE DIFFERENTIAL    *
160   REM *                                                                     *
170   REM *                                                                     *
180   REM *                                                                     *
190   REM *                                                                     *
200   REM ***********************************************************************
210   REM
220   REM
230   REM ****************************INPUT***********************************
240    GOSUB 360
250   REM
260   REM
270   REM ************************COMPUTATIONS*******************************
280    GOSUB 670
290   REM
300   REM
310   REM **************************OUTPUT***********************************
320    GOSUB 770
330   REM
340   REM
350   REM
360   REM ***********************************************************************
370   REM *                              INPUT                                  *
380   REM ***********************************************************************
390    CLS
400   PRINT "PLEASE ENTER THE FOLLOWING DATA:"
410   PRINT
420   INPUT "                           DOMESTIC INTEREST RATE (%): ",RD
430    IF CHOICE = 1 THEN RETURN
440   INPUT "                            FOREIGN INTEREST RATE (%): ",RF
450    IF CHOICE = 2 THEN RETURN
460   INPUT "   SPOT EXCHANGE RATE (DOMESTIC CURRENCY/FOREIGN CURRENCY): ",SPOT
470    IF CHOICE = 3 THEN RETURN
480   INPUT "FORWARD EXCHANGE RATE (DOMESTIC CURRENCY/FOREIGN CURRENCY): ",FORWD
490    IF CHOICE = 4 THEN RETURN
500   INPUT "                          TIME TO FORWARD DELIVERY (DAYS): ",T
510    IF CHOICE = 5 THEN RETURN
520   PRINT: PRINT
530   PRINT TAB(10);"CHOICE";TAB(20)"ITEM TO CHANGE";TAB(55);"CURRENT VALUE"
540   PRINT TAB(10);"------";TAB(20)"--------------";TAB(55);"-------------"
```

```
550 PRINT TAB(10);"0";TAB(20);"DO COMPUTATIONS"
560 PRINT TAB(10);"1";TAB(20);"DOMESTIC INTEREST RATE (%):";TAB(55);RD
570 PRINT TAB(10);"2";TAB(20);" FOREIGN INTEREST RATE (%):";TAB(55);RF
580 PRINT TAB(10);"3";TAB(20);"        SPOT EXCHANGE RATE:";TAB(55);SPOT
590 PRINT TAB(10);"4";TAB(20);"     FORWARD EXCHANGE RATE:";TAB(55);FORWD
600 PRINT TAB(10);"5";TAB(20);" DAYS TO FORWARD DELIVERY :";TAB(55);T
610 PRINT:PRINT
620 INPUT "CHOOSE VARIABLE TO CHANGE OR TYPE '0' TO DO COMPUTATIONS",CHOICE
630  ON CHOICE GOSUB 420,440,460,480,500,
640  IF CHOICE = 0 THEN RETURN
650  GOTO 520
660 REM **********************************************************************
670 REM *                          COMPUTATIONS                              *
680 REM **********************************************************************
690 REM CHANGE RATES TO DECIMALS FOR COMPUTATIONS
700  RD = RD/100
710  RF = RF/100
720  IRDIF = (RD-RF)*(T/365)
730  IMPDIF = (1+RF)*((FORWD-SPOT)/SPOT)*(T/365)
740  IRDIF = INT(IRDIF*1000000!)/10000
750  IMPDIF = INT(IMPDIF*1000000!)/10000
760 REM **********************************************************************
770 REM *                            OUTPUT                                  *
780 REM **********************************************************************
790 PRINT:PRINT
800 PRINT "                    ACTUAL INTEREST RATE DIFFERENTIAL = ";IRDIF
810 PRINT "INTEREST RATE DIFFERENTIAL IMPLIED FROM FORWARD MARKET = ";IMPDIF
820 PRINT
830 INPUT "DO COMPUTATIONS AGAIN WITH MODIFIED DATA? (Y/N) ",A$
840  IF A$ = "Y" THEN GOTO 230
850 END
```

6
A Model for Pricing Convertible Bonds

A convertible bond is part bond and part option. Like other bonds, the convertible bond pays a periodic, specified coupon, and like a bond, it has a senior claim to payment. If the coupon payments are not met, the convertible bond holders have recourse through a claim on the assets of the firm.

But the convertible bond also has a conversion feature that gives the bondholder the right to convert the bond into a specified number of shares of stock at a specified price. This conversion feature is like a call option: it gives the bondholder the right to buy stock at a predetermined exercise price. Obviously, if the stock of the firm is significantly higher than this exercise price, the option value of the convertible bond will exceed its bond value. The bond will be worth more as potential stock than as a bond.

When the bond is converted, the firm will issue additional stock according to the agreements of the bond. This stock will dilute the value of shares outstanding. For example, if initially there are ten million shares outstanding, and the conversion of the bonds gives the bondholders the right to one million shares, then the total number of shares outstanding after conversion will be eleven million shares. If the value of the firm claimed by the equity itself has not changed, each share now will be worth less money. Each share will give rights to one eleven-millionth of the firm rather than one ten-millionth of the firm. This means that in evaluating conversion strategies, the postconversion value of the shares received by the bondholder must be considered, since this will differ from the preconversion share value. This adjustment is made by reducing the share value according to a *dilution* factor; in the example just cited, the dilution factor will be 1/11.

Typically, the convertible bond has a call feature that allows the firm to call the bond back for a specified price. Usually there are some restrictions on this feature, such as a minimum number of years before the bond can be called. A common restriction is that the bond cannot be called until five years after it has been issued. Also, the redemption price typically is initially higher than par value, and only drops toward par value over time, so the bondholder is guaranteed more return the earlier the bond is called.

The call provision dampens the value of the conversion option to some degree. The bond is likely to be called back if the stock begins to appreciate very far beyond the range of the redemption price. This means the potential

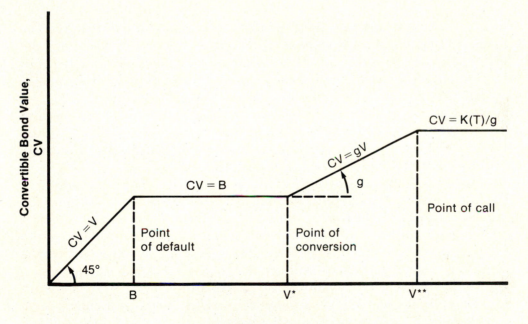

Figure 6-1. The value of a convertible bond.

for sizable gains through stock appreciation are lost to the bondholder. A callable convertible bond is complicated by the fact that the call feature leads to two conflicting options on the bond. The bondholder has the option to exchange the bond for stock, while the bond issuer has the option to call the bond back for a cash payment.

The particulars of the bond pricing, dilution factor, and call features are obviously important in pricing the bond. These are too complex to list in the daily bond market quotes, but they are available in other sources, such as Moody's Manual.

Since we know how to price bonds and how to price options, it seems reasonable that we can combine these two to price convertible bonds. In this chapter we will show how this can be done.

THE RELATIONSHIP BETWEEN THE VALUE OF A CONVERTIBLE BOND AND THE VALUE OF THE FIRM

Consider a simple discount bond with a conversion and call feature. The discount bond gives a payment of B dollars at the end of the year, and furthermore, if it is converted, the bond can be exchanged for a fraction g of the postconversion equity of the firm. Figure 6-1 traces the value of a convertible bond as the value of the firm varies. If the value of the firm is below B, then the assets of the firm are not sufficient to pay off the bondholders. The firm then goes into default, and the bondholders get claim to the assets of the firm. If the value of the firm is above B then the bondholders can get the payment B, so that at maturity the bond will be worth at least B dollars.

However, if the value of the firm is high enough, it will be in the interest of the bondholders to convert the bond and take a share of the equity value of the firm. In particular, if the fraction that they receive of the value of the firm is greater than B, the bondholders will convert. This will be the case if the overall value of the firm is greater than B/g. This is depicted in Figure 6-1 by the increasing slope in the value line above the point V^*. The line rises at a rate g equal to the fraction of the value of the firm that they receive.

The call provision is represented by the final turn in the profit line at point V^{**}. There is the conversion value gV equals the effective call price, $K(T)/g$, and it is better for the firm to exercise its option to redeem the bonds than to let the bondholders take a claim to any further increases in the firm's value.

PRICING CONVERTIBLE BONDS

The simplest case to consider in valuing convertible bonds is a pure discount convertible bond without a call provision. In this case, the value of the convertible bond is simply equal to the value of an ordinary discount bond plus a warrant or option that entitles the bondholder to purchase a fraction of the equity of the company equal to the conversion value of the bond upon payment of an exercise price equal to the principal of the bond. That is, the value of the convertible, CV, is

$$CV = F(V,T,B) + C(gV,T,B).$$

In this equation, F( ) is the value of the discount bond, and C( ) is the value of the call option giving the right to buy a fraction of the firm worth gV dollars for an exercise price of B.

For a callable convertible bond, as we have already discussed, the pricing becomes more difficult, because we now must consider the possibility of two options. The procedure for valuing a callable convertible depends pivotally on the specification of the call provision. The program for this chapter uses a general numerical approach that can determine the convertible's price for fairly complex call features and coupon payment streams.

The effect of the call feature on the convertible bond can be illustrated by assuming the price at which the bond can be called decreases at a compounding rate over time, much like an interest rate discounting factor.

Let ρ be the rate at which the call price decreases over time. If the value of ρ is less than the prevailing riskless interest rate r, then the optimal call policy for the firm will be to call the bonds when the value of the firm reaches $V(T)=K(T)/g$.

Under this simple call structure, the convertible bond price can now be stated as the sum of three terms:

$$CV = F(V,T,B) + C(gV,T,B) - W(V,T,B;g,\rho).$$

This expression for the price of the convertible bond is similar to the price for the noncallable convertible bond. The only difference is the addition of a third term, W( ). This third term reflects the value of the call provision to the issuer of the bond. Since whatever value is gained by the issuer is lost to the bondholder, this third term will reduce the price of the bond. The value of W is fairly complex, but can be expressed in terms of the difference in two call option prices.

In the special case where the rate of increase in the price for calling the bond equals the interest rate, the value of the callable convertible bond reduces to the price of a pure discount bond plus the price of a call option, although with the terms of the call option differing slightly from the terms of the call option represented in the pricing of the noncallable bond.

USING THE CONVERTIBLE BOND PRICING MODEL

The pricing model for convertible bonds requires inputs of the bond coupon rate and the current market yield for bonds that are equivalent to the convertible bond but without the bond feature, the terms of the call provision, the dilution factor g, and the conversion rate, which specifies the number of shares of stock the bond can be converted into. It also requires the parameters necessary for computing the options price: the time to maturity, the riskfree interest rate, and the volatility of the stock.

CONVERTIBLE BOND PRICING MODEL

Computational Procedure

i = counter to increment the number of time periods
j = counter to increment the stock price
$B(i)$ = underlying bond value in period i
$CP(i)$ = call price in period i
$S(i,j)$ = stock price j for period i
$C(i,j)$ = value of the option underlying the convertible bond in period i given a stock price j
$CV(i,j)$ = convertible bond value in period i given a stock price of j
g = dilution factor
c = conversion ratio

The value of the convertible bond in period i, given a stock value $S(i,j)$, will be the lower of the call price $CP(i)$, or the market value of the convertible bond. The market value of the convertible bond will in turn be the larger of the value of the bond if converted, $(1-g) \cdot c \cdot S(i,j)$, or the value of the bond if not converted, $B(i,j) + C(i,j)$. Thus the convertible bond value in period i for stock price j, can be expressed as

$$CV(i,j) = Min[CP(i), Max((1-g) \cdot c \cdot S(i,j), B(i,j) + C(i,j))].$$

This leads to a system that is solved numerically using finite differences, leading finally to the current period convertible bond price.

The option value is computed recursively, using a method similar to that described in Chapter 22.

Trading Strategy

- Buy the convertible bond if its model price, CV, is greater than its market price.
- Sell the convertible bond if its model price, CV, is less than its market price.

```
10    REM  *****************************************************************
20    REM *                   CONVERTIBLE BOND PRICING                     *
30    REM *                                                                *
40    REM *    THIS PROGRAM USES THE ARBITRAGE PRICING METHODS OF OPTION   *
50    REM *    PRICING TO DETERMINE THE CORRECT PRICE FOR CONVERTIBLE BONDS.*
60    REM *    THE PROGRAM EMPLOYS A NUMERICAL SOLUTION WHICH ALLOWS FOR    *
70    REM *    STOCK DIVIDENDS AND PERIODIC COUPON PAYMENTS, AS WELL AS     *
80    REM *    A CALL PROVISION.                                           *
90    REM *                                                                *
100   REM *    VARIABLES USED:                                             *
110   REM *                    S = STOCK PRICE                             *
120   REM *                    B = PAR VALUE OF THE BOND                   *
130   REM *                    K = DISCOUNT RATE FOR THE BOND              *
140   REM *                    R = RISKFREE INTEREST RATE                  *
150   REM *                   CR = CONVERSION RATIO (THE NUMBER OF SHARES OF *
160   REM *                        STOCK RECEIVED WHEN BOND IS CONVERTED)  *
170   REM *                CL(I) = CALL PRICE FOR THE BOND                 *
180   REM *                    D = QUARTERLY DOLLAR DIVIDEND PAYMENT       *
190   REM *                    G = DILUTION FACTOR                         *
200   REM *               COUPON = SEMI-ANNUAL DOLLAR COUPON PAYMENT       *
210   REM *                    V = VOLATILITY OF THE STOCK                 *
220   REM *                    T = YEARS TO MATURITY FOR THE BOND          *
230   REM *                                                                *
240   REM  *****************************************************************
250   Y1=0
260   DIM SE(60),NU(60),CP(60,60),COUPON(120),CL(20),BCALL(60),TCOUPON(120)
270   DIM TDIVIDEND(120),PLUS(60),MINUS(60),DIV(60)
280   REM
290   REM
300   GOSUB 1370:REM*********************INPUT DATA*********************
310   REM
320   REM
330   GOSUB 470:REM*********************DO COMPUTATIONS*********************
340   REM
350   REM
360   GOSUB 1900:REM*********************OUTPUT DATA*********************
370   REM
380   REM
390   END:REM*************************STOP PROGRAM*********************
400   REM
410   REM
420   REM*****************************************************************
430   REM                     SUBROUTINE TO DO COMPUTATIONS
440   REM*****************************************************************
450   REM
460   REM
470   REM INITIALIZE VALUES
480   REM
490   PN=CINT(T*2) :REM SET NUMBER OF PERIODS; 30 PERIODS IS SET AS THE MINIMUM
500   IF PN<=30 THEN PN=30
510   PL=(T*365)/PN
520   D=D*2    :REM CONVERT DIVIDEND INTO SEMI-ANNUAL TERMS
530   D=1-D/S
540   TPERIODS=T/PN
```

```
550   RH=(R/100+1)^TPERIODS
560   KH=(K/100+1)¨TPERIODS
570   UP=EXP(V*SQR(TPERIODS))
580   DN=1/UP
590   P=(RH-DN)/(UP-DN)
600   REM
610   REM DETERMINE PERIODS WHEN STOCK WILL GO EXDIVIDEND
620   REM
630   FOR L=0 TO (T*2)
640     TDIVIDEND(L)=CINT((PN/T)*.5*L)
650   NEXT L
660   FOR I=0 TO PN
670     NU(TDIVIDEND(I))=N : N=N+1
680   NEXT I
690   REM
700   REM SET UP ARRAYS FOR GRID OF STOCK PRICE CHANGES
710   REM
720   FOR I=0 TO PN
730     PLUS(I) = UP^I
740     MINUS(I) = DN^I
750     DIV(I) = D^NU(I)
760   NEXT I
770   REM
780   REM DETERMINE STOCK PRICES AND VALUE OF BOND IF CONVERTED IN LAST PERIOD
790   REM
800   FOR I=0 TO PN
810     SE(I)=S*(MINUS(PN-I))*(PLUS(I))*(DIV(PN))
820     SE(I)=SE(I)*(1-G)*N
830   NEXT I
840   REM
850   REM DETERMINE PERIODS WITH COUPON PAYMENTS
860   REM
870   FOR L=0 TO (T*2)
880     TCOUPON(L)=CINT((PN/T)*.5*L)
890   NEXT L
900   FOR I=0 TO PN
910     COUPON(TCOUPON(I))=COUPON
920   NEXT I
930   REM
940   REM CALCULATE PRICES AT WHICH BOND WILL BE CALLED
950   REM
960   FOR I=0 TO PN
970     LIM=CINT(T/5)
980     FOR L=1 TO LIM
990       IF ((5*PN/T)*(L-1)<=I AND I<(5*PN/T)*L) THEN BCALL(I)=CL(L)
1000    NEXT L
1010   NEXT I
1020   REM DETERMINE CONVERTIBLE BOND VALUES IN LAST PERIOD
1030   FOR J=0 TO PN
1040     CV1=SE(J)*CR*(1-G)
1050     IF B>CV1 THEN CV1=B
1060     IF CV1>BCALL(1) THEN CV1=BCALL(1)
1070     CP(PN,J)=CV1
1080   NEXT J
```

```
1090 REM
1100 REM WORKING BACKWARD, DETERMINE CALL/PUT VALUES IN PRECEEDING PERIODS
1110 REM
1120  FOR I=PN-1 TO 0 STEP -1
1130    FOR J=0 TO I
1140      C1=MINUS(I-J)*PLUS(J)*DIV(I)*S*(1-G)*CR
1150      C2=(P*CP(I+1,J+1)+(1-P)*CP(I+1,J))/RH + COUPON(I)/KH
1160      IF C1>=C2 THEN CP(I,J)=C1 ELSE CP(I,J)=C2
1170    IF CP(I,J)>BCALL(I) THEN CP(I,J)=BCALL(I)
1180 REM COUNTER TO MONITOR THE TIME IN THE LOOP
1190      FOR IT=0 TO PN STEP 10
1200        IF I=PN-IT AND J=0 THEN PRINT "CURRENTLY ON ITERATION ";IT
1210      NEXT IT
1220    NEXT J
1230  NEXT I
1240 REM
1250 REM DETERMINE CONVERTIBLE BOND VALUE IN CURRENT PERIOD
1260 REM
1270  CV=CP(0,0)
1280 RETURN
1290 REM
1300 REM
1310 REM*******************************************************************
1320 REM                        SUBROUTINE TO INPUT DATA
1330 REM*******************************************************************
1340 REM
1350 REM
1360 PRINT "YOU MAY ENTER THE FOLLOWING VARIABLES:"
1370 PRINT TAB(10);"CURRENT STOCK PRICE ($)";TAB(55):INPUT ;S
1380  IF Y1=1 THEN RETURN
1390 PRINT TAB(10);"BOND PAR VALUE ($)";TAB(55):INPUT ;B
1400  IF Y1=2 THEN RETURN
1410 PRINT TAB(10);"ANNUAL RISKFREE INTEREST RATE (%)";TAB(55):INPUT ;R
1420  IF Y1=3 THEN RETURN
1430 PRINT TAB(10);"QUARTERLY DIVIDEND ($)";TAB(55):INPUT ;D
1440  IF Y1=4 THEN RETURN
1450 PRINT TAB(10);"TIME TO MATURITY (YEARS)";TAB(55):INPUT ;T
1460  IF Y1=5 THEN RETURN
1470 PRINT TAB(10);"VOLATILITY OF STOCK";TAB(55):INPUT ;V
1480  IF Y1=6 THEN RETURN
1490 PRINT TAB(10);"DILUTION FACTOR (SET AT 1 IF NO DILUTION)";TAB(55):INPUT ;G

1500  IF Y1=7 THEN RETURN
1510 PRINT TAB(10);"CONVERSION RATIO";TAB(55):INPUT ;CR
1520  IF Y1=8 THEN RETURN
1530 PRINT TAB(10);"DISCOUNT RATE FOR BOND (%)";TAB(55):INPUT ;K
1540  IF Y1=9 THEN RETURN
1550 PRINT TAB(10);"SEMI-ANNUAL COUPON PAYMENT ($)";TAB(55):INPUT ;COUPON
1560  IF Y1=10 THEN RETURN
1570 PRINT TAB(10);"BOND CALL PRICE FOR:"
1580 PRINT TAB(15);"THE NEXT 5 YEARS";TAB(55):INPUT ;CL(1)
1590  IF CINT(T/5)<2 GOTO 1630
1600  FOR I=2 TO CINT(T/5)
1610 PRINT TAB(15);"THE FOLLOWING 5 YEARS";TAB(55):INPUT CL(I)
```

```
1620   NEXT I
1630 PRINT
1640 PRINT
1650 PRINT "YOU MAY CHANGE ANY OF THE VALUES ENTERED ABOVE AS FOLLOWS:"
1660 PRINT TAB(10);"CHOICE";TAB(20);"ITEM TO CHANGE";TAB(55);"CURRENT VALUE"
1670 PRINT TAB(10);"------";TAB(20);"--------------";TAB(55);"-------------"
1680 PRINT TAB(10);"0";TAB(20);"COMPUTE CONVERTIBLE BOND PRICE"
1690 PRINT TAB(10);"1";TAB(20);"CURRENT STOCK PRICE ($)";TAB(55);S
1700 PRINT TAB(10);"2";TAB(20);"BOND PAR VALUE";TAB(55);B
1710 PRINT TAB(10);"3";TAB(20);"ANNUAL INTEREST RATE (%)";TAB(55);R
1720 PRINT TAB(10);"4";TAB(20);"QUARTERLY DIVIDEND ($)";TAB(55);D
1730 PRINT TAB(10);"5";TAB(20);"TIME TO MATURITY (YEARS)";TAB(55);T
1740 PRINT TAB(10);"6";TAB(20);"VOLATILITY";TAB(55);V
1750 PRINT TAB(10);"7";TAB(20);"DILUTION FACTOR (0 TO 1)";TAB(55);G
1760 PRINT TAB(10);"8";TAB(20);"CONVERSION RATIO";TAB(55);CR
1770 PRINT TAB(10);"9";TAB(20);"DISCOUNT RATE FOR BOND (%)";TAB(55);K
1780 PRINT TAB(9);"10";TAB(20);"SEMI-ANNUAL COUPON PAYMENT";TAB(55);COUPON
1790 PRINT
1800 PRINT
1810 INPUT "WHICH CHOICE DO YOU DESIRE (0-10)";Y1
1820   ON Y1 GOSUB 1370,1390,1410,1430,1450,1470,1490,1510,1530,1550
1830   IF Y1=0 THEN RETURN
1840 PRINT
1850 PRINT
1860   GOTO 1650
1870 REM
1880 REM
1890 REM*********************************************************************
1900 REM                        SUBROUTINE TO OUTPUT DATA
1910 REM*********************************************************************
1920 REM
1930 REM
1940 PRINT:PRINT
1950 PRINT TAB(10);"THE BOND VALUE=";TAB(42);:PRINT USING "####.##";CV
1960 PRINT:PRINT
1970 REM
1980 REM RETURN T AND D TO ORIGINAL VALUES
1990 REM
2000   TPERIOD=TPERIOD*PN
2010   D=S-S*D
2020   D=D*.5
2030 INPUT "DO YOU WISH TO GO AGAIN WITH MODIFIED DATA (Y/N)";A3$
2040   IF A3$="Y" THEN GOSUB 1630:GOTO 320
2050 RETURN
```

7
Bond Swaps to Improve Portfolio Performance

A bond swap, as its name implies, is the trading of one bond for another bond. The bonds in the swap may vary in terms of coupon rate, time to maturity, or the segment of the market they represent. Bond swaps may be used for yield improvements, to take advantage of shifts in interest rate levels, or to take advantage of changes in the intermarket yield spreads.

The recent volatility of interest rates demands that far more attention be given to the value of bond swaps, and particularly to the source of the apparent returns to the swap. Slight miscalculations in interest rates can be disastrous for swaps whose profits depend on interest rate changes or reinvestment rate assumptions. Therefore, it is important to be able to pinpoint what portion of the realized yield accruing to the swap is sensitive to these factors.

The program for this chapter separates the return to a swap into three parts: the coupon payments; the interest generated by the reinvestment of these coupon payments, referred to as the *interest on interest;* and the capital gain or loss resulting from bond price changes. The *realized compound yield* is the sum of these elements of return, and the *value of the swap*, reported in the program along with these other values, is the difference between the realized yield to the bond that is to be purchased and the realized yield of the bond that is currently held.

There are four principle types of bond swaps. The simplest is called a *substitution swap*. This is a swap from one bond into another bond that is a close substitute, but that allows a larger realized compound yield. A second type of swap is the *yield pickup swap*, which involves shifting from one bond to another bond with a higher coupon yield. This is done simply to capture the higher coupon without any expectation of interest rate shifts leading to capital gains. A third swap is the *rate anticipation swap*. The rate anticipation swap involves moving from one bond to another in a way that capitalizes on anticipated changes in the market interest rate. Finally, there is the *intermarket spread swap*. The swap involves moving from one segment of the bond market to another segment, in anticipation of changes in the basis, the interest rate differential between the market segments. There are many other types of swaps as well, engaged in for tax purposes, for liquidity, or for altering the risk characteristics of the bond portfolio. We will illustrate two of these swaps—the substitution swap, and the rate anticipation swap.

APPLYING THE BOND SWAP PROGRAM: TWO EXAMPLES

The Substitution Swap

The substitution swap involves trading one bond for another bond of similar market and risk characteristics, but with a higher realized yield. Suppose the bond currently held has a coupon rate of 7⅛%, a par value of $1000, and a current market price of $632.50. The yield to maturity for this bond is 12.11%.

The candidate for the swap is a bond with a 12¼% coupon rate, and is currently selling at par. This means its yield to maturity equals its coupon rate. If both bonds are comparable in terms of risk and the market segment they represent, then a swap into the 12¼% bond will lead to a pickup of 14 basis points in yield to maturity.

The bond that is currently held is priced far below the bond to be purchased. To equate the dollar value of the bond to be purchased with the bond to be sold, we will sell 1.581 of the bond held for each one bond purchased. Table 7-1 shows the results of the swap when this proportion of the bonds held are sold for each bond purchased.

In Table 7-1, the first column on the left compares the coupon return generated for each of the bonds. The bond to be purchased gives a slightly higher coupon return; $122.50 per year, reflecting the 12.25% coupon rate. The

TABLE 7-1. Bond Swap Evaluation[a, b]

	CUMULATIVE COUPON RETURN	INTEREST ON INTEREST	BOND PRICE	CAPITAL GAIN	REALIZED YIELD	VALUE OF SWAP
Year 1						
Bond Held	112.65	3.45	997.37	-2.63	11.35	
Bond Purchased	122.50	3.75	1000.00	0	12.63	1.28
Year 2						
Bond Held	225.29	21.56	1007.20	7.20	25.41	
Bond Purchased	245.00	23.44	1000.00	0	26.84	1.43
Year 3						
Bond Held	337.94	56.17	1018.26	18.26	41.24	
Bond Purchased	367.50	61.09	1000.00	0	42.86	1.62
Year 4						
Bond Held	450.59	109.38	1030.72	30.72	59.07	
Bond Purchased	490.00	118.95	1000.00	0	60.89	1.82
Year 5						
Bond Held	563.23	183.52	1044.76	44.76	79.15	
Bond Purchased	612.50	199.58	1000.00	0	81.21	2.06
Year 6						
Bond Held	675.88	281.25	1060.56	60.56	101.77	
Bond Purchased	735.00	305.86	1000.00	0	104.09	2.32

TABLE 7-1. Bond Swap Evaluation[a, b] *(continued)*

	CUMULATIVE COUPON RETURN	INTEREST ON INTEREST	BOND PRICE	CAPITAL GAIN	REALIZED YIELD	VALUE OF SWAP
Year 7						
Bond Held	788.52	405.54	1078.37	78.37	127.25	
Bond Purchased	857.50	441.02	1000.00	0	129.85	2.60
Year 8						
Bond Held	901.17	559.74	1098.42	98.42	155.94	
Bond Purchased	980.00	608.71	1000.00	0	158.87	2.93
Year 9						
Bond Held	1013.82	747.64	1121.00	121.00	188.25	
Bond Purchased	1102.50	813.04	1000.00	0	191.55	3.30

[a]The bond held has a par value of **$1000**, current price of $632.50, 19 years to maturity, and a coupon rate of 7⅛%. The bond to be purchased has a par value of $1000, current price of $1000, nine years to maturity, and a coupon rate of 12.25%.

[b]1,581 of the bonds held are being sold for each bond purchased in this evaluation.

bond currently held gives an annual coupon of $112.65, an amount that is 1.581 times the coupon rate of 7.125%.

The next column is the interest on interest. This is the interest income that accrues to the bondholder by reinvesting the coupon payments at the prevailing market rate. The market rate for both bonds is assumed to be the same in this example, 12.25%. The interest on interest naturally will accrue faster on the bond to be purchased, since it provides a larger coupon for reinvestment. As this example illustrates, the interest on interest can be a substantial part of the overall bond value. By year 9, when the bond to be purchased matures, the interest on interest is nearly as large as the total value of the coupon payments themselves, and is far larger than the capital gain from the bonds. Naturally, the interest on interest will be a more significant factor the longer the bond is held. It is also a very uncertain part of the bond value, since shifts in the reinvestment rate can have a dramatic impact on it.

The next column "Bond Price" traces the path of the bond price over time. The bond price stays at par for the bond to be purchased, and increases toward par for the bond that is currently held. Since more than one of these bonds is being considered in the swap, the total value of this bond position increases steadily above $1000, bringing a capital gain by year 9 of just over $121. The capital gain, the difference between the bond's market price and par value, is shown in the next column.

The yield resulting from these three factors are then reported in the next column as the *realized yield* for the bond. The difference between the realized yield for the bond currently held and the bond that is to be purchased determines the value of the swap. The value of the swap is positive in this case, giving a 128 basis point advantage the first year, and increasing up to a 330 basis point advantage by year 9.

The breakdown of the bond swap into its constituent parts facilitates risk analysis of the swap strategy. The importance of the interest on interest in the success of the strategy is apparent from Table 7-1. Over 42% of the value of the bond to be purchased is due to interest on interest, compared to slightly less than 40% of the value of the bond held. While the coupon payments and, to a large part, the capital gain are not interest rate dependent, the interest on interest is closely tied to future market rates. The program, therefore, opens up to inspection an area of concern for this particular bond swap.

RATE ANTICIPATION SWAPS

A rate anticipation swap is motivated by a predicted change in market bond yields. As we already noted in the introduction to the bond section, different bonds will react in different ways to changes in interest rates. In particular, bond prices change more in percentage terms with changes in interest rates the longer the time remaining to maturity, and the lower the coupon rate. For an investor who believes interest rates are on the rise, this means a natural strategy is to shift from longer term bonds to shorter term bonds, and from low coupon bonds to higher-coupon bonds. For declining market interest rates, the opposite strategy of moving from shorter to longer maturity bonds, and from higher to lower coupon bonds will be most profitable.

We will illustrate the rate anticipation bond swap by considering a move out of the 8⅛s of 2005 Treasury bond when the market rate is thought to be going up. Suppose this bond is currently selling at $745, giving it a yield to maturity of 11.33%. The investor predicts interest will rise slightly. Since this bond has both a long time to maturity and a comparatively low coupon rate, it will be one of the big losers if interest rates do rise.

Consider two possible swaps. The first is to a shorter maturity Treasury bond, one with only four years to maturity, and a coupon rate of 8¼. This bond almost matches the coupon rate on the bond currently held. It is priced at 905, giving it a yield to maturity of 11.27%.

The second candidate for the swap also has just four years to maturity, but has a coupon rate of 14%, far higher than the other two. It is priced at 1087.5 to yield 11.21%, just six basis points lower than the yield to maturity of the 8¼ bond.

Since the yields of the bonds are virtually identical, the relationship between bond coupon rates and price volatility discussed above would suggest the higher coupon bond is the best choice in the swap. Table 7-2 compares the value of each of these swaps. It is based on the output of the swap program at the end of this chapter. This table verifies that the higher coupon bond, the 14, is a better candidate for the swap, although only slightly better. The value of a swap to the 14, shown in Table 7-2A, is 341 basis points over a one-year holding period, compared to 337 basis points for the 8¼, and is 483 basis points after four years, compared to 478 basis points for the 8¼.

TABLE 7-2. Bond Swap Evaluation*

	CUMULATIVE COUPON RETURN	INTEREST ON INTEREST	BOND PRICE	CAPITAL GAIN	REALIZED YIELD	VALUE OF SWAP
A						
Year 1						
Bond Held	81.25	2.44	708.48	-36.52	6.33	
Bond Purchased	140.00	4.20	1049.17	-38.33	9.74	3.41
Year 2						
Bond Held	162.50	15.22	712.36	-32.64	19.47	
Bond Purchased	280.00	26.22	1034.65	-52.85	23.30	3.83
Year 3						
Bond Held	243.75	39.62	716.72	-28.28	34.24	
Bond Purchased	420.00	68.27	1018.33	-69.17	38.54	4.30
Year 4						
Bond Held	325.00	77.08	721.62	-23.38	50.83	
Bond Purchased	560.00	132.82	1000.00	-87.50	55.66	4.83
B						
Year 1						
Bond Held	81.25	2.44	708.48	-36.52	6.33	
Bond Purchased	82.50	2.47	907.80	2.80	9.70	3.37

TABLE 7-2. Bond Swap Evaluation* *(continued)*

B

	CUMULATIVE COUPON RETURN	INTEREST ON INTEREST	BOND PRICE	CAPITAL GAIN	REALIZED YIELD	VALUE OF SWAP
Year 2						
Bond Held	162.50	15.22	712.36	-32.64	19.47	
Bond Purchased	165.00	15.45	935.03	30.03	23.26	3.79
Year 3						
Bond Held	243.75	39.62	716.72	-28.28	34.24	
Bond Purchased	247.50	40.23	965.62	60.62	38.49	4.25
Year 4						
Bond Held	325.00	77.08	721.62	-23.38	50.83	
Bond Purchased	330.00	78.27	1000.00	95.00	55.61	4.78

*The bond held has a par value of $1000, current price of $745, 21 years to maturity, and a coupon rate of 8⅛%. The bond being considered in Table 7-2A has a par value of $1000, current of $1000, current price of $1087.50, and a coupon rate of 14%. The bond being considered in Table 7-2B for purchase has a par value of $1000, current price of $905, and a coupon rate of 8¼%. Both of the bonds considered for purchase have four years to maturity.

The difference is not substantial, but the first impulse is to go with the 14, since it does have a slight edge. However, a closer inspection of where the swap value for the 14 is coming from may lead to second thoughts. The bulk of the value for the 8¼ is in the capital gain. That gain is not interest-rate-dependent over the four-year period, since it must sell for par at maturity. But the movement toward par value leads to an unavoidable capital loss for the 14. It is selling at a premium, and will drop to par at maturity for a loss of $87.50. The gain from the 14 is through coupon return, and even more significantly, through interest on interest. The coupon return, of course, is not affected by changes in the market interest rate. But the interest on interest is. If interest rates subsequently drop, the reinvestment rate for the coupons will drop, and the interest on interest will drop. The value of the swap into the 14 may therefore be more risky, since it is more interest rate dependent.

This example serves as an illustration of the insight that can be gained by breaking up the swap into its component parts. Each aspect of the swap is affected by different factors, and the swap program provides a useful tool for analyzing the sensitivity of the swap to market uncertainties.

One important aspect of many bond swaps, indeed the motivating factor for some swaps, is the tax effect of shifting from one bond to another. Different bonds will lead to different patterns of interest and capital gains, with varying tax consequences. The complex and individual nature of the tax consequence for alternative strategies force us to forego a discussion of these tax effects. However, their importance deserves mentioning.

```
10    REM *************************************************************************
20    REM *                         BOND SWAP ANALYSIS                            *
30    REM *                                                                       *
40    REM * THIS PROGRAM WILL ANALYZE THE RELATIVE VALUE OF TWO BONDS AND         *
50    REM * COMPARE THE BONDS IN TERMS OF COUPON RETURN, INTEREST ON INTEREST,    *
60    REM * CAPITAL GAINS, AND REALIZED YIELD.                                    *
70    REM *                                                                       *
80    REM * VARIABLES USED:   C = ANNUAL COUPON RATE                              *
90    REM *                   P = PAR VALUE OF BOND                               *
100   REM *                   N = NUMBER OF YEARS TO MATURITY                     *
110   REM *                   K = DISCOUNT RATE                                   *
120   REM *                   M = NUMBER OF DIVIDEND PAYMENTS PER YEAR            *
130   REM *                   D = DAYS TO NEXT PAYMENT                            *
140   REM *                   R = RANGE OF YEARS                                  *
150   REM *                   Q = QUANTITY TO BE USED IN THE SWAP                 *
160   REM *                PMKT = CURRENT MARKET PRICE OF BOND                    *
170   REM *                                                                       *
180   REM *                                                                       *
190   REM *                                                                       *
200   REM *                                                                       *
210   REM *************************************************************************
220   REM
230   X=2 :REM CHOOSE NUMBER OF BONDS TO ANALYZE
240   REM DIMENSION ARRAYS
250   DIM C(X),P(X),N(X),K(X),M(X),D(X),PMKT(X),INCOME(X,100),INTEREST(X,100)
260   DIM PFMKT(X,100),GAIN(X,100),REALYIELD(X,100),CAPGAIN(X,100),VALU(100)
270   DIM ANNUITY(100),PRINCIPAL(100)
280   REM
290   REM
300   GOSUB 400:REM*********************INPUT*********************************
310   REM
320   REM
330   GOSUB 610:REM*******************COMPUTATIONS****************************
340   REM
350   REM
360   GOSUB 1190:REM*********************OUTPUT*******************************
370   REM
380   REM
390   REM *************************************************************************
400   REM *                              INPUT                                    *
410   REM *************************************************************************
420   CLS :REM CLEARS SCREEN
430   FOR J = 1 TO 2
440     IF J = 1 THEN GOTO 470
450   PRINT "ENTER THE FOLLOWING DATA FOR BOND TO BE PURCHASED:"
460     GOTO 480
470   PRINT "ENTER THE FOLLOWING DATA FOR BOND HELD:"
480   INPUT "          ANNUAL COUPON RATE(%):   ",C
490     C=C*.01 :REM CONVERT TO DECIMAL
500   INPUT "                    PAR VALUE:   ",P
510   INPUT "          CURRENT MARKET PRICE:   ",PMKT
520   INPUT "            YEARS TO MATURITY:   ",N
530   INPUT "         ANNUAL DISCOUNT RATE(%):   ",K
540     K=K*.01 :REM CONVERT TO DECIMAL
```

```
550 INPUT "NUMBER OF COUPON PAYMENTS PER YEAR:   ",M
560 INPUT "        DAYS TO NEXT COUPON PAYMENT:   ",D
570 INPUT "        QUANTITY INVOLVED IN SWAP:   ",Q
580 PRINT:PRINT
590 REM
600 REM ***********************************************************************
610 REM *                          COMPUTATIONS                               *
620 REM ***********************************************************************
630 REM
640   PMKT = PMKT*Q :REM ADJUST CURRENT PRICE FOR NUMBER OF BONDS HELD
650 REM COMPUTE COUPON INCOME AND INTEREST ON INTEREST TO YEAR I
660 REM
670   FOR I = 1 TO N
680     INCOME(J,I) = C*P*I*Q
690     INTEREST(J,I) = (((((1 + K/M)^(M*I) -1)/(K/M))*(C/M)*P*Q) - INCOME(J,I)
700   NEXT I
710 REM
720 REM COMPUTE VALUE OF BOND IN YEAR I
730 REM
740   ENDCOUPON=C*P*Q/M
750   DISCOUNT=(1+K/M)^(D/30/12/M)
760   TAG=C*P*Q/M*(1-D/30/12/M)
770   FOR I = 1 TO N
780     ANNUITY(I)=C*P*Q/M*(1-(1/(1+K/M)^(M*(N-I))))/K/M
790     PRINCIPAL(I)=P*Q/(1+K/M)^(M*(N-I))
800     PFMKT(J,I) =(ANNUITY(I)+PRINCIPAL(I)+ENDCOUPON)/DISCOUNT-TAG
810   NEXT I
820 REM
830 REM COMPUTE CAPITAL GAIN
840 REM COMPUTE TOTAL DOLLAR GAIN TO YEAR I
850 REM COMPUTE REALIZED COMPOUND YIELD TO YEAR I
860 REM
870   FOR I=1 TO N
880     CAPGAIN(J,I)=PFMKT(J,I)-PMKT
890     GAIN(J,I)=PFMKT(J,I)+INCOME(J,I)+INTEREST(J,I)-PMKT
900     REALYIELD(J,I) = GAIN(J,I)/PMKT*100
910   NEXT I
920   C(J)=C:P(J)=P:N(J)=N:K(J)=K:M(J)=M:D(J)=D:PMKT(J)=PMKT
930   NEXT J :REM REPEAT LOOP FOR BOND PURCHASED
940 REM FIX PERIOD FOR ANALYSIS
950 IF N(1) < N(2) THEN N=N(1)
960 ELSE N=N(2)
970 REM
980 REM DETERMINE VALUE OF SWAP
990 REM
1000  FOR I=1 TO N
1010    VALU(I) = REALYIELD(2,I) - REALYIELD(1,I)
1020  NEXT I
1030 REM
1040 REM ROUND VALUES
1050 REM
1060  FOR J=1 TO X
1070    FOR I=1 TO N
1080      INTEREST(J,I)=INT((INTEREST(J,I)+.005)*100)/100
```

```
1090     PFMKT(J,I)=INT((PFMKT(J,I)+.005)*100)/100
1100     CAPGAIN(J,I)=INT((CAPGAIN(J,I)+.005)*100)/100
1110     REALYIELD(J,I)=INT((REALYIELD(J,I)+.005)*100)/100
1120     VALU(I)=INT((VALU(I)+.005)*100)/100
1130     INCOME(J,I)=INT((INCOME(J,I)+.005)*100)/100
1140   NEXT I
1150   NEXT J
1160 REM
1170 REM
1180 REM ********************************************************************
1190 REM *                            OUTPUT                               *
1200 REM ********************************************************************
1210 REM
1220   GOSUB 1240
1230   GOTO 1290
1240 CLS :REM CLEARS SCREEN
1250 PRINT"               COUPON    INTEREST ON  BOND  CAPITAL  REALIZED  VALUE OF
1260 PRINT"               RETURN      INTEREST   PRICE   GAIN     YIELD     SWAP"
1270 PRINT"               ------    -----------  -----  -------  -------  -------"
1280 RETURN
1290   FOR I = 1 TO N
1300 PRINT "YEAR ";I
1310 PRINT TAB(3);"BOND H";TAB(15);INCOME(1,I);TAB(23);INTEREST(1,I);
1320 PRINT TAB(35);PFMKT(1,I);TAB(46);CAPGAIN(1,I);TAB(56);REALYIELD(1,I)
1330 PRINT TAB(3);"BOND P";TAB(15);INCOME(2,I);TAB(23);INTEREST(2,I);
1340 PRINT TAB(35);PFMKT(2,I);TAB(46);CAPGAIN(2,I);TAB(56);REALYIELD(2,I);
1350 PRINT TAB(66);VALU(I)
1360 PRINT
1370   IF I/4=INT(I/4) THEN INPUT "PRESS RETURN TO CONTINUE",Q$
1380   IF (I/4 = INT(I/4)) AND (I<N) THEN GOSUB 1240
1390   NEXT I
1400 REM
1410 REM *************TO RERUN PROGRAM WITH DIFFERENT BONDS *****************
1420 REM
1430 PRINT:PRINT
1440 INPUT "WOULD YOU LIKE TO ANALYZE ANOTHER POSSIBLE SWAP?    (Y/N)",AGAIN$
1450   IF AGAIN$ = "Y" THEN GOTO 300
1460 END
```

8
Immunization: Risk Management Strategies for Bond Portfolios

The greatest risk in a bond portfolio is not the risk of default. By holding a widely diversified set of high quality bonds, the maximum loss from default can be kept negligible. The greatest risk for bonds arises from changes in interest rates.

Interest rates affect the bond portfolio in two ways. First, they affect the price of the bonds, leading to capital gains or losses if the bond is sold before maturity. Second, they lead to changes in the reinvestment rate for coupon payments, affecting the returns that are generated on the coupons from the bond. The first effect is well known by anyone who has dabbled in the bond market. As interest rates rise, bond prices drop so that the return on the bonds matches the interest rate. But the second effect is equally important. And, significantly, the effect of interest rates on coupon reinvestment rates is the opposite of their effect on the bond price itself. If interest rates rise, the coupon payments can be reinvested at a higher rate.

The counteracting effects of interest rate changes on the value of the bond and on the reinvestment rate suggest that by properly balancing the two effects, a bond position can be created with a value that on net is unaffected by interest rate changes. That is, a bond position can be formed where the impact of interest rate changes on the bond price is exactly offset by the impact of the interest rates on the returns from reinvestment of the coupons.

For many bond portfolio managers, the most important objective is to assure the capital invested will appreciate to a predetermined amount by some future date. For example, a pension fund will have a predetermined outflow of funds each year, and a given capital base to invest to meet those outflows. If the pension fund simply invests the capital in bonds without concern for the implications of interest rates on the bond portfolio value, interest rates may shift adversely, leaving them with a shortfall at the time the pension payments must be made. The same problems can occur on the individual level when funds are set aside to cover a future expense, such as college education or a retirement annuity.

The bond portfolio management technique for reducing interest rate risk on the bond portfolio value is called *immunization*. Immunization, while borrowed from the biological literature, does not generally lead to the complete eradication of interest rate risk that the term might at first suggest. It does, however, allow the variation of the portfolio value to be kept within generally acceptable levels.

DURATION: A MEASURE OF THE AVERAGE TIME TO PAYMENT

Two bonds may have the same time to maturity, but still be so different in their coupon payments as to be far from equivalent. For example, compare a ten-year pure discount or zero coupon bond (a bond that pays its face value in ten years, but pays no coupon payments before that time) with a typical ten-year corporate bond that pays a coupon payment in semiannual installments each year in addition to paying face value at its maturity date. The discount bond makes no payments before maturity. Changes in the reinvestment rate are therefore of no concern to the holder of that bond. The reinvestment rate will make a difference for the corporate bond, however. If the reinvestment rate goes up, the bondholder can take the coupon payments, reinvest them at the higher rate, and substantially increase the total return to the bond. And, of course, if the interest rates drop below the coupon rate, the bondholder cannot even get the return promised by the bond on his reinvestment of the coupons. In that case, the actual ten-year return to the corporate bond will be lower than it will for the discount bond, which gives the same return to the investment throughout the ten-year time period.

This situation suggests that we need to have a better measure of comparison between bonds than their time to maturity. One such measure is called *duration*. Duration measures the 'average' time to receipt of the payments due the bondholder. For a zero coupon bond, the duration equals the time to maturity of the bond, since no payments are made before maturity. But for a coupon paying bond, some of the payments are made over the course of the time the bond is outstanding. Thus its duration will be less than its time to maturity. And the larger the coupon payments relative to the face value, the smaller its duration will be.

Duration is determined by looking at the length of time to each payment, and the present value of the payment that is made at each of those times. The calculation of duration is illustrated with a simple three-year bond in Table 8-1. This bond has a coupon of 10%, paying a $100 coupon in one year and again in two years. Then, in three years the bond matures and pays a final coupon and its face value of $1000. Column (3) of Table 8-1 computes the present value of each of these payments. The discount factor we use here is the yield to maturity for the bond. In this case, we are assuming the yield to maturity for the bond equals the coupon payment of 10%, although that obviously need not always be the case. Next, in column (4), we determine the present value of each payment as a proportion of the total value of the bond. The bond's value

TABLE 8-1   The Calculation of Duration

(1) TIME WHEN FUTURE PAYMENT WILL BE MADE (IN YEARS)	(2) AMOUNT OF PAYMENT ($)	(3) PRESENT VALUE OF PAYMENT AT 10%	(4) PRESENT VALUE OF PAYMENT AS PROPORTION OF CURRENT BOND VALUE	(5) CALCULATION OF DURATION (COLUMN (1) MULTIPLIED BY COLUMN (4))
1	100	90.91	.091	.091
2	100	82.64	.083	.166
3	1100	826.45	.826	2.478
		1000.00	1.000	
Duration (In Years):				2.735

is simply the sum of the present value of all the payments the bond makes, $1000.00. The calculation of duration is then completed by multiplying the proportion of the bond payment that will be made by the time before that payment is made. That is, we multiply column (4) by column (1), and sum the values up to get the time of duration, 2.735 years.

THE USE OF DURATION IN PORTFOLIO IMMUNIZATION

Duration provides the primary tool for immunizing a portfolio. The usefulness of duration arises from the following important observation: *The realized yield for a bond will equal the bond's yield to maturity if the investment horizon of the investor equals the duration of the bond.* That is, interest rate effects will not change the returns generated by a bond if the bond is held for a length of time equal to its duration. At the time of duration, the capital gain or loss will offset the gain or loss from shifts in the reinvestment rate.

This is illustrated in Figure 8-1. The price gain that results from a drop in the interest rate is initially high, and decreases as the time period to maturity approaches, while the loss from coupon reinvestment opportunities is initially low and increases as the time to maturity approaches. These two factors balance out at the duration of the bond (d on the figure).

Table 8-2 illustrates the immunization effect for the bond used in Table 8-1. Suppose we have an investment horizon of 2.735 years, the duration of the three-year bond used in Table 8-1. As Table 8-2A shows, if the interest rate stays at 10% throughout the holding period, our realized yield will be 10%, and we will have a dollar return of $1,298.42.

If the interest rate drops to 8% immediately after we purchase the bond and stays at that level for the remainder of the holding period, we will have a capital gain, as the bond will have a terminal value of $1,077.88 compared to a value of $1,077.88 for the 10% interest rate. However, we will lose money on the reinvestment of the coupons. For example, while the first coupon payment, reinvested at the 10% rate, would return $118.04, at 8% it only returns $114.29. And the second coupon returns $105.83 at 8% compared to $107.31 at a 10% reinvestment rate. The interest rate effect on the terminal bond value and the coupon reinvestment opportunities cancel out, so that the total return in the two cases is essentially the same: $1,298.42 at 10% reinvestment rate versus $1,298.00 at the 8% reinvestment rate.

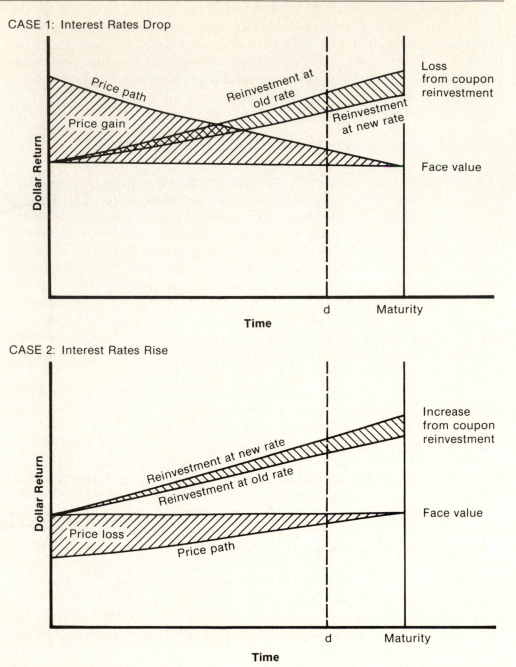

Figure 8-1. The effect of interest rate changes on the bond price and the returns to coupon reinvestment.

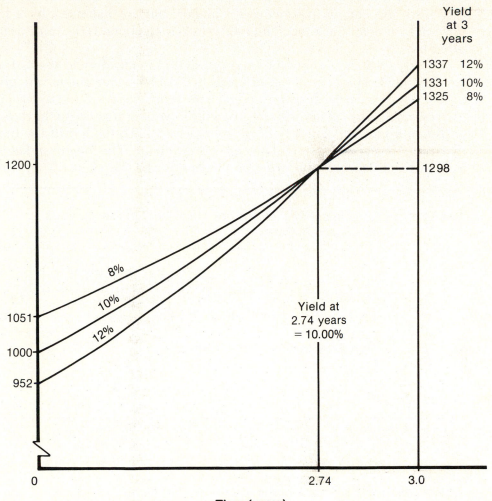

Figure 8-2. Realized yield and immunization for various reinvestment rates. Adapted from Investment Management by Sarkis J. Khoury. Copyright © 1983 by Macmillan Publishing Company.

The same is true if interest rates increase. The right-hand column of the top half of Table 8-2 shows what happens if interest rates increase to 12%. In this case, the coupon payments are higher, but are balanced by a lower terminal value for the bond. The total return to the bond is the same as in the other two cases.

Figure 8-2 shows how the total return and realized yield varies for the reinvestment rates considered in Table 8-2. An 8% reinvestment rate gives a higher return up to the duration, and then the return is dominated by the higher interest rates. The 12% interest rate gives the lowest total return to the duration, and then gives the highest total return thereafter. To the left of the time of duration, the capital gains and loss effects dominate. The lower market interest rates will increase the price of the bonds. To the right of the time of

TABLE 8-2   Comparison of Returns and Realized Yield for Various Reinvestment Rates

	REINVESTMENT RATE		
	8%	10%	12%
Bond With Duration Equal to Investment Horizon			
Coupon Value of the First Coupon	114.29	118.04	121.80
Coupon Value of the Second Coupon	105.83	107.31	108.75
Terminal Bond Value	1077.88	1073.08	1068.06
Total Return	1298.00	1298.43	1298.61
Realized Yield (%)	10.00	10.00	10.00
Bond With Time to Maturity Equal to Investment Horizon			
Coupon Value of the First Coupon	114.29	118.04	121.80
Coupon Value of the Second Coupon	105.83	107.31	108.75
Terminal Bond Value	1100.00	1100.00	1100.00
Total Return	1320.12	1325.35	1330.55
Realized Yield (%)	9.83	10.00	10.15

duration, the reinvestment effect dominates. The higher reinvestment rates on the coupons at that point will have more of an effect on prices than will the capital gains or losses on the bond price. At the time of the bond's duration, all the rates are equal, they all give a realized return of 10%.

Thus, if we had an obligation to pay out 1,298 dollars in two years and eight months, holding this bond would virtually assure that our investment would grow to provide the necessary funds. But the same cannot be said for other bond strategies.

In contrast to the strategy of holding a bond with duration equal to the time horizon of the investment, consider holding a bond with a time to maturity equal to the investment horizon. This case is worked out in the bottom half of Table 8-2. Now the terminal value of the bond is unaffected by the interest rate. Since the bond is being held to maturity, it will return face value no matter what the prevailing reinvestment rate is in the market. The value of the coupons, however, will be affected by the reinvestment rate. As in Table 8-2, a higher reinvestment rate will increase the dollar returns from the coupons, and a lower reinvestment rate will decrease their dollar returns. The net effect is for a decrease in the interest rate to drop the total returns and realized yield, while an increase in the interest rate increases total returns and realized yield.

IMMUNIZATION STRATEGIES

For a one-bond portfolio, the point that interest rates do not have an impact on the realized yield of bonds held to the time of duration implies a simple strategy for immunization: Buy a bond with a duration equal to your desired time horizon. Of course, a bond portfolio is made up of more than one bond. But the same strategy can be easily generalized: Select a portfolio of bonds so that the duration of the portfolio is equal to your investment time horizon. The duration of the portfolio, d_p, is simply equal to the duration of each bond weighted by the proportion of your portfolio made up by each bond:

$$d_p = \Sigma \; w_i d_i,$$

where w_i is the proportion of the total dollar portfolio value invested in bond i, and d_i is the duration of bond i.

There will undoubtedly be a number of combinations of bonds that can lead to any particular level of portfolio duration. The best combination, subject to the bonds all being of sufficiently high quality, will be that combination that leads to the highest portfolio yield subject to the appropriate portfolio duration. This is essentially the bond portfolio counterpart of the objective of stock portfolio diversification, the objective of finding the stock portfolio that gives the highest expected return subject to a given level of risk.

This bond portfolio objective can be stated in the following way:

Maximize portfolio yield to maturity:

$$Y = \Sigma \, w_i Y_i$$

subject to portfolio duration being equal to the investment time horizon, H:

$$d_p = H.$$

This problem is stated in the form of a linear programming problem. In addition to making the calculations for duration, the computer program for this chapter can construct the optimal portfolio once the necessary information, the coupon payments, time to maturity, yield to maturity, and time horizon H have been specified.

Other considerations are also important in immunization besides getting the highest expected return. Obviously, the set of bonds under consideration should be of high enough quality and from a broad enough cross-section of firms to keep default risk down to an acceptable level. A second consideration is which structure of bonds gives the best immunization. As we have already mentioned, immunization is rarely perfect, there will always be some shift of the yield curve that will undo part of the efforts to immunize. In particular, most immunization strategies are only perfect if the shifts in the yield curve are linear. The effects of immunization strategies, while still potentially valuable, may not be complete for other yield curve shifts.

The immunized portfolio can be constructed with bonds that all have a duration close to that of the investment time horizon; with some bonds that have a duration much shorter than the time horizon and others that are much longer than the time horizon; or, with bonds that are evenly spread out along a wide range of durations. These portfolios are called bullet, barbell, and ladder portfolios, respectively. Studies suggest the best choice is to use the bullet strategy of constructing the portfolio with bonds that all have durations near the target duration of the portfolio. The bullet portfolio will give more protection over the range of typical yield-curve shifts.

IMMUNIZATION

Computational Procedure

For each bond, compute duration:

$$d = \frac{\sum\limits_{t=1}^{N} t[C/(1+r)^t] + [(FV\ N)/(1+r)^N]}{\sum\limits_{t=1}^{N} [C/(1+r)^t] + [FV/(1+r)^N]}$$

where

  d = duration
  t = time period
  N = periods to maturity
  C = coupon payment in dollars
  r = yield to maturity
  FV = face value
  (Note that the denominator is simply the market price of the bond.)

Solve the linear programming problem:

$$\text{Max} \quad Y_p = \sum_{i=1}^{N} w_i\, Y_i$$

subject to

$$d_p = \sum_{i=1}^{N} w_i\, d_i = H,$$

$$\sum_{i=1}^{N} w_i = 1,$$

$$w_i \geq 0 \text{ for all } i,$$

where

Y_p = realized portfolio yield
w_i = proportion of portfolio made up of bond i
Y_i = yield to maturity of bond i
d_p = portfolio duration
d_i = duration of bond i
H = investment time horizon

```
10   REM  ***********************************************************************
20   REM  *                       IMMUNIZATION PROGRAM                          *
30   REM  *                                                                     *
40   REM  * THIS PROGRAM USES A LINEAR PROGRAM BASED ON THE BOUNDED SIMPLE      *
50   REM  * ALGORITHM TO FIND THE BOND PORTFOLIO THAT MEETS A SPECIFIED         *
60   REM  * TARGET DURATION WITH THE HIGHEST YIELD.                             *
70   REM  *                                                                     *
80   REM  * VARIABLES USED:                                                     *
90   REM  *                 Y = YIELD TO MATURITY                               *
100  REM  *                 D = DURATION OF BOND                                *
110  REM  *                 H = INVESTMENT TIME HORIZON                         *
120  REM  *                 N = NUMBER OF DIFFERENT BONDS IN THE PROGRAM        *
130  REM  *                                                                     *
140  REM  ***********************************************************************
150  REM
160  DIM A(50,100), NME(50), X(100)
170  REM
180  REM  ***********************INPUT SUBROUTINE*****************************
190  REM GOSUB 2705
200  REM
210  REM  **********************LINEAR PROGRAM OPTIMIZATION*****************************
220  REM GOSUB 5020
230  REM
240  REM  ***********************OUTPUT SUBROUTINE*****************************
250  REM GOSUB 6000
260  REM
270  REM  ***********************************************************************
280  REM  *                        INPUT SUBROUTINE                            *
290  REM  ***********************************************************************
300  REM
310  CLS
320  PRINT TAB(15);" MENU FOR BOND IMMUNIZATION PROGRAM"
330  PRINT TAB(15);"1.INPUT INITIAL DATA"
340  PRINT TAB(15);"2 MODIFY EXISTING DATA
350  PRINT TAB(15);"3.QUIT"
360  INPUT " WHICH OPTION DO YOU CHOOSE (1,2 OR 3) : ",CHOICE
370  ON CHOICE GOSUB 400,570,1880
380  GOTO 310
390  REM
400  REM  ***********************************************************************
410  REM  *              INPUT ROUTINE FOR IMMUNIZATION PROGRAM                 *
420  REM  ***********************************************************************
430  CLS
440  PRINT TAB(15);"   BOND IMMUNIZATION PROGRAM"
450  INPUT "             NUMBER OF BONDS : ",N
460   M=2:NM=N+M:NR=3:NC=NM+1
470  INPUT "        INVESTMENT TIME HORIZON : ",H
480   FOR I = 1 TO N
490  PRINT "  "
500  PRINT  TAB(20);"    YIELD OF BOND ";I;" : ";
510  INPUT "  ",Y(I)
520  PRINT  TAB(20);" DURATION OF BOND ";I;" : ";
530  INPUT "  ",D(I)
540   NEXT I
```

```
550    GOSUB 820
560  RETURN
570  REM ****************************************************************
580  REM *              SUBROUTINE TO MODIFY EXISTING DATA              *
590  REM ****************************************************************
600  CLS
610  REM
620  REM
630  PRINT TAB(15);" MENU FOR MODIFYING EXISTING DATA"
640  PRINT TAB(15);"1. CHANGE INVESTMENT HORIZON"
650  PRINT TAB(15);"2. CHANGE YIELD FOR A GIVEN BOND"
660  PRINT TAB(15);"3. CHANGE DURATION FOR A GIVEN BOND"
670  PRINT TAB(15);"4. NO MORE CHANGES"
680  INPUT " WHICH OPTION DO YOU SELECT (1,2,3,OR 4) : ",CHOICE
690  CLS
700  ON CHOICE GOTO 710,730,760,790
710  INPUT "INPUT NEW INVESTMENT HORIZON : ",H
720    GOTO 600
730  INPUT "WHICH BOND YIELD IS TO BE CHANGED : ",I
740  INPUT "                 NEW YIELD VALUE : ",Y(I)
750    GOTO 600
760  INPUT "WHICH BOND DURATION IS TO BE CHANGED : ",I
770  INPUT "                 NEW DURATION VALUE : ",D(I)
780    GOTO 600
790  CLS
800    GOSUB 820
810  RETURN
820  REM ****************************************************************
830  REM *           SUBROUTINE FOR OPTIMIZING LINEAR PROGRAM            *
840  REM ****************************************************************
850  PRINT " PROCESSING . . . "
860    IPRT=0
870    A(1,NC)=1:A(2,NC)=H
880    DINF=100
890  FOR J = 1 TO N
900    A(1,J)=1:A(2,J)=D(J)
910    A(3,J)=-Y(J) - DINF*(A(1,J)+A(2,J))
920    X(J)=0
930  NEXT J
940    A(3,NC)=A(3,NC)-DINF*(A(1,NC)+A(2,NC))
950  FOR I=1 TO M:NME(I)=I+N:A(I,I+N)=1:NEXT I
960    IF IPRT<=0 GOTO 1010
970    GOSUB 1730
980    REM
990  REM SELECT ENTERING VARIABLE
1000   REM
1010   JC=0
1020   CBAR=-.0001
1030   FOR J=1 TO NM
1040     IF A(NR,J)>= CBAR GOTO 1060
1050     CBAR=A(NR,J):JC=J
1060   NEXT J
1070   IF JC=0 GOTO 1510
1080     RR=10000000#
```

```
1090 REM
1100 REM SELECT LEAVING VARIABLE
1110 REM
1120  FOR I=1 TO M
1130   IF A(I,JC)<.0001 GOTO 1170
1140   R5=A(I,NC)/A(I,JC)
1150   IF R5>=RR GOTO 1170
1160   RR=R5:IR=I
1170  NEXT I
1180  GOTO 1350
1190 REM
1200 REM SELECT ENTERING VARIABLE FOR PRIMAL INFEASIBLE PIVOT
1210 REM
1220  RR=-10000000#
1230  FOR J=1 TO NM:IF A(IR,J)>-.0001 GOTO 1280
1240   IF ABS(A(IR,J))<.0001 GOTO 1280
1250   R5=A(NR,J)/A(IR,J)
1260   IF R5<=RR GOTO 1280
1270   JC=J:RR=R5
1280  NEXT J
1290  IF JC=NME(IR) GOTO 1310
1300   GOTO 1350
1310 PRINT "NO FEASIBLE SOLUTION":STOP
1320 REM
1330 REM PIVOT EXCHANGE
1340 REM
1350  IZ=IZ+1:A0=A(IR,JC)
1360  JD=NME(IR):NME(IR)=JC
1370  FOR I=1 TO NR:IF I=IR GOTO 1410
1380  FOR J=1 TO NC:IF J=JC GOTO 1400
1390   A(I,J)=A(I,J)-(A(IR,J)*A(I,JC))/A0
1400  NEXT J
1410  NEXT I
1420  FOR J=1 TO NC:A(IR,J)=A(IR,J)/A0:NEXT J
1430  FOR I=1 TO NR:A(I,JC)=0:NEXT I:A(IR,JC)=1:IF IPRT<=0 GOTO 1450
1440   GOSUB 1730
1450   GOTO 1010
1460   IP=JC:GOTO 1010
1470 REM
1480 REM ***********************************************************************
1490 REM *               OUTPUT RESULTS OF LINEAR PROGRAMMING COMPUTATIONS    *
1500 REM ***********************************************************************
1510  CLS
1520  INF=0:YP=0
1530  FOR I=1 TO M
1540   IF NME(I) <= N THEN 1560
1550   INF=1:GOTO 1580
1560   X(NME(I))=A(I,NC)
1570   YP=YP + X(NME(I))*Y(NME(I))
1580  NEXT I
1590  IF INF=1 THEN 1690
1600 PRINT TAB(15);" BOND      WEIGHT      YIELD       DURATION"
1610 PRINT TAB(15);"  ----      ------      -----       --------"
1620  FOR I = 1 TO N
```

```
1630 PRINT USING "                    ###       ####.##      ######.##    ######.##";
I;X(I);Y(I);D(I)
1640   NEXT I
1650 PRINT "     "
1660 PRINT TAB(15);"      AVERAGE YIELD OF BOND PORTFOLIO : ";YP
1670 PRINT TAB(15);"   AVERAGE DURATION OF BOND PORTFOLIO : ";H
1680   GOTO 1700
1690 PRINT TAB(15);"   PORTFOLIO CANNOT ACHIEVE TARGET DURATION"
1700 INPUT " TYPE RETURN KEY WHEN YOU WANT TO CONTINUE ",A$
1710 RETURN
1720 REM
1730 REM **********************************************************************
1740 REM *                      MATRIX PRINT SUBROUTINE                       *
1750 REM **********************************************************************
1760 REM
1770 PRINT
1780 PRINT "ITERATION ";IZ
1790   FOR JJ=1 TO NC STEP 5:J9=JJ+4:IF J9>NC THEN J9=NC
1800 PRINT
1810 PRINT "BVAR",:FOR J=JJ TO J9:PRINT J,:NEXT J:IF J9<JJ+4 THEN PRINT
1820 PRINT
1830   FOR I=1 TO NR:PRINT NME(I),
1840   FOR J=JJ TO J9:A9=INT(10000*A(I,J))/10000:PRINT A9,:NEXT J:PRINT
1850   NEXT I
1860   NEXT JJ
1870 RETURN
1880 CLS
1890 END
```

Bond Strategies References*

The essentials of bond pricing can be found in most intermediate investment texts. The more sophisticated, professional strategies of cash-futures arbitrage and basis trading are covered in great detail in Kidder Reports, a research newsletter. Two books by Stigum (1978, 1981) cover the money markets and government bond markets with sensitivity to the institutional realities of these markets.

The covered interest arbitrage strategy for taking advantage of interest rate—exchange rate imbalances across currencies is discussed in Frenkel and Levich (1977) and in Holley, Beidleman, and Greenleaf (1979). These papers also consider the feasibility of covered interest arbitrage and the practical problems in implementing this strategy successfully.

The use of contingent claim analysis on option pricing theory in pricing convertible bonds is presented by Ingersoll (1977a). Other studies of convertible bond prices that pay particular attention to the effect of the call provision are Ingersoll (1977b), and Brennan and Schwartz (1977).

Homer and Leibowitz (1972) give an excellent discussion of bond swaps. Their analysis is further amplified by Seix (1983).

The investment strategy of bond portfolio immunization was first suggested by Macaulay (1938). Expansions of the basic principles of immunization are developed by Fisher and Weil (1971), Bierwag (1977), Bierwag and Khang (1979), and Kaufman, Bierwag, and Toeus (1983). A more practical view is presented by Christensen, Feldstein, and Fabozzi (1983). Variations on the immunization strategy are proposed by Leibowitz and Weinberger (1982) and Platt and Latainer (1984).

*Refer to the Bibliography at the back of the book for complete citations.

II
STOCK ANALYSIS

9
An Introduction to Stock Analysis

It is difficult to keep from seeming trite when addressing the topic of stock market analysis. Along with the weather and politics, it is a perennial topic of discussion. There always seems to be at least one book on investments on the best seller list. Books with advice on how to make a million in the stock market have been filling shelves ever since traders first gathered on the curbside of Wall Street.

While walking through the investments section of our library yesterday, I passed by a wall filled with books related to the stock market. Some were recollections of the past century. Two books, *Ten Years in Wall Street*, published in 1870, and the even more definitive *Fifty Years on Wall Street*, published in 1908, recounted the staid old men who dominated the market of that era. Other books were investment classics from the earlier part of this century, such as John Burr Williams' *The Theory of Investment Value*, and Graham and Dodd's *Security Analysis*. Still others, such as *Reminiscences of a Stock Operator*, gave personal reminiscences of life in the stock market.

The stock market and investment world of these men seems far different from that of today. It was both exclusive and colorful. It had larger than life characters who could shape the entire investment world. It was filled with legends of shrewd traders bootstrapping their way up to positions of market domination through clever, opportunistic strategies.

Of course, the greatest difference of all goes far beyond the attitudes of the market participants. The computer revolution of the past decade separates the stock market today as an era distinct from all the decades that have preceded it. Stock quotes can be monitored and subjected to computer analysis by anyone, anywhere in the country on a realtime or close to realtime basis; detailed information is disseminated quickly and widely. Computers can tap data banks to do large-scale data analysis that was impossible just a few years ago.

THE WORLD OF QUANTITATIVE INVESTMENT ANALYSIS: MODERN PORTFOLIO THEORY

It is interesting that this information revolution, which has given us such immense data and computer capabilities, has coincided with the application of quantitative, computer-intensive theories to stock analysis and portfolio management. These theories generally go under the heading of *modern portfolio theory*, or simply MPT. Two critical concepts that have emerged as part of modern portfolio theory—the capital asset pricing model (CAPM) and the concept of optimal portfolio diversification—have become staples for the large investment firms. A number of so-called beta services provide online quantitative stock analysis based on these models to hundreds of clients. And even the most traditional, conservative firms have bowed to the new trend by peppering their research groups with those versed in quantitative analysis.

If modern portfolio theory has made some inroads into the investment profession, it has completely dominated investment thinking in the academic community. A look at the academic journals in finance such as the *Journal of Finance*, the *Journal of Business*, or the *Journal of Financial Economics* is enough to show that the current orientation in academics is squarely one of quantitative, mathematical analysis. And as would be expected, investment courses in the better M.B.A. programs mimic this academic orientation.

The abandonment of classical techniques of stock analysis in the academic world is more than the result of the seductive new tools of computer technology. The enthusiasm for the new, more quantitative or analytical methods has been spurred by three considerations.

First, as already mentioned, the technology is in place to freely benefit from quantitative methods that can be expressed succinctly in computer-executable form, and that use the standard types of data in abundance in the investments area. This not only eases the application of these methods but also facilitates the testing of hypotheses. The interest in new directions for research is partly dependent on the ease of empirical verification. And this is now more easily done for statistical tests than for hypotheses based on subjective or isolated instances.

Second, the approach of modern portfolio theory is very rich in its variations and in the breadth of its applicability. The capital asset pricing model, for example, is not restricted in its explanation of the risk-return tradeoffs to just one particular industry, or one particular type of stock. It can be used to explain any stock, and can be further applied to other areas, such as the capital budgeting problem in corporate finance. In any field of science, the theory that will be the most attractive is that which leads to explanations in the widest number of areas.

Third, the existing framework for fundamental analysis—a framework tied to the study of balance sheets and attempts to relate projected earnings to stock prices—has intellectual limitations that make it a poor foundation for the elucidation of general principles of stock price behavior. This framework, however, continues to be used successfully by many investment analysts. But for those interested in researching the deeper questions of market behavior and the elements of asset pricing, this framework simply does not seem to lead in any new directions, and it pales beside the broad scope of modern portfolio theory.

LIMITATIONS TO THE QUANTITATIVE APPROACH TO STOCK ANALYSIS

In view of the sophisticated, scientific tools we now bring to bear on stock analysis, it is tempting to look back at an earlier era with some smugness. Or, just let the records of that past era of "soft, anecdotal" analysis continue collecting dust until the inventory department of the library finally gets around to clearing off the shelves. Certainly such analysis has no place in the modern portfolio theory revolution—a new world of betas, covariance coefficients, and the orthogonal factor loadings of arbitrage pricing theory.

Unfortunately, revolution can lead to excesses and new theory can emerge as an all-encompassing orthodoxy. As a result, the former methods are discarded without a trace, and principals of the new method can be applied far beyond reasonable bounds. In the investment field, this has occurred as the tools of modern portfolio theory have become increasingly devoted to finding mispriced stocks. It was only a decade or so after the tools of modern portfolio theory became well rooted in academics that they have reshaped themselves and have taken over the function of security analysis, a function that had been diminished by the revolution.

It is natural to try to use these tools to fulfill the void left behind by the casting off of the more traditional security analysis. But the fact is that in doing so they are being used to attempt to fill a void they simply were not designed to fill. Used in isolation, the methods of modern portfolio theory say nothing about how to find a mispriced stock. Indeed, these methods were at first part of the package of the efficient market approach to investments, an approach containing the random walk hypothesis. This approach states that stocks do not move in any predictable or forecastable way, and that attempts to find mispriced stocks would be fruitless.

For example, the most popular model of modern portfolio theory, the capital asset pricing model, is a model that shows the correct way to measure the risk of a stock, and the proper tradeoff between risk and return. Used in isolation, it says nothing about determining the course of future stock prices or forecasting future stock returns. Yet many firms provide services that dazzle the investor with an array of sophisticated computer methods that purport to use the capital asset pricing model to pinpoint mispriced stocks.

And, the foundation for the quantitative revolution in investments, the tools of diversification and portfolio strategy, likewise say nothing about determining future stock prices. They are valuable techniques for combining stocks to eliminate the avoidable, stock-specific risks. But that function, useful though it is, has little to do with the traditional role of stock analysis—that of predicting the future direction of stock prices.

The traditional, accounting-data-based tools of fundamental analysis and the more quantitative approach of modern portfolio theory present the two extremes to stock analysis in the investment world today. Each approach, taken on its own, can give only a part of the picture. It is when they are taken *together* that the full potential of their methods can be tapped. But just as there are barriers between the fundamental and technical analyst, or between the technical analyst and the efficient market advocate, there seems to be little interaction between these two approaches to stock analysis.

Looking through the programs in this section of the book, we seem to side with modern portfolio theory. Only one of the chapters, Chapter 13, deals with the more traditional methods for pricing stocks. This is the inevitable result of writing a book that deals specifically with computer-intensive strategies. Granted, it is possible to computerize a number of traditional fundamental methods by screening stocks according to accounting ratios and earnings performance, for example. But this requires a substantial data base that would be beyond the resources of most of those using this book. However, the intention here is not to slight the more traditional approach to fundamental analysis. Indeed, as we run through the chapters in this section, we will suggest ways to combine profitably the traditional and the MPT approaches.

There are better ways to start this section on computer-oriented methods of stock analysis than to state that these quantitative methods are of limited value. And, lest the stock traders thumb past this section of the book without a glance, I should restate that this section is not comprised exclusively of modern portfolio theory methods.

Even in terms of modern portfolio theory, saying the methods are limited is not saying they are valueless. On the contrary, they have extended our understanding of the market in significant ways. They have led to the development of investment methods both for creating strategies and measuring performance that far surpass any used in the past. They are tools that will be useful for those who want to filter out stocks that are potentially mispriced. However, enthusiasm for these methods has led to their having been overextended beyond their usefulness, and, to the exclusion of other potentially useful stock analysis techniques. One value of dusting off the books of the past is that some perspective is gained. The pendulum has swung very far toward the new, efficient market, quantitative methods in stock analysis, and it will certainly swing back.

OVERVIEW OF STOCK ANALYSIS PROGRAMS

This section on stock analysis contains three types of programs. The majority of the programs deal with the important issue of portfolio diversification strategies. The programs in Chapter 10, "Diversification Strategies for Stock Portfolio Management," show how the stocks the investor holds can best be combined to reduce or possibly even eliminate unnecessary risk. The program in Chapter 11 extends this analysis to stock portfolios that include option positions. Option strategies, especially the strategy of covered call writing, have become popular over the past decade and can be helpful in achieving certain investment objectives. This program allows the investor to prepare a detailed picture of the effect an option-stock strategy will have on the characteristics of the portfolio return.

Chapter 12 covers the computations necessary to apply capital asset pricing model. The program uses a regression technique to determine the beta of a stock from the stock's past return history. It also will compute the alpha of the stock, an indicator of whether the stock has achieved returns that are either extraordinarily high or below normal for its level of market risk. The program also gives the statistical measures necessary to evaluate the accuracy of the beta and alpha estimates.

These methods are an important part of the stock analysis process and should be used *after* the stock price forecast has been made. It is not enough to have a forecast for the returns to a stock. The risk of the stock must also be measured, and the expected return must then be related to the riskiness of those returns to assess whether the stock is a good buy. The capital asset pricing model, as already indicated, cannot be of much assistance in projecting the future return potential of a stock. But it does provide the construct for evaluating those risk-return tradeoffs. It can be used to tell whether, *given* a particular forecast for future stock prices, the risk of the stock is low enough to make the stock a favorable purchase.

For example, the CAPM can be merged with traditional fundamental analysis by taking the analyst's forecast of returns—based, for example, on earnings and dividend forecasts—and then predicting the future risk of these forecasts. These risk and return forecasts can then be placed within the capital asset pricing model framework to determine the future equilibrium price. This is discussed in more detail in Chapter 12.

The final chapter of the section, Chapter 13, cuts across the grain of modern portfolio theory and develops a computer application of one of the most widely held traditional methods of stock valuation—the three-stage dividend growth model, a flexible model for pricing stocks.

10
Diversification Strategies for Stock Portfolio Management

Portfolio strategies must be measured in two dimensions—risk and return. The risk-return tradeoff is central to all investments; a strategy with a higher expected payoff is obviously more desirable, but it generally only comes at the price of taking on greater risk. This means a successful portfolio strategy can be designed by starting from either of two directions. The objective can be either to find stocks that are mispriced in an effort to obtain higher than average returns and absorb whatever the risk is in taking those positions, or it can be to take the returns the market gives, but mix the portfolio in a way that results in the minimum possible risk. That is, the strategy can take either return maximization or risk minimization as its starting point. It can either focus on stock picking or on risk management.

This is, of course, an oversimplified view of alternative investment strategies, since there is a tradeoff between the objective of risk and return; one objective is never pursued in isolation to the complete exclusion of the other. But it does relate two distinct styles of investment management. For example, most small, individual investors emphasize stock selection. They try to find the stocks that will lead to the highest expected return, while giving only passing consideration to the impact of their individual positions on the risk of the overall portfolio. The implications of individual trades on portfolio risk and diversification are generally ignored, or are treated as an unavoidable and unalterable part of being in the market.

Some large institutional investors, on the other hand, spend far more time worrying about portfolio risk and diversification than they do trying to pick winners. I know of one pension fund with over five billion dollars in equity that devotes only 5% of its portfolio to active management—the task of trying to spot underpriced stocks—and 95% of its portfolio to passive management—the task of selecting stocks to eliminate diversifiable risk. (It is worth mentioning that they use fifteen analysts for the 5% in active management, and only three to manage the remaining 95% of the assets in the passive fund.) The relative weights of active and passive management, of money devoted to picking winners compared to money devoted to reducing risk, do not vary far from this for other large pension funds.

Since expected return and risk must be looked at together, it does not really matter whether a portfolio has achieved an attractive level of return for the risk taken by finding stocks with a high potential, or has achieved it by combining stocks in a way that keeps risk at a minimum. The end result will be the same. Put another way, even the shrewdest stock picker can be done in by inadequate risk management. There is always some level of risk that will wipe away the benefits of pinpointing underpriced stocks.

And, as we show in this chapter, there is essentially no cost to diversifying portfolio risk. Unlike stock selection methods, which pit the investor in a zero-sum game requiring deep analysis and astute judgment, the task of optimal diversification is fairly straightforward, and its benefits are open to all investors.

THE PRINCIPLE OF DIVERSIFICATION

A Simple Example

Consider three companies that have returns that are a function of the economic climate. Firms X and Y are cyclical—they do well when the economy is doing well, and do poorly when the economy is doing poorly. Firm Z is counter-cyclical—it does well when the economy is doing poorly, and does poorly when the overall economy is doing well.

Table 10-1A shows the rate of return of the firms under each of the three states of the economy. The probability of each state occurring is shown on the row at the top. Given the returns of the companies in each state, and the probability of that state occurring, the expected returns for the firms are calculated in the last column on the right.

The risk from holding Firm X is higher than for Firm Y or Z. The returns for Firm X may vary 16%, dropping to 2% in a recession, and rising to 18% in a boom. Firms Y and Z, however, only vary by 8% from the recession to boom economy. But the expected return to Firm X is also higher—10% compared to 8% for the other two firms. Firms Y and Z have the same level of risk and expected return. The difference between them is that Firm Y is cyclical, with

---

TABLE 10-1

A

RETURN

	Recession	Normal	Boom	Expected Return
Probability	.3	.4	.3	
Firm				
X	2%	10%	18%	10%
Y	4%	8%	12%	8%
Z	12%	8%	4%	8%

B

RETURN

	Recession	Normal	Boom	Expected Return
Portfolio				
X and Y	3%	9%	15%	9%
X and Z	7%	9%	11%	9%

returns that vary in the same direction of the economy, while Firm Z, is countercyclical, doing best when the economy is doing poorly.

Rather than holding the stock of just one of the firms, suppose an investor diversifies by holding two of the three firms. Will the diversification reduce his risk? In Table 10-1B we show the returns for a portfolio containing Firms X and Y, and for a portfolio containing Firms X and Z, with the two firms in both cases being held in the portfolio in equal amounts. Both portfolios give the same expected return of 9%, but the portfolio consisting of Firms X and Y has far more risk; it has returns that vary from a recession low of 3% to a high during economic booms of 15%, while the range of returns from the X and Z portfolio only varies from 7% to 11%. For the typical investor, who is risk averse, the portfolio of stocks X and Z will be more attractive.

What makes the one portfolio effective in diversifying risk while the other is not? The answer is the correlation between stocks. If two stocks are highly correlated, as are X and Y, then diversification cannot reduce risk. When the one stock does well, the other is likely to do well, and when the one does poorly, the other is likely to do poorly, so the two stocks only serve to amplify the variability in returns. But to the extent that the stocks react differently to the important sources of risk in the economy, diversification will serve to reduce risk.

Indeed, if there is *no* correlation between stocks, (if the stocks are stochastically independent), or better yet, if there is *negative* correlation between stocks, then diversification cannot only reduce risk, it can actually eliminate risk. For independent assets, the law of averages (or, more precisely, the Law of Large Numbers), assures that the random variations in the individual assets will tend to balance one another out. While it is likely some assets will have unfavorable returns and below-average performance, others are likely to do above average. Overall, these random variations will cancel, leaving a return to the overall portfolio of assets that is very close to the expected return.

As an aside, it is worth mentioning that this same argument lets insurance companies estimate their annual claims very accurately. By insuring a large number of different individuals, the Law of Large Numbers allows insurance companies to determine their losses within very tight bounds. Because of this, they can set the premium payments close to the expected loss they will face, with little or no extra premium being added for the risk that claims might exceed their expectations. It is also the reason why it is possible to insure against only a limited class of events. In particular, the risks that are insured have to be independent of one another for the Law of Large Numbers to apply. Generally, the risk of fires, traffic accidents, and deaths are independent across the broad set of the population, and so these are insurable losses. Business losses, crop failures, unemployment, deaths due to war, are all examples of losses that are not independent. If they occur to one person they are more than likely to occur to many people. These losses are not, strictly speaking, insurable losses, and insurance is only available because government subsidies compensate for the nondiversifiable risk.

The Limits to Diversification

If diversification works so neatly, why not hold a wide range of different stocks and completely eliminate risk? The reason brings us back to the example of Table 10-1: If risks are positively correlated, we cannot completely diversify risk. There will be some element of risk that is shared by all the stocks, and this risk will remain even after we have spread our investments out across the stocks.

In the economy, there are certain risks that affect virtually all firms— inflation, interest rates, tax reforms, energy prices, and the risk of war. No matter how widely we spread out our investments, we cannot eliminate these risks because they are common to all firms. We can eliminate some risk, however. Risks such as the death of a key executive, the risk that a pharmaceutical company has been manufacturing a drug that has been found to cause cancer, or that a technological change will make a company's product obsolete, are independent from one sector of the economy to another. These diversifiable risks are called *nonsystematic risks*, because they are not inherent in the economic system. The economywide, nondiversifiable risks are called *systematic risks*. They are the risks that will be unavoidable in the stock market.

MEASURING PORTFOLIO PERFORMANCE

We generally assume stock portfolios have returns that are normally distributed. The normal distribution is the distribution that gives rise to the bell-shaped distribution curve seen in Figure 10-1. The attractive feature of this

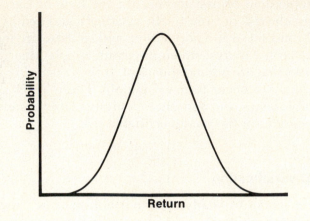

Figure 10-1. Portfolio returns typified by the normal distribution.

assumption is that the shape of the normal distribution can be fully described by just two terms—the mean or expected return, and the variance of returns. These two terms give immediate intuition to the risk-return tradeoffs just mentioned. The risk is measured by the variance, or spread of the distribution, while the potential for return is measured by the mean of the distribution.

Two methods for measuring the expected return and variance of stock portfolios are used in the program in this chapter. The first method, originally proposed by Harry Markowitz in the fifties, is to compute the variance of the stock portfolio as the sum of the variance and covariance terms of all the stocks in the portfolio, weighted by their relative proportion in the portfolio. This method is the one that immediately comes to mind for computing portfolio variance, since it is the correct method from a statistical standpoint. However, it is also very complex computationally for even moderate-size portfolios, requiring a large number of inputs.

The second method, developed by William Sharpe, reduces the amount of data necessary for the computation of the portfolio variance. This reduction is not without a price. It naturally results in a solution that is only an approximation of the actual variance. However, the results are still accurate enough to meet virtually all practical applications.

The Markowitz Model

We denote the covariance between stock i and j as σ_{ij}. If i equals j, so that we have σ_{ii}, then that is the variance of stock i, which is also represented by σ_i^2. The proportion of the portfolio held in stock i will be denoted by w_i. For example, if the total value of the portfolio is $100,000, and the market value of stock i is $15,000, then w_i equals .15. Using this notation, the portfolio variance, σ_p^2, of a portfolio of N stocks will be

$$\sigma_p^2 = \sum_{i=1}^{N} \sum_{j=1}^{N} w_i\, w_j\, \sigma_{ij}.$$

A look at this expression for the portfolio variance shows why this method of computing the portfolio variance is so computationally tedious. The portfolio variance is made up of the double summation of all the variance and covariance terms for all the stocks in the portfolio. Each stock has a covariance with every other stock as well as a variance term for itself. This means the number of terms that must be entered in making this computation goes up geometrically with the number of stocks in the portfolio. A three-stock portfolio only has six variance—covariance terms—σ_1^2, σ_{12}, σ_{13}, σ_2^2, σ_{23}, σ_3^2—while a portfolio with 100 stocks will have over 5000 such terms.

The expected return of the portfolio is easier to compute. It is the weighted average of the expected returns to each individual stock in the portfolio. If we denote the expected return to stock i by $\bar{r}_i$, the expected return to the portfolio $\bar{r}_p$ will be

$$\bar{r}_p = \sum_{i=1}^{N} w_i \bar{r}_i.$$

The Sharpe Single-Index Model

Considering the large number of terms the Markowitz method requires, it is easy to see why another approach is desirable, even if it does lead to slight errors. The Sharpe method begins with the assumption that the returns to all stocks are related according to the simple equation

$$r_i = r_F + \beta_i (r_M - r_F) + u_i.$$

This equation says the return of each stock is determined by the excess return to the market above the risk-free rate and by an error term u_i. The error term is assumed to be independent from stock to stock and also is assumed to be independent of the market return. This independence assumption means that any interrelationship between stocks will come only through their joint dependence on the market return.

Having the interrelationship come in this way eliminates the multiplicity of covariance terms in the computation of the portfolio variance. In particular, if all stock returns are generated according to this single-index model, the expected return to the portfolio will be

$$\bar{r}_p = \sum_{i=1}^{N} w_i(r_F + \beta_i(r_M - r_F)) = r_F + (r_M - r_F) \sum_{i=1}^{N} w_i\beta_i,$$

and the portfolio variance will be

$$\sigma_p^2 = \left[\sum w_i\beta_i \right]^2 \sigma_M^2 + \sum w_i^2 \sigma_i^2.$$

The portfolio variance now only depends on the weight of each stock in the portfolio, w_i, the beta coefficient of each stock, the variance of the market return, σ_M^2, and the variance of the residual error for each stock, σ_i^2. This is a significant saving in the data necessary to do the computations. For example, a 100-stock portfolio now requires just 301 inputs, less than a tenth of the number of inputs required by the Markowitz method.

OPTIMAL DIVERSIFICATION:
FINDING THE MINIMUM-VARIANCE PORTFOLIO

The Markowitz and Sharpe models not only provide a means of measuring the return and variance of the portfolio, they also provide the first step in developing portfolio diversification strategies. Once we know how to measure risk and return, we can begin looking at alternative risk-return tradeoffs. We can try to find that combination of risk and return that best meets our investment objectives.

We already described how the tradeoffs between returns and risk can be rephrased in mean-variance terms when returns are typified by a normal distribution. The investor may key in on a maximum acceptable level of variance and then search for the portfolio that achieves the highest possible expected return without exceeding that risk. Or, the investor may key in on a minimum required expected return, and then search for the portfolio that leads to the lowest variance while meeting that return objective.

That is, the portfolio diversification trading strategy can be stated as follows:

- Find the portfolio that gives the highest expected return subject to the variance of return not exceeding a specified level; or
- Find the portfolio that gives the lowest variance of return subject to the expected return not being below a specified level.

Both statements of the objective are essentially the same.

For each level of expected return, there will be one portfolio that gives that level of expected return with the least variance. For the investor who has that level of expected return for a return objective, this minimum variance portfolio will be the best one to hold. It will be the optimal investment portfolio—the portfolio that is the best diversified given the expected return objectives. Any other portfolio meeting the investor's return objectives will, by assumption, do so only at the cost of higher variance, and will therefore be less desirable.

Suppose we take a set of stocks, and for each level of expected return, we find the portfolio that achieves that return with the least variance. (This technique is discussed a bit later in this chapter. The programs in this chapter are designed to do this.) Doing this will trace out a curve as in Figure 10-2. This curve relates a specific variance to each expected return. The curve is upward-sloping, as we would expect, since a higher expected return is only obtained at the cost of a higher variance.

It is possible to hold other portfolios that would have an expected return-variance tradeoff falling below this curve. For example, it may be perfectly possible to find a mix of stocks that will fall at point A in Figure 10-2. But there is no reason to hold that portfolio, since a different mix of stocks can put you at point B, where you would have the same expected return with less risk, or at point C, where you would have the same risk and a higher expected return. On the other hand, it is not possible to find a portfolio that will put you above the curve, since by assumption, the curve represents the minimum-variance portfolio for each expected return.

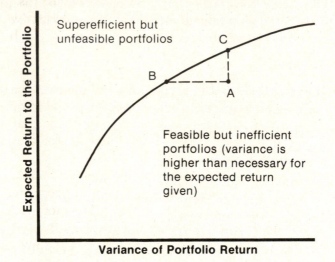

Figure 10-2. The efficient portfolio frontier. The portfolios below the efficient portfolio frontier are attainable, but are inefficient. They have a variance of return that is higher than necessary for the expected return they generate. The portfolios above the efficient portfolio frontier are superefficient, but are unattainable. They have a variance of return that is lower than what is possible in the market for the expected return they generate. The set of portfolios, then, that give the best possible risk-return tradeoff attainable are on the efficient portfolio frontier.

Because of this, the curve is called the *efficient portfolio frontier*. It sketches out the perimeter of feasible portfolios that lead to optimal diversification. Every investor will want to have a portfolio that is on this frontier. We now discuss the methods used in this chapter's programs that determine the mix of stocks on the frontier.

THE QUADRATIC PROGRAMMING APPROACH TO PORTFOLIO OPTIMIZATION

The portfolio manager's task of finding the portfolio that gives the lowest variance of return for a given expected return can be restated as: Minimize the portfolio variance subject to the portfolio expected return being equal to or greater than a given value.

The measure of portfolio variance that is used in this programming problem will depend on whether the Sharpe or the Markowitz method is specified. The measure of expected return is the same for both methods, however.

This problem is called a quadratic programming problem because the variance of the portfolio, σ_p^2, involves squared, or quadratic, terms.

The most immediate application of the quadratic optimization method is to find the portfolio mix that will produce the lowest risk; that is, to find the weights of each asset that lead to the lowest variance for whatever level of expected return that is specified.

Table 10-2 shows the optimal proportions of stocks to hold for a particular ten-stock portfolio. The second column shows the proportions calculated when the variance is specified using the Markowitz method, and the third column shows the proportions for the Sharpe method. The objective in this case was to minimize the portfolio variance subject to achieving an expected return of at least 15%. A comparison of the weights given to each stock and the variance and expected returns calculated by the two methods indicates how small the loss in accuracy is for the Sharpe method. The error from the Sharpe method depends on how well the β of the stocks encompasses the information in the variance/covariance matrix.

The efficient portfolio frontier can be traced out using both of these methods by varying the level of expected return to be achieved in the programming problem. There will be a different level of minimum variance

TABLE 10-2 Optimal Portfolio Composition

STOCK	MARKOWITZ METHOD	SHARPE METHOD
Aluminum Company of America	10.0	12.1
Avon	8.8	8.5
Bank of America	12.5	12.2
Ford	5.7	4.9
General Electric	6.2	5.8
IBM	20.2	17.5
Mobil Oil	13.0	13.2
Pfizer	2.4	3.3
Safeway	14.4	15.0
United Airlines	6.8	7.5
Total	*100.0*	*100.0*

possible for each expected return that is used in the quadratic program. Each pair of expected return and variance returned by the program gives one point on the efficient portfolio frontier. An alternative for tracing out the efficient portfolio frontier uses the Sharpe method to evaluate the effect of adding more stocks to the portfolio, one at a time, in a way that brings the portfolio from a high-variance, high-expected return position to a low-variance, low-expected return position. This method requires less computational power than the formal quadratic programming method does, but it only gives an approximation to the true frontier. Furthermore, this method will not be useful for constructing the minimum variance portfolio, since it constructs each of its points by using fewer of the stocks than are actually available for use.

OPTIMAL DIVERSIFICATION

Computational Procedure

Markowitz Method:

w_i = proportion of funds in the portfolio placed in stock i
$\bar{r}_i$ = expected return to stock i
$\bar{r}_p$ = expected return to the portfolio
σ_{ij} = covariance of returns stock i and j
σ_p^2 = variance of returns of the portfolio
K = a user-selected constant that is the target-expected return

Find the set of w_i to solve the problem:

Minimize: $\sigma_p^2 = \sum_i \sum_j w_i w_j \sigma_{ij}$

Subject to: $\bar{r}_p = \sum_i w_i \bar{r}_i = K, \sum w_i = 1$

Sharpe Method:

r_F = risk-free interest rate
β_i = the stock's beta
$\bar{r}_M$ = expected return to the market
u_i = error term
σ_i^2 = variance of u_i
σ_M^2 = variance of market return

Find the set of w_i to solve the problem:

Minimize: $\sigma_p^2 = [\sum w_i \beta_i]^2 \sigma_M^2 + \sum w_i^2 \sigma_i^2$

Subject to: $\bar{r}_p = \sum w_i(r_F + \beta_i(\bar{r}_M - r_F)) = K, \sum w_i = 1.$

Both of these are quadratic programming problems that are solved in the computer program by a modified simplex algorithm solving for the Kuhn-Tucker conditions.

Trading Strategy

Hold stocks within the portfolio according to the weights, w_i, that are given to the stocks in the optimization.

```
10   REM ***********************************************************************
20   REM *-                    DIVERSIFICATION PROGRAM                         *
30   REM *                                                                     *
40   REM * THIS PROGRAM USES A QUADRATIC PROGRAMMING TECHNIQUE TO FIND THE     *
50   REM * COMBINATION OF STOCKS WHICH GIVE THE SPECIFIED LEVEL OF EXPECTED    *
60   REM * RETURN WITH THE LOWEST VARIANCE OF RETURN.  THE PROGRAM EMPLOYS     *
70   REM * METHODS WHICH ARE COMPUTATIONALLY INTENSIVE, AND MAY LEAD TO        *
80   REM * SOME INACCURACY UNLESS THE COMPUATIONS ARE DONE IN FLOATING POINT   *
90   REM * PRECISION.                                                          *
100  REM *                                                                     *
110  REM *              N       =   NUMBER OF STOCKS                           *
120  REM *              R(I)    =   EXPECTED RETURN ON STOCK I                 *
130  REM *              S(I,J)  =   COVARIANCE OF STOCKS I AND J               *
140  REM *              K       =   TARGET EXPECTED RETURN                     *
150  REM *              SP      =   PORTFOLIO VARIANCE                         *
160  REM *              RP      =   PORTFOLIO EXPECTED RETURN                  *
170  REM *              W(I)    =   WEIGHT  OF STOCK I IN  OPTIMAL PORTFOLIO   *
180  REM ***********************************************************************
190  REM
200   DIM CAP(50), B(2,50), A(52,105), NME(52), X(100), ARET(50), C(50,50)
210  REM
220  REM ****************************MENU***************************************
230   GOSUB 350
240  REM
250  REM ********************** INPUT SUBROUTINE *******************************
260   GOSUB 490
270  REM
280  REM **********************MAIN QUADRATIC SUBROUTINE************************
290   GOSUB 1880
300  REM
310  REM ********************** OUTPUT SUBROUTINE ******************************
320   GOSUB 3710
330  REM
340   CLS:   REM CLEARS SCREEN
350  PRINT TAB(30)  "DIVERSIFICATION MENU."
360  PRINT TAB(30)  "********************"
370  PRINT TAB(25)  "1.   MARKOWITZ METHOD:INPUT INITIAL DATA"
380  PRINT TAB(25)  "2.   MARKOWITZ METHOD:MODIFY EXISTING DATA"
390  PRINT TAB(25)  "3.   SHARPE METHOD:INPUT INITIAL DATA"
400  PRINT TAB(25)  "4.   SHARPE METHOD:MODIFY EXISTING DATA"
410  PRINT TAB(25)  "5.   EXIT TO BASIC."
420  PRINT: INPUT "WHICH COMPUTATION WOULD YOU LIKE TO RUN : ",CHOICE
430  ON CHOICE GOSUB 460,770,1040,1380,1830
440   GOTO 280
450  REM
460  REM ***********************************************************************
470  REM *                        INPUT SUBROUTINE                            *
480  REM ***********************************************************************
490   CLS-:REM CLEARS SCREEN
500  INPUT " NUMBER OF STOCKS: ",N
510   M=2
520   NM = N + M
530   NR = NM
540   NC = 2 * NM + 1
```

```
550   M0 = M
560   N0 = NM + N
570 INPUT " TARGET EXPECTED RETURN (%): ",E
580 PRINT
590   FOR I=1 TO N
600 PRINT " EXPECTED RETURN OF STOCK ";I;" : ";
610 INPUT " ",ARET(I)
620   NEXT I
630 PRINT
640   FOR I = 1 TO N
650   FOR J = I TO N
660 PRINT " COVARIANCE OF STOCK ";I;" AND STOCK ";J;" :";
670 INPUT " ",C(I,J)
680   C(J,I)=C(I,J)
690   NEXT J
700   NEXT I
710   GOSUB 1850 : REM SUBROUTINE FOR SOLVING QUADRATIC PROGRAM
720   GOSUB 3910 : REM SUBROUTINE FOR MARKOWITZ OUTPUT
730 PRINT "        "
740 PRINT " TYPE RETURN WHEN YOU WISH TO CONTINUE"
750 INPUT " ",A$
760   GOTO 340
770 REM *********************************************************************
780 REM *        SUBROUTINE FOR MODIFYING DATA FOR MARKOWITZ METHOD         *
790 REM *********************************************************************
800   CLS
810 REM MENU FOR MAKING CHANGES IN DATA FOR MARKOWITZ METHOD
820 PRINT TAB(15);" MENU FOR CHANGES IN DATA FOR MARKOWITZ DATA :"
830 PRINT TAB(15);"1. CHANGE TARGET RETURN"
840 PRINT TAB(15);"2. CHANGE RETURN FOR A GIVEN STOCK"
850 PRINT TAB(15);"3. CHANGE COVARIANCE FOR A GIVEN PAIR OF STOCKS"
860 PRINT TAB(15);"4. NO MORE CHANGES"
870 INPUT "WHICH OPTION DO YOU SELECT(1,2,3,OR 4) : ",CHOICE
880   CLS
890   ON CHOICE GOTO 900,920,950,990
900 INPUT "INPUT NEW TARGET RETURN : ",E
910   GOTO 800
920 INPUT "WHICH STOCK WILL HAVE NEW EXPECTED RETURN : ",I
930 INPUT "              INPUT NEW EXPECTED RETURN : ",ARET(I)
940   GOTO 800
950 INPUT "WHICH PAIR OF STOCKS WILL HAVE NEW COVARIANCE (I,J) : ",I,J
960 INPUT "              INPUT NEW COVARIANCE VALUE : ",C(I,J)
970   C(J,I)=C(I,J)
980   GOTO 800
990   GOSUB 1850
1000   GOSUB 3910
1010 PRINT " TYPE RETURN WHEN YOU WISH TO CONTINUE"
1020 INPUT " ",A$
1030   GOTO 340
1040 REM *********************************************************************
1050 REM *                INPUT ROUTINE FOR SHARPE METHOD                    *
1060 REM *********************************************************************
1070 INPUT " NUMBER OF STOCKS: ",N
1080   M=2
```

```
1090   NM = N + M
1100   NR = NM
1110   NC = 2 * NM + 1
1120   M0 = M
1130   N0 = NM + N
1140 INPUT " TARGET EXPECTED RETURN (%): ",E
1150 INPUT " VARIANCE OF MARKET RETURN : ",SM
1160 INPUT " RISKFREE RATE OF RETURN : ",RF
1170 INPUT " MARKET RATE OF RETURN : ",RM
1180   FOR I = 1 TO N
1190 PRINT " BETA OF STOCK ";I;" : ";
1200 INPUT " ",BETA(I)
1210 PRINT " VARIANCE OF RESIDUAL OF STOCK ";I;" : ";
1220 INPUT " ",SU(I)
1230 PRINT "   "
1240   ARET(I) = RF + (RM-RF)*BETA(I)
1250   NEXT I
1260   FOR I = 1 TO N
1270   FOR J = 1 TO N
1280   C(I,J) =   BETA(I)*BETA(J)*SM
1290   IF I<> J THEN 1310
1300   C(I,J) = C(I,J) + SU(I)
1310   NEXT J
1320   NEXT I
1330   GOSUB 1850
1340   GOSUB  3910
1350 PRINT " PRESS RETURN TO CONTINUE"
1360 INPUT "    ",A$
1370   GOTO 340
1380 REM ****************************************************************************
1390 REM *            SUBROUTINE FOR MODIFYING DATA FOR SHARPE METHOD            *
1400 REM ****************************************************************************
1410 CLS
1420 REM
1430 REM MENU FOR MODIFYING DATA FOR THE SHARPE METHOD
1440 REM
1450 PRINT TAB(15)" MENU FOR MODIFYING DATA FOR THE SHARPE METHOD"
1460 PRINT TAB(15);"1. CHANGE TARGET RETURN"
1470 PRINT TAB(15);"2. CHANGE VARIANCE OF MARKET RETURN"
1480 PRINT TAB(15);"3. CHANGE RISKFREE RATE OF RETURN"
1490 PRINT TAB(15);"4. CHANGE MARKET RATE OF RETURN"
1500 PRINT TAB(15);"5. CHANGE BETA VALUE OF A GIVEN STOCK"
1510 PRINT TAB(15);"6. CHANGE VARIANCE OF RESIDUAL OF A GIVEN STOCK"
1520 PRINT TAB(15);"7. NO MORE CHANGES"
1530 INPUT "WHICH OPTION DO YOU SELECT (1,2,3,4,5,6 OR 7) : ",CHOICE
1540   CLS
1550   ON CHOICE GOTO 1560,1580,1600,1620,1640,1670,1700
1560 INPUT " INPUT NEW TARGET RETURN : ",E
1570   GOTO 1410
1580 INPUT "INPUT NEW VARIANCE OF MARKET RETURN : ",SM
1590   GOTO 1410
1600 INPUT "INPUT NEW RISKFREE RATE OF RETURN : ",RF
1610   GOTO 1410
1620 INPUT " INPUT NEW MARKET RATE OF RETURN : ",RM
```

```
1630   GOTO 1410
1640 INPUT "WHICH STOCK WILL HAVE A NEW BETA VALUE : ",I
1650 INPUT "INPUT NEW BETA VALUE : ",BETA(I)
1660   GOTO 1410
1670 INPUT "WHICH STOCK WILL HAVE A NEW VARIANCE OF  RESIDUAL VALUE : ",I
1680 INPUT "INPUT NEW VARIANCE OF RESIDUAL VALUE : ",SU(I)
1690   GOTO 1410
1700   FOR I = 1 TO N
1710    ARET(I) = RF + (RM-RF)*BETA(I)
1720   FOR J = 1 TO N
1730    C(I,J) =   BETA(I)*BETA(J)*SM
1740    IF I<> J THEN 1760
1750    C(I,J) = C(I,J) + SU(I)
1760   NEXT J
1770   NEXT I
1780   GOSUB 1850
1790   GOSUB  3910
1800 PRINT " TYPE RETURN WHEN YOU WISH TO CONTINUE"
1810 INPUT "  ",A$
1820 RETURN
1830  CLS
1840  GOTO 4270
1850 REM *********************************************************************
1860 REM *                MAJOR LOOP - QUADRATIC PROGRAMMING                 *
1870 REM *********************************************************************
1880 PRINT "PROCESSING . . ."
1890   FOR I=1 TO NR
1900   FOR J=1 TO NC
1910    A(I,J)=0
1920   NEXT J
1930   NEXT I
1940 REM       *****************************************************
1950 REM       RIGHT-HAND SIDE CONSTRAINTS
1960 REM       *****************************************************
1970    A(1,NC)=1
1980    A(2,NC)=E
1990 REM
2000   FOR J=1 TO N
2010    A(M0+J,NC)=0
2020   NEXT J
2030 REM *****************************************************
2040 REM LEFT-HAND SIDE CONSTRAINTS
2050 REM *****************************************************
2060 REM
2070   FOR J=1 TO N
2080    B(1,J)=0
2090    B(2,J)=1
2100    CAP(J)=B(2,J)-B(1,J)
2110    A(1,J) = 1
2120    A(2,J)=ARET(J)
2130   NEXT J
2140 REM
2150   FOR I=1 TO M
2160   FOR J=1 TO N
```

```
2170    A(M0+J,N0+I)=-A(I,J)
2180    A(M0+J,NC)=A(M0+J,NC)-10*A(I,J)
2190    A(I,NC)=A(I,NC)-B(1,J)*A(I,J)
2200   NEXT J
2210   NEXT I
2220  REM ****************************************************
2230  REM VARIANCE-COVARIANCE MATRIX
2240  REM ****************************************************
2250   FOR I=1 TO N
2260   FOR J=1 TO N
2270    A(M0+I,J)= -C(I,J)/1000
2280   NEXT J
2290   NEXT I
2300   FOR I=1 TO NM
2310    NME(I)=I+N
2320    A(I,I+N)=1
2330   NEXT I
2340    IZ=0
2350    JN=0
2360    IP=0
2370    IF IPRT = 0 THEN 2470
2380  PRINT  "  ROW         VARIABLE       VALUE "
2390  PRINT " "
2400   FOR I=1 TO NM
2410  PRINT I,NME(I),A(I,NC)
2420   NEXT I
2430  PRINT " "
2440  REM ****************************************************
2450  REM SELECT ENTERING VARIABLE
2460  REM ****************************************************
2470   IR=0
2480    TOL = .001
2490    IF IP <> 0 THEN 2640
2500   CBAR=-TOL
2510   FOR I=1 TO NM
2520    IF A(I,NC) >= CBAR THEN 2550
2530    CBAR= A(I,NC)
2540    IR=I
2550   NEXT I
2560    IF IR = 0 THEN 3700
2570    JC=NME(IR)
2580    IF JC <= NM THEN 3000
2590    JC=JC-NM
2600    IF ABS(A(IR,JC))<TOL THEN 2650
2610    RR=A(IR,NC)/A(IR,JC)
2620    IF RR > TOL THEN 2700
2630    GOTO 2650
2640    JC=JN+NM
2650    RR=1000000
2660    IR = 0
2670  REM ****************************************************
2680  REM SELECT LEAVING VARIABLE
2690  REM ****************************************************
2700    IF JC>N THEN 2740
```

```
2710    CAP0=ABS(CAP(JC))
2720    IF CAP0>RR THEN 2740
2730    RR=CAP0:IR=-1
2740    FOR I=1 TO NM
2750     JD=NME(I)
2760     IF JD <= NM THEN 2830
2770     IF JC <= NM THEN 2920
2780     IF JD <> IP+NM THEN 2920
2790     IF ABS(A(I,JC)) < TOL THEN 2920
2800     R5= A(I,NC)/A(I,JC)
2810     IF R5 < 0 THEN 2920
2820     GOTO 2890
2830     IF ABS(A(I,JC)) < TOL THEN 2920
2840     IF A(I,JC) < -TOL THEN 2860
2850     R5= A(I,NC)/A(I,JC):GOTO 2890
2860     IF JD>N GOTO 2920
2870     CAP1=ABS(CAP(JD))
2880     R5=(CAP1-A(I,NC))/-A(I,JC)
2890     IF R5 >= RR THEN 2920
2900     RR=R5
2910     IR=I
2920    NEXT I
2930    IF IR > 0 THEN 3060
2940    IF IR<0 THEN 3560
2950 PRINT "UNBOUNDED SOLUTION."
2960    GOTO 4270
2970 REM ***********************************************
2980 REM SELECT ENTERING VARIABLE FOR PRIMAL INFEASIBLE PIVOT
2990 REM ***********************************************
3000 PRINT " "
3010 PRINT "NO FEASIBLE SOLUTION."
3020    GOTO 4270
3030 REM      ***********************************************
3040 REM       SET MARKERS FOR NON-STANDARD SOLUTION
3050 REM      ***********************************************
3060    IF IP > 0 THEN 3110
3070    IF NME(IR) > NM THEN 3150
3080    IP = JC
3090    JN = NME(IR)
3100    GOTO 3190
3110    IF NME(IR) > NM THEN 3150
3120    IF NME(IR) = IP THEN 3150
3130    JN = NME(IR)
3140    GOTO 3190
3150    IP = 0
3160 REM           ***********************************************
3170 REM           EXCHANGE
3180 REM           ***********************************************
3190    IZ=IZ+1
3200    JD=NME(IR):NME(IR)=JC
3210    IF JD>NM THEN 3300
3220    IF A(IR,JC)>0 THEN 3300
3230 REM  COMPLEMENT LEAVING PRIMAL VARIABLE AND ITS DUAL
3240    CAP(JD)=-CAP(JD)
```

```
3250   A(IR,NC)=ABS(CAP(JD))-A(IR,NC)
3260   FOR J=1 TO NM2:A(IR,J)=-A(IR,J):NEXT J
3270   A(IR,JD)=1
3280   JD1=JD+NM
3290   FOR I=1 TO NM:A(I,JD1)=-A(I,JD1):NEXT I
3300   AO= A(IR,JC)
3310   FOR I=1 TO NM
3320    IF I = IR THEN 3370
3330   FOR J=1 TO NC
3340    IF J = JC THEN 3360
3350    A(I,J) = A(I,J) -(A(IR,J)*A(I,JC))/AO
3360   NEXT J
3370   NEXT I
3380   FOR J=1 TO NC
3390    A(IR,J) = A(IR,J)/AO
3400   NEXT J
3410   FOR I=1 TO NM
3420    A(I,JC)=0
3430   NEXT I
3440   A(IR,JC)=1
3450   IF IPRT = 0 THEN 2470
3460 PRINT     "  ROW          VARIABLE        VALUE "
3470 PRINT " "
3480   FOR I=1 TO NM
3490 PRINT I,NME(I),A(I,NC)
3500   NEXT I
3510 PRINT " "
3520 GOTO 2470
3530 REM
3540 REM UPDATE WORKING MATRIX WHEN THERE IS NO EXCHANGE
3550 REM
3560   IZ=IZ+1:IR=0:JC1=JC+NM:CAP(JC)=-CAP(JC)
3570   FOR I=1 TO NM
3580    A(I,NC)=A(I,NC)-A(I,JC)*CAP0
3590    A(I,JC)=-A(I,JC)
3600    A(I,JC1)=-A(I,JC1)
3610    IF NME(I)<> JC1 THEN 3630
3620    IR=I
3630   NEXT I
3640   IF IR=0 THEN 2470
3650   FOR J=1 TO NC:A(IR,J)=-A(IR,J):NEXT J
3660   GOTO 3450
3670 REM *********************************************************
3680 REM OUTPUT
3690 REM *********************************************************
3700 PRINT " "
3710   INF=0
3720   FOR J=1 TO N
3730    IF CAP(J) >0 THEN 3750
3740    X(J)=B(2,J):GOTO 3760
3750    X(J)=B(1,J)
3760   NEXT J
3770   FOR I=1 TO NM
3780    JD=NME(I)
```

```
3790    IF JD > N THEN 3850
3800    IF CAP(JD)<0 THEN 3830
3810    X(JD) = X(JD)+A(I,NC)
3820    GOTO 3880
3830    X(JD)=X(JD)-A(I,NC)
3840    GOTO 3880
3850    IF JD>NM GOTO 3880
3860    IF A(I,NC)< TOL THEN 3880
3870    INF=1
3880    NEXT I
3890    RETURN
3900 REM ****************************************************************
3910 REM *        SUBROUTINE FOR OUTPUT FOR MARKOWITZ METHOD            *
3920 REM ****************************************************************
3930    CLS
3940    IF INF =0 GOTO 3970
3950 PRINT "  TARGET RETURN CANNOT BE ACHIEVED."
3960    RETURN
3970    F1=0
3980    F2=0
3990    FOR I=1 TO N
4000    F1=F1+X(I)
4010    F2=F2+X(I)*ARET(I)
4020    NEXT I
4030    V3=0
4040    FOR I=1 TO N
4050    V3=V3 + C(I,I)*X(I)^2
4060    IF I=N GOTO 4110
4070    L1=I+1
4080    FOR J=L1 TO N
4090    V3=V3 + C(I,J)*X(I)*X(J)*2
4100    NEXT J
4110    NEXT I
4120    V3=SQR(V3)
4130 REM ****************************************************************
4140 REM *                     OUTPUT SUBROUTINE                       *
4150 REM ****************************************************************
4160 REM
4170 PRINT "STOCK         WEIGHT         EXPECTED RETURN      STD. DEV."
4180 PRINT "-----         ------         ---------------      ---------"
4190    FOR I=1 TO N
4200 PRINT USING "###        ####.##         ######.##          ######.#";
I;X(I)*100;ARET(I);SQR(C(I,I))
4210    NEXT I
4220 PRINT "              ------         ---------------      ---------"
4230 PRINT USING "          ####.##         ######.##          ######.#";
F1*100;F2;V3
4240 PRINT " "
4250 PRINT " "
4260    RETURN
4270    END
```

11
Evaluating the Characteristics of Optioned Portfolios

The key to the diversification methods discussed in Chapter 10 is to encapsulate the important characteristics of the portfolio in two parameters—the mean and the variance of the return. The investor need only specify the desired expected return, and the portfolio that will lead to that expected return with the least risk, as measured by the variance or standard deviation of the return, can immediately be calculated. It should be recognized that this simple risk-return tradeoff is only possible because the distribution of returns to the portfolio depends only on the mean and variance of returns. That is, since the stocks are assumed to follow a normal distribution, once we know the mean and the variance, we know everything about the returns.

As discussed in the last chapter, the normal distribution has the familiar bell shape depicted in Figure 11-1A. The returns are symmetric around the mean; there is an equal chance of having returns a given distance above the mean as of having returns that same distance below the mean. Such a return distribution has a number of desirable properties. For example, if each stock is normally distributed, then a portfolio made up of a number of stocks will also be normally distributed. And, as just mentioned, the normal distribution is very easy to characterize since it depends on only two parameters, the mean and variance.

But there is no reason to think that these properties, convenient though they may be, will fit the preferences or objectives of the investor. For example, a conservative investor may want to have protection against large losses, while retaining some of the upside potential from the portfolio. Such an investor may prefer a portfolio with returns that are distributed like those in Figure 10-1B.

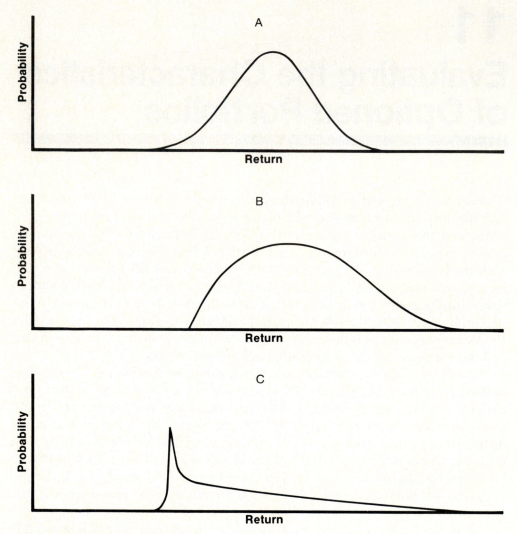

Figure 11-1. Alternative return distributions.

With this distribution, the investor continues to have the potential for reasonable gains—although not as large as the gains possible for the pure stock portfolio depicted in Figure 10-1A—while having very little potential for a large loss. Or, a risk-averse investor who is confident of his or her portfolio selection may want a levered investment to generate a very high payoff if his beliefs turn out to be correct, but only if it can be done without risking catastrophic losses if the market turns against him. This investor may prefer a portfolio with returns like those in Figure 11-1C. Rather than the typical tradeoff of achieving the potential for large gains by taking an increased risk of large losses, here the tradeoff involves a sacrifice of potential moderate gains to achieve the increased potential for very high gains.

These types of returns are not possible by trading in stocks alone. They are possible to achieve by combining the stock position with a position in options. The use of options in portfolio management allows an investor to "mold" the returns of the portfolio to better fit a particular set of investment objectives. Indeed, the range of returns that can be created through the use of option markets makes traditional portfolio management based on two-dimensional mean-variance tradeoffs obsolete.

The program in this chapter allows the investor to evaluate the effects option strategies can have on the portfolio return characteristics. This program can be an extremely valuable tool for portfolio management, since it allows an investor to adjust the portfolio strategy to better meet investment objectives and risk profiles.

DETERMINING THE RETURN CHARACTERISTICS OF PORTFOLIOS WITH OPTION POSITIONS

Determining the effect options will have on portfolio returns is a complex issue. Unlike the relationship between one option and one stock, which can be plotted using the profit profile described in Chapter 27, calculating the return for a portfolio of options and stocks requires evaluating the return on each individual stock conditional on the return of all the other stocks in the portfolio. The reason for this can be illustrated by the following example. Suppose an investor holds 100 shares of two different stocks and writes an option on each of the stocks. Both stocks are initially at $90 a share, and each option has an exercise price of $100. Assume the stock portfolio increases in value from

$18,000 to $20,000 by the time the options expire. What will the value of the portfolio be with the option position?

As Table 11-1 shows, the portfolio value all depends on how each of the two stocks moved to lead to the $20,000 value. If both stocks increased to $100 per share, then the full value of the stock appreciation will be realized, and the optioned portfolio will be worth $20,000. (Here we are ignoring any proceeds from writing the options.) On the other hand, if one of the stocks increases to $110 per share while the other stays at $90, the one stock will be called away at the option exercise price of $100, and the writer will only gain the first ten dollars of appreciation in the stock price. The optioned portfolio in this case will only be worth $19,000. Obviously, there are any number of other possibilities for the behavior of the two stocks, and any number of possible values for the optioned portfolio for any return to the underlying stock portfolio.

TABLE 11-1   Returns to a Portfolio of Two Stocks with Call Options Written on Each Stock

---

Portfolio Value at Time Options Are Written

> Price of Stock A = $90
> Price of Stock B = $90

> Price of Portfolio = $18,000

Write a Call Option on Both Stocks, with E = $100.

Portfolio Value at Option Expiration

Case 1: Price of Stock A = $100
Price of Stock B = $100
> Value of Stock Portfolio = $20,000
> Value of Stock Portfolio *with* Option Position = $20,000

Case 2: Price of Stock A = $110
Price of Stock B = $ 90
> Value of Stock Portfolio = $20,000
> Value of Stock Portfolio *with* Option Position = $19,000

There is a way around this problem, however. There is an approximation algorithm that can be used to generate the return distribution of portfolios with option positions. The algorithm is based on the use of the expected value of the optioned portfolio conditional on the return to the stock portfolio. This algorithm assumes that all stocks held by the investor have returns generated by the single index model:

$$r_i = r_f + \beta_i(r_m - r_f) + u_i$$

where:

r_i = the return to stock i
r_f = the return to the riskless asset (such as treasury bills)
β_i = the systematic risk to firm i
r_m = the return to the index
u_i = a random error term for firm i

The single index model we are using here is identical to the single index model used in the Sharpe method of generating the efficient portfolio frontier in Chapter 10. This model is also similar to the capital asset pricing model relationship presented in Chapter 12, but has an error term added that is assumed to be normally distributed and is also assumed to be independent from firm to firm. This means that securities are assumed to be related only through their relationship with the index return, r_m. It is useful to note that the index here does not necessarily need to be the market return, although that is the interpretation that will lead to the capital asset pricing model. In other settings, such as when considering the effect of options on foreign exchange positions or on commodity futures, a different index may be applicable.

The algorithm itself is fairly complex, and so we leave the details to the program description at the end of the chapter. The important point in making use of it is to know that since it relies on the single index model, the beta of each stock, the riskfree interest rate, the expected return on the market, and the residual error term, u_i, will all be required inputs. Another required input will be the proportion of each stock to be converted by the option position. This proportion is denoted by the portfolio alpha. An alpha of .5 means that half of each stock is covered with an option. So, for example, if the portfolio has 2000 shares of IBM, an alpha of .5 means 10 options will be written. (Recall that an option covers 100 shares of stock, so 10 options cover 1000 shares of IBM.)

EXAMPLES OF OPTION-PORTFOLIO STRATEGIES

The method for evaluating option-portfolio strategies are illustrated here by three popular strategies: writing covered calls, protective put buying, and call option/paper buying. Needless to say, these three can only begin to cover the many strategies that are possible and that can be analyzed with the program. But they provide a representative look at how options alter the return characteristics of a stock portfolio.

Writing Covered Call Options

Writing covered call options is a popular option strategy used by portfolio managers. Writing call options seems to hold out the best of two worlds. If the stock appreciates and is called away, the portfolio still gains the option premium, and also receives dividends for the period before exercise. And if the option is out of the money, the portfolio will gain the stock appreciation up to the exercise price. If the stock declines in price, the loss is buffered by the option premium, so the total loss from the position will be less than if no option were written.

Figure 11-2 presents the return distribution that results from writing call options on the underlying stock portfolio. Curve A is the distribution of the underlying stock portfolio when no options are written. As shown in Table 11-2, this reference portfolio has an expected semi-annual return of 8.04% and a standard deviation of return of 14.98%. Since the return is assumed to be normally distributed, the mean and variance are sufficient statistics for the distribution.

However, the distribution becomes more complex as an increasing proportion of call options is written on the stocks in the portfolio. Curves B, C, and D show the portfolio return distribution when the proportion of the portfolio covered by call options, which we denote by α, rises from zero to 25%, 50%, and 75%, respectively. The exercise price of all the options in this strategy is assumed to equal the current stock price. That is, the exercise return is 0%. With this and all other strategies, the time to expiration is six months.

The two apparent characteristics of this strategy on the portfolio returns are, first, the truncation of the righthand portion of the distribution, and second, the shift to the right in the distribution. Essentially, writing a call option involves selling the desirable righthand tail of the distribution, with the payment reflected in the option premium received. The truncation results from the sale of part of the tail, from having the stock called away if it rises above the exercise price. The shift results from the premium value added to the portfolio, which reduces the initial investment base required to purchase the stocks.

　　The change in the shape of the return distributions is evident from

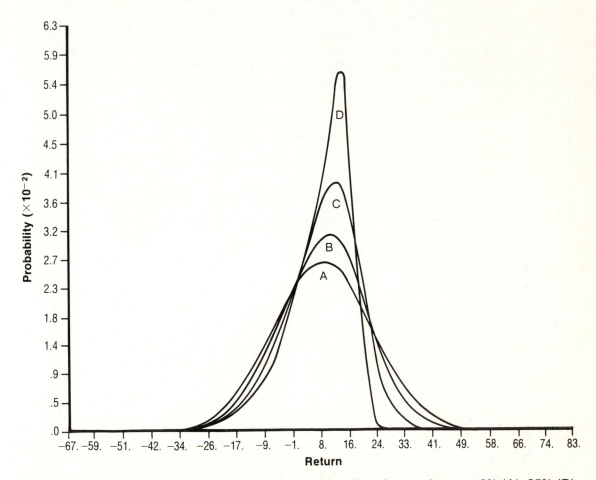

Figure 11-2. Return distribution of a portfolio with call options written on 0% (A), 25% (B), 50% (C), and 75% (D) of the stock portfolio. The exercise price of the options is equal to the current stock price.

reference to Table 11-2. For the underlying portfolio with $\alpha = 0$, the probability of receiving a return below –20% is 3.07%. (This probability is computed by summing the probabilities of receiving below –40%, –30% to –40%, and –20% to –30%.) This probability diminishes as the portfolio is covered with option positions, and the distribution shifts to the right. For the case of $\alpha = 1.0$, the probability of receiving a return below –20% drops to .77%. The truncation on the righthand side is more pronounced—the probability of receiving a return above 20% is 0 for $\alpha = 1.0$, compared to over 21.25% for the underlying portfolio.

The effect of this strategy on the mean, variance, and skewness of the distribution and the portfolio beta is shown in Table 11-2. The expected return for the fully covered portfolio is 6.56%, compared to 8.04% for the reference portfolio of underlying stocks. While the expected return drops by 18%, the

TABLE 11-2 Probability of Returns for Writing Call Options
(Exercise Return is 0%)

Return Interval (Semi-Annual)	PROPORTION OF THE PORTFOLIO COVERED (α)				
	0	.25	.50	.75	1.0
Below –40	.07	.05	.03	.02	.01
–30 –40	.49	.33	.24	.16	.11
–20 –30	2.51	1.86	1.34	.94	.65
–10 –20	8.37	6.83	5.34	4.01	2.89
0 –10	18.14	17.19	15.45	13.05	10.31
10 0	25.62	29.14	33.35	38.26	44.51
20 10	23.55	27.91	34.39	42.25	41.52
30 20	14.10	13.26	9.29	1.31	0.00
40 30	5.50	3.05	.55	0.00	0.00
40+	1.65	.36	.01	0.00	0.00
Mean	8.04	7.70	7.34	6.96	6.56
Standard Deviation	14.98	12.91	10.78	8.67	6.72
Skewness	0.00	–.25	–.63	–1.22	–2.12
β	.95	.82	.68	.53	.37

standard deviation of the portfolio drops by over 50%, from 14.98% to 6.72%. The beta of the portfolio drops by over a half, from .95 to .37.

Covered call option writing significantly alters the risk-return tradeoff; in terms of standard deviation, it reduces risk. However, the steep reduction in risk as measured by standard deviation can be misleading. Most of the drop in variance occurs in that part of the distribution where high variance is desirable—in the righthand tail. It is natural to have more compensation in expected return for a drop in standard deviation when that drop occurs from the covered call strategy than when it occurs from a strict stock-riskless asset tradeoff, since in the latter case the desirable righthand side and the undesirable lefthand side of the distribution are affected symmetrically.

Buying Put Options

In two obvious respects, buying put options is the mirror image of writing covered call options. While writing covered calls truncates the righthand side of the distribution and shifts the distribution to the right, buying puts truncates the lefthand side of the distribution and shifts the distribution to the left. The truncation results from the price of the put option increasing to offset any decline in the stock price. The shift results as the cost of the put premium decreases the investment base of the portfolio.

Figure 11-3 shows the returns for the put option strategy with α = .25, .50, and .75 (Curves B, C, and D, respectively), and the return distribution of the reference stock portfolio (Curve A). The values are tabulated in Table 11-3. These figures are all generated for options purchased at the money (i.e., for an exercise return of 0%).

The most obvious characteristic of the put option strategy is the reduction of downside risk and the maintenance of upside potential. The probability of receiving a severe loss can be reduced and even brought to zero with the appropriate option strategy. This is as would be expected, since analytically put options can be characterized as an insurance contract to protect the purchaser from a decline in the price of the underlying stock.

As Table 11-3 indicates, both the expected return and standard deviation drop as the proportion of the portfolio with put options held increases. For α = 1.0, the expected return is 6.67% compared to 8.04% for the reference portfolio, and the standard deviation is 9.64% compared to 14.98%.

A more interesting comparison is between this put option strategy and the covered call writing strategy. The two strategies have much the same effect on expected return. For $\alpha = 1.0$, the expected return for the put strategy is virtually identical to that of the call strategy—6.67%, compared to 6.56%. But the standard deviation for the put strategy is actually higher—9.64% compared to 6.72% for covered call writing. If variance is used as a proxy for risk, covered call writing will be preferred to buying puts. But variance is not a suitable proxy

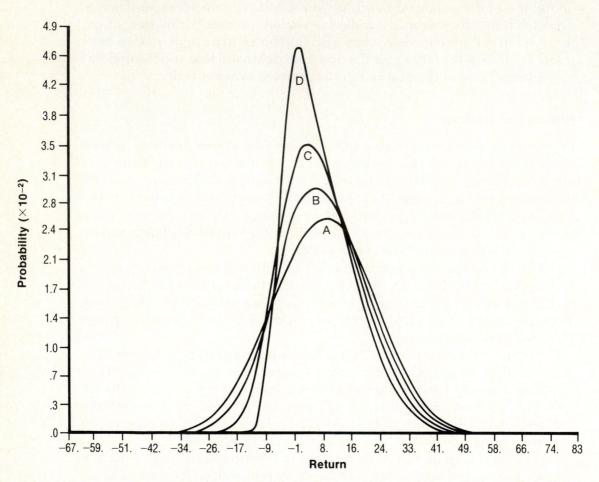

Figure 11-3. Return distribution of a portfolio with put options purchased on 0% (A), 25% (B), 50% (C), and 75% (D) of the stock portfolio. The exercise price of the options is equal to the current stock price.

for risk, since the option strategies reduce variance asymmetrically. The call truncates the righthand side of the distribution, and thereby reduces the desirable upside variance. The put, on the other hand, eliminates the variance more on the undesirable lefthand portion of the return distribution. It is clear that more than variance is needed in assessing risk of the option portfolio strategies.

The insurance characteristics of buying put options are apparent in Figure 11-3. But while the probability of having a large loss can be made arbitrarily small, the protection does not come without a cost. One obvious cost is the price paid for the option; this is reflected in the lefthand shift of the distribution. Another less obvious cost is reflected in the increase in probability mass just above the point of truncation. That is to say, while the probability of

TABLE 11-3 Probability of Returns for Purchasing Put Options (Exercise Return is 0%)

Return Interval (Semi-Annual)	PROPORTION OF THE PORTFOLIO COVERED (α)				
	0	.25	.50	.75	1.0
Below −40	.07	0.00	0.00	0.00	0.00
−40 −30	.49	.09	0.00	0.00	0.00
−30 −20	2.51	1.23	.18	0.00	0.00
−20 −10	8.37	7.58	5.32	1.28	0.00
−10 0	18.14	20.90	24.58	29.22	31.10
0 10	25.62	28.43	31.42	34.48	37.46
10 20	23.55	23.53	23.06	22.15	20.85
20 30	14.10	12.65	11.13	9.60	8.15
30 40	5.50	4.42	3.50	2.71	2.07
40+	1.65	1.16	.80	.55	.36
Mean	8.04	7.68	7.34	7.00	6.67
Standard Deviation	14.98	13.50	12.11	10.81	9.64
Skewness	0.00	.22	.47	.74	1.11
β	.95	.86	.76	.67	.59

a very low return declines, the probability mass associated with the very low return is just pushed up slightly, and consequently the probability of a moderately low return increases. As is shown in Table 11-3, the probability of receiving a return below –20% declines from 3.07% for $\alpha = 0$ to .18% for $\alpha = .5$, and to 0.0 for $\alpha = .75$ and for $\alpha = 1.0$. But the probability of receiving a return

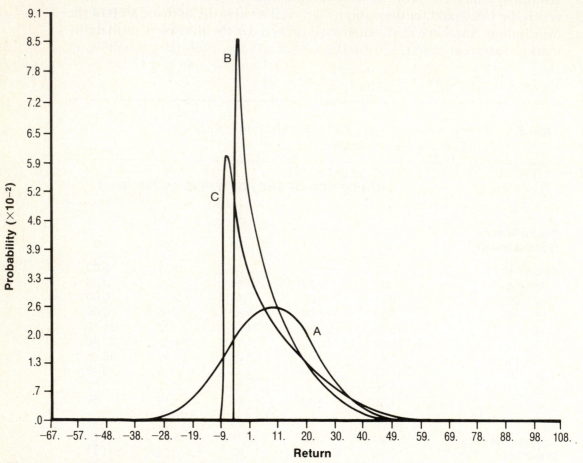

Figure 11-4. Return distribution of a portfolio of call options, with 1.15 options purchased for every 100 shares of stock in the reference portfolio (B), and with 1.685 options purchased for every 100 shares of stock in the reference portfolio (C). (A) is the reference portfolio.

between –10% to 0% increases from 18.14% for $\alpha = 0$ to 24.58% for $\alpha = .5$, and to 31.10% for $\alpha = 1$.

Call Option/Paper Buying

Call options are conventionally viewed as highly levered, speculative securities. But it is now widely recognized that the leverage and risk of options can be reduced to convert the strategy of buying call options into a prudent, low-risk strategy. Indeed, by holding a sufficiently small proportion of the portfolio in call options, with the remainder held in a low-risk money market instrument, portfolio risk can be reduced substantially below that of the underlying stock portfolio.

Figure 11-4, Curve B shows the return distribution for a call/paper strategy long in call options and long in bonds. Ten percent of the portfolio funds are held in call options, with the remainder held in money market instruments. Given the price of the options, with our data set, this strategy leads to $\alpha = 1.15$, where the options are held in place of the underlying stocks. Figure 11-4, Curve C gives the return distribution of the "share-equivalent" portfolio—the option portfolio that matches the price movement of the underlying stocks. Since the share-equivalent, derived as the inverse of the hedge ratio, is an instantaneous measure, the actual share-equivalent will vary over time, and this static option portfolio will not exactly match the stock price movement over any finite time horizon.

The option/paper strategy dramatically truncates the left side of the distribution, since the maximum loss is limited to the fraction of the portfolio in calls less the interest on the paper, and still allows for some appreciation should the underlying stocks increase in value. As α increases, the distribution spreads out, the truncated left tail shifts down, and the right tail extends further to the right. Table 11-4 also shows the result of holding all the portfolio in options—the extreme case of this strategy. Here, 11.5 options are held in place of each 100 shares of stock of the underlying portfolio. In this case, the distribution truncates at –100% return, and the right tail extends well beyond that of the underlying portfolio. Roughly a third of the probability mass rests below –40%, a third rests between –40% and 40%, and a third rests above 40%.

As with buying options on the stocks in the portfolio, the call/paper strategy concentrates much of the mass near the point of truncation. While there is no risk of a return below –10%, there is over a .40 probability of a return between –10% and 0% for the portfolio with $\alpha = 1.685$.

OPTION-STOCK PORTFOLIO ANALYSIS STRATEGY

The three strategies just illustrated only begin to cover the many strategies that may be profitable to pursue. The program for this chapter is very general, and can analyze a virtually unlimited number of strategies involving combinations of puts, calls, and stock. The program can also be applied to applications of hedging using futures contracts and the related calls and puts on futures.

TABLE 11-4　Probability of Returns for Call/Paper Buying

Return Interval (Semi-Annual)	OPTION POSITION RELATIVE TO STOCK POSITION IN REFERENCE PORTFOLIO (α)				
	0	**1.0**	**1.15**	**1.685**	**11.5**
Below −40	.07	0.00	0.00	0.00	37.38
−40　−30	.49	0.00	0.00	0.00	4.41
−30　−20	2.51	0.00	0.00	0.00	4.06
−20　−10	8.37	0.00	0.00	0.00	3.77
−10　　0	18.14	29.23	33.11	40.37	3.54
0　10	25.62	43.42	37.73	26.36	3.32
10　20	23.55	19.32	18.85	16.50	3.14
20　30	14.10	6.44	7.60	9.41	2.97
30　40	5.50	1.38	2.20	4.60	2.80
40+	1.65	.20	.51	2.76	34.58
Mean	8.04	6.19	6.37	6.974	21.25
Standard Deviation	14.98	8.49	9.65	13.560	106.12
Skewness	0.00	1.23	1.23	1.230	1.23
β	.95	.51	.58	.810	6.34

THE SINGLE INDEX ALGORITHM FOR DETERMINING THE RETURN DISTRIBUTION OF DYNAMIC PORTFOLIO STRATEGIES AND PORTFOLIOS WITH OPTION POSITIONS

Computational Procedure

Assume stock returns are generated by the single index model:

$$r_i = r_f + \beta_i(r_m - r_f) + u_i$$

where

r_i = the return to stock i
r_f = the return to the riskless asset (such as treasury bills)
β_i = the systematic risk to firm i
r_m = the return to the index
u_i = a random error term for firm i
σ_i = standard deviation of the error term u_i

The conditional expected return on the shares of stock i with a call option written on a proportion α_i of the total shares of stock held in the portfolio is:

$$E(\tilde{r}_i'|r_m) = E(\tilde{r}_i|r_m, r_i \leq r_i^e) \text{ prob } (r_i \leq r_i^e|r_m)$$
$$+[(1 - \alpha_i)E(\tilde{r}_i|r_m, r_i \geq r_i^e) + \alpha_i r_i^e] \text{ prob } (r_i \geq r_i^e|r_m) \tag{1}$$

where r_i^e is the return to stock i at which the stock price will equal the exercise price of the option.

The aggregate conditional expected return on the optioned portfolio is

$$E(\tilde{r}_{op}|r_m) = \Sigma\omega_i E(\tilde{r}_i'|r_m) = \Sigma\omega_i \bar{r}_i + \Sigma\omega_i \, \alpha_i(1-\emptyset(y_i))(r_i^e - \bar{r}_i - \bar{U}_i). \tag{2}$$

where

$\emptyset (\cdot)$ is the standard normal cumulative distribution function
$y_i = (r_i^e - \bar{r}_i)/\sigma_i$, $\bar{U}_i$ is the mean of the error term for stock i given that $u_i < (r_i^e - \bar{r}_i)$
ω_i is the proportion of the portfolio made up by stock i

The conditional expected return on the *total* investment portfolio can be written as the return from any funds invested in the riskless asset, *plus* the proceeds or cost of the option position, *plus* the expected return on the combined option-stock portfolio:

$$E(\tilde{r}|r_m) = \omega_f r_f + \omega_c(1 + r_f) + E(\tilde{r}_{op}|r_m) \tag{3}$$

The single index algorithm computes Equation (3), conditional on a range of values for r_m, and assigns a probability weighting to each resulting expected total portfolio return according to the probability of the corresponding index return. The single index algorithm may be summarized as follows:

INDEX ALGORITHM

Step 1.   Compute the expected return on the total portfolio conditional on r_m using Equation (3).

Step 2.   Assign a cumulative probability to the resulting total portfolio return equal to the probability of the corresponding value of r_m.

Step 3.   Interate Step 1 and Step 2 for all admissible values of r_m to trace out the cumulative probability distribution for the total portfolio return. Using the estimated points in the cumulative distribution, calculate the height of the density function at each point consistent with the cumulative probability distribution.

This algorithm takes advantage of the Law of Large Numbers, and so it is more accurate for portfolios having many stocks. However, it has been tested extensively and is reasonably accurate for many portfolios having as few as five stocks.

```
10    REM ***********************************************************
20    REM *              OPTION-STOCK PORTFOLIO STRATEGY ANALYSIS    *
30    REM *                                                          *
40    REM *                                                          *
50    REM * THIS PROGRAM USES AN ALGORITHM BASED ON THE SINGLE INDEX OR  *
60    REM * MARKET MODEL TO DETERMINE THE RETURN DISTRIBUTION THAT WILL  *
70    REM * RESULT WHEN OPTIONS ARE WRITTEN OR PURCHASED ON AN UNDERLYING *
80    REM * STOCK PORTFOLIO.  THE PROGRAM ALLOWS FOR THE PURCHASE AND SALE *
90    REM * OF BOTH PUT AND CALL OPTIONS, AND ASSUMES AN INVESTMENT TIME  *
100   REM * HORIZON OF ONE YEAR.                                      *
110   REM *                                                          *
120   REM * VARIABLES USED:                                          *
130   REM *              PSTCK( ) = ARRAY OF STOCK PRICES            *
140   REM *              PCLL( ) = ARRAY OF CALL OPTION PRICES       *
150   REM *              PPT( ) = ARRAY OF PUT OPTION PRICES         *
160   REM *              EXCLL( ) = EXERCISE PRICE FOR CALL OPTIONS  *
170   REM *              EPR( ) = EXERCISE PRICE FOR PUT OPTIONS     *
180   REM *    C1ALP( ),C2ALP( ) = PROPORTION OF STOCK COVERED WITH CALLS *
190   REM *    P1ALP( ),P2ALP( ) = PROPORTION OF STOCK COVERED WITH PUTS  *
200   REM *              THETA( ) = WEIGHT OF STOCK IN THE PORTFOLIO *
210   REM *              CGAMMA( ) = RATIO OF CALL TO STOCK PRICE    *
220   REM *              PGAMMA( ) = RATIO OF PUT TO STOCK PRICE     *
230   REM *              DIV( ) = ARRAY OF DOLLAR DIVIDENDS          *
240   REM *              RDIV( ) = ARRAY OF DIVIDEND YIELDS          *
250   REM *              NM = NUMBER OF ITERATIONS                   *
260   REM *              NSTK = NUMBER OF STOCKS IN THE PORTFOLIO    *
270   REM *              RF = ANNUAL RISKFREE RATE                   *
280   REM *                                                          *
290   REM ***********************************************************
300   REM
310   REM
320   REM DIMENSION ARRAYS
330   REM
340   DIM AX(10),U(10),G(250,4),D(250),BETA(60),STD(60),STDNORM(60),THETA(60)
350   DIM PGAMMA(60),CGAMMA(60),PT(60),CT(60),DIV(60),RDIV(60),C1ALP(60)
360   DIM C2ALP(60),P1ALP(60),P2ALP(60),PSTCK(60),EXCLL(60),EPT(60)
370   DIM PCLL(60),PPT(60),IPRET(60),ICRET(60),IDIV$(60)
380   REM
390   REM READ IN DATA FOR GAUSSIAN QUADRATURE
400   REM
410   DATA  .06667,.06667,.14945,.14945,.21908
420   DATA  .21908,.26926,.26926,.29552,.29552
430   DATA  -.97390,.97390,-.86506,.86506,-.67940
440   DATA  .67940,-.43339,.43339,-.14887,.14887
450   FOR I = 1 TO 10: READ AX(I): NEXT I
460   FOR I = 1 TO 10: READ U(I): NEXT I
470   REM
480   REM SET ENTRY FLAGS FOR DATA ENTRY AND CHANGE
490   REM
500   U1NOP$ = "INIT":U2NOP$ = "CLR"
510   YSBS$ = "YES":NOBS$ = "NO"
520   UNFG$ = U2NOP$:OPFG$ = U2NOP$:MDFG$ = U2NOP$
530   FGBS$ = NOBS$:SFFG$ = U2NOP$
540   NM = 100:NX = NM - 1
```

```
550   REM
560   REM ****************************************************************
570   REM *                         MAIN MENU FOR INPUT                      ⅄
580   REM ****************************************************************
590   REM
600    CLS
610   PRINT "     OPTION AND STOCK": PRINT " PORTFOLIO ANALYSIS PROGRAM"
620   PRINT: PRINT
630   INPUT "          PRESS RETURN TO CONTINUE";A$
640    CLS
650   PRINT "********  DATA ENTRY MODULE  ********"
660   PRINT :PRINT "     COMMAND                      STATUS": PRINT
670   PRINT "1. STOCK PORTFOLIO"; TAB( 30);UNFG$
680   PRINT "2. MARKET DATA"; TAB( 30);MDFG$
690   PRINT "3. OPTION DATA"; TAB( 30);SFFG$
700   PRINT "4. OPTION STRATEGY"; TAB( 30);OPFG$
710   PRINT "5. BLACK-SCHOLES PRICING"; TAB( 30);FGBS$
720   PRINT "6. DISPLAY INPUTS"; TAB( 30);"ACTIVE"
730   PRINT "7. PROCESSOR"; TAB( 30);"ACTIVE"
740   PRINT "8. EXIT"; TAB( 30);"ACTIVE": PRINT
750   INPUT "ENTER NUMBER OF OPTION DESIRED ->";LDFG
760    ON LDFG GOSUB 810,1550,1650,2300,2670,2880,3270,5850
770    GOTO 640
780   REM
790   REM ***************** STOCK PORTFOLIO ROUTINE ********************
800   REM
810    CLS
820   INPUT "HOW MANY STOCKS WILL YOU HAVE IN YOUR PORTFOLIO (UP TO 60)";NSTK
830    CLS
840   PRINT "SPECIFY ITEM:": PRINT "1. BETA"
850   PRINT "2. RESIDUAL STANDARD ERROR (%)"
860   PRINT "3. PORTFOLIO WEIGHT (%)"
870   PRINT "4. STOCK PRICE"
880   PRINT "5. DOLLAR DIVIDEND OR YIELD (%)"
890   PRINT "6. EXIT"
900   PRINT : INPUT "ENTER NUMBER OF DESIRED SELECTION ->";SPITM
910    IF SPITM < > 6 THEN 940
920    UNFG$ = U1NOP$:FGBS$ = NOBS$
930    RETURN
940    PRINT: PRINT "1. ENTER COMMON DATA FOR ALL"
950    PRINT "2. ENTER DATA FOR EACH SEPARATELY"
960    INPUT "ENTER DESIRED MODE: ->";ENTMD
970    IF ENTMD < 1 OR ENTMD > 2 THEN 940
980    IF ENTMD = 2 THEN  GOSUB 1140: GOTO 830
990    IF SPITM = 5 THEN 1070
1000   INPUT "-ENTER VALUE:   ";SVL
1010    ON SPITM GOSUB 1030,1040,1050,1060,1070
1020    GOTO 830
1030    FOR I = 1 TO NSTK:BETA(I) = SVL: NEXT I: RETURN
1040    FOR I = 1 TO NSTK:STD(I) = SVL: NEXT I: RETURN
1050    FOR I = 1 TO NSTK:THETA(I) = SVL: NEXT I: RETURN
1060    FOR I = 1 TO NSTK:PSTCK(I) = SVL: NEXT I: RETURN
1070   PRINT : PRINT "DO YOU WANT TO SPECIFY A DIVIDEND YIELD"
1080   PRINT "INSTEAD OF A DOLLAR DIVIDEND? (Y/N)";IDIV$
```

```
1090    INPUT "-ENTER VALUE: ";SVL
1100      FOR I = 1 TO NSTK:IDIV(I) = IDIV: NEXT I
1110      IF IDIV$ = "Y" GOTO 1130
1120      FOR I = 1 TO NSTK:DIV(I) = SVL: NEXT I: GOTO 830
1130      FOR I = 1 TO NSTK:RDIV(I) = SVL: NEXT I: GOTO 830
1140    REM   INDIVIDUAL DATA ENTRY
1150    INPUT "SPECIFY STOCK # (1 THRU ";NSTK;" (999 TO EXIT))";ISTK
1160      IF ISTK = 999 THEN   RETURN
1170      IF SPITM <  > 5 THEN 1250
1180    PRINT "DO YOU WANT TO SPECIFY A DIVIDEND YIELD";
1190    PRINT " INSTEAD OF A DOLLAR DIVIDEND? (Y/N)"
1200    INPUT; IDIV$(ISTK)
1210    PRINT "-ENTER VALUE:   ";
1220      IF IDIV$(ISTK) = "Y" THEN   INPUT " ";RDIV(ISTK)
1230      IF IDIV$(ISTK) = "N" THEN   INPUT " ";DIV(ISTK)
1240      GOTO 1150
1250    PRINT "-ENTER VALUE:   ";
1260      IF SPITM = 1 THEN   INPUT " ";BETA(ISTK)
1270      IF SPITM = 2 THEN   INPUT " ";STD(ISTK)
1280      IF SPITM = 3 THEN   INPUT " ";THETA(ISTK)
1290      IF SPITM = 4 THEN   INPUT " ";PSTCK(ISTK)
1300      GOTO 1150
1310    REM INITIALIZE OPTION AND DIVIDEND ARRAYS
1320      IFX = 0
1330      FOR J = 1 TO NSTK
1340      IF IPRET(J) = 1 THEN EPT(J) = PSTCK(J) * (1 + PT(J) / 100)
1350      IF ICRET(J) = 1 THEN EXCLL(J) = PSTCK(J) * (1 + CT(J) / 100)
1360      IF PSTCK(J) <  = 0 THEN 1450
1370      IF IDIV(J) = 1 THEN DIV(J) = PSTCK(J) * RDIV(J) / 100
1380      RDIV(J) = (DIV(J) / PSTCK(J)) * 100
1390      PGAMMA(J) = PPT(J) / PSTCK(J)
1400      CGAMMA(J) = PCLL(J) / PSTCK(J)
1410    REM COMPUTE EXERCISE RETURN AS A PERCENT OF STOCK PRICE
1420      PT(J) = (EPT(J) / PSTCK(J) - 1) * 100
1430      CT(J) = (EXCLL(J) / PSTCK(J) - 1) * 100
1440      GOTO 1500
1450    PRINT "THE STOCK PRICE IS NOT POSITIVE FOR"
1460    PRINT "OPTIONED STOCK ";J
1470    INPUT "PRESS RETURN TO CONTINUE";A$
1480      IFX = 1
1490      RETURN
1500      NEXT J
1510      RETURN
1520    REM
1530    REM ******************** MARKET DATA INPUT SUBROUTINE **************
1540    REM
1550      CLS
1560    PRINT "ENTER:"
1570    INPUT "   ANNUAL RISKLESS RATE ";RF
1580    INPUT "   EXPECTED MARKET RETURN";AVRM
1590    INPUT "   MARKET STANDARD DEVIATION";RMSTD
1600      MDFG$ = U1NOP$:FGBS$ = NOBS$
1610      RETURN
1620    REM
```

```
1630    REM ******************** OPTION DATA INPUT SUBROUTINE **************
1640    REM
1650     CLS
1660    PRINT "SPECIFY ITEM:"
1670    PRINT "1. PUT EXERCISE PRICE OR RETURN (%)"
1680    PRINT "2. CALL EXERCISE PRICE OR RETURN (%)"
1690    PRINT "3. PUT OPTION PRICE"
1700    PRINT "4. CALL OPTION PRICE"
1710    PRINT "5. EXIT"
1720    INPUT "    ->";SPITM
1730     IF SPITM = 5 THEN SFFG$ = U1NOP$:FGBS$ = NOBS$: GOSUB 1320: RETURN
1740    PRINT : PRINT "1. ENTER COMMON DATA FOR ALL"
1750    PRINT "2. ENTER DATA FOR EACH SEPARATELY": PRINT
1760    INPUT "ENTER DESIRED MODE ->";ENTMD
1770     IF ENTMD < 1 OR ENTMD > 2 THEN 1740
1780     IF ENTMD = 1 THEN 2000
1790    PRINT
1800    INPUT "SPECIFY STOCK # (1 THRU ";NSTK;", 999 TO EXIT) ->";ISTK
1810     IF ISTK = 999 THEN 1650
1820     IF SPITM < 3 THEN 1870
1830    PRINT "-ENTER VALUE: ";
1840     IF SPITM = 3 THEN  INPUT " ";PPT(ISTK)
1850     IF SPITM = 4 THEN  INPUT " ";PCLL(ISTK)
1860     GOTO 1800
1870    PRINT : PRINT "DO YOU WANT TO SPECIFY AN EXERCISE RETURN"
1880    PRINT "INSTEAD OF AN EXERCISE PRICE? (1=YES 2=NO)";
1890     IF SPITM = 1 THEN  INPUT "->";IPRET(ISTK)
1900     IF SPITM = 2 THEN  INPUT "->";ICRET(ISTK)
1910     IF SPITM = 1 AND IPRET(ISTK) < > 1 THEN 1970
1920     IF SPITM = 2 AND ICRET(ISTK) < > 1 THEN 1970
1930    PRINT "ENTER VALUE: "
1940     IF SPITM = 1 THEN  INPUT " ";PT(ISTK)
1950     IF SPITM = 2 THEN  INPUT " ";CT(ISTK)
1960     GOTO 1800
1970     IF SPITM = 1 THEN  INPUT " ";EPT(ISTK)
1980     IF SPITM = 2 THEN  INPUT " ";EXCLL(ISTK)
1990     GOTO 1800
2000     IF SPITM = 3 THEN  INPUT "-ENTER VALUE:   ";SVL
2010     FOR I = 1 TO NSTK:PPT(I) = SVL: NEXT I
2020     IF SPITM = 4 THEN  INPUT "-ENTER VALUE:   ";SVL
2030     FOR I = 1 TO NSTK:PCLL(I) = SVL: NEXT I
2040     IF SPITM > 2 THEN 1650
2050    PRINT : PRINT "DO YOU WANT TO SPECIFY AN EXERCISE RETURN"
2060    PRINT "INSTEAD OF AN EXERCISE PRICE? (1-YES 2-NO)";
2070     IF SPITM = 1 THEN  INPUT "->";IPRET
2080     IF SPITM = 2 THEN  INPUT "->";ICRET
2090     IF SPITM = 1 THEN 2130
2100     IPRET = 0
2110     FOR I = 1 TO NSTK:ICRET(I) = ICRET: NEXT I
2120     GOTO 2150
2130     FOR I = 1 TO NSTK:IPRET(I) = IPRET: NEXT I
2140     ICRET = 0
2150    INPUT "-ENTER VALUE:   ";SVL
2160     IF IPRET = 2 OR ICRET = 2 THEN 2220
```

```
2170    IF SPITM = 1 THEN 2200
2180    FOR I = 1 TO NSTK:CT(I) = SVL: NEXT I
2190    GOTO 1650
2200    FOR I = 1 TO NSTK:PT(I) = SVL: NEXT I
2210    GOTO 1650
2220    IF SPITM = 1 THEN 2250
2230    FOR I = 1 TO NSTK:EXCLL(I) = SVL: NEXT I
2240    GOTO 1650
2250    FOR I = 1 TO NSTK:EPT(I) = SVL: NEXT I
2260    GOTO 1650
2270    REM
2280    REM *************** OPTION STRATEGY INPUT SUBROUTINE ***************
2290    REM
2300    FOR I = 1 TO NSTK
2310     C1ALP(I) = 0:C2ALP(I) = 0:P1ALP(I) = 0:P2ALP(I) = 0
2320    NEXT I
2330    CLS
2340    PRINT "OPTION STRATEGY SELECTION (EACH CAN BE CHOSEN ONLY ONCE):"
2350    PRINT: PRINT "1. SELL (WRITE) CALL OPTIONS"
2360    PRINT "2. PURCHASE CALL OPTIONS"
2370    PRINT "3. PURCHASE PUT OPTIONS"
2380    PRINT "4. SELL PUT OPTIONS"
2390    PRINT "5. EXIT"
2400    INPUT "->";STGY
2410    IF STGY = 5 THEN  RETURN
2420    PRINT
2430    PRINT "NOW SPECIFY THE FRACTION OF THE STOCK"
2440    PRINT "COVERED BY THE OPTION POSITION (IN PERCENT)"
2450    OPFG$ = U1NOP$
2460    PRINT "1.ENTER COMMON DATA FOR ALL"
2470    PRINT "2.ENTER DATA FOR EACH SEPARATELY"
2480    PRINT " ": INPUT "ENTER DESIRED MODE  ->";ENTMD
2490    IF ENTMD < 1 OR ENTMD > 2 THEN 2460
2500    IF ENTMD = 1 THEN 2590
2510    INPUT "SPECIFY STOCK # (1 THRU ";NSTK;", 999 TO EXIT) ->";ISTK
2520    IF ISTK = 999 THEN  RETURN
2530    PRINT "ENTER VALUE: ";
2540    IF STGY = 1 THEN  INPUT "VALUE:   ";C1ALP(ISTK)
2550    IF STGY = 2 THEN  INPUT "VALUE:   ";C2ALP(ISTK)
2560    IF STGY = 3 THEN  INPUT "VALUE:   ";P1ALP(ISTK)
2570    IF STGY = 4 THEN  INPUT "VALUE:   ";P2ALP(ISTK)
2580    GOTO 2510
2590    INPUT "-ENTER VALUE: ";SVL
2600    IF STGY = 1 THEN  FOR I = 1 TO NSTK:C1ALP(I) = SVL: NEXT I
2610    IF STGY = 2 THEN  FOR I = 1 TO NSTK:C2ALP(I) = SVL: NEXT I
2620    IF STGY = 3 THEN  FOR I = 1 TO NSTK:P1ALP(I) = SVL: NEXT I
2630    IF STGY = 4 THEN  FOR I = 1 TO NSTK:P2ALP(I) = SVL: NEXT I
2640    RETURN
2650    REM
2660    REM *********** BLACK SCHOLES PRICING INPUT SUBROUTINE *************
2670    CLS
2680    INPUT "DO YOU WANT TO USE THE BLACK-SCHOLES PRICES? (Y/N)"; IBS$
2690    IF IBS$ < > "Y" AND IBS$ < > "N" THEN 2670
2700    IF IBS$ = "N" THEN FGBS$ = NOBS$: RETURN
```

```
2710    FGBS$ = YSBS$
2720    FOR I = 1 TO NSTK
2730      IF PSTCK(I) <= 0 THEN PRINT "STOCK PRICE NOT POSITIVE FOR STOCK ";I
2740      IF PSTCK(I) <= 0 THEN INPUT "PRESS RETURN TO CONTINUE";A$: RETURN
2750      SIG = (BETA(I) * RMSTD) ^ 2 + STD(I) ^ 2
2760      IF PT(I) < = - 100 THEN 2790
2770      R2 = PT(I): GOSUB 4720:PGAMMA(I) = P
2780      PPT(I) = PSTCK(I) * PGAMMA(I)
2790      IF CT(I) < = - 100 THEN 2820
2800      R2 = CT(I): GOSUB 4720:CGAMMA(I) = C
2810      PCLL(I) = PSTCK(I) * CGAMMA(I)
2820    NEXT I
2830    PRINT : INPUT "OPTION PRICES CALCULATED, PRESS RETURN TO CONTINUE";A$
2840    RETURN
2850    REM
2860    REM *****************DATA CHECK SUBROUTINE ************************
2870    REM
2880    CLS
2890    PRINT "STOCK  BETA    STDERR  WT    PRICE DIV"
2900    PRINT "-----  ----    ------  ---   ----- ---"
2910    FOR I = 1 TO NSTK
2920    PRINT I;
2930      X$ =   STR$ ( INT (BETA(I) * 100) / 100: PRINT  TAB( 8);X$;
2940      X$ =   STR$ ( INT (STD(I) * 100) / 100: PRINT  TAB( 15);X$;
2950      X$ =   STR$ ( INT (THETA(I) * 100) / 100: PRINT  TAB( 23);X$;
2960      X$ =   STR$ ( INT (PSTCK(I) * 100) / 100: PRINT  TAB( 29);X$;
2970      X$ =   STR$ ( INT (DIV(I) * 100) / 100: PRINT  TAB( 35);X$
2980    NEXT I
2990    INPUT "PRESS RETURN TO CONTINUE";A$
3000    CLS
3010    PRINT "RISKLESS RATE MARKET RETURN MARKET STD"
3020    PRINT "------------- ------------- ----------"
3030    PRINT : PRINT  TAB( 4);RF; TAB( 19);AVRM; TAB( 33);RMSTD
3040    PRINT  TAB( 10);"CALLS"; TAB( 27);"PUTS"
3050    PRINT "------------------- ------------------"
3060    PRINT "  BUY  SELL       EX BUY  SELL       EX"
3070    PRINT "#   %     %    PRI PRI %     %    PRI PRI"
3080    PRINT "-- ---  ----  --- --- ---  ----  --- ----"
3090    FOR I = 1 TO NSTK
3100    PRINT I;
3110      X$ =   STR$ ( INT (C2ALP(I) * 10) / 10: PRINT  TAB( 4);X$;
3120      X$ =   STR$ ( INT (C1ALP(I) * 10) / 10: PRINT  TAB( 9);X$;
3130      X$ =   STR$ ( INT (PCLL(I) * 10) / 10: PRINT  TAB( 14);X$;
3140      X$ =   STR$ ( INT (EXCLL(I) * 10) / 10: PRINT  TAB( 20);X$;
3150      X$ =   STR$ ( INT (P1ALP(I) * 10) / 10: PRINT  TAB( 24);X$;
3160      X$ =   STR$ ( INT (P2ALP(I) * 10) / 10: PRINT  TAB( 29);X$;
3170      X$ =   STR$ ( INT (PPT(I) * 10) / 10: PRINT  TAB( 36);X$;
3180      X$ =   STR$ ( INT (EPT(I) * 10) / 10: PRINT  TAB( 40);X$
3190    NEXT I
3200    INPUT "PRESS RETURN TO CONTINUE";A$
3210    RETURN
3220    REM
3230    REM *******************************************************************
3240    REM *                   MAIN COMPUTATION SUBROUTINE                  *
```

```
3250   REM  ***********************************************************
3260   REM
3270    ARFTHT = 0:APTHT = 0:XX =  - 5
3280   REM THE VALUE OF XX DETERMINES THE NUMBER OF STANDARD DEVIATIONS AROUND THE
3290   REM MEAN RETURN THAT WILL BE USED IN COMPUTING THE DISTRIBUTION
3300    GOSUB 1320
3310    IF IFX = 1 THEN RETURN
3320    IF NSTK < 1 GOTO 3410
3330    CC = 0
3340    FOR I = 1 TO NSTK
3350     APTHT = APTHT + THETA(I) * (PGAMMA(I) * (P2ALP(I) - P1ALP(I)))/100
3360     APTHT = APTHT + THETA(I) * (CGAMMA(I) * (C1ALP(I) - C2ALP(I)))/100
3370     ARFTHT = ARFTHT + THETA(I)/100
3380    NEXT I
3390    ARFTHT = 1 - ARFTHT
3400    IF RMSTD > 0 GOTO 3420
3410   INPUT "VARIABLES NOT INITIALIZED; PRESS RETURN TO CONTINUE"; A$: RETURN
3420    CN = 1 / (RMSTD * 2.50663)
3430   PRINT : PRINT "STARTING PROCESSING"
3440    FOR M9 = 1 TO NM
3450     R = (AVRM + RMSTD * XX) - (M9 - 1) * RMSTD * 2 * XX / NX
3460     ROP = 0
3470      FOR J = 1 TO NSTK
3480       SIG = (BETA(J) * RMSTD) ^ 2 + STD(J) ^ 2
3490       IF C1ALP(J) = 0 AND C2ALP(J) = 0 THEN 3610
3500       RXC = CT(J) + RDIV(J) - RF - BETA(J) * (R - RF)
3510       IF STD(J) = 0 THEN STD(J) = .000001
3520       ZV = RXC / STD(J): GOSUB 4830
3530       CXC = N
3540       UMAX = RXC
3550       DX =  - 5
3560       UBAR = 0
3570       U1MN = STD(J) * DX + UBAR
3580       GOSUB 4970:CUX = SM :REM MEAN ERROR TERM
3590       ROPTAIL = ((1-CXC) * RXC + CUX + CGAMMA(J) * 100)/100
3600       ROP = ROP + THETA(J) * (C1ALP(J) - C2ALP(J)) * ROPTAIL
3610       IF P1ALP(J) = 0 AND P2ALP(J) = 0 THEN 3730
3620       RXP = PT(J) + RDIV(J) - RF - BETA(J) * (R - RF)
3630       IF STD(J) = 0 THEN STD(J) = .000001
3640       ZV = RXP / STD(J): GOSUB 4830
3650       PCX = N
3660       UBAR = 0
3670       DX = 5
3680       U1MN = RXP
3690       UMAX = STD(J) * DX + UBAR
3700       GOSUB 4970:PUX = SM
3710       ROPTAIL = (PCX * RXP + PUX - PGAMMA(J) * 100)/100
3720       ROP = ROP + THETA(J) * (P1ALP(J) - P2ALP(J)) * ROPTAIL
3730       ROP = ROP + THETA(J) * (RF + BETA(J) * (R - RF))/100
3740      NEXT J
3750     CC = CC + 1:CY = CC -  INT (CC / 10) * 10
3760     IF CY = 0 THEN  PRINT "ITERATION #: ";CC;" OF ";NM
3770     RPP = (ARFTHT + APTHT) * RF + ROP
3780     R1PROB = CN *  EXP ( - ((R - AVRM) * (R - AVRM)) / (2 * RMSTD * RMSTD))
```

```
3790      G(M9,1) = RPP
3800      G(M9,2) = R
3810      D(M9) = R1PROB
3820      IF M9 = 1 THEN 3850
3830      XZ =  ABS (G(M9,1) - G(M9 - 1,1))
3840      IF XZ <  = .01 THEN G(M9,1) = G(M9 - 1,1)
3850     NEXT M9
3860     REM
3870     REM ********* NORMALIZATION OF DISTRIBUTION FUNCTION **************
3880     REM
3890      SUM = 0
3900      FOR J = 1 TO NX
3910       I = J + 1
3920       SUM = SUM + (G(I,2) - G(J,2)) * (D(I) + D(J)) / 2
3930      NEXT J
3940      G(1,4) = 0
3950      FOR J = 1 TO NX
3960       I = J + 1
3970       G(I,4) = G(J,4) + 100 * (G(I,2) - G(J,2)) * (D(I) + D(J)) / (2 * SUM)
3980      NEXT J
3990      IW = 1: GOSUB 5120
4000      FLG = 0
4010      FOR J = 1 TO NX
4020       I = J + 1
4030       IF G(I,1) <  > G(J,1) THEN 4060
4040       IF J = 1 THEN FLG = 1
4050       GOTO 4100
4060       A = G(I,4) - G(J,4)
4070       IF FLG = 1 THEN A = G(I,4)
4080       G(I,3) = A / (G(I,1) - G(J,1))
4090       FLG = 0
4100      NEXT J
4110      G(1,3) = 0
4120      IW = 2: GOSUB 5120
4130      G(NM,3) = 0
4140     REM
4150     REM ***********************************************************************
4160     REM *                        OUTPUT SUBROUTINE                            *
4170     REM ***********************************************************************
4180     REM
4190      I1 = 1
4200      GOSUB 5300
4210      CLS
4220     PRINT "MEAN RETURN :";SX: PRINT "STD DEV :";S2: PRINT "SKEWNESS :";S3
4230     PRINT "BETA :";SB
4240     INPUT "PRESS RETURN TO CONTINUE";A$
4250      CLS
4260     REM
4270     REM ***************** MAIN MENU FOR OUTPUT ********************
4280     REM
4290     PRINT "***** OUTPUT MODULE *****": PRINT
4300     PRINT "1. CALCULATE PROBABILITIES"
4310     PRINT "2. CALCULATE PARTIAL BETAS"
4320     PRINT "3. EXAMINE PROBABILITY ARRAY"
```

```
4330    PRINT "4. EXIT"
4340    INPUT "->";CH
4350     ON CH GOTO 4370,4500,4570,4680
4360     GOTO 4250
4370    INPUT "SPECIFY MINIMUM ANNUAL RETURN (%); (999 TO EXIT)";MINRR
4380    INPUT "SPECIFY MAXIMUM ANNUAL RETURN (%)"; MAXRR
4390    INPUT "INCREMENT OF RETURNS"; RINC
4400     IF MINRR = 999 THEN 4250
4410     IF MAXRR <  = MINRR THEN 4370
4420     INC = (MAXRR - MINRR) / RINC
4430     FOR K = 1 TO INC
4440      RAMN = MINRR + (K - 1) * RINC
4450      RBMAX = RAMN + RINC
4460       GOSUB 5630
4470    PRINT : PRINT "MIN = ";RAMN;" MAX = ";RBMAX;" PROB = ";PMXMN
4480     NEXT K
4490     GOTO 4370
4500    INPUT "SPECIFY MINIMUM MARKET RETURN (999 TO EXIT)"; RDMN
4510    INPUT "SPECIFY MAXIMUM MARKET RETURN"; RCMAX
4520     IF RDMN = 999 THEN 4250
4530     I1 = 0
4540     GOSUB 5300
4550    PRINT : PRINT " MIN = ";RDMN;" MAX = ";RCMAX;" BETA = ";SB
4560     GOTO 4500
4570    CC = 0
4580    PRINT "  MARKET      PORTFOLIO            CUMULATIVE"
4590    PRINT "  RETURN       RETURN     DENSITY    DISTRIBUTION": PRINT
4600     FOR I = 1 TO NM
4610      CC = CC+1:CY = CC - INT(CC/20)*20
4620      IF CY = 0 THEN INPUT "PRESS RETURN TO CONTINUE ->";A$
4630      IF CY = 0 THEN PRINT: PRINT "  MARKET      PORTFOLIO
        CUMULATIVE":
PRINT "  RETURN       RETURN     DENSITY    DISTRIBUTION": PRINT
4640    PRINT USING "####.###    "; G(I,2), G(I,1),G(I,3),G(I,4)
4650     NEXT I
4660    INPUT "PRESS RETURN TO CONTINUE";A$
4670     GOTO 4250
4680     RETURN
4690    REM
4700    REM **********CALCULATION OF BLACK-SCHOLES OPTION PRICE ************
4710    REM
4720     X = (1 -  EXP ( - RF / 100) * RDIV(I) / 100) / (1 + R2 / 100)
4730     D1 = ( LOG (X) + (RF / 100 + SIG / 20000)) /  SQR (SIG / 10000)
4740     D2 = D1 -  SQR (SIG / 10000)
4750     ZV = D1: GOSUB 4830:N1 = N:ZV = D2: GOSUB 4830
4760     C = (1 -  EXP ( - RF / 100) * RDIV(I) / 100) * N1
4770     C = C -  EXP ( - RF / 100) * (1 + R2 / 100) * N
4780     P = ((100 + R2 + RDIV(I)) / 100) *  EXP ( - RF / 100) - (1 - C)
4790     RETURN
4800    REM
4810    REM SUBROUTINE TO CALCULATE CUMULATIVE NORMAL DISTRIBUTION FUNCTION
4820    REM
4830     Z1 =  ABS (ZV)
4840     IF Z1 >  = 5 THEN 4910
4850     Z2 = 1 / (1 + .2316419 * Z1)
```

```
4860    Z3 = .3989423 *  EXP ( - ZV * ZV / 2)
4870    N = (((((1.330274*Z2-1.821256)*Z2+1.781478)*Z2-.3565638)*Z2+.3193815)
4880    N = 1 - Z3 * Z2 * N
4890    IF ZV >  = 0 THEN  RETURN
4900    N = 1 - N: RETURN
4910    IF ZV >  = 0 THEN 4930
4920    N = 0: RETURN
4930    N = 1: RETURN
4940    REM
4950    REM ***** GAUSSIAN QUADRATURE CALCULATION OF MEAN ERROR TERM *******
4960    REM
4970    N1 = 10
4980    Y = UBAR + STD(J) *  - 5
4990    YY = UBAR + STD(J) * 5
5000    IF U1MN <  = Y THEN U1MN = Y
5010    IF UMAX <  = U1MN THEN SM = 0: RETURN
5020    SM = 0
5030    FOR I = 1 TO N1
5040     X = ((UMAX - U1MN) * U(I) + UMAX + U1MN) / 2
5050     STDNORM(J) = STD(J) * 2.506627
5060     SM = SM+AX(I)*X*((UMAX-U1MN)/2)*EXP(-(((UBAR-X)/STD(J))^2)/2)/(STDNORM(J))
5070    NEXT I
5080    RETURN
5090    REM
5100    REM ****SUBROUTINE TO GROUP THE PROBABILITY OF MULTIPLE POINTS *****
5110    REM
5120    IF IW = 1 THEN 5190
5130    FOR J = 1 TO NX
5140     I = J + 1
5150     IF G(I,1) <  > G(J,1) THEN 5170
5160     G(I,3) = G(J,3)
5170    NEXT J
5180    RETURN
5190    FOR K = 1 TO NX
5200     J = NM - K
5210     I = J + 1
5220     SS =  ABS (G(I,1) - G(J,1))
5230     IF SS > .001 THEN 5250
5240     G(J,1) = G(I,1)
5250    NEXT K
5260    RETURN
5270    REM
5280    REM *** SUBROUTINE TO CALCULATE THE MEAN, VARIANCE, AND SKEWNESS ***
5290    REM
5300    IF I1 = 1 THEN 5440
5310    JM = 1
5320    FOR J = 1 TO NM
5330     IF RDMN >  = G(J,2) THEN JM = J
5340     IF RCMAX < G(J,2) THEN 5360
5350     J1MAX = J: GOTO 5370
5360     IF J = 1 THEN 5390
5370    NEXT J
5380     GOTO 5420
5390    PRINT "NO CALCULATION POSSIBLE--LIMITS MAY BE OUTSIDE THE RANGE OF"
```

```
5400    PRINT "MARKET RETURNS OR MAY BE TOO CLOSE TO EACH OTHER"
5410    INPUT "PRESS RETURN TO CONTINUE";A$: RETURN
5420     IF JM >  = J1MAX THEN 5390
5430     GOTO 5450
5440     JM = 1:J1MAX = NM
5450     SM = 0
5460     FOR J = JM TO J1MAX:SM = SM + D(J): NEXT J
5470     SX = 0:SR = 0:S4 = 0:S2 = 0:S3 = 0:S5 = 0
5480     FOR J = JM TO J1MAX
5490      SX = SX + G(J,1) * D(J) / SM
5500      SR = SR + G(J,2) * D(J) / SM
5510      S2 = S2 + G(J,1) * G(J,1) * D(J) / SM
5520      S5 = S5 + G(J,2) * G(J,2) * D(J) / SM
5530      S4 = S4 + G(J,1) * G(J,2) * D(J) / SM
5540     NEXT J
5550     S2 =   SQR (S2 - SX * SX)
5560     S5 = S5 - SR * SR
5570     SB = (S4 - SX * SR) / S5
5580     FOR J = JM TO J1MAX:S3 = S3 + D(J) * ((G(J,1) - SX) / S2) ^ 3 / SM: NEXTJ
5590     RETURN
5600    REM
5610    REM * SUBROUTINE TO CALCULATE THE PROBABILITY BETWEEN TWO POINTS *
5620    REM
5630     I3 = 1:I2 = NM:I4 = 0
5640     FOR J = I3 TO I2
5650      IF RAMN > G(J,1) THEN 5690
5660      IF J = I3 THEN P1MN = G(J,4): GOTO 5710
5670      P1MN = G(J-1,4)+(G(J,4)-G(J-1,4))*(RAMN-G(J-1,1))/(G(J,1)-G(J-1,1))
5680      GOTO 5710
5690      IF J = I2 THEN I4 = 1
5700     NEXT J
5710     IF I4 = 1 THEN PMXMN = 0: RETURN
5720     I5 = 0
5730     FOR I = I3 TO I2
5740      J = I2 - I + 1
5750      IF RBMAX < G(J,1) THEN 5800
5760      IF I = I3 THEN P2MX = G(J,4): GOTO 5820
5770      PT = G(J + 1,4)
5780      P2MX = G(J,4) + (PT - G(J,4)) * (RBMAX - G(J,1)) / (G(J + 1,1) - G(J,1))
5790      GOTO 5820
5800      IF I = I2 THEN I5 = 1
5810     NEXT I
5820     IF I5 = 1 THEN PMXMN = 0: RETURN
5830     PMXMN = P2MX - P1MN
5840     RETURN
5850    END
```

12

The Capital Asset Pricing Model

What expected return does an investment need in order to be a good buy? If two investment opportunities are available, one having an expected return of 12% and the other having an expected return of 20%, which would you take?

The immediate reaction most people have is to choose the investment with the 20% expected return. However, the expected return figures alone are not enough to make the decision. For example, suppose the first investment gives a guaranteed 12% return (as could an investment in treasury bills), while the second investment gives a 20% return but involves an equal chance of a 200% loss (as would a $20,000 investment resulting in the investor's either having to pay a total of $40,000 or making a 240% gain). (This sort of payoff structure is typical of investments in futures contracts.) Or, what if the second investment involves an equal chance of either increasing your wealth tenfold or leaving you impoverished the rest of your life? It is clear that the choice between these two investments, as is the choice between any two investments, can only be measured by looking at both the expected payoff *and* the risk involved.

The market mechanism must price stocks to give a risk-return tradeoff that will make the investments desirable to hold. If an investment is priced too high, so that the rate of return generated per dollar investment is too low for the risk involved, investors will sell the stock, bringing the price down. Similarly, if an investment is priced too low, so that it has a very attractive rate of return, then the price will be bid up. This seems like a simple argument straight out of an Economics 101 class. However, we have skirted the difficult issue: What do we mean by a return being too high or too low for the amount of risk? How do we even measure risk? The capital asset pricing model, or CAPM, addresses this issue. It sets forth a method for measuring risk, and in doing so gives us a valuable tool for determining the fair market price for stocks and other assets. Before discussing the CAPM in the world of stocks, we will take a look at the relationship between risk and asset prices in a more simplified setting.

ASSET PRICING IN MARBLEHEAD

Marblehead is an imaginary province that has marbles as its primary investment vehicle. The supply of marbles is carefully controlled by the king, who at his pleasure either increases or taxes the citizens' holdings of marbles according to the marble's color. One time he might decree that all green marbles can be brought to the palace and exchanged for three blue marbles each. Another time he might extract a tax of two-thirds of all blue marbles held. Everyone wants to have as many marbles as possible, but if they lose too many of their marbles, they are banished forever. This naturally leads to risk-averse behavior in their marble investment strategy.

As a visitor to the province, I approached a marble investment manager, who gave me a tour of the vaults where the numerous accounts he managed were stored. "You'll notice I try very hard to keep each of my clients' marble portfolios well balanced. There is some tendency toward the darker colors, especially blue, but that just reflects the preponderance of these marbles in the economy."

"Yes, I see that. And there are only a few white marbles in the portfolios. Those must be very rare."

"Oh yes, the albinos. They are only issued every few years, so we don't see many of them."

"So are they the most valuable, then?", I asked.

"No, not at all. You see, the king has a fine sense of contrast, and so whenever he taxes the darker marbles, which he regularly does, he taxes holdings of the albinos as well. It doesn't do much good to hold them for diversification, since they pretty much get taxed or increased at the same time the larger holding of the dark colors do. So they are priced about the same as the blues—maybe a bit higher."

"Well, then, what marbles are the most valuable?"

"Oh, the crimsons are the most sought after by far. They are not as rare as the albinos, and thank goodness, they are really a great hedge."

"They're a safe investment, you mean?"

He gave a little chuckle and rolled a crimson around in his palm and said, "Safe? The king is as fickle about crimson as you'll ever see. One day he triples the supply, the next he taxes half of them away. They are the most volatile marble of all. Why, I employ three clerks who do nothing else but monitor the inflows and outflows of these."

I was a bit perplexed at this. "Well, if they are not all that rare, and they are so risky, what makes them so valuable? Do they appreciate?"

"No more than any of the others. I keep charts on them all, and the rate of return on any of the marbles is pretty much the same. It is related to the rate of economic growth in the province, near as I can tell."

The broker strolled down the brightly lit corridor, past more vaults, bouncing a marble in his hand as if to test its weight. He continued, "To tell you why the crimsons are so highly valued, first I need to tell you how I price a marble. I look at my clients' portfolios, and I ask myself, 'What effect will adding one more of this or that color marble have on the risk of the overall portfolio? How will this extra marble affect the chances he will, God forbid, lose his marbles?' Now from that perspective, you can see the blues and albinos are pretty much awash. If the king taxes the blues, he is likely to take the albinos as well. And *that* is the time you really need some other colors around that don't go well with the darks. You know, when the blues move, most all the darks move, and they make up so much of the portfolio, maybe seventy or eighty percent of it."

"This seems a bit strange. You're saying color itself doesn't matter, only how one color moves with the overall portfolio?"

"That's right. We're in the investment business here, not in aesthetics. Color itself doesn't mean a thing to me. It is how the total number of marbles changes that is important. And it just happens that the way the different marbles move in the market is related to their color."

"Then, I suppose colors that really don't relate well with the darker marbles are worth the most. Marbles that are taxed and increased independent of the king's interest in the blues."

"Oh, yes. The yellows, pinks, all hardly have anything to do with the movement in the systematic colors—that is what we call the blues and other colors that make up most of the market. But the best of all is one that *clashes* with the systematic colors. And that's what makes crimson so valuable. It is volatile as can be, but when the king is interested in the blues, he virtually rids himself of the crimson. Its an evident pattern—the times the blues and other systematic colors are taxed, he unloads crimsons on the market. And when the systematic colors are increased, he pulls some crimsons back. So while they are volatile, they are volatile in a way that counteracts the general flow of marbles in the market. And *that* is what gives them their value. Looking at it from my perspective as a portfolio manager, they are not risky at all. They are more like portfolio insurance. So long as you've got some crimsons, or the other nonsystematics for that matter, you've got stability in the ups and downs in the market."

THE CAPITAL ASSET PRICING MODEL

The capital assets pricing model can be developed in three steps. The critical step is the one we just discussed—that the proper measure of the risk of an asset is its contribution to the risk of the investor's portfolio. Preceding this step are two others. The first is that all investors will try to diversify as best as possible, leading them all to hold a broad portfolio reflecting the behavior of the market overall. And the second is that, in addition to stocks, investors can take a position in a risk-free asset. They can use the risk-free asset to lever up their stock position, or to reduce their position in stocks. We will introduce each of these steps now in more detail.

---

1. **Diversification leads all investors to hold the market portfolio.** The market can be thought of as the best diversified portfolio that can be held. It is the portfolio constructed by holding every stock in a proportion equal to its proportion of the total market value of all available stocks. If a portfolio manager were to hold the best diversified portfolio possible, the manager would end up holding the market portfolio. If he were not holding it, the manager could always reduce the nonsystematic component of the portfolio risk by adding some of the stocks that were not currently held. The capital asset pricing model starts with this idea—that in optimally diversifying, everyone will end up holding the same

portfolio—the market portfolio. The market portfolio is one portfolio on the efficient portfolio frontier, depicted by the point M in Figure 12-1. This figure is the same as Figure 10-2 in Chapter 10.

2. **The risk-free asset expands investment opportunities.** The CAPM introduces a very important investment vehicle in addition to stocks. This vehicle is a risk-free asset—an asset that can be borrowed or loaned with no risk of default. The counterpart to the risk-free asset in the marketplace can be thought of as Treasury bills. The risk-free asset is at point R on Figure 12-2, with an expected return r_F and zero variance. By borrowing and lending with the risk-free asset, the investor who holds the market portfolio, M, can move anywhere along the line (RM).

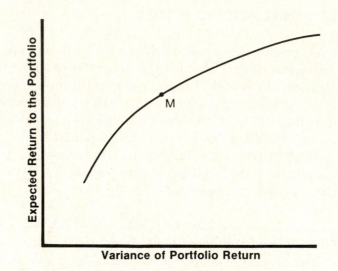

Figure 12-1. The efficient portfolio frontier. This figure is identical to Figure 10-2 in Chapter 10. It depicts the best attainable tradeoffs between expected return and variance. Point M is the market portfolio, the portfolio consisting of all stocks in the market, each stock held in proportions equal to its proportion of total market value.

This line is the efficient portfolio frontier when there is risk-free borrowing and lending. No one will hold a portfolio of stocks other than the market portfolio since combining this portfolio with the risk-free asset can always lead to more favorable returns. From Figure 12-2, it is evident we can determine the market portfolio as the portfolio that is the tangent point for the risk-free asset and the efficient portfolio frontier.

If a fraction λ of an investor's money is loaned out at the risk-free rate, then the investor will have an expected return on the line segment between R and M. The expected returns will be comprised of the λ fraction of the portfolio that is in the risk-free asset times the return to that

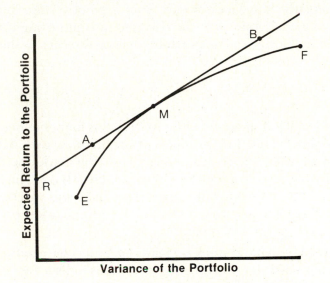

Figure 12-2. The efficient portfolio frontier when there is a riskless asset. By holding the market portfolio and levering or unlevering that position by either borrowing or lending part of the investment funds through the riskfree asset, the investor can be anywhere on the line RMB. This gives a better risk-return tradeoff than the efficient portfolio frontier that results when only stocks are used (the portfolio frontier is represented by the line EMF).

asset, plus the remaining $(1-\lambda)$ of the portfolio in the stock times the expected return to the stock, or the portfolio return, r_P, will be

$$E(r_P) = \lambda\ r_F + (1-\lambda)\ E(r_M).$$

For example, if 50% of this investor's funds are placed in the risk-free asset $(\lambda = .5)$, the investor will have the expected return-variance tradeoff of point A—halfway between R and M. The variance of the returns will similarly be a weighting of the variance of the market and the risk-free asset—the latter, of course, having a variance of return of zero.

Similarly, the investor can be at a point on the line above M by borrowing an amount λ at the risk-free rate and using it to lever up the position in the stock. The portfolio expected return in this case will be

$$E(r_P) = -\lambda\ r_p + (1+\lambda)\ E(r_M).$$

Naturally, as is indicated in Figure 12-2, this higher expected return also entails higher risk. For example, if an investor with $10,000 borrows another $10,000, any return realized from the market will increase two-fold relative to the original $10,000 investment base. The investor would be at point B, with twice the return potential—and variability in possible returns—as he would have if he just held the market portfolio without levering the position.

3. **Risk for an individual stock is measured by its contribution to the overall risk of the portfolio.** The principle previously discussed of how marbles are priced in "Marblehead" carries over directly to asset pricing in our more complex economy. The risk of an asset can only be measured with respect to the environment where it is being used. The variability of an asset, as measured by the asset's own variance, is not the proper way to measure its risk. We must take the wider view of what the variance of the asset does to the portfolio in which it is placed. A stock that has wide swings in price may actually be more highly valued than another stock that is stable if its price swings are countercyclical to the overall portfolio. For then its very variability will moderate the risk of the overall portfolio. When other stock prices drop, that stock will increase in value, thereby

conserving the portfolio value. On the other hand, a stock that moves right along with almost every other stock in the market, a stock that is highly cyclical, will be no more prized than the blue or albino marbles in Marblehead. This principle means that risk is measured by the variability of the stock only to the extent it is related to the variability of the overall portfolio.

As we saw in Chapter 10, any stock movements that are independent of the overall market will be washed out when many stocks are held. When one stock is up, another is as likely to be down, and the net effect will be of little impact. Using the terminology introduced in that chapter, the only risk that is important for the risk-return tradeoff that determines asset pricing is *systematic risk*. This is the marketwide risk all stocks share. The *nonsystematic risk*, the risk that is stock-specific, will be diversified away in a large portfolio, while the systematic risk will remain.

When dealing with individual stocks, then, as opposed to the portfolio itself, risk should be measured by the covariance of returns with the market rather than by the variance of returns, in keeping with the principle of risk just discussed. The covariance of the return on stock i with the market is denoted by $cov(r_i, r_m)$.

To illustrate the expected return-risk tradeoffs for individual stocks we have redrawn the RM line of Figure 12-2 in Figure 12-3. Figure 12-3 differs from Figure 12-1 and Figure 12-2 by replacing the portfolio variance with the covariance of the stock and the market on the x axis. The risk-free asset and the market portfolio still fall on the line, since the risk-free asset has zero covariance with the market, and the covariance of the market with itself is simply equal to its variance.

It is possible to have a stock that has a negative covariance with the market. Such a stock would fall on the RM line to the left of the risk-free asset, at a point like N. As the line suggests, it would then have an expected return that is lower than the return to the risk-free asset, even though its returns are uncertain. The reason is that it is in fact less risky from the viewpoint of the portfolio than is the risk-free asset. While the risk-free asset contributes no additional risk or variability when it is added to the stock portfolio, this stock, having negative covariance with the portfolio, actually *reduces* the risk of the portfolio. It will counterbalance the movement of the other stocks. Like the crimsons, it will be up in value when everything else is down, and thereby will moderate the swings in portfolio value. Unfortunately, in practice there is no counterpart in our market for the crimson marbles of "Marblehead." Virtually all stocks have positive covariance with the market, and therefore reinforce some component of the risk of the other stocks in the portfolio. But the lower their covariance with the market, the less of an effect they will have

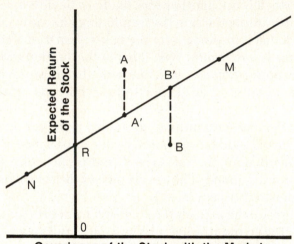

Figure 12-3. The security market line. The line NRM gives the risk-return tradeoffs for all stocks when the market is in equilibrium. For individual stocks, risk is measured by the covariance of the stock with the market portfolio. A stock with expected return and covariance with the market like that depicted by point A will be attractive from a risk-return standpoint. Bidding for the stock will drive its price back down to the security market line at point A'. Similarly, a stock at point B will be sold, and this will lead to a price drop that will increase expected return and move it up to the line at point B'.

on the risk, and the lower their expected return will need to be to have people willing to hold them.

THE SECURITY MARKET LINE

The three steps in the development of the CAPM lead to one vital implication for the price of stocks. Suppose you hold a portfolio on the RM line in Figure 12-3, and observe a stock with an expected return and with a covariance with the market portfolio depicted by point A. Since it is above the line, adding it to your portfolio will give you a higher return for the level of risk than you can get from any combination of the market and risk-free asset alone. Put another way, it gives a higher expected return for the amount of systematic risk than is available in the market as a whole. Investors will bid for this stock to add it to their portfolio, raising its market price and thereby lowering the expected return per dollar invested in the stocks until it finally comes into line with the risk-return tradeoffs possible in the rest of the market. This point is shown in the figure by A′. A stock with a risk-return tradeoff like that depicted by point B will be sold, since it underperforms the possibilities available in the rest of the market. The selling pressure will force the price down, raising its expected return per dollar invested until it falls on the line at point B′.

In equilibrium, then, all stocks will be on the line RM. This line is called the *security market line*. For any degree of systematic risk a stock has, we can determine its fair market return by seeing what expected return corresponds to that level of covariance with the market. We can make the measurement of systematic risk easier to interpret by dividing the covariance of the stock's return with the market return, denoted by $Cov(r_i, r_M)$, by the variance of the market return, $Var(r_M)$, i.e., by measuring the risk of a stock i by $Cov(r_i, r_M)/Var(r_M)$. This term is commonly called the *beta* of the stock. The beta coefficient gives us a nice, intuitive range of values for risk. Since the covariance of the market with itself is equal to its variance, $Cov(r_M, r_M)/Var(r_M)$ is equal to one. Thus, a stock with a beta greater than one is riskier, in terms of systematic risk, than is the market overall. Such a stock will tend to react more to market movements than will the market itself. A stock with a beta of 1.5 would on average be expected to go up 15% if the market rose 10%, and similarly drop 1.5 times the amount of a market decline. And a beta of less than 1 indicates a stable, low-risk stock, as compared to the overall market. The security market line is redrawn in terms of the beta of the stock in Figure 12-4.

Restating the systematic risk of a stock in terms of its beta, we can write the equation for the security market line in Figure 12-4 as

$$(\bar{r}_i - r_F) = \beta_i(\bar{r}_M - r_F).$$

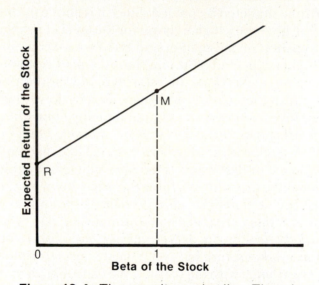

Figure 12-4. The security market line: The relationship between expected return and the beta of a stock. Here the security market line is drawn in terms of the expected return and the beta of the stock. The beta measures the co-variance of a stock with the market, but is adjusted so that stocks that are riskier than the market have a beta above 1, and those that are less risky than the market have a beta of less than 1. The higher the beta of a stock, the greater its systematic risk, and the higher its expected return should be.

This is the basic equation of the capital asset pricing model. It states that the excess expected return of a stock above the risk-free rate will be equal to the excess expected return of the market above the risk-free rate multiplied by the

TABLE 12-1 Betas for Representative Stocks

COMPANY	BETA
Aetna Life and Casualty	.80
Aluminum Company of America	1.10
Avon Products	.83
Boeing	1.80
Chase Manhattan	.95
Coleco Industries	1.60
Disney Productions	1.15
Dow Chemical	1.38
Exxon	.85
General Electric	.95
General Motors	.70
International Business Machines	.80
Mattel	2.05
Merrill Lynch	2.30
McDonnell Douglas	1.55
NCR	1.37
National Semiconductor	2.00
Penney, J. C.	.65
Proctor and Gamble	.60
RCA	1.15
Resorts International	1.00
Safeway Stores	.75
Sears and Roebuck	.70
Southern	.30
Standard Oil of California	1.20
Superior Oil	1.48
Tandy	1.95
Trans World Corporation	2.00
United Airlines	1.65
U.S. Steel	1.30

beta of a stock. If the excess return to the market is 10% (for example if $r_F = 5\%$ and $\bar{r}_M = 15\%$), then the excess expected return to a stock with a beta of 1.5 will be 15%.

Table 12-1 shows the historical betas of thirty stocks, calculated using monthly data over a five-year period. These stocks represent a wide range of industries and levels of risk. As would be expected, the betas are low for the regulated companies, and high for growth stocks. One interesting stock is Merrill Lynch. Merrill Lynch has a beta of 2.30, the largest beta listed. Yet, it is not an unusually volatile stock. The reason for the high beta is that Merrill Lynch is very highly correlated with the market. Its profits are, after all, linked directly with the fortunes of the stock market. Systematic risk, therefore, makes up a much larger part of its total risk. The other extreme in this table is Southern Company, an electric utility. Utilities are generally low-risk industries, with risks that are not closely tied to the market. They are further insulated from the market by the regulatory system.

USING THE CAPITAL ASSET PRICING MODEL IN EQUITY TRADING STRATEGIES

There are two issues in the use of the CAPM. The first is estimating or forecasting the beta of the stock. The second is using the resulting beta to formulate an investment strategy.

There are a number of services that provide estimates for stock betas. A number of these are expensive, computer timesharing services such as BARRA or Wilshire Associates. These services can run tens of thousands of dollars a year. They are obviously designed for the large institutional investor. There are also publications available through subscription or from brokerage firms that list betas. One of the most popular of these is Value Line, although its beta estimates have tended to underestimate the beta values for the high beta stocks.

The program in this chapter estimates the beta of a stock directly from the historical stock price data. It rephrases the security market line as an ordinary least squares regression, and estimates the beta as a coefficient of the regression. This method is the most widely used and theoretically justifiable technique for determining the stock's beta.

Once the beta has been estimated, the work of the stock analyst is only half done. The beta gives a measure of risk, but the investor must also provide an estimate of the return expected over the investment horizon. This can be estimated using other tools, such as the three-stage growth model seen in Chapter 13. But in the final analysis, the estimate of future returns must be based on individual subjective analysis.

Once the future expected return and the beta of the stock are determined, these values can be put into the CAPM. If the excess expected return is greater than the stock's beta times the excess of the market return over the risk-free rate, i.e., if $\bar{r}_i - r_F > \beta_i(\bar{r}_M - r_F)$, then the return on the stock is greater than it should be for its risk, and it is a buy. On the other hand, if $(\bar{r}_i - r_F) < \beta_i(\bar{r}_M - r_F)$, then the stock is overpriced—its expected return is too low for its beta, and it is a sell. In the regression framework, these inequalities can be represented by a constant term. If, in running the security market line regression we find a nonzero intercept, i.e., if the CAPM leads to an equation like

$$\bar{r}_i - r_F = \alpha_i + \beta_i(\bar{r}_M - r_F),$$

where the α_i is significantly different from zero, then the stock is mispriced. If α_i is positive, the stock has too high an expected return, if α_i is negative, it has too low an expected return. Appropriately enough, this constant term is called the stock's *alpha*. For example, if the alpha equals 3%, the expected return to the stock is 3% higher than it should be given its beta. The final output of the CAPM in determining mispricing, then, is the alpha of the stock.

The CAPM program in this chapter can calculate the historical beta and alpha, as well as the historical mean return to the stock and the market, using the ordinary least-squares regression technique. Doing so simply requires inputting the historical time series data for the stock, the market, and the risk-free rate. A reasonably accurate result requires at least five years of data, (monthly or quarterly is best), so this program makes significant demands on data availability.

It is also possible to compute the appropriate ex post expected return for a stock using the long-term historical relationship between market return and the risk-free rate reported by Ibbotson and Sinquefield (1976). This study showed that over a fifty-year period, the average expected return of the market over the risk-free rate, $(r_M - r_F)$, was 8.7%. This relationship can be used as the basis of the CAPM calculation rather than relying on time series regressions. The data requirements for this are far less demanding, all that is needed is the stock's beta and the risk-free rate. Of course, such a simple approach will work only if this fifty-year value makes sense in the current market environment.

The relationship between the historical and the future values of beta must be kept in mind in applying the programs in this chapter. For stock trading, it is the *future* beta and alpha that are important. The results of the regression analysis will be useful for trading only if it is believed the historical relationships still apply.

An alternative to the techniques just described is to forecast the expected return of the stock and its beta using fundamental methods, such as by looking at earnings forecasts, industry and firm growth, and the economic outlook. These forecasts can then be fed into the CAPM to determine the fair market price for the stock. If the stock price differs from this model price, a trading opportunity is open.

THE CAPITAL ASSET PRICING MODEL

Computational Procedure

Perform the regression

$$r_t - r_{Ft} = \alpha + \beta(r_{Mt} - r_{Ft}) + \epsilon_t$$

where

r_t = stock return for period t
r_{Ft} = risk-free rate for period t
r_{Mt} = market return for period t
ϵ_t = zero-mean error term for period t
α = a regression coefficient, the stock's alpha
β = a regression coefficient, the stock's beta

The regression is performed using ordinary least squares. Also reported is the R^2 of the regression and the t statistics for the two coefficients.

Trading Strategy

- Buy the stock if α is greater than zero.
- Sell the stock if α is less than zero.

The t statistic is used to determine if the value of α differs significantly from zero.

```
10   REM ***************************************************************
20   REM *         STOCK ANALYSIS BASED ON THE CAPITAL ASSET PRICING MODEL      *
30   REM *                                                                      *
40   REM * THIS PROGRAM USES ORDINARY LEAST SQUARES REGRESSION ANALYSIS TO      *
50   REM * COMPUTE THE BETA AND ALPHA FOR A SECURITY.  THE BETA IS USED IN      *
60   REM * THE CAPITAL ASSET PRICING MODEL TO MEASURE THE SYSTEMATIC RISK       *
70   REM * OF THE SECURITY, AND THE ALPHA IS USED TO MEASURE THE PERFORMANCE    *
80   REM * OF THE SECURITY GIVEN ITS LEVEL OF SYSTEMATIC RISK.                  *
90   REM *                                                                      *
100  REM *   VARIABLES USED:                                                    *
110  REM *                                                                      *
120  REM *              RS( ) = ARRAY OF EACH PERIOD'S RETURN ON STOCK          *
130  REM *              RM( ) = ARRAY OF EACH PERIOD'S RETURN ON MARKET         *
140  REM *              RF( ) = ARRAY OF EACH PERIOD'S RISK FREE RETURN         *
150  REM *               Z( ) = FOR EACH PERIOD Z(I) = RS - RF                  *
160  REM *               X( ) = FOR EACH PERIOD X(I) = RM - RF                  *
170  REM *          SERROR( ) = ARRAY OF EACH PERIOD'S ERROR FACTOR             *
180  REM *              MEANZ = MEAN OF ALL VALUES OF Z                         *
190  REM *              MEANX = MEAN OF ALL VALUES OF X                         *
200  REM *                DX2 = SUM OF ALL X DEVIATIONS SQUARED                 *
210  REM *                DZ2 = SUM OF ALL Z DEVIATIONS SQUARED                 *
220  REM *               BETA = BETA COEFFICIENT                                *
230  REM *              ALPHA = ALPHA COEFFICIENT                               *
240  REM *             TALPHA = T STATISTIC FOR ALPHA                           *
250  REM *              TBETA = T STATISTIC FOR BETA                            *
260  REM *                 SP = STARTING PERIOD                                 *
270  REM *                 NP = NUMBER OF PERIODS                               *
280  REM *                                                                      *
290  REM *                                                                      *
300  REM ***************************************************************
310  REM
320  REM
330   DIM RS(100), RM(100), RF(100), Z(100), X(100), SERROR(100)
340  REM
350  REM
360  REM ***************************ENTER DATA***************************
370   GOSUB 500
380  REM
390  REM
400  REM ***********************DO COMPUTATIONS***********************
410   GOTO 900
420  REM
430  REM
440  REM **************************PRINT OUTPUT**************************
450  REM
460  REM
470  REM **************************PROGRAM END**************************
480  REM
490  REM
500  REM ***************************************************************
510  REM                      SUBROUTINE TO ENTER DATA
520  REM ***************************************************************
530  REM
540   CLS:  REM CLEARS SCREEN AND HOMES CURSOR
550   SP=1: REM SET STARTING PERIOD
```

```
560  I=1:   REM INITIALIZE COUNTER FOR DATA ENTRY
570 PRINT "ENTER '999' IN ANY OF THE THREE POSITIONS TO END DATA ENTRY"
580 PRINT "FOR PERIOD";I;"ENTER:"
590 INPUT "                    RETURN ON STOCK:",RS(I)
600  IF RS(I) =999 THEN GOTO 670
610 INPUT "                    RETURN ON MARKET:",RM(I)
620  IF RM(I)=999 THEN GOTO 670
630 INPUT "                RISK FREE RETURN:",RF(I)
640  IF RF(I) = 999 THEN GOTO 670
650  I=I+1
660  GOTO 580
670  I=I-1 :REM DECREMENTS COUNTER ON LAST ENTRY
680  NP=I
690 REM
700  CLS :REM CLEARS SCREEN AND HOMES CURSOR
710 REM
720 REM
730 PRINT "PERIOD        RETURN ON STOCK      RETURN ON MARKET      RISKFREE RETURN"
740 PRINT"_____   _____    _____    _____ "
750  FOR I= 1 TO NP
760 PRINT TAB(4)I;TAB(19)RS(I);TAB(39)RM(I);TAB(59)RF(I)
770   IF I=NP THEN GOTO 790
780  NEXT I
790 INPUT "ENTER PERIOD TO CHANGE OR '0'TO CONTINUE";CP
800  IF CP<>0 THEN I=CP
810  IF CP=0 THEN RETURN
820 PRINT"THE RETURN ON STOCK FOR PERIOD";CP;"IS: ",RS(I):PRINT
830 INPUT"                    NEW RETURN: ",RS(I):PRINT
840 PRINT" THE RETURN ON THE MARKET FOR PERIOD";CP;"IS: ",RM(I):PRINT
850 INPUT"                        NEW RETURN: ";RM(I):PRINT
860 PRINT"THE RISKFREE RETURN FOR PERIOD";CP;"IS: ",RF(I):PRINT
870 INPUT "                    NEW RETURN: ",RF(I)
880  GOTO 730
890  REM
900 REM ********************************************************************
910 REM *                    COMPUTATIONS                                  *
920 REM ********************************************************************
930 REM
940 REM DEFINE 'X' AND 'Z'
950 REM
960  FOR I=1 TO NP
970   Z(I)=RS(I)-RF(I)
980   X(I)=RM(I)-RF(I)
990  NEXT I
1000 REM
1010 REM COMPUTE MEANS FOR 'X' AND 'Z'
1020 REM
1030  FOR I=1 TO NP
1040   SUMZ=SUMZ + Z(I)
1050   SUMX=SUMX + X(I)
1060   NEXT I
1070  MEANZ=SUMZ/NP
1080  MEANX=SUMX/NP
1090 REM COMPUTE ALPHA AND BETA
1100  FOR I=1 TO NP
```

```
1110    SUMDXDZ=SUMDXDZ + (Z(I)-MEANZ)*(X(I)-MEANX)
1120    DX2=DX2 + (X(I) -MEANX)^2
1130   NEXT I
1140   BETA = SUMDXDZ/DX2
1150   ALPHA = MEANZ - BETA*MEANX
1160   FOR I = 1 TO NP
1170     SERROR(I) = Z(I) - ALPHA - BETA*X(I)
1180   NEXT I
1190  REM COMPUTE S2
1200   SUMERROR=0
1210   FOR I = 1 TO NP
1220     SUMERROR = SUMERROR + SERROR(I)^2
1230   NEXT I
1240   S2 = (1/(NP-2))*SUMERROR
1250  REM COMPUTE SALPHA2, SBETA2, TBETA, AND TALPHA
1260   SALPHA2 = S2*(1/NP + (MEANX^2/DX2))
1270   SBETA2 = S2/DX2
1280   TBETA = BETA/(SQR(SBETA2))
1290   TALPHA = ALPHA/(SQR(SALPHA2))
1300  REM COMPUTE R2
1310   FOR I = 1 TO NP
1320    DZ2 = DZ2 + (Z(I) - MEANZ)^2
1330   NEXT I
1340   R2 = (BETA^2)*DX2/DZ2
1350  REM
1360  REM COMPUTE STANDARD ERROR FOR ALPHA AND BETA
1370  REM
1380   SSALPHA2 = (SQR(SALPHA2))
1390   SSBETA2 = (SQR(SBETA2))
1400  REM****************************************************************
1410  REM*                            OUTPUT                           *
1420  REM****************************************************************
1430   CLS : REM CLEARS SCREEN AND HOMES CURSOR
1440  PRINT:PRINT:PRINT
1450  PRINT "                         BETA = ";BETA
1460  PRINT "               STANDARD ERROR = ";SSBETA2
1470  PRINT "                   T for BETA = ";TBETA
1480  PRINT:PRINT
1490  PRINT "                        ALPHA = ";ALPHA
1500  PRINT "               STANDARD ERROR = ";SSALPHA2
1510  PRINT "                  T for ALPHA = ";TALPHA
1520  PRINT:PRINT:PRINT
1530  PRINT "                    R-SQUARED = ";R2
1540  REM
1550  REM ***************TO RERUN PROGRAM WITH DIFFERENT FIGURES***************
1560  REM
1570  PRINT:PRINT:PRINT:PRINT:PRINT
1580  INPUT "WOULD YOU LIKE TO REPEAT THIS PROCESS?    (Y/N)";PREPEAT$
1590   IF PREPEAT$ = "Y" THEN GOTO 360
1600  END
```

13
The Dividend Capitalization Model for Stock Valuation

Stock is equity, and equity implies ownership. Stock does not give ownership to any particular physical asset of the company, rather, it gives a claim on the company's future stream of earnings. Therefore, we can look at the value of stock as the present value of the future earnings of the company that the stockholders will receive. If we knew the future stream of earnings of the company, and the appropriate discount rate for converting those future earnings into current dollars, we could easily value the stock.

We can go further than this to say that the value of stock is the present value of the future *dividends* due the stockholder. This is because ultimately the only way the stockholder can actually receive any earnings is through dividend payments. Of course, the stockholder can sell the stock to another investor, and receive the value of the stock in that way, but the investor who has bought the stock will in turn only receive a return through future dividend payments. Thus, the final determining factor of stock value will be future dividends.

Unfortunately, the value of future earnings or future dividends is difficult to project with any accuracy. Unlike bond valuation, where the coupon payments and the maturity value of the bond are carefully spelled out, the returns due the stockholder are uncertain, depending as they do on the future prospects for the firm, the industry, and the overall economy. We have already alluded to the difficulties in making earnings projections in the introduction to this section. Here we will skirt the issue of how the future dividends are forecast. The model we will develop in this chapter will take the projected pattern of future dividends as given.

A SIMPLE DIVIDEND GROWTH MODEL

The returns to a stock investment come either as dividends or as price appreciation. In a simple one-period setting, an investor's return is simply

$$r = (P_1 - P_0)/P_0 + D/P_0, \tag{1}$$

where

P_0 = the price at the start of the period
P_1 = the price at the end of the period, (adjusted for the dividend payment)
D = the dollar dividend payment, paid at the end of the period

The first term is the return generated by the price change from the start to the end of the period, and the second term is the return generated by the dividend. For example, if the dividend payment D is \$5, and the initial stock price P_0 is \$100, then the return from the dividend will be 5%.

This formula can be restated to show the current price as a function of the dividend payment, projected end-of-period price, and discount rate:

$$P_0 = P_1/(1+r) + D/(1+r). \tag{2}$$

That is, the current price of the stock should equal the discounted future price and the discounted dividends.

If the investor has an investment horizon of many years, then the argument is the same, but with the return being determined by the dividends received over the total number of time periods the stock is held, and by the price at the end of the holding period. For example, if the investor holds the stock for T time periods, and then sells the stock at the end of period T, the current price should equal the discounted value of the dividends received through period T plus the present value of the price at the end of period T:

$$P_0 = D_1/(1+r)+D_2/(1+r)^2+D_3/(1+r)^3+\cdots+D_T/(1+r)^T+P_T/(1+r)^T$$

$$= \sum_{t=1}^{T} D_t/(1+r)^t + P_T/(1+r)^T. \tag{3}$$

It is apparent that the price in period T can be expressed in terms of the dividends from period T on, since these are what will accrue to whomever buys the stock in that period. So, ultimately, we can just set the price as the present value of all dividends that will be paid out in perpetuity:

$$P_0 = \sum_{t=1}^{\infty} D_t/(1+r)^t. \tag{4}$$

This is the essence of the dividend capitalization model, sometimes also called the dividend discount model. The whole idea is to set the stock price equal to the present value of all the dividends that will be paid on the stock for time immemorial.

Stated in the form presented here, this model appears not to have much practical value, since it seems unreasonable to have to project dividends out to infinity. Of course, the discount factor in the denominator makes it a little easier, since dividends very far out in the future will have a negligible present value, and will not be an issue in determining the current price.

Things can be simplified even further by assuming the company, and thus earnings and dividends, is growing at a constant rate. This assumption transforms the dividend capitalization model into what is known as the Gordon growth model. In the Gordon growth model, we assume dividends grow at a constant rate g. That is, the dividend in any future period t equals the initial period's dividend payment D_0 multiplied by the growth factor $(1+g)^t$. So we can rewrite Equation (4) as

$$P_0 = \sum_{t=1}^{\infty} D_0(1+g)^t/(1+r)^t.$$

If we make the further assumption that the growth rate g is less than the discount rate r, this infinite series can be expressed in the simple form

$$P_0 = D/(k-g),$$

where

$$D = D_0(1+g).$$

That is, the current stock price is equal to the projected dividend discounted by the difference between the company's discount rate k and its growth rate g. For example, for a company with a projected $5 dividend, a discount rate of 10%, and a growth rate of 6%, the price of the stock should be

$$P_0 = 5/(.1-.06) = 125.$$

FIRM VALUATION USING EARNING GROWTH PROJECTIONS

The dividend capitalization model can easily be modified to use earnings growth forecasts rather than dividend growth forecasts.

Earnings are related to dividends through the payout ratio. In particular, dividends are simply earnings times the payout ratio.

Let E be projected earnings, b the retention rate, (so 1–b is the payout ratio), and r the return on retained earnings. Projected dividends equal $(1-b)E$, and the growth rate of the firm, g, is br. We can therefore restate the relationship of the simple dividend capitalization equation as

$$P_0 = \frac{D}{k-g} = \frac{(1-b)E}{k-br}.$$

By this substitution, the stock of the firm can be valued as a function of earnings growth. The program for this chapter allows either dividends or earnings to be used in the stock valuation.

A THREE-STAGE GROWTH MODEL

The valuation model just described, simple though it is, actually does a pretty good job at valuing certain types of companies. As the assumptions suggest, the model will best fit those companies that are in a constant growth phase—companies in the more mature industries with an established market position, such as Proctor and Gamble, General Mills, or Kodak. This growth model also does well for valuing regulated firms. These firms typically grow at a rate that reflects the economic or demographic growth in the region they serve. Indeed, the Gordon growth model is often applied in its pristine form by regulators to determine the fair rate of return for regulated utilities.

Still, the model is quite restrictive. Many companies are not in a stable, constant growth phase. For example, high growth companies experience growth far above the discount rate, thus violating one of the assumptions for obtaining the simple expression of the Gordon growth model. These companies are also not expected to sustain a rate of high growth forever. The typical pattern of a successful emerging company is high growth followed by a gradual slowing to a more permanent, constant growth rate. An IBM or Tandy may have an initial spurt of growth of 25% or more, compared to the normal growth rate for S/P 500 companies of around 8% to 10%. After a few years, these companies face a maturing market or increasing competition, and the growth rate gradually settles down closer to the normal growth rate. Obviously, a company cannot sustain supernormal growth forever without finally engulfing the whole economy.

The program we present in this chapter adjusts the Gordon growth model to allow the flexibility of dealing with companies that manifest this more complex pattern of growth. It allows for a first stage of supernormal growth, where the growth rate might exceed the average growth rate of the market, and might exceed the discount rate for the company. A second stage marks the period of maturation, where growth gradually drops. We assume in the program that this decline in the growth rate is linear. That is, if the growth rate drops from, say, 20% to 10% over five years, then the growth rate is assumed to drop by 2% per year. The third and final growth stage is the constant growth stage discussed earlier in the chapter. In this stage, the company has stabilized to a pattern of growth that appears to be constant for the foreseeable future.

Figure 13-1A shows the growth pattern of earnings (and dividends) through these three stages. The slope of the curve represents the growth rate, which is shown in Figure 13-1B.

Using the Three-Stage Growth Program

The three-stage growth program can be used to find the fair value for the current stock price given the discount rate and other inputs, or can be used to solve for the discount rate implied by the current market price.

This latter option is especially interesting when the dividend capitalization model is applied in conjunction with the capital asset pricing model of Chapter 12. The discount rate from the dividend capitalization model can be compared to the discount rate the company should have given its beta as measured by the capital asset pricing model. If the discount rate that equates future dividends to the current market price is greater than the fair discount rate as determined by the CAPM, then dividends may be unduly discounted, and the stock could be underpriced. This two-pronged approach is used by a number of prominent portfolio management groups. It is attractive in that it combines the fundamental information implicit in the dividend growth model analysis with the risk analysis from the CAPM.

The three-stage growth model requires inputs of the growth rate for the period of high growth, the normal growth rate once its growth stabilizes, the time high growth is terminated, and the period of transition to the normal growth rate. These inputs are obviously highly subjective, and are all subject to a high degree of variation. The effective use of this program is, therefore, perhaps more sensitive to data variations than any other program in the book. But, as I mentioned in the introduction to this section, such is the nature of stock analysis.

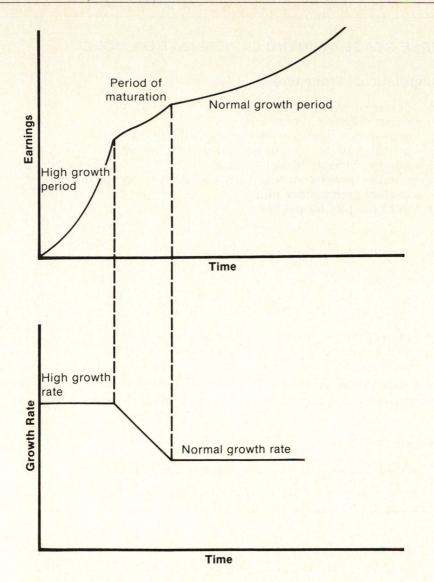

Figure 13-1. Earnings and growth rate in the three-stage growth model. (Adapted from Farrell: *Guide to Portfolio Management,* p. 137. New York, McGraw-Hill, 1983. With permission)

THREE-STAGE DIVIDEND CAPITALIZATION MODEL

Computational Procedure

D_o = current dollar dividend
$D(t)$ = dollar dividend at time t
g_h = growth rate during initial high-growth period
g_n = growth rate during final normal-growth period
T_h = number of years of high growth
T_M = number of years for transition from high to normal growth
P_o = current period stock price
k = discount rate for the firm

The current price of the firm is, then,

$$P_o = \sum_{t=1}^{T_h} D_o(1+g_h)^t/(1+k)^t + 1/(1+k)^{T_h} \sum_{t=T_h}^{T_M} D(t)/(1+k)^t + (1/(1+k)^{T_h+T_M})D(T_h+T_M)(1+g_n)/(k-g_n).$$

These three terms represent the value of the high-growth period, period of maturation, and normal growth period, respectively.

Trading Strategy

- Buy the stock if the market price is less than P_o.
- Sell the stock if the market price is greater than P_o.

```
10   REM  *****************************************************************
20   REM  *                THREE STAGE DIVIDEND GROWTH MODEL              *
30   REM  *                                                              *
40   REM  * THIS PROGRAM USES THE THREE STAGE GROWTH DIVIDEND CAPITALIZATION *
50   REM  * MODEL TO VALUE STOCK AND TO COMPUTE THE RATE OF RETURN THAT CAN  *
60   REM  * BE EXPECTED FROM A STOCK.  THE PROGRAM ALLOWS THE USE OF EARNINGS *
70   REM  * GROWTH AND PAYOUT RATIOS AS WELL AS DIVIDEND GROWTH TO MAKE THE   *
80   REM  * COMPUTATION.                                                  *
90   REM  *                                                              *
100  REM  * VARIABLES USED:                                              *
110  REM  *                                                              *
120  REM  *                  P = PAYOUT RATIO                            *
130  REM  *                  G = GROWTH RATE                             *
140  REM  *                  R = DISCOUNT RATE                           *
150  REM  *                EPS = EARNINGS PER SHARE                      *
160  REM  *                DIV = DIVIDEND PER SHARE                      *
170  REM  *              PRICE = PRICE PER SHARE                         *
180  REM  *                 PE = PRICE/EARNINGS RATIO                    *
190  REM  *                                                              *
200  REM  *****************************************************************
210  REM
220  DIM G(50),P(50),N(50),R(50),EPS(50),DIV(50),PRICE(50)
230  DIM PE(50),G1(50),P1(50),R1(50)
240  REM
250  REM
260  REM  ********************INPUT THE DATA***************************
270  GOSUB 370
280  REM
290  REM  ******************DO CALCULATIONS***************************
300  GOSUB 910
310  REM
320  REM  ****************OUTPUT THE RESULTS**************************
330  GOSUB 1370
340  REM
350  REM  ********************REITERATE*******************************
360  GOTO 250
370  REM
380  REM  *****************************************************************
390  REM  *                    INPUT SUBROUTINE                         *
400  REM  *****************************************************************
410  PRINT
420  PRINT "WHAT OPTION DO YOU WISH TO RUN:"
430  PRINT "    1) STOCK PRICE VALUATION"
440  PRINT "    2) DISCOUNT RATE"
450  PRINT "    3) EXIT"
460  PRINT
470  INPUT "ENTER YOUR CHOICE (1, 2, OR 3)";C1
480  IF C1<1 OR C1>4 THEN C1=4
490  ON C1 GOTO 500,500,2520,480
500  PRINT
510  PRINT "WHAT DO YOU WISH TO BASE THE CALCULATIONS ON:"
520  PRINT "    1) EARNINGS"
530  PRINT "    2) DIVIDENDS"
540  PRINT
```

```
550 INPUT "ENTER YOUR CHOICE (1 OR 2) ";C2
560 IF C2<1 OR C2>2 THEN C2=3
570 PRINT
580 IF C2=1 THEN INPUT "ENTER THE CURRENT EPS ",EPS0
590 IF C2=2 THEN INPUT "ENTER THE CURRENT DIVIDEND ",EPS0
600 IF EPS0 > 0 THEN GOTO 630
610 PRINT "PLEASE ENTER A POSITIVE NUMBER"
620 GOTO 580
630 P(1) = 100
640 IF C2=1 THEN INPUT "ENTER THE PHASE 1 PAYOUT RATIO (%) ",P(1)
650 IF C1=1 THEN INPUT "ENTER THE PHASE 1 DISCOUNT RATE (%) ",R(1)
660 INPUT "ENTER THE PHASE 1 GROWTH RATE (%) ",G(1)
670 INPUT "ENTER THE LENGTH OF PHASE 1 (YEARS) ",N(1)
680 P(2) = 100
690 IF C2=1 THEN INPUT "ENTER THE PHASE 2 PAYOUT RATIO (%) ",P(2)
700 IF C1=1 THEN INPUT "ENTER THE PHASE 2 DISCOUNT RATE (%) ",R(2)
710 P(1)=P(1)/100 : R(1)=R(1)/100 : G(1)=G(1)/100 : P(2)=P(2)/100
720 R(2)=R(2)/100
730 INPUT "ENTER THE LENGTH OF PHASE 2 (YEARS) ",NN
740 S = NN+1
750 T = NN+N(1)
760 FOR I = 2 TO NN+1
770    P(I) = P(2)
780    R(I) = R(2)
790    N(I) = 1
800    NEXT I
810 PT = 100
820 IF C2=1 THEN INPUT "ENTER THE PHASE 3 PAYOUT RATIO (%) ",PT
830 IF C1=1 THEN INPUT "ENTER THE PHASE 3 DISCOUNT RATE (%)",RT
840 INPUT "ENTER THE PHASE 3 GROWTH RATE (%)",GRT
850 PT=PT/100 : RT=RT/100 : GRT=GRT/100
860 FOR I = 2 TO NN+1
870    G(I) = G(1) + ((GRT-G(1))/(NN+1))*(I-1)
880    NEXT I
890 RETURN
900 REM
910 REM ****************************************************************
920 REM *                    CALCULATION SUBROUTINE                   *
930 REM ****************************************************************
940 REM
950 REM    INITIALIZING ARRAYS
960 REM
970 FOR J=0 TO T+1
980    G1(J) = 0
990    P1(J) = 0
1000   R1(J) = 0
1010   DIV(J) = 0
1020   EPS(J) = 0
1030   PE(J) = 0
1040   PRICE(J) = 0
1050   NEXT J
1060 REM
1070 REM    LOAD ARRAYS: EARNINGS GROWTH,PAYOUT, & DISCOUNT RATE
1080 REM
```

```
1090 FOR J=1 TO S
1100    IF J=1 THEN I=1
1110    IF J<>1 THEN GOTO 1130
1120    IF I=1 THEN GOTO 1140
1130    I=N(J-1)+I
1140    FOR K=I TO (N(J)+(I-1))
1150       G1(K)=G(J)
1160       P1(K)=P(J)
1170       R1(K)=R(J)
1180       NEXT K
1190    NEXT J
1200 G1(T+1) = GRT
1210 P1(T+1) = PT
1220 R1(T+1) = RT
1230 REM
1240 REM    CALCULATING THE PRICE IN PERIOD T
1250 REM
1260 EPS(0)=EPS0
1270 FOR I=1 TO T
1280    EPS(I)=EPS(I-1)*(1+G1(I))
1290    DIV(I) = P1(I)*EPS(I)
1300    NEXT I
1310 EPS(T+1)=EPS(T)*(1+GRT)
1320 ON C1 GOTO 1330,1350
1330 PRICE(T)=(PT*EPS(T+1))/(RT-GRT)
1340 PRICE(T+1) = PRICE(T)*(1+GRT)
1350 DIV(T+1) = EPS(T+1)*PT
1360 RETURN
1370 REM *************************************************************
1380 REM *                    OUTPUT SUBROUTINE                      *
1390 REM *************************************************************
1400 ON C1 GOTO 1410,2140
1410 PRINT
1420 PRINT TAB(14);
1430 IF C2=1 THEN PRINT "           EPS          ";
1440 IF C2=2 THEN PRINT "    DIVIDEND    ";
1450 PRINT "PAYOUT          PRICE      PRICE/"
1460 PRINT TAB(10);"YEAR";
1470 IF C2=1 THEN PRINT "      EPS ";
1480 PRINT "   GROWTH    RATIO DIVIDEND PER SHARE ";
1490 IF C2=1 THEN PRINT "EARNINGS RATIO "
1500 IF C2=2 THEN PRINT "DIVIDEND RATIO"
1510 PRINT TAB(10);"_____";
1520 IF C2=1 THEN PRINT "     _____";
1530 PRINT "   _____   _____ _____   _____  _____ "
1540 FOR I=1 TO T
1550    J=T-I
1560    PRICE(J)=(PRICE(J+1)+DIV(J+1))/(1+R1(J+1))
1570    NEXT I
1580 FOR I=0 TO T+1
1590    PE(I)=PRICE(I)/EPS(I)
1600    NEXT I
1610 PRINT "PHASE 1";
1620 FOR I=0 TO N(1)
```

```
1630    P100 = P1(I)*100
1640    G100 = G1(I)*100
1650    PRINT TAB(10);
1660    PRINT USING " ###";I;
1670    IF C2=1 THEN PRINT USING" #,###.##";EPS(I);
1680    PRINT USING " #,###.## #,###.##";G100,P100;
1690    PRINT USING " #,###.## #,###.##    #,###.##";DIV(I),PRICE(I),PE(I)
1700    COUNT=COUNT + 1
1710    IF COUNT=18 THEN GOSUB 2000
1720    NEXT I
1730 IF T>N(1)+1 THEN PRINT "PHASE 2";
1740 FOR I=N(1)+1 TO T
1750    P100 = P1(I)*100
1760    G100 = G1(I)*100
1770    PRINT TAB(10);
1780    PRINT USING " ###";I;
1790    IF C2=1 THEN PRINT USING" #,###.##";EPS(I);
1800    PRINT USING " #,###.## #,###.##";G100,P100;
1810    PRINT USING " #,###.## #,###.##    #,###.##";DIV(I),PRICE(I),PE(I)
1820    COUNT=COUNT+1
1830    IF COUNT=18 THEN GOSUB 2000
1840    NEXT I
1850 PRINT TAB(10);"_____";
1860 IF C2=1 THEN PRINT "      _____";
1870 PRINT "    _____      _____ _____   _____ _____ "
1880 PRINT "PHASE 3";
1890 I = T+1
1900    P100 = P1(I)*100
1910    G100 = G1(I)*100
1920   COUNT=COUNT+1
1930   IF COUNT=18 THEN GOSUB 2000
1940    PRINT TAB(10);
1950    PRINT USING " ###";I;
1960    IF C2=1 THEN PRINT USING" #,###.##";EPS(I);
1970    PRINT USING " #,###.## #,###.##";G100,P100;
1980    PRINT USING " #,###.## #,###.##    #,###.##";DIV(I),PRICE(I),PE(I)
1990 PRINT
2000 INPUT"TO CONTINUE, PRESS RETURN", Y$
2010 COUNT=0
2020 RETURN
2030 ON C1 GOTO 2100,2040
2040 PRINT USING " THE DISCOUNT RATE IS ###.##%";IRR
2050 PRINT
2060 IF C1=1 THEN INPUT "ANOTHER PRICE/EARNINGS RATIO (Y=1 OR N=2)";AN
2070 IF C1=2 THEN INPUT "ANOTHER PRICE/DIVIDEND RATIO (Y=1 OR N=2)";AN
2080 IF AN<1 OR AN>2 THEN AN=3
2090 ON AN GOTO 2140,2130,2060
2100 PRINT
2110 INPUT"TO CONTINUE, PRESS RETURN ", Y$
2120 COUNT=0
2130 RETURN
2140 IF C2=1 THEN INPUT"ENTER CURRENT PRICE/EARNINGS RATIO",PE0
2150 IF C2=2 THEN INPUT"ENTER THE CURRENT PRICE/DIVIDEND RATIO",PE0
2160 PRICE0 = PE0*EPS0
```

```
2170 REM ***********************************************************
2180 REM *                 DISCOUNT RATE SUBROUTINE                *
2190 REM ***********************************************************
2200 RN = 1
2210 IRR = 10
2220 FOR J = 1 TO 100
2230 XIRR = IRR
2240 IF XIRR/100=GRT THEN XIRR=XIRR*(1.01)
2250 PRICE(T)=PT*EPS(T+1)/(XIRR/100-GRT)
2260 IF J=1 THEN GOTO 2290
2270 IF X0>0 THEN EVEN = 1
2280 IF X0<0 THEN EVEN = 2
2290 XX = 0
2300 FOR I = 1 TO T
2310 XX = XX+(DIV(I)*(1/((1+(XIRR/100))^I)))
2320 NEXT I
2330 X0 = (PRICE0)-XX-(PRICE(T)*(1/((1+(XIRR/100))^T)))
2340 IF ABS(X0)<=(.01) THEN GOTO 2470
2350 IF X0>0 AND J=1 THEN GOTO 2440
2360 IF X0<0 AND J=1 THEN GOTO 2450
2370 IF X0>0 THEN BINDX = 1
2380 IF X0<0 THEN BINDX = 2
2390 IF X0>0 AND BINDX=EVEN THEN GOTO 2440
2400 IF X0>0 AND BINDX<>EVEN THEN GOTO 2430
2410 IF X0<0 AND BINDX=EVEN THEN GOTO 2450
2420 IF X0<0 AND BINDX<>EVEN THEN GOTO 2430
2430 RN = RN*2
2440 IF X0>0 THEN IRR = IRR-(1/RN)
2450 IF X0<0 THEN IRR = IRR+(1/RN)
2460 NEXT J
2470 FOR J=1 TO T+1
2480 R1(J) = IRR/100
2490 NEXT J
2500 PRICE(T+1) = PRICE(T)*(1+GRT)
2510 GOTO 1410
2520 STOP
2530 END
```

Stock Analysis References*

There are many texts that detail the approach to stock selection covered in this section, an approach generally called modern portfolio theory. Several good references on this topic include Elton and Gruber (1981), Francis (1984), Sharpe (1978), and Garbade (1982).

The notion of portfolio diversification strategies and risk measurement is developed by Markowitz (1952, 1959). The Sharpe model can be found in Sharpe (1963). A readable article on the relationship between risk and return in asset pricing is Modigliani and Pogue (1974). The technique for combining stock selection with optimal diversification is presented in Treynor and Black (1973).

The description and use of option portfolio strategies is presented in Bookstaber and Clarke, *Option Strategies for Institutional Investment Management,* (1983). This book presents a broad, detailed look at strategies, and algorithms for describing these strategies. Other discussion of these strategies is in Bookstaber and Clarke (1981, 1983a). The use of historical data to evaluate option portfolio strategies is discussed in the two papers by Merton, Scholes, and Gladstein (1978, 1982). Another approach to option portfolio strategies is in Rubinstein and Leland (1981).

The capital asset pricing model was developed by Sharpe (1964), Lintner (1965), and Mossin (1966). Jensen (1972) contains an early review of the empirical studies on the CAPM. A later discussion of empirical tests of the CAPM can be found in Roll (1977).

The dividend growth model has roots that go far back in the investment literature. Formulations can be found in Williams (1958), in Graham, Dodd, and Cottle (1962), and in Gordon (1962). The three-stage growth model presented here originates from Molodovsky, May, and Chottiner (1965). It is also discussed in Farrell (1983).

*Refer to Bibliography at the back of the text for complete citations.

III
TECHNICAL SYSTEMS

14
An Introduction to Technical Trading Systems

Depending on your investment upbringing, this section is either the only important section in the book, or else compromises the integrity of everything else in the book. Either technical trading *is* the system for speculative investments, or else technical trading is the catch basin for those who would have become astrologers in an earlier age. The latter view is the first article of faith among the dominant academic religion of efficient markets, and to discuss technical systems, much less to write about them and advocate their use, is to risk excommunication. The efficient market school does not approve of any trading method that makes abnormal profits, especially one based on so obvious and readily available an information source as past prices. The most universally accepted form of the efficient market hypothesis, often called the random walk hypothesis, is that past prices give no information about the future price. The hypothesis immediately implies that technical systems based on past prices are of no value.

Unfortunately, (or fortunately, for those who are doing so successfully), there are many investors who have not been swayed by the arguments for efficient markets, and still persist in the following the irrational, if not heathen ritual of looking at the entrails of past prices to try to divine the future. And perhaps it is just luck, but there are those who are quite content making profits in doing so. So in the true spirit of ecumenicism, I have added to a book that would otherwise receive the imprimator and Nihil Obstat of the academic community a section on technical systems. Before I discuss some of the general trading rules for the technical systems that follow, I will explain why almost I am persuaded to be a technician.

AN EFFICIENT MARKET CATECHISM

Harold Williamson entered the Wall Street office of Suliman, Abbott and Green five minutes before his 4:30 P.M. appointment, and exactly five minutes later was invited into William Crandon's office. After a few brief pleasantries, Williamson got down to business.

"I am an aerospace engineer, but ever since graduate school I have been studying the market, trying out different trading strategies. Five years ago I narrowed myself down to three strategies, and have been trading them with small amounts of money since then. I am now convinced that they work, and I want to use my track record to attract more capital."

Crandon was sitting straight up in his chair, with his hands folded like a choirboy's. "I don't want to pry into what you might consider proprietary, but could you give me some idea of the nature of your strategies? For example, are they arbitrage strategies to take advantage of relative mispricing, or do they involve some unusual information resource?"

"Oh, no. None of that." He gave a triumphant waving gesture with his hands. "All these strategies need are past prices. All I do is put the past prices into my computer, and then out come the buy and sell rules."

Crandon took off his glasses and put them on the table. He rubbed his temples with the index finger and thumb of his right hand, and slumped back slightly.

"We are of course always interested in updating our investment methods to include more sophisticated methods; sophisticated and to some extent proven methods, that is. But I am afraid we are not really interested in using technical systems. We simply have evolved to a level of understanding of the markets that would foreclose any rule based on something as simple as past prices from working."

"But it does work. It is proven. I have the track record now to prove it." He laid out a looseleaf folder and a bundle of supporting documents on the table.

Crandon pushed them aside gently to make room to rest his forearm. "I'm sure you think it works. In fact, I'm sure it has worked over the past years. I would not dispute that. But some rule is always going to end up working after the fact. If I took a thousand investors, and had each come into my office, throw a dart at a stock, and then track that stock over the next year, half of them would have done better than average, just by chance. And if I had those five hundred or so winners come back again next year, half of that group would again do better than average just by chance. I could do it again and again, and finally I would have around twenty-five investors who would have beat the market five years in a row. But do you think I would put them in an office with a golden dart and follow their stock picks the next year? Of course not. The problem is there is no way to tell who is going to hit the right stock before the fact. For all I know, you are just one of those who has, by luck, hit them right. There is no reason to think the pattern you have discovered will continue any more than to think the darts of the five-time winners will continue to hit the right stocks."

"Well, that may be, but it seems you have nothing to lose by trying. At least I do have a track record. How can you be sure there isn't something to it without trying it?"

"I suppose I can't in the particular. But I know enough about these markets to know in general that no simple system of past prices can really do the job. If it was that simple, everyone would have caught onto it by now, and its very popularity would eliminate the profits for all those trading by it."

"Not if they had as little money to trade with as I have. I think the market is big enough to absorb a few million people with my account size without anyone noticing. But in any case, it really isn't that simple a system. It is actually quite complex, and I don't think many people would stumble onto it."

"Well *you* did. And you should realize the arguments are even stronger against it if it is a complex system. After all, there is a much larger set of complex systems that could work just by chance over some time period."

"Really." Crandon shook his head and gave a leathery smile. "I never could buy something that involves torque ratios, triple peaked prime resistance levels, and that sort of thing."

Williamson started to speak, but Crandon raised his arm and continued.

"My argument is simply this: Just by luck out of every thousand investors, there will be a few dozen who end up with a favorable track record. There will also be a few dozen who go completely broke. Of course, I never see them. But you can bet the ones who have done much better than average will end up at my door." Crandon paused for a moment and gave a laugh. "And if I put $10 on each system I've seen work in the past, I'd go broke too. I can't go simply on the basis of your past performance. I can always find investors with good *past* performance. I can have our computer run through various technical trading rules and pop out those that had good past performance if I wanted to do that sort of thing. And somebody, just by luck, will have been dealt the royal flush and have great performance for five, or even ten or more years. But I need to look at rules that make sense for the future, that have some chance of beating the market. I'm not an efficient market advocate. I wouldn't be in this business if I were. But I know enough to understand you've got to dig a little deeper than past prices if you are going to find something that works. That much I do know."

He started up from his chair, and leaned over to hand the notebook and bundle of papers back to Williamson.

"I'm sorry Mr. Williamson, that I can't be more positive about your system's potential. But I suppose it all boils down to this. Past prices are free for everyone to look at. If your systems really worked, everyone would be using it already."

Williamson gave a forced smile and a shrug, and left the office. As he closed the door behind him, he looked back and said, "Not if everyone in the market is like you."

WHY SHOULD TECHNICAL SYSTEMS WORK?

When taken within the framework it is presented, the efficient market hypothesis is very persuasive. The assumptions underlying the efficient market hypothesis are that first, there are many rational investors in the market carefully considering all sources of information and trading on any information that gives an extraordinary rate of return. Second, all information is available and is received simultaneously by all investors. The result of this is that no one trader can make money on new information: No sooner does a trader get information and try to trade in anticipation of what that information will mean for the security price than every other trader tries to do the same thing. The end result is that the price moves to the correct level given the new information before anyone can complete their transaction and profit from it.

Since past prices are the most readily available of any information, and certainly are made available simultaneously to all investors, any information content in past prices would be instantaneously inputed into the current price. The end result would then be that the past prices would have no information about the security price. This is the essence of a random walk—there is nothing in the past prices that tells anything about the future price path.

That would seem to pretty much do it for any technical system, then. If a technical system—or any other system—really worked, then everyone would flock to it, and its very success would be its downfall. The profits would be bid away through its popularity.

But the efficient market school itself presents the best refutation of this argument. Like Mr. Crandon, there are many investors who will never be satisfied that a method is really profitable. No reasonable amount of past performance figures will convince them that the extraordinary returns of the past are any more than a statistical fluke. After all, no system turns a huge profit every time, and no system is completely devoid of risks. The science of measuring just what makes an extraordinary return is an inexact one, and gives further room for the skeptic to steer away from apparently profitable systems. And it is not just efficient market people who fall into this category. There are fundamental traders who will never look at a chart no matter how well the chartist at the next desk has been doing, there are chartists who will never look at a balance sheet, and, naturally, there are the index funds manned by those of the efficient market school who will not trade on any information at all.

There is, after all, an element of religion in investing. Beliefs are simply held to as articles of faith, and are not easily displaced. And, as Mr. Crandon illustrates, the structure of the market is such that the skeptic cannot be easily persuaded. It may well be that the rational traders in the market will not flock all that quickly to plug the profit gap of successful systems. A profitable system may be sustained.

But why is there any reason for a rule based on past prices to work in the first place? Why should past prices tell anything about the course of future prices? Well, for one reason or another, many traders have not been convinced by Crandon's arguments, and do trade on past prices. If the demand for buying or selling is based largely on past prices, the resulting price movements necessary to clear the markets will also be based on past prices. That is, the very fact that many traders—in some markets the large majority of speculative traders—trade using past prices will lead the past prices to have an impact on future prices. This is not to say that every rule based on past prices is going to work. Indeed, it may be that no trader can come across a technical trading rule that actually works. There may be a technical rule that works, but that is too complex to discover. And the technical traders themselves will face some of the problems of the more skeptical traders. They will need to convince themselves a profitable rule really is profitable, and not just a one-shot quirk, should they stumble on it. It may be that those who trade on the rule begin to see significant enough profits to suspect they have stumbled onto something, but there is no way they can convince others, or possibly even themselves, that it has been more than a lucky streak. Still, while their "luck" keeps running, they will continue to trade based on the rule; and depending on the complexity and profitability of the rule, they may be the only ones to use it for some time.

Past prices and other market data may also be a key to the course of future prices if there are information flows—that is, if information moves from one group in the market to another group with lags. The best illustration of this is what happens with inside information. As the information goes from the top executives and their acquaintances, to the middle-level executives, to the well-connected analysts, to the market at large, the amount of trading on that information will vary. At first, the information will be known first hand to a small group. That group, because of its small size and the injunctions against insider trading, will have a different impact on the market than the trading that will occur when the information is known to the next group. The next group, however, while larger and less restricted in trading, has the information only second or third hand, which will give a different pattern to the trading they may do. As the information takes its course, a distinctive pattern may emerge in the price movement of the stock—a pattern that may be exploitable before the information is fully discounted by the market.

There is no reason to believe the resulting pattern will be readily detected, or will be so distinctive as to guarantee a profit every time. Indeed, if that were the case, the efficient market argument against technical trading rules would gain in strength.

THE SCIENCE BEHIND THE ART OF TECHNICAL ANALYSIS

Technical analysis is pattern analysis; the technical analyst tries to discern pattern in past prices and other market data that can then be related to a pattern that can be anticipated in future prices. And when it comes to pattern recognition, no computer or mathematical system can beat the human eye. Scientists have difficulty in getting sophisticated computers to see the pattern of well-defined objects we scan across with our every glance. And the problems of pattern detection are far more complex when dealing with stock prices. There the patterns are not well defined, and can vary along any number of dimensions. Take, for example, the simple head and shoulder pattern many chartists look for. The pattern is characterized by three peaks, the middle peak higher than the other two. But the relative heights may vary, there may be some slope to the peaks, one pattern may emerge over a twenty-day period, and another over sixty-five days. It would be very difficult to program a computer to scan prices for head and shoulder patterns, pennants, or resistance levels. To put it into a computer, the pattern must be stated in precise mathematical form, and many stock price patterns are too complex and qualitative to put down precisely.

Thus, we come to think of charting as a fine art. The chartist is regarded as a mystic because what he is doing is too complex for the current tools of science. One might argue the chartist is doing statistical analysis to find recurring patterns, but analysis that cannot yet be parameterized given the mathematical limitations of our current statistical methods.

A number of prominent statisticians have recognized the limitations the mathematical methods place on their analysis. An article in the September 1982 issue of *Science* discusses a computer graphics system developed by statisticians at Stanford and Harvard "to make use of the uniquely human ability to recognize meaningful patterns in . . . data." These statisticians are now *looking* at data rather than crunching the data through routines based on mathematical analysis, and "are seeing patterns in data that would never have been picked up with standard statistical techniques." What is now appearing at the frontiers of statistics has been done by chartists for years.

The technical systems in this section do not include charting. However, I regard charting not as a strange mystical art, but as holding the full picture while the technical trading rules only see a part. A technical trading rule can only capture a part of what is in the data. It is constrained, limited, by its mathematical form. It is not that charting is an art while computer-aided technical systems are a science. It is that these technical systems are a partial approximation of what may potentially be available, but the approximation is necessary because the fuller picture is beyond our present abilities to place in quantifiable form.

TRADING WITH TECHNICAL SYSTEMS

Every technical system in this section has its own set of trading rules and a market environment where it performs the best. However, there are a few underlying rules that apply to every technical system.

1. **Optimize the performance of technical trading strategies.** All but one of the trading methods in this section, the band-width strategy, are well known among technicians. But there still remains considerable variation even among those who use the same trading systems. Every system has a set of parameters that must be set by the trader. For example, the moving average systems require the input of the length of each moving average, and whether one or two moving averages will be used. The trading rules also can vary for some of the systems. The relative strength index, for example, does not have any one universally accepted trading rule associated with it.

   What set of parameters will give the greatest profit? That naturally varies from system to system, but it also varies from commodity to commodity, and will even vary from time to time for any one commodity. The best parameter settings also depend on what the trading objectives are—that is, on what is meant by "greatest profit." There may be some settings that give a higher profit on average, but with greater chance of a larger intertrade drawdown. The "best system" and "greatest profit" can only be determined when the resource base, investment time horizon, and risk preferences of the trader are all taken into account.

   For this reason, I have not been specific about the best parameter values in the systems I discuss. The large number of futures, and the variability in the price behavior in these futures, would doom any attempt at listing the best parameters to failure. But I have actually done better than provide parameter values. I have included the tools to allow the investor to determine the optimal parameter values for himself. Chapter 20 on optimization presents programs for finding the optimal parameters for any particular commodity.

2. **Mix trading systems.** Like the blind men who each feel a different part of an elephant, each trading system focuses in on a different aspect of the

pattern of past prices. If we pit the rigidity of the trading systems against the complexity of the actual price patterns, we will inevitably find times that the system fails; no system can capture everything that is happening in the market. If each system gives only a part of the picture, it seems sensible that combining several systems together will give a more complete picture.

Several systems can indeed be combined either to compliment each other's information, or to give verification of the other's trading signal. One of the best examples of two trading rules that compliment each other's information is to combine the Trend Measurement System with a trend-following rule, such as the volatility or moving average methods. The trend following rules work best when the market is trending, and the Trend Measurement System gives a measure of just how much trend there is in the market. An example of two rules that give verification of one another's trading signals is mixing the moving average and volatility methods. Both the moving average and the volatility rules give signals of trends, but each relies on the data in a different way, each looks at the data from a different perspective. When both of those perspectives signal a trend, there is all the more reason to take a position. And if the two do not agree, there is reason to take the position off.

3. **Diversify to eliminate risk.** The concept of diversification is almost second nature to the portfolio manager. Indeed, the major portion of the portfolio manager's time is devoted to creating a mix of securities that best spreads out risk. The technical trader can also gain from the benefits of diversification. These benefits can accrue in two ways.

First, rather than trading in only one commodity, the trader should apply the system to a number of commodities. The market conditions in one commodity may go against a particular technical system, but if the technical system is a sound one, such circumstances should be the exception rather than the rule. By applying the system in a number of separate markets, the trader puts the Law of Large Numbers on his side, and does not need to worry about the chances that he has happened to trade in the wrong market at the wrong time.

Diversification can also be applied before the technical system is used. Rather than trading a number of commodities and applying the technical system separately to each one, a set of stocks or commodities with similar characteristics can be placed in a portfolio, with the system then applied to the price of the portfolio. The portfolio will not be affected by the commodity or stock-specific variations. Its price movement will be less erratic than the price movement of any of its individual components. The result will be a price series with fewer false starts and less noise. Examples of these portfolios might include holdings across a particular industry, or holdings of a market basket of foreign exchange.

4. **Do not second guess the system.** One of the objectives of technical systems is to create a set of rules that are not subjective, a set of rules that can be followed without the emotions inherent in trading. The technical system should pass or fail on its own merits. If subjective opinion is interspersed with the signals generated by the system, it is impossible to know whether the system has been successful, or whether the human element has tipped the scales.

TECHNICAL PROGRAMS OVERVIEW

The technical programs in this section all look at the world in two dimensions—price and time. There are other rules that include more market data, such as volume, odd-lot trades, or short interest. Certainly adding these other variables cannot reduce the strength of the system, but if, as some technicians would argue, past prices truly are a reflection of other pertinent information in the market, then this other data will be superfluous. (It is interesting that the technical trader and the disciple of efficient markets would both argue that all the information in the market is imbedded in the market price. The principle point of departure for these two radically different views is whether the information is also fully discounted in the *current* price or not.) In any case, the technical systems based on price movements over time are rich enough to provide a fertile ground for profitable trading strategies.

Technical trading rules can be broken down into three types. The first type, and by far the most popular, is the trend-following rule. Trend-following rules are designed to pick the turning point of the market, and the development of major price directional shifts in price movements. They obviously will do the best in periods of wide market movement, and will be unsuccessful in flat markets. The best known trend-following system is the moving average system, but virtually all of the widely used trading systems are trend-following systems.

The second type of trading rule is an antitrend rule. This is a rule that generates buy and sell signals from the sideways vibrations of flat markets. The antitrend rule will do the best in a market devoid of any sizable price movements. Although it can be adapted for use in trending markets, many complications arise in hedging the trades from the directional movements in the market. The third type of trading rule is designed to determine whether the market is in a trending or antitrending mode. The trend movement index system is designed to do this. This system can also be adjusted for use as an antitrend system.

The manifest characteristic of any technical system is an abundance of calculations. These computer programs will allow a level of analysis, comparison, and optimization of technical systems that is practically impossible without the use of a computer.

15
The Moving Average System

Moving averages are the simplest and most popular trend-following systems. Taking a moving average of past prices is an obvious way of smoothing out erratic movements in the past prices, and revealing only the more pronounced trends. As a widely used and long-standing system, moving averages have developed numerous variations. Moving averages may be used singly—or two moving averages, one short and one long, may be tracked against one another. The past prices may be averaged directly, or more sophisticated averaging techniques, such as double smoothing or exponential smoothing may be used. Furthermore, any of a number of past prices may be used in computing the moving average.

By far the most common price to use is the closing price of the day. The closing price is generally considered by technicians to be the "correct" price of the day, and it is the principle price used in calculating trends. However, some technical systems, such as the volatility system, are designed to use the high and the low prices, and the moving average system can be used in this way as well. For example, the average of the high and low price of the day can be used to give intraday smoothing of the moving average. Generally, this will not give stop and reverse signals that differ from those using the closing prices.

THE MOVING AVERAGE CALCULATION

An n-day moving average is simply the average of the closing prices over the past n days. For example, the ten-day moving average calculated for day t will be

$$MA_t(10) = \frac{1}{10} (P_t + P_{t-1} + P_{t-2} + \ldots + P_{t-9}) = \frac{1}{10} \sum_{i=1}^{10} P_{t-i+1}.$$

Each following time period, the price ten days back is eliminated from the moving average calculation, and the current price is added. Moving averages with 5-, 20-, and 100-day lengths are plotted against the underlying Treasury bill contract price in Figures 15-1–15-3. The implication of the moving average calculation that is immediately apparent from these figures is that any one price only has a small effect on the overall average. The moving average will therefore be slower to respond to changes in market conditions than the current price itself. Slight aberrations in the price will also be moderated in the moving average. Only persistent and significant price changes will lead to a significant change in the moving average. The longer term the moving average, the more slowly it will change with changes in the price level.

Because the moving average is slow to react to sudden short-term shifts in prices, it will not give a signal during nondirectional, volatile price vibrations, and will avoid whipsawing during abrupt retracements. However, this feature brings with it sluggishness in reacting to developing trends, and may also lead to small repeated losses in flat markets until a new trend begins. The obvious tradeoff, then, in setting the critical parameter of the moving average length, is between the increased sensitivity to the start of new trends that will come by having a short moving average, and the elimination of false starts that comes with the longer moving averages.

Two variations on the standard moving average calculation deserve mentioning. These are exponentially smoothed moving averages, and doubly smoothed moving averages.

Exponentially Smoothed Moving Averages

Exponential smoothing gives comparatively more weight to the more recent prices in the moving average calculations. The weight given to the less recent prices drops exponentially the further back the prices are. In the standard moving average calculation with n past prices, each price is given a weight of 1/n. With exponential smoothing, the weights decline according to the geometric progression

$$1, a, a^2, a^3, ..., a^n, ...$$

The resulting exponentially smoothed moving average is then

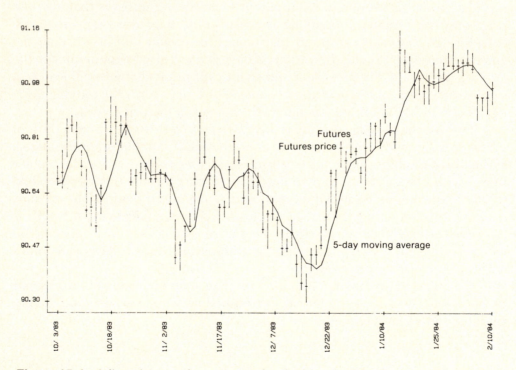

Figure 15-1. A five-day moving average for the March 1984 Treasury bill contract.

$$E_t = \frac{P_t + aP_{t-1} + a^2P_{t-2} + \ldots + a^nP_{t-n} + \ldots}{1 + a + a^2 + \ldots + a^n + \ldots}.$$

The smoothing constant, a, is restriced to be between zero and one, so that it becomes smaller as it is raised to higher powers.

Although this moving average appears to be more complex than the standard moving average, it actually reduces to a very simple form. By applying a lag operator, it can be shown that the exponential moving average can be expressed as

$$E_t = E_{t-1} + a(P_t - E_{t-1}).$$

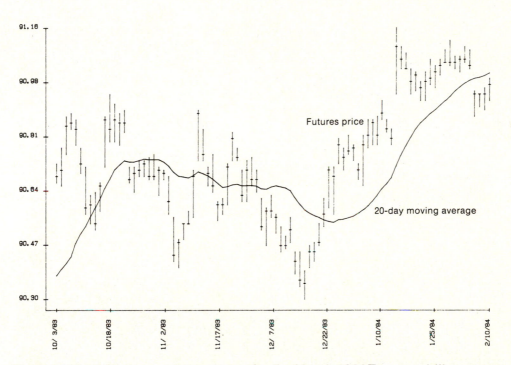

Figure 15-2. A 20-day moving average for the March 1984 Treasury bill contract.

Thus, once the exponential moving average over the first n periods is calculated, the moving average for each successive period can be easily calculated from it by substitution.

Exponential smoothing replaces the number of past periods, n, with a smoothing constant, a. The exponential smoothing is done over all past periods, although obviously the effect of price very far in the past will have a negligible effect on the average. Dropping the value of a has much the same effect as dropping the number of days included in the standard moving average. As a general rule of thumb, an exponentially smoothed moving average with a=.5 is roughly comparable to a standard two-day moving

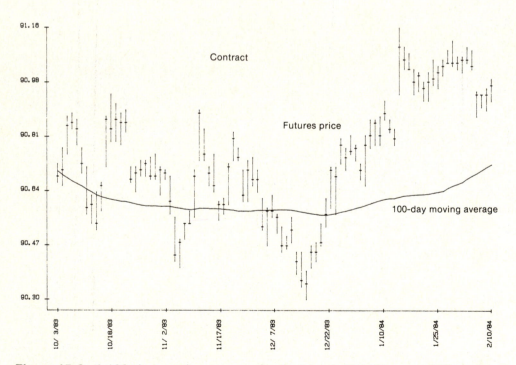

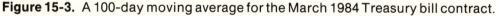

Figure 15-3. A 100-day moving average for the March 1984 Treasury bill contract.

average, one with a=.1 is comparable to a 10-day, and one with a=.05 is comparable to a 20-day standard moving average. Figures 15-4 and 15-5 compare the standard and exponential moving averages. Note that the exponential moving average is slightly slower than its counterpart from the standard moving average, especially at the turning points.

Doubly Smoothed Moving Averages

With double smoothing, the past prices are broken up into subintervals, with each of these being averaged, and then the resulting averages are used in the

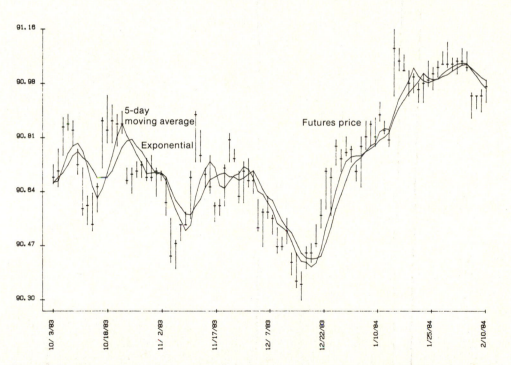

Figure 15-4. A comparison of a five-day moving average and an exponential moving average with a=.2 for the March 1984 Treasury bill contract.

moving average calculation. For example, if we use the high, low, and close of each day, we can combine them into an average of the form

$$P_1 = (H_1 + L_1 + C_1)/3,$$
$$P_2 = (H_2 + L_2 + C_2)/3,$$
$$P_3 = (H_3 + L_3 + C_3)/3, \ldots$$

We then use these averages, P_1, P_2, P_3, … as the prices in the moving average calculation. It should be clear that double smoothing can also be applied to exponential smoothing.

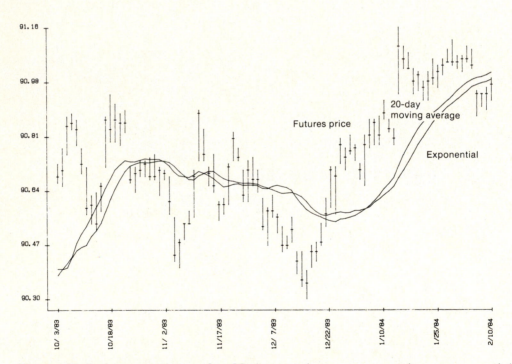

Figure 15-5. A comparison of a 20-day moving average and an exponential moving average with a=.05 for the March 1984 Treasury bill contract.

TRADING WITH THE MOVING AVERAGE SYSTEM

The fact that a change in prices will have a less than one-for-one impact on the moving average assures that a rising trend will rise more quickly than a moving average of that trend, and, similarly, a dropping trend will drop more quickly than a moving average of that trend. That is, the moving average will lag behind the market, causing the moving average to be below the price of a bull market and be above the price in a bear market.

This leads to the basic trading signal for single moving average systems:

- Buy when a rising price crosses above the moving average.
- Sell when a declining price crosses below the moving average.

The price is only considered to have crossed the moving average if the price *closes* across the moving average; intraday movements do not count.

TRADING WITH A TWO-MOVING AVERAGE SYSTEM

When two moving averages are used, the longer moving average is used to trace out the long-term trend, and the shorter moving average is used as a timing device to time when to move long and short in that trend. The shorter moving average may vary in length from a few days to fifteen or twenty days, while the long-term moving average may vary in length from twenty days for the more volatile commodities, to over two hundred days for stocks.

When two moving averages are used, one short and one long, the trading rule is similar to when one moving average is used, but the short-term average acts as a smoothed proxy for the price:

- Buy when the rising short-moving average crosses above the longer moving average.
- Sell when the declining short-moving average crosses below the longer moving average.

As stated, the moving average system is a trend-following stop/reverse system. The moving average system will do well when there is a trend, but will churn small gains and losses if the market is flat. The moving average system is always in the market. The signal shifts from buy to sell and back again as the market price cuts across the moving average line. One way to give added protection against being whipsawed in a flat market is to add stops above and below the crossing point. The trading rules will then become:

- Buy when the rising price crosses and penetrates x points above the moving average.

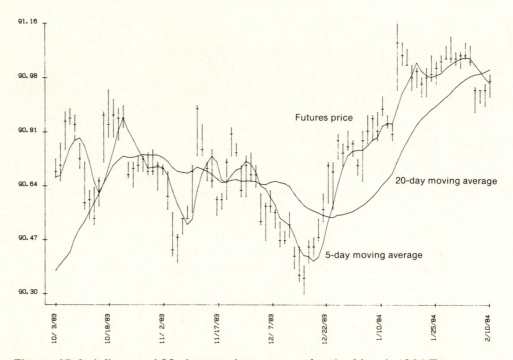

Figure 15-6. A five- and 20-day moving average for the March 1984 Treasury bill contract.

● Sell when the declining price crosses and penetrates x points below the moving average.

The effect of a system with two moving averages is shown in Figures 15-6 and 15-7. Figure 15-6 combines a five- and 20-day moving average, while Figure 15-7 combines a five- and 100-day moving average. Both catch the major trend in mid-December, and the smaller dip at the start of December. The two averages react differently in the volatile market period of October and November. The five- and 20-day average is quicker to call the end of a

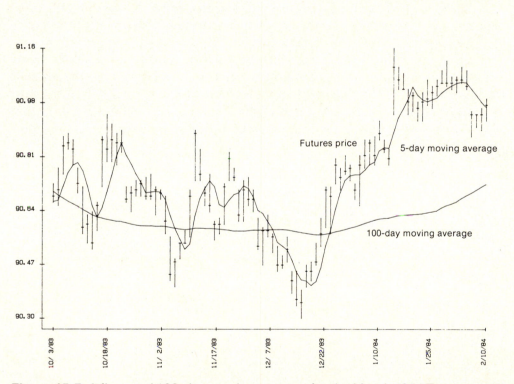

Figure 15-7. A five- and 100-day moving average for the March 1984 Treasury bill contract.

trend. It turns back to a short position in early February, while the five- and 100-day combination remains long.

FINDING THE OPTIMAL MOVING AVERAGE SYSTEM

The most important element in the moving average system is the proper selection of the length of the moving averages. There will always be a set of moving average lengths in the two-average system that will give profits, and there will be a small subset of these profitable values that will do the best. Unfortunately, the optimal moving average length will vary for each commodity, and even within each commodity, it will vary as market conditions change.

Optimization of the moving average length is critical for getting the most success out of the moving average system. This can only be done by simulating trading over past data with various moving average lengths and finding those that have done the best. If the current market conditions, average trend lengths, and volatility of the commodity price are similar to those that existed during the time of the data used in the optimization program, then the best moving average lengths for the past data will also apply to the current trading period. The programs for optimizing the moving average system are presented later in this section.

THE MOVING AVERAGE SYSTEM

Computational Procedure

The N-day moving average for day t is

$$MA_t\,(N) = \frac{1}{N} \sum_{i=1}^{N} P_{t-i+1}$$

where

P_i = closing price of day i.

Trading Strategy

Single moving average system:

- Buy when a rising price crosses above the moving average.
- Sell when a declining price crosses below the moving average.

Double-moving average system:

- Buy when the rising short-moving average crosses above the longer moving average.
- Sell when the declining short-moving average crosses below the longer moving average.

```
10   REM   ********************************************************************
20   REM   *                        MOVING AVERAGE SYSTEM                     *
30   REM   *                                                                  *
40   REM   * THIS PROGRAM APPLIES THE MOVING AVERAGE TRADING SYSTEM FOR TWO   *
50   REM   * MOVING AVERAGES.  IT WILL ALSO DO A SINGLE MOVING AVERAGE IF THE *
60   REM   * SHORT MOVING AVERAGE IS SPECIFIED TO CONTAIN ONLY ONE DAY.       *
70   REM   *                                                                  *
80   REM   *      VARIABLES USED:                                             *
90   REM   *                      CLOS( ) = ARRAY OF DAILY CLOSING PRICES     *
100  REM   *                      ARRY$( ) = ARRAY OF SHORT AND LONG POSITIONS*
110  REM   *                      SMOV( ) = ARRAY OF SHORT MOVING AVERAGE     *
120  REM   *                      LMOV( ) = ARRAY OF LONG MOVING AVERAGE      *
130  REM   *                      JS = STARTING DAY                           *
140  REM   *                      SJ = DAYS IN SHORT MOVING AVERAGE           *
150  REM   *                      LJ = DAYS IN LONG MOVING AVERAGE            *
160  REM   *                      M = NUMBER OF DAYS TYPED IN (DATA)          *
170  REM   *                      TTLPROFIT = TOTAL PROFITS                   *
180  REM   *                      CURPROFIT = CURRENT PROFITS                 *
190  REM   *                      DAYPROFIT = THE DAY PROFITS                 *
200  REM   *                      XLAST = CLOSING PRICE OF PREVIOUS DAY       *
210  REM   *                                                                  *
220  REM   ********************************************************************
230  DIM CLOS(100),ARRY$(100),SMOV(100),LMOV(100)
240  CLS : REM CLEAR SCREEN AND HOME CURSOR
250   JS = 1
260  REM
270  REM   ***************************INPUT********************************
280  REM
290   GOSUB 500
300  REM
310  REM   *********RETRIEVE THE NUMBER OF DAYS FOR THE MOVING AVERAGE**********
320  REM
330   GOSUB 780
340  REM
350  REM   *************COMPUTE THE SHORT AND LONG MOVING AVERAGE***************
360  REM
370   GOSUB 900
380  REM
390  REM   *****************COMBINE THE TWO MOVING AVERAGES********************
400  REM
410   GOSUB 1020
420  REM
430  REM   *****************COMPUTE AND PRINT THE RESULTS*********************
440  REM
450   GOSUB 1120
460  REM
470  REM
480  REM
490  REM
500  REM   ********************************************************************
510  REM   *                     SUBROUTINE TO ENTER DATA                     *
520  REM   ********************************************************************
530  CLS : REM CLEARS SCREEN AND HOMES CURSOR
540  I = 1 : REM INITIALIZE COUNTER FOR DATA ENTRY
```

```
550 PRINT "ENTER `999' AS CLOSING PRICE TO END DATA ENTRY"
560 PRINT "ENTER CLOSING PRICE FOR DAY";I; : INPUT CLOS(I)
570  IF CLOS(I) = 999 THEN GOTO 600
580  I = I + 1
590  GOTO 560
600  I = I - 1 : REM DECREMENTS COUNTER ON LAST ENTRY
610  LASTDAY = I :M = I
620  START = 1
630  CLS : REM CLEARS SCREEN AND HOMES CURSOR
640 PRINT " DAY        CLOSING PRICE"
650 PRINT " ---        -------------"
660  FOR I = START TO START + 19
670 PRINT TAB(2)I;TAB(15)CLOS(I)
680   IF I = LASTDAY THEN GOTO 700
690  NEXT I
700  INPUT "ENTER DAY TO CHANGE OR `0' TO CONTINUE";DAY
710  IF DAY = 0 AND I < LASTDAY THEN START = I : GOTO 630
720  IF DAY = 0 THEN GOTO 760
730 PRINT "THE CLOSING PRICE FOR DAY";DAY;" IS";CLOS(DAY);
740  INPUT "NEW PRICE";CLOS(DAY)
750  GOTO 630
760 INPUT "HOW MANY DAYS IN THE SHORT MOVING AVERAGE";SJ
770 INPUT "HOW MANY DAYS IN THE LONG MOVING AVERAGE";LJ
780 REM ******************************************************************
790 REM *            SUBROUTINE TO COMPUTE SHORT MOVING AVERAGE         *
800 REM ******************************************************************
810  SUM = 0
820  FOR I = 1 TO SJ
830   SUM = SUM + CLOS(I)
840   SMOV(I) = 0
850  NEXT I
860  SMOV(SJ) = SUM/SJ
870  FOR I = SJ + 1 TO M
880   SMOV(I) = (SMOV(I-1) * SJ - CLOS(I-SJ) + CLOS(I)) / SJ
890  NEXT I
900 REM ******************************************************************
910 REM *            SUBROUTINE TO COMPUTE LONG MOVING AVERAGE          *
920 REM ******************************************************************
930  SUM = 0
940  FOR I = 1 TO LJ
950   SUM = SUM + CLOS(I)
960   LMOV(I) = 0
970  NEXT I
980  LMOV(LJ) = SUM/LJ
990  FOR I = LJ + 1 TO M
1000   LMOV(I) = (LMOV(I-1) * LJ - CLOS(I-LJ) + CLOS(I)) / LJ
1010  NEXT I
1020 REM ******************************************************************
1030 REM *            SUBROUTINE TO COMBINE THE TWO MOVING AVERAGES      *
1040 REM ******************************************************************
1050  SL$ = " "
1060  FOR I = 1 TO M
1070   ARRY$(I) = " "
1080    IF SMOV(I) = 0 OR LMOV(I) = 0 THEN GOTO 1110
```

```
1090    IF SMOV(I) > LMOV(I) AND SL$ <> "L" THEN SL$ = "L":ARRY$(I) = "L"
1100    IF SMOV(I) < LMOV(I) AND SL$ <> "S" THEN SL$ = "S":ARRY$(I) = "S"
1110   NEXT I
1120  REM ****************************************************************
1130  REM *            SUBROUTINE TO COMPUTE PROFITS AND DISPLAY RESULTS        *
1140  REM ****************************************************************
1150   CLS : REM CLEARS SCREEN AND HOMES CURSOR
1160  PRINT "  DAY     PRICE        AVE 1        AVE 2        POSITION    PROFIT"
1170  PRINT "  ---    ----------   ----------   ----------   --------   ----------"
1180    SL$ = " "
1190    TTLPROFIT = 0
1200    XLAST = CLOS(1)
1210    CURPROFIT = 0
1220    DAYPROFIT = 0
1230    FOR I = 1 TO M
1240      PROFIT = 0
1250      IF ARRY$(I) <> " " THEN GOTO 1270
1260      GOTO 1310
1270      IF SL$ = "S" THEN PROFIT = XLAST - CLOS(I)
1280      IF SL$ = "L" THEN PROFIT = CLOS(I) - XLAST
1290      XLAST = CLOS(I)
1300      SL$ = ARRY$(I)
1310      IF SL$ = "S" THEN CURPROFIT = XLAST - CLOS(I)
1320      IF SL$ = "L" THEN CURPROFIT = CLOS(I) - XLAST
1330      TTLPROFIT = TTLPROFIT + PROFIT
1340      DAYPROFIT = TTLPROFIT + CURPROFIT
1350      SMOV(I) = INT(SMOV(I) * 100)/100
1360      LMOV(I) = INT(LMOV(I) * 100)/100
1370  PRINT TAB(3)I;TAB(9)CLOS(I);TAB(21)SMOV(I);TAB(33)LMOV(I);TAB(48)ARRY$(I);
1380  PRINT TAB(57)DAYPROFIT
1390    NEXT I
1400  PRINT
1410    TTLPROFIT = TTLPROFIT + CURPROFIT
1420  PRINT TAB(30) "TOTAL PROFIT IS";TTLPROFIT
1430  REM
1440  REM  WILL ALLOW THE USER TO REPEAT THE PROGRAM WITH NEW PARAMETERS
1450  REM
1460  PRINT
1470  INPUT "WOULD YOU LIKE TO REPEAT THE PROCESS";AN$
1480    IF AN$ = "Y" THEN GOTO 760
1490  END
```

16

The Parabolic System:
A Variation on
Moving Averages

Like the moving average system discussed in Chapter 15, the parabolic system develops trading signals by taking a smoothed average of past prices. The essential difference between the moving average and parabolic system is the averaging technique used. The parabolic system takes a particular *weighted* average of past prices, rather than a simple moving average. The weighting scheme of the parabolic system is designed to adjust the trading stop as a function both of the direction of price movement and of the time over which the movement takes place. The stop moves slowly at first, and accelerates once the trend has become established. This adjustment method is ideal in markets characterized by large trends coupled with periods of sideways movement. The adjustment of the stops is intended to let the parabolic system ride the trends, while holding the stop back during short-term swings in price.

The stop in the parabolic system is a weighted average of the market price at the time the trading position is initiated and the sum of the market prices after the position is initiated. Denoting the market price at the initiation of the position by P_o, and the price i days after the initiation of the position by P_i, the stop for day t will be

$$S_t = (1-A)P_o + A \sum_{i=1}^{N} P_{t-i}.$$

The parameter A which determines the weight between the two price measures is called the *acceleration factor*. It will dictate how quickly the stop starts to move with a market upswing or downswing. The acceleration factor is always between 0 and 1. The lower A is set, the more gradual the stop will adjust. If A is set at 0, the stop will remain at P_0, while if it is set at 1, it will move up one-for-one with the market price. Generally, the acceleration factor is kept fairly low, between .01 and .2. The lower the acceleration factor, the more protection there is from reversals, while the higher the acceleration factor, the more profit will be captured from trends.

Figures 16-1 and 16-2 trace the parabolic system for cocoa and Deutsch

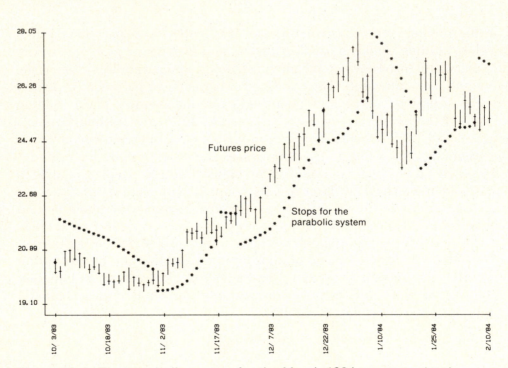

Figure 16-1. The parabolic system for the March 1984 cocoa contract.

Mark futures, respectively. The gradual acceleration of the stop forms a smooth parabolic curve; hence, the name of the system.

The trading rule for the parabolic system is quite simple:

- Buy when the price moves above the stop.
- Sell when the price moves below the stop.

Like the moving average system, the parabolic system as stated here is a stop/reverse system, which means the trader is never out of the market; the position is always either long or short, and a passage through the stop reverses

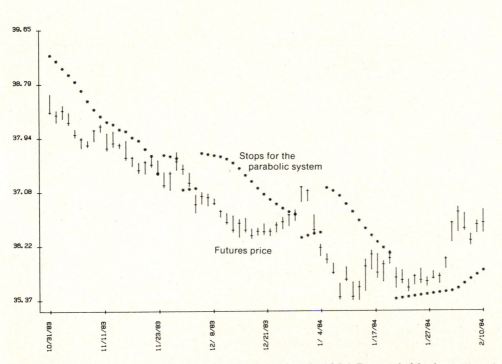

Figure 16-2. The parabolic system for the March 1984 Deutsch Mark contract.

the position. Obviously, this leads to repeated small losses if the market fails to establish a trend. The parabolic system, and for that matter, the other stop/ reverse systems, can be adapted to put the investor in or out of the market depending on the strength of the buy and sell signals.

A number of prices can be used for the parabolic system. The most simple method is to use the closing prices. A slightly more sophisticated variation of the system uses the high and low prices of the day; for a long position, the high of the day is used, for a short position, the low of the day is used. If the stop is based on the closing price, the position needs to be evaluated using the opening price of the next day. It is also wise to set a minimum distance between the stop and the current market price, even when the calculation for the stop brings it closer. The ideal minimum distance for the stop should be determined with a view towards the volatility or sideways potential in the market. The trend measurement system in Chapter 19 can be helpful for this.

THE PARABOLIC SYSTEM

Computational Procedure

The stop for day t using an N-day parabolic system is

$$S_t(N) = (1-A)P_o + A \sum_{i=1}^{N} P_{t-i},$$

where
A = acceleration factor
P_o = price at the time the position is initiated
P_i = price i days after the position is initiated at date t.

Trading Strategy

- Buy when the price moves above the stop $S_t(N)$.
- Sell when the price moves below the stop $S_t(N)$.

```
10   REM   *******************************************************************
20   REM   *                     PARABOLIC TRADING SYSTEM                    *
30   REM   *                                                                 *
40   REM   * THIS PROGRAM APPLIES THE PARABOLIC TRADING SYSTEM TO HIGH, LOW, *
50   REM   * AND CLOSING PRICES, OR TO CLOSING PRICES, AT THE USER'S OPTION. *
60   REM   * THE PROGRAM ALSO CALCULATES AND DISPLAYS THE TRADING POSITION   *
70   REM   * AND THE PROFITS AND LOSSES.                                     *
80   REM   *                                                                 *
90   REM   *        VARIABLES USED: HIG( ) = ARRAY OF DAILY HIGH PRICES      *
100  REM   *                        LOW( ) = ARRAY OF DAILY LOW PRICES       *
110  REM   *                       CLOS( ) = ARRAY OF DAILY CLOSING PRICES   *
120  REM   *                      ARRY$( ) = ARRAY OF SHORT OR LONG POSITIONS*
130  REM   *                        STP( ) = ARRAY OF DAILY STOPS            *
140  REM   *                             M = NUMBER OF OBSERVATIONS IN THE DATA *
150  REM   *                            AF = ACCELERATING FACTOR FOR THE CONSTANT *
160  REM   *                        ALIMIT = CEILING LIMIT FOR THE CONSTANT  *
170  REM   *                           SL$ = SHORT OR LONG SIGNALS           *
180  REM   *                      TTLPROFIT = TOTAL PROFITS                  *
190  REM   *                      CURPROFIT = CURRENT PROFITS                *
200  REM   *                      DAYPROFIT = THE DAY PROFIT                 *
210  REM   *                          XLAST = CLOSING PRICE OF PREVIOUS DAY  *
220  REM   *                                                                 *
230  REM   *******************************************************************
240   DIM HIG(100),LOW(100),CLOS(100),STP(100),ARRY$(100)
250    JS = 1
260  REM
270  REM   **************************INPUT THE DATA************************
280   GOSUB 400
290  REM
300  REM   *****IF ONLY THE CLOSING PRICE IS GIVEN, FIND THE HIGH AND LOW*******
310   GOSUB 1050
320  REM
330  REM   ***************RUN THE PARABOLIC SYSTEM*************************
340   GOSUB 1200
350  REM
360  REM   **********PRINT THE RESULTS, STOPS, POSITIONS, AND PROFIT**********
370   GOSUB 1770
380  REM
390  REM   ****************************************************************
400  REM   *                 SUBROUTINE TO INPUT DATA                     *
410  REM   ****************************************************************
420    CLS : REM CLEAR SCREEN AND HOME CURSOR
430  PRINT "ARE YOU GOING TO TYPE IN:"
440  PRINT "1) THE HIGH, LOW, AND CLOSING PRICES"
450  PRINT "2) OR ONLY THE CLOSING PRICES"
460  INPUT ISERIES
470    ON ISERIES GOTO 490,820
480    GOTO 390
490    CLS : REM CLEAR SCREEN AND HOME CURSOR
500    I = 1
510  PRINT "ENTER HIGH  PRICE FOR DAY #";I; : INPUT HIG(I)
520    IF HIG(I) = 999 THEN GOTO 610
530  PRINT "ENTER LOW   PRICE FOR DAY #";I; : INPUT LOW(I)
540    IF LOW(I) = 999 THEN GOTO 610
```

```
550 PRINT "ENTER CLOSE PRICE FOR DAY #";I; : INPUT CLOS(I)
560  IF CLOS(I) = 999 THEN GOTO 610
570 PRINT : REM PRINTS BLANK LINE BETWEEN DAYS
580  IF ED = 1 THEN ED = 0 : RETURN
590  I = I + 1 : REM INCREMENT DAY COUNTER
600  GOTO 510
610  I = I - 1 : LASTDAY = I : M=I : START = 1
620  CLS : REM CLEAR SCREEN AND HOME CURSOR
630 PRINT "DAY       HIGH       LOW       CLOSE"
640 PRINT "---       --------   --------  --------"
650  FOR I = START TO START + 19
660 PRINT TAB(1)I;TAB(9)HIG(I);TAB(19)LOW(I);TAB(29)CLOS(I)
670   IF I = LASTDAY THEN GOTO 690
680  NEXT I
690 INPUT "ENTER DAY TO CHANGE OR `0' TO CONTINUE";DAY
700  IF DAY = 0 AND I < LASTDAY THEN START = I : GOTO 620
710  IF DAY = 0 THEN RETURN
720  I = DAY
730 PRINT "CURRENT VALUES ARE:"
740 PRINT "DAY       HIGH       LOW       CLOSE"
750 PRINT "---       --------   --------  --------"
760 PRINT TAB(1)DAY;TAB(9)HIG(I);TAB(19)LOW(I);TAB(29)CLOS(I)
770 PRINT "ENTER NEW DATA:"
780 PRINT : REM SEPARATE WORDS ON SCREEN
790  ED = 1 : REM GO INTO EDIT MODE
800  GOSUB 510
810  GOTO 620
820 REM **************** LOAD DATA FOR CLOSING PRICE ONLY *****************
830  CLS : REM CLEAR SCREEN AND HOME CURSOR
840  I = 1 : REM INITIALIZE DAY COUNTER
850 PRINT "ENTER `999' AS CLOSING PRICE TO END DATA ENTRY"
860 PRINT "ENTER CLOSING PRICE FOR DAY";I; : INPUT CLOS(I)
870  IF CLOS(I) = 999 THEN GOTO 900
880  I = I + 1
890  GOTO 860
900  I = I - 1: LASTDAY = I : M = I : START = 1
910  CLS : REM CLEAR SCREEN AND HOME CURSOR
920 PRINT " DAY       CLOSING PRICE"
930 PRINT " ---       -------------"
940  FOR I = START TO START + 19
950 PRINT TAB(2)I;TAB(15)CLOS(I)
960   IF I = LASTDAY THEN GOTO 980
970  NEXT I
980 INPUT "ENTER DAY TO CHANGE OR `0' TO CONTINUE";DAY
990  IF DAY = 0 AND I < LASTDAY THEN START = I : GOTO 910
1000  IF DAY = 0 THEN RETURN
1010 PRINT "THE CLOSING PRICE FOR DAY";DAY;" IS";CLOS(DAY);
1020 INPUT "NEW PRICE";CLOS(DAY)
1030  GOTO 910
1040 REM *******************************************************************
1050 REM *         SUBROUTINE TO FIND HIGH AND LOW LOOKING BACK `X' DAYS       *
1060 REM *******************************************************************
1070  IF ISERIES <> 2 THEN GOTO 320
1080 INPUT "HOW MANY DAYS IN THE BACKWARD LOOK";JS
```

```
1090  FOR I = JS TO M
1100   XLOW = 9999 : XHIG = -9999
1110   FOR K = I - JS + 1 TO I
1120    IF XLOW > CLOS(K) THEN XLOW = CLOS(K)
1130    IF XHIG < CLOS(K) THEN XHIG = CLOS(K)
1140   NEXT K
1150   LOW(I) = XLOW
1160   HIG(I) = XHIG
1170  NEXT I
1180  RETURN
1190 REM ***************************************************************
1200 REM *              SUBROUTINE TO RUN THE PARABOLIC SYSTEM         *
1210 REM ***************************************************************
1220 INPUT "WHAT IS THE INCREMENT FOR THE STEP SIZE";AF
1230 INPUT "WHAT IS THE LIMIT FOR THE STEP SIZE";ALIMIT
1240   ITIME = 0
1250   ARRY$(1) = " "
1260   ARRY$(2) = " "
1270   SL$ = "L"
1280   LSIP = LOW(1)
1290   EP = LOW(1)
1300   STP(2) = LOW(1)
1310   SSIP = HIG(1)
1320   C = 0
1330   IF CLOS(1) <= CLOS (2) THEN GOTO 1370
1340   SL$ = "S"
1350   EP = HIG(1)
1360   STP(2) = HIG(1)
1370   FOR I = 3 TO M
1380    ITIME = ITIME + 1
1390    ARRY$(I) = " "
1400    IF C = 0 THEN STP(I) = EP : GOTO 1420
1410    STP(I) = STP(I-1) + C * (EP - STP(I-1))
1420    C = C + AF
1430    IF C > ALIMIT THEN C = ALIMIT
1440    IF SL$ <> "L" THEN GOTO 1570
1450    IF STP(I) > LOW(I-1) OR STP(I) > LOW(I-2) AND ITIME <> 1 THEN GOTO 1470
1460    GOTO 1490
1470    IF LOW(I-1) < LOW(I-2) THEN STP(I) = LOW(I-1) : GOTO 1490
1480    STP(I) = LOW(I-2)
1490    IF STP(I) <= LOW(I) THEN GOTO 1570
1500    SL$ = "S"
1510    ARRY$(I) = "S"
1520    SSIP = LOW(I)
1530    EP = LSIP
1540    C = 0
1550    ITIME = 0
1560    GOTO 1740
1570    IF SL$ <> "S" THEN GOTO 1700
1580    IF STP(I) < HIG(I-1) OR STP(I) < HIG(I-2) AND ITIME <> 1 THEN GOTO 1600
1590    GOTO 1620
1600    IF HIG(I-1) > HIG(I-2) THEN STP(I) = HIG(I-1) : GOTO 1620
1610    STP(I) = HIG(I-2)
1620    IF STP(I) >= HIG(I) THEN GOTO 1700
```

```
1630    SL$ = "L"
1640    ARRY$(I) = "L"
1650    LSIP = HIG(I)
1660    EP = SSIP
1670    C = 0
1680    ITIME = 0
1690    GOTO 1740
1700    IF SSIP > LOW(I) AND SL$ = "S" THEN SSIP = LOW(I)
1710    IF LSIP < HIG(I) AND SL$ = "L" THEN LSIP = HIG(I)
1720    IF SL$ = "S" THEN EP = SSIP
1730    IF SL$ = "L" THEN EP = LSIP
1740    NEXT I
1750    RETURN
1760 REM ********************************************************************
1770 REM *         SUBROUTINE TO PRINT RESULTS, STOPS, POS, AND PROFITS        *
1780 REM ********************************************************************
1790    CLS : REM CLEAR SCREEN AND HOME CURSOR
1800 PRINT "DAY     HIGH       LOW        CLOSE      STOP       POSITION  PROFIT"
1810 PRINT "---     --------   --------   --------   --------   --------  ---------"
1820    SL$ = " "
1830    TTLPROFIT = 0  : CURPROFIT = 0  : DAYPROFIT = 0
1840    XLAST = CLOS(1)
1850    FOR I = 1 TO M
1860      PROFIT = 0
1870      IF ARRY$(I) = " " THEN GOTO 1920
1880      IF SL$ = "S" THEN PROFIT = XLAST - CLOS(I)
1890      IF SL$ = "L" THEN PROFIT = CLOS(I) - XLAST
1900      XLAST = CLOS(I)
1910      SL$ = ARRY$(I)
1920      IF SL$ = "S" THEN CURPROFIT = XLAST - CLOS(I)
1930      IF SL$ = "L" THEN CURPROFIT = CLOS(I) - XLAST
1940      TTLPROFIT = TTLPROFIT + PROFIT
1950      DAYPROFIT = TTLPROFIT + CURPROFIT
1960      IF I < JS THEN GOTO 2010
1970      DAYPROFIT = INT(DAYPROFIT * 100 + .001)/100
1980      STP(I) = INT(STP(I) * 100 + .5)/100
1990      PRINT TAB(1)I;TAB(6)HIG(I);TAB(16)LOW(I);TAB(26)CLOS(I);TAB(36)STP(I);
2000      PRINT TAB(49)ARRY$(I);TAB(56)DAYPROFIT
2010    NEXT I
2020    TTLPROFIT = TTLPROFIT + CURPROFIT
2030 PRINT
2040 PRINT TAB(30) "TOTAL PROFIT";TTLPROFIT
2050 INPUT "WOULD YOU LIKE TO REPEAT THIS PROCESS";AN$
2060   IF AN$ = "Y" THEN GOTO 330
2070 END
```

17
The Volatility System

One of the greatest difficulties with trend-following systems is their inability to distinguish between the start of a trend and the sideways movement of a flat but volatile market. If a trend-following system is fine tuned to react quickly to any indications of a trend, then it will have frequent losses in a flat market, especially if the futures prices are choppy. The system simply cannot discriminate between short up and down movements and the start of a trend.

There is a way around the whipsawing that will occur with a trend-following system in these markets—to simply wait until the price level has moved more than is typical for a sideways movement before taking a position in the market. For example, with the moving average system, this can be accomplished by increasing the length of the moving average, or using a short-term moving average in place of the daily market price. With the parabolic system, this is done by keeping the stop away from the price until the trend is established, thereby allowing for some breathing room for small, short-term price reversals.

The problem with using these techniques is that they keep you from getting into the market at the start of the price swing. Part of the profit is lost while the system decides whether the movement really is a trend. In fact, if the parameters of these trend-following systems are not selected properly, the system may not get you in until the trend is more than halfway established, and may not close you out until the price has more than halfway recovered again.

The volatility system is designed specifically to adjust for this sort of sideways variability. The more choppy the market becomes, the further the stop in the volatility system moves from the price.

THE MEASUREMENT OF VOLATILITY

The concept of volatility we are interested in has to do with the amount the futures price might move up or down without that movement indicating a shift in the direction of the price (i.e., without that movement indicating the start of a new trend). We might think of the volatility as the noise inherent in the futures price. A noisy price will be likely to move erratically about the trend. For example, an upward price movement in a volatile market might be marked by sudden, brief declines and retracements.

Ideally, the volatility measure we use should measure the variance of price movements *around the trend.* That is, a commodity with smooth and distinct trends, where the daily price change during up trends is always up, and during down trends is always down, would not be considered a volatile commodity for our purposes here. Indeed, this sort of commodity would be ideal for trend-following systems. There would be no erratic movements in the price that could be mistaken for a trend. Any price shift could be followed from the outset, with the next change in the direction of the price being an unambiguous signal that the trend was at an end. There would be no risk of mistaking a brief dip in the price for the start of a downward trend, and there would be no risk of missing a trend by mistaking it for a temporary retracement.

Unfortunately, it is difficult to distinguish between trends and choppy price movements in making volatility calculations. It is difficult to find a satisfactory definition of a trend that will be agreed upon by all traders in all markets. In many cases, two traders may disagree whether a price movement is a trend or a short-term movement. We will therefore use volatility measures that consider the extent of variability of the futures price without regard to whether that price is part of trend or noise.

The most obvious volatility measure is the standard deviation of price movements. Volatility is measured in this way in the option pricing methods discussed in Chapter 27. The standard deviation looks at the variation in the price around the average or mean price. If we denote the average price by $\overline{P}$, then the standard deviation of the price is estimated by first taking the square of the difference between $\overline{P}$ and each of the daily prices to get the variance of the price,

$$\sigma^2 = \frac{1}{n-1} \sum_{i=1}^{N} (P_i - \overline{P})^2$$

and then taking the square root of this. The resulting standard deviation is denoted by σ. (The difference between the prices is squared because we do not care whether the daily price is less than or greater than the average price, only the distance it is from the price. By squaring the difference, we get a positive number no matter whether the difference is positive or negative.)

The standard deviation can be used to tell how likely the price is to move around its average. An alternative measure of volatility is to look at how likely prices are to move without regard to the average price. To do this, we measure the *total* distance prices have moved rather than the distance they have moved around their average value. This is most effectively done on an intraday basis by measuring the absolute value of the difference between the high and low price. (If the price gaps up or down, then the greater of the difference between yesterday's close and today's high or the distance between yesterday's close and today's low is used rather than the difference between today's high and low.) These prices can then be averaged over a number of days to get a value for the average distance of price movements. For example, denoting the high for day i by H_i, and the low by L_i, the N-day volatility will be

$$V(N) = \frac{1}{N} \sum_{i=1}^{N} |H_i - L_i|$$

This volatility index has several attractive features that make it superior to the standard deviation in developing a volatility trading system.

First, the calculation does not require the specification of the average price level. Since the average price level may vary wildly depending on the length of the average and on the market behavior over the recent past, eliminating the average price level from the calculation also eliminates a major potential source of error.

Second, and more importantly, measuring the volatility as the average total distance of price movements rather than as the average distance of price movements around the mean goes partially toward the ideal volatility measure which does not include trend movements in the volatility estimate.

This point is illustrated in Figure 17-1. Price profile A is marked by a very distinct trend, and almost no price variability around the trend. As just discussed, such price behavior would not be regarded as volatility, because it is unlikely that the trends will be confused with choppy sideways price movements. Price profile B depicts prices that combine occasional trends with very erratic sideways movement. It would be far easier to confuse the start of trends with short-term sideways vibrations in markets with this sort of price movement. We would regard price profile B as being more volatile than A from a technical trading standpoint. Yet the standard deviation of A is higher than B. This is so because the peaks and troughs of the trends in A are so far from the average price level. The volatility index V(N) only looks at the distance the prices travel, without regard for how far their travels take them from the mean. It will therefore give less weight to trends than the standard deviation will, and it will show B to be more volatile than A.

TRADING WITH THE VOLATILITY SYSTEM

The volatility system is a trend-following, reversal system. That is, it develops stops based on the likelihood a price movement is a trend, and it is always in the market, reversing from short to long and back as the price moves through the stop.

The stop is set a distance from the daily price that is proportional to the volatility index. The volatility index is multiplied by a parameter K, (called the volatility constant), and the stop is placed that distance from the current day's price. If the current position is long in the futures, then the stop is set below the current price; if the current position is short in the futures, then the stop is set above the current price.

The trading rule for this system is:

- Go short if the close drops more than $K^*V(N)$ from the previous close.
- Go long if the close rises more than $K^*V(N)$ from the previous close.

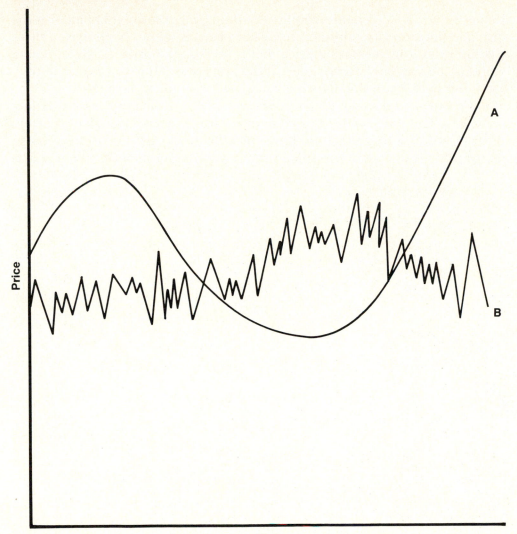

Figure 17-1. A comparison of volatility for two types of price movements. The price movement A is far more regular than B and has more distinct trends. However, in terms of its variance, it is more volatile than B. This suggests that for trend-following systems, another measure of volatility is needed to describe the noisiness of the price movement.

In these rules, K*V(N), the volatility constant times the volatility index is the distance the stop is established from the previous close. Note that in these trading rules it is the closing price that is used as the price for determining whether the stop has been violated. If the price passes the stop during the day but is not past the stop at the close, the position is not reversed.

Figures 17-2 through 17-4 trace the volatility system for several volatility constants. The stop has the desired effect of hovering far enough away from the price to avoid the false starts during the sideways markets. The stop has the undesirable property of dropping further away from the price when a dra-

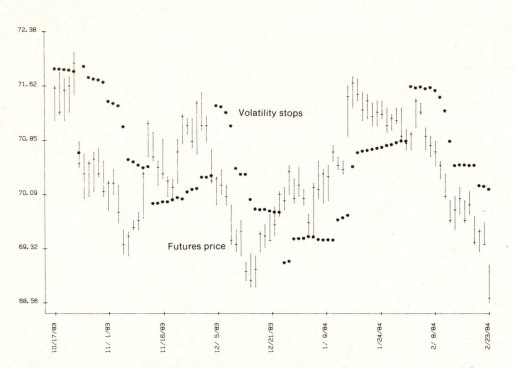

Figure 17-2. The volatility system for the March 1984 Treasury bond futures contract. The volatility constant is 2.0.

matic trend is underway. This is because the volatility index cannot fully distinguish the price movement of a trend from nondirectional volatility. However, as has already been shown, this effect is less pronouned with the volatility index than it would be if the variance or standard deviation is used as the volatility measure.

These figures make it clear that the critical parameter for this system is the volatility constant. If it is not properly selected, the stop will be too far from the price to signal the start of a trend, or will be so close to the price that it has false starts during periods of erratic, flat prices. The volatility constant will

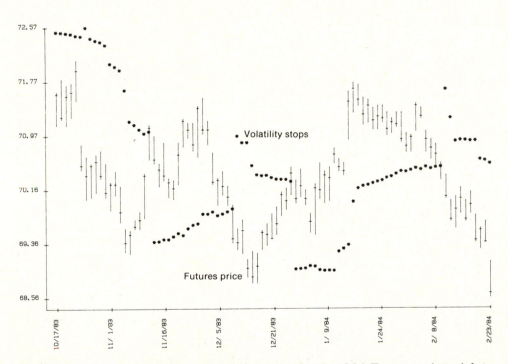

Figure 17-3. The volatility system for the March 1984 Treasury bond futures contract. The volatility constant is 3.0.

generally have a value near 3.0, but as with the other technical systems, the optimal value should be determined from simulation studies. The program for doing this is presented in the chapter on optimization. The volatility system is not as sensitive to the specification of the number of days used in the average for the volatility index as it is to the specification for the volatility constant. Generally, an average over the last one to three weeks is used.

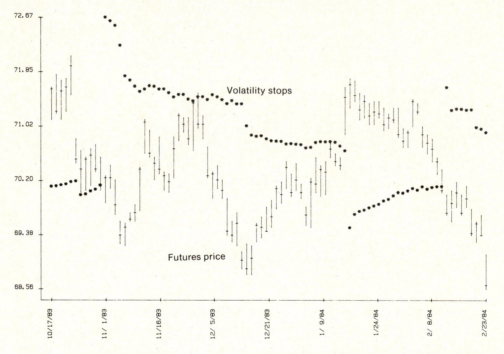

Figure 17-4. The volatility system for the March 1984 Treasury bond futures contract. The volatility constant is 4.0.

VOLATILITY SYSTEM

Computational Procedure

The N-day volatility for day t is measured as

$$V_t(N) = \frac{1}{N} \sum_{i=1}^{N} D_{t-i+1} ,$$

where D_i is the maximum of

    a. $| H_i - C_{i-1} |$
    b. $\ \ H_i - L_i$
    c. $| L_i - C_{i-1} |$

where

    H_i = high for day i
    C_i = close for day i
    L_i = low for day i

Trading Strategy

- Sell if the close drops more than $K^*V(N)$ from the previous close.
- Buy if the close rises more than $K^*V(N)$ from the previous close.

K is the volatility constant, and will generally take on values near 3.0.

```
 10   REM   *******************************************************************
 20   REM   *                    TECHNICAL VOLATILITY PROGRAM                 *
 30   REM   *                                                                 *
 40   REM   *     THIS PROGRAM APPLIES THE VOLATILITY TRADING SYSTEM TO HIGH,  *
 50   REM   *   LOW, AND CLOSING PRICES OR TO CLOSING PRICES ONLY.   IT        *
 60   REM   *   COMPUTES AND DISPLAYS THE TRADING POSITION AND THE PROFITS     *
 70   REM   *   AND LOSSES.                                                    *
 80   REM   *                                                                 *
 90   REM   *      VARIABLES USED: HIG( ) = ARRAY OF DAILY HIGH PRICES         *
100   REM   *                      LOW( ) = ARRAY OF DAILY LOW PRICES          *
110   REM   *                     CLOS( ) = ARRAY OF DAILY CLOSING PRICES      *
120   REM   *                    ARRY$( ) = ARRAY OF SHORT OR LONG POSITIONS   *
130   REM   *                      STP( ) = ARRAY OF DAILY STOPS               *
140   REM   *                          M = NUMBER OF OBSERVATIONS IN THE DATA  *
150   REM   *                   T1,T2,TR = VARIATIONS OF THE TRUE RANGE        *
160   REM   *                       AVTR = AVERAGE TRUE RANGE FOR `X' DAYS     *
170   REM   *                          C = CONSTANT                           *
180   REM   *                        AVC = AVERAGE RANGE TIMES THE CONSTANT    *
190   REM   *                        SIC = SIGNIFICANT CLOSE                   *
200   REM   *                        SL$ = SHORT OR LONG SIGNALS               *
210   REM   *                   TTLPROFIT = TOTAL PROFITS                      *
220   REM   *                   CURPROFIT = CURRENT PROFITS                    *
230   REM   *                   DAYPROFIT = THE PROFIT TO DATE                 *
240   REM   *                       XLAST = CLOSING PRICE OF PREVIOUS DAY      *
250   REM   *                                                                 *
260   REM   *******************************************************************
270   DIM HIG(100),LOW(100),CLOS(100),STP(100),ARRY$(100)
280   JS = 1
290   REM
300   REM   *****************************INPUT*********************************
310   REM
320    GOSUB 540
330   REM
340   REM   *****IF ONLY THE CLOSING PRICE IS GIVEN, FIND THE HIGH AND LOW ******
350   REM
360    GOSUB 1280
370   REM
380   REM   ************GET PARAMETERS FOR VOLATILITY SYSTEM*******************
390   REM
400   REM
410   REM   ********************RUN THE VOLATILITY SYSTEM*********************
420   REM
430    GOSUB 1430
440   REM
450   REM   ***********PRINTS THE RESULTS, STOPS, POSITIONS, AND PROFIT**********
460   REM
470    GOSUB 1930
480   REM
490   REM   *********WILL ALLOW USER TO REPEAT PROCESS WITH NEW PARAMETERS*******
500   REM
510   REM
520   REM
530   REM
540   REM   *******************************************************************
```

```
550 REM *                    SUBROUTINE TO INPUT DATA                      *
560 REM *****************************************************************
570  CLS : REM CLEAR SCREEN AND HOME CURSOR
580 PRINT "ARE YOU GOING TO TYPE IN:"
590 PRINT "1) THE HIGH, LOW, AND CLOSING PRICES"
600 PRINT "2) OR ONLY THE CLOSING PRICES"
610 INPUT ISERIES
620  ON ISERIES GOTO 640,990
630  GOTO 540
640  CLS : REM CLEAR SCREEN AND HOME CURSOR
650  I = 1
660 PRINT "ENTER HIGH  PRICE FOR DAY #";I; : INPUT HIG(I)
670  IF HIG(I) = 999 THEN GOTO 760
680 PRINT "ENTER LOW   PRICE FOR DAY #";I; : INPUT LOW(I)
690  IF LOW(I) = 999 THEN GOTO 760
700 PRINT "ENTER CLOSE PRICE FOR DAY #";I; : INPUT CLOS(I)
710  IF CLOS(I) = 999 THEN GOTO 760
720 PRINT TAB(40) "ENTER `999' TO END DATA ENTRY"
730  IF ED = 1 THEN ED = 0 : RETURN
740  I = I + 1 : REM INCREMENT DAY COUNTER
750  GOTO 660
760  I = I - 1
770  LASTDAY = I : M = I
780  START = 1
790  CLS : REM CLEAR SCREEN AND HOME CURSOR
800 PRINT "DAY       HIGH       LOW        CLOSE"
810 PRINT "---       --------   --------   --------"
820  FOR I = START TO START + 19
830 PRINT TAB(1)I;TAB(9)HIG(I);TAB(19)LOW(I);TAB(29)CLOS(I)
840   IF I = LASTDAY THEN GOTO 860
850  NEXT I
860 INPUT "ENTER DAY TO CHANGE OR `0' TO CONTINUE";DAY
870  IF DAY = 0 AND I < LASTDAY THEN START = I : GOTO 790
880  IF DAY = 0 THEN RETURN
890  I = DAY
900 PRINT "CURRENT VALUES ARE:"
910 PRINT "DAY       HIGH       LOW        CLOSE"
920 PRINT "---       --------   --------   --------"
930 PRINT TAB(1)DAY;TAB(9)HIG(I);TAB(19)LOW(I);TAB(29)CLOS(I)
940 PRINT "ENTER NEW DATA:"
950 PRINT : REM SEPARATE WORDS ON SCREEN
960  ED = 1 : REM GO INTO EDIT MODE
970  GOSUB 660
980  GOTO 790
990 REM ***************** LOAD DATA FOR CLOSING PRICE ONLY *****************
1000  CLS : REM CLEAR SCREEN AND HOME CURSOR
1010  I = 1 : REM INITIALIZE DAY COUNTER
1020 PRINT "ENTER `999' AS CLOSING PRICE TO END DATA ENTRY"
1030 PRINT "ENTER CLOSING PRICE FOR DAY";I; : INPUT CLOS(I)
1040  IF CLOS(I) = 999 THEN GOTO 1070
1050  I = I + 1
1060  GOTO 1030
1070  I = I - 1 : REM DECREMENTS COUNTER ON LAST ENTRY
1080  LASTDAY = I : M = I
```

```
1090    START = 1
1100   CLS : REM CLEAR SCREEN AND HOME CURSOR
1110  PRINT " DAY          CLOSING PRICE"
1120  PRINT " ---          --------------"
1130   FOR I = START TO START + 19
1140  PRINT TAB(2)I;TAB(15)CLOS(I)
1150    IF I = LASTDAY THEN GOTO 1170
1160   NEXT I
1170  INPUT "ENTER DAY TO CHANGE OR `0' TO CONTINUE";DAY
1180   IF DAY = 0 AND I < LASTDAY THEN START = I : GOTO 1100
1190   IF DAY = 0 THEN GOTO 1230
1200  PRINT "THE CLOSING PRICE FOR DAY";DAY;" IS";CLOS(DAY);
1210  INPUT "NEW PRICE";CLOS(DAY)
1220   GOTO 1100
1230  REM ***********************************************************************
1240  REM *         SUBROUTINE TO FIND HIGH AND LOW LOOKING BACK `X' DAYS       *
1250  REM ***********************************************************************
1260   IF ISERIES <> 2 THEN GOTO 1410
1270  INPUT "HOW MANY DAYS IN THE BACKWARD LOOK";JS
1280   FOR I = JS TO M
1290    XLOW = 9999
1300    XHIG = -9999
1310    FOR K = I - JS + 1 TO I
1320     IF XLOW > CLOS(K) THEN XLOW = CLOS(K)
1330     IF XHIG < CLOS(K) THEN XHIG = CLOS(K)
1340    NEXT K
1350    LOW(I) = XLOW
1360    HIG(I) = XHIG
1370   NEXT I
1380  REM ***********************************************************************
1390  REM *                 SUBROUTINE TO RUN THE VOLATILITY SYSTEM             *
1400  REM ***********************************************************************
1410  INPUT "HOW MANY DAYS IN THE MOVING AVERAGE";J1
1420  INPUT "WHAT IS THE VALUE FOR THE CONSTANT";C
1430   TR = 0
1440   T1 = 0
1450   T2 = 0
1460   SUMTR = 0
1470   AVTR = 0
1480   SL$ = "L"
1490   IF CLOS(J1 + 3) >CLOS(1) THEN SL$ = "S"
1500   SIC = CLOS(1)
1510   FOR I = 3 TO M
1520    STP(I) = 0
1530    ARRY$(I)  = " "
1540    J = I - 1
1550    TR = HIG(J) - LOW(J)
1560    T1 = HIG(J) - CLOS(J-1)
1570    T2 = CLOS(J-1) - LOW(J)
1580    IF TR < T1 OR TR < T2 THEN GOTO 1600
1590    GOTO 1620
1600    IF TR < T1 THEN TR = T1
1610    IF TR < T2 AND T2 > T1 THEN TR = T2
1620    IF I > J1 + 3 THEN GOTO 1660
```

```
1630    SUMTR = SUMTR + TR
1640    AVTR = SUMTR / J1
1650    IF I <= J1 + 3 THEN GOTO 1890
1660    X = J1
1670    AVTR =(AVTR * (X-1) + TR)/ X
1680    ARC = AVTR * C
1690    IF SL$ = "L" THEN GOTO 1710
1700    GOTO 1780
1710    STP(I) = SIC - ARC
1720    IF LOW(I) < STP(I) THEN 1740
1730    GOTO 1780
1740    SL$ = "S"
1750    ARRY$(I) = "S"
1760    SIC = CLOS(I)
1770    GOTO 1890 : REM NEXT I
1780    IF SL$ = "S" THEN GOTO 1800
1790    GOTO 1870
1800    STP(I) = SIC + ARC
1810    IF HIG(I) > STP(I) THEN 1830
1820    GOTO 1870
1830    SL$ = "L"
1840    ARRY$(I) = "L"
1850    SIC = CLOS(I)
1860    GOTO 1890 : REM NEXT I
1870    IF CLOS(I) < SIC AND SL$ = "S" THEN SIC = CLOS(I)
1880    IF CLOS(I) > SIC AND SL$ = "L" THEN SIC = CLOS(I)
1890   NEXT I
1900  REM ********************************************************************
1910  REM *          SUBROUTINE TO PRINT RESULTS, STOPS, POS, AND PROFITS          *
1920  REM ********************************************************************
1930   CLS : REM CLEAR SCREEN AND HOME CURSOR
1940  PRINT "DAY    HIGH       LOW       CLOSE     STOP      POSITION  PROFIT"
1950  PRINT "---    --------  --------  --------  --------  --------  ---------"
1960    SL$ = " "
1970    TTLPROFIT = 0
1980    XLAST = CLOS(1)
1990    CURPROFIT = 0
2000    DAYPROFIT = 0
2010    FOR I = 1 TO M
2020      PROFIT = 0
2030      IF ARRY$(I) <> " " THEN GOTO 2050
2040      GOTO 2090
2050      IF SL$ = "S" THEN PROFIT = XLAST - CLOS(I)
2060      IF SL$ = "L" THEN PROFIT = CLOS(I) - XLAST
2070      XLAST = CLOS(I)
2080      SL$ = ARRY$(I)
2090      IF SL$ = "S" THEN CURPROFIT = XLAST - CLOS(I)
2100      IF SL$ = "L" THEN CURPROFIT = CLOS(I) - XLAST
2110      TTLPROFIT = TTLPROFIT + PROFIT
2120      DAYPROFIT = TTLPROFIT + CURPROFIT
2130      IF I < JS THEN GOTO 2180
2140      DAYPROFIT = INT(DAYPROFIT * 100 )/100
2150      STP(I) = INT(STP(I) * 100)/100
2160  PRINT TAB(1)I;TAB(6)HIG(I);TAB(16)LOW(I);TAB(26)CLOS(I);TAB(36)STP(I);
```

```
2170 PRINT TAB(49)ARRY$(I);TAB(56)DAYPROFIT
2180   NEXT I
2190   TTLPROFIT = TTLPROFIT + CURPROFIT
2200 PRINT
2210 PRINT TAB(30) "TOTAL PROFIT = ";TTLPROFIT
2220 INPUT "WOULD YOU LIKE TO REPEAT THIS PROCESS";AN$
2230   IF AN$ = "Y" THEN GOTO 1230
2240 END
```

18
Momentum Indicators

The technical systems we have looked at up to this point depend on the past price level. For example, the moving average system takes the average price over a given past number of days as its input. The parabolic system adds a stop to the average of past prices which makes the timing of price movements more important. The volatility system takes us a little further away from looking strictly at the levels of past prices, since it also gauges the variability of daily price fluctuations in determining its stops.

The momentum indicators do not look at the price levels at all but at the changes in price. Rather than looking at the direction of price movement, the momentum indicators look at the rate of change in price movement. They therefore provide a sense of the pace of the market, giving a measure of whether the market is heating up or cooling off.

The analogy between the price level systems and the momentum systems is the same as that between velocity and acceleration. To know where an object is going for the next instant, it is sufficient to know the velocity of that object. But to know if a change in direction is imminent, we must know the acceleration of the object. If the rate of acceleration is high, then it is likely the present course will be continued. If the acceleration is negative, then we might expect a shift to a different course.

It is always hazardous to stretch analogies between the physical world and the investment markets too far. There seems to be no end to systems

237

developed using some appeal to the laws of physics; systems based on the second law of thermodynamics, the gravitational constant or on the engineering principles of torque. It might be argued that momentum systems fit in this group. The basic principle in this case is Newton's second law of motion: A body in motion tends to stay in motion. The greater the momentum in the market price, the more likely it will be to continue in its present course. If thinking about the momentum system in these terms helps give a feel for its application, fine. If it makes you more suspicious of its value, then it may be easier to simply look at it as a method for extracting more information out of the past prices. The fact is that the momentum systems have been used and improved on by technical traders for years, and many traders will tell you that for whatever reason, they do work.

MOMENTUM INDICATORS

The simplest measure of momentum is to take the difference between today's price and the price a number of days in the past. For example, a simple 10-day momentum value is calculated by subtracting the price 10 days ago from the price today:

$$M_t(10) = P_t - P_{t-10}.$$

If the price moves at a constant rate, this value will be constant, no matter what direction the price is moving. It will only take on different values with changes in the rate of price movement.

As Figure 18-1 shows, the momentum value will fluctuate above and below the zero line. A crude trading strategy is to sell when the momentum drops from positive to negative and buy when the momentum rises from negative to positive. In practice, it is better to establish some band above and below the zero line for the buy and sell range.

Momentum will move away from the zero line less frequently the longer the moving average. Therefore, there is a tradeoff with this momentum indicator much like that for the moving average system: The longer the moving average of momentum, the lower the probability of a false start, but the greater the likelihood of missing profit opportunities.

It is interesting to note the relationship between this simple momentum estimate and the moving average of prices. Just as the momentum varies with the rate of change in past prices, so it varies with the rate of change in the moving average of past prices. If we represent the 10-day moving average as of time t by $MA_t(10)$, then we can show the 10-day momentum value as 10 times the difference between today's 10-day moving average and yesterday's 10-day moving average:

$$M_t(10) = 10[MA_t(10) - MA_{t-1}(10)].$$

THE RELATIVE STRENGTH INDEX

A more sophisticated momentum indicator is the relative strength index (RSI) proposed by J. Welles Wilder. This system divides price changes into two groups: daily positive price changes, and daily negative price changes. The

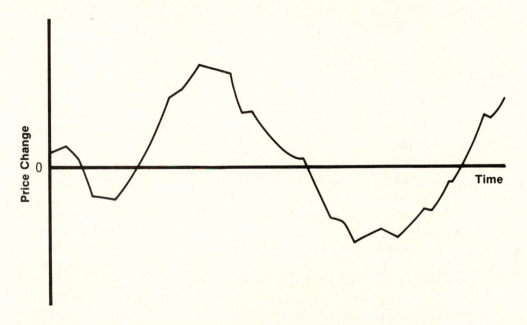

Figure 18-1. Momentum as measured by the price change of a commodity.

ratio of the average positive and negative price changes is calculated, and then this is normalized to give a value between 0 and 100. If we denote the daily price change by Δp, then the average positive price change is

$$UP = \frac{1}{N} \sum_{\Delta p > 0} \Delta p$$

and the average negative price change is

$$DN = \frac{1}{N} \sum_{\Delta p < 0} \Delta p.$$

The relative strength averaged over the last N periods is then just UP/DN, and the relative strength index is calculated as

$$RSI = 100 - \frac{100}{1 + (UP/DN)}.$$

The relative strength index has a number of attractive features as a momentum indicator. First, it is based on a moving average of the price changes. This keeps the index from overreacting to sudden, short-term movements. Second, since the relative strength is normalized, the relative strength index calculation takes on values between 0 and 100, giving an absolute scale or measuring market momentum.

Figure 18-2 superimposes the relative strength index on the futures price of cocoa, and Figure 18-3 shows the RSI for the Deutsch Mark futures. The tendency for momentum to signal imminent changes is clear in these figures. The peaks and troughs of the RSI often occur several days before the price level changes direction.

THE ACCUMULATION/DISTRIBUTION OSCILLATOR

Another popular momentum indicator is the A/D, or Accumulation/Distribution Oscillator developed by Jim Walters and Larry Williams. The basis for their system is buying power (BP), defined as the difference between the daily high and opening prices, and selling power (SP), defined as the difference between the daily close and low. They combine these two measures to calculate the daily raw figure (DRF),

$$DRF = \frac{1}{2}\,[(BP + SP)/(high-low)].$$

The daily raw figure is between –1 and 1. It reaches its maximum value of 1 when trading opens at the low and closes at the high, and reaches its minimum value of –1 when trading opens at the high and closes at the low. A

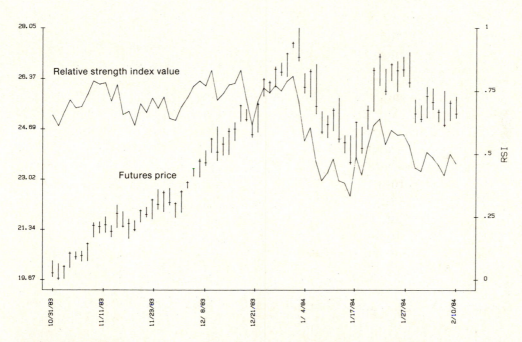

Figure 18-2. The relative strength index for the March 1984 cocoa futures contract.

measure that varies between minus and plus one as the daily raw figure does is often termed an *oscillator*.

The A/D system makes automatic adjustments for variations in the trading range, since the difference between the high and low are entered in the divisor of the daily raw figure. And, like the relative strength index, the A/D system imposes an absolute scale for measuring momentum.

The daily raw figure is fairly erratic, and does require some smoothing to give a dependable reading of the current momentum in the market. This can be easily done by taking a moving average of the DRF.

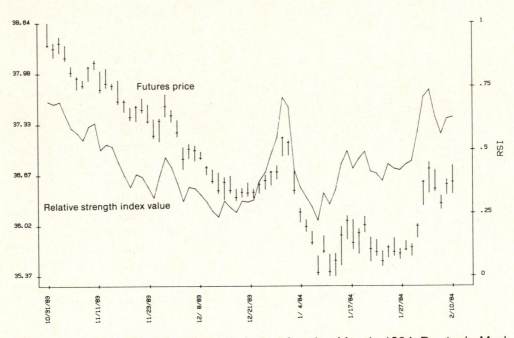

Figure 18-3. The relative strength index for the March 1984 Deutsch Mark contract.

TRADING STRATEGIES WITH MOMENTUM INDICATORS

Momentum indicators signal overbought and oversold markets. The attractive feature of the momentum indicators is that they signal when turning points are imminent. By contrast, the trend-following systems based on price levels, such as the moving average and volatility systems, can only signal a trend after the trend has become established. This means part of the profit opportunity is lost before the trade is made. But with the momentum indicators, the turning point is signaled before it is reached, leaving the full run of the trend available for exploitation. The general trading rule for all momentum indicators is:

- Sell when the momentum exceeds the critical upper bound depicting an overbought market.
- Buy when the momentum drops below the critical lower bound depicting an oversold market.

For example, a general rule of thumb for the RSI is that the market is overbought when the index rises above 75 and is oversold when the index drops below 25. But clearly careful optimization of these bounds can only enhance profits beyond those possible with this rough rule.

The values for the bounds are obviously important decision parameters. Also important is the trading rule associated with these bounds. The momentum indicators leave some leeway for the trading rule. For example, the investor can trade when the momentum crosses the bound, or when the momentum stays above the bound for a given number of days, or when the momentum crosses the bound and then begins to turn back. Or, instead of following the momentum of the price itself, the momentum of the nonsystematic portion of the price movement (that portion of the price movement that differs from the overall trend of the market) can be used as the basis for the momentum strategy. Washing out the market effect on the futures or stock price, and then applying the momentum strategies to the residual price movement is a strategy with high potential.

The momentum indicators can be adapted to take more market information into account by using both price change *and* trading volume. This sort of a measure would be a bit truer to the concept of momentum, with the volume being thought of as the mass behind the market movement.

As with the other technical systems discussed to this point, computer simulations present an essential tool in finding the parameters and the precise strategy that gives the optimal profit.

THE RELATIVE STRENGTH INDEX

Computational Procedure

The N-day relative strength index for day t is

$$RSI_t(N) = 100 - [100/(1+(UP_t(N)/DN_t(N)))].$$

where

$$UP_t(N) = \frac{1}{N} \sum_{\substack{i=1 \\ \Delta P_i > 0}}^{N} \Delta P_{t-i+1},$$

and

$$DN_t(N) = \frac{1}{N} \sum_{\substack{i=1 \\ \Delta P_i < 0}}^{N} \Delta P_{t-i+1}$$

$$\Delta P_i = \text{daily price change for period i}$$

Trading Strategy

- Sell when the RSI is above the given upper bound (usually around 75).
- Buy when RSI is below the given lower bound (usually around 25).

```
10   REM   ************************************************************
20   REM   *                    THE RELATIVE STRENGTH INDEX           *
30   REM   *                                                          *
40   REM   * THIS PROGRAM CALCULATES THE RELATIVE STRENGTH INDEX GIVEN THE *
50   REM   * HIGH, LOW, AND CLOSING PRICE FOR EACH DAY IN THE BACKWARD LOOK. *
60   REM   *                                                          *
70   REM   *       VARIABLES USED: HIG( ) = ARRAY OF DAILY HIGH PRICES *
80   REM   *                       LOW( ) = ARRAY OF DAILY LOW PRICES *
90   REM   *                      CLOS( ) = ARRAY OF DAILY CLOSING PRICES *
100  REM   *                       RSI( ) = DAILY RELATIVE STRENGTH INDEX *
110  REM   *                      ARRY( ) = WORK ARRAY                *
120  REM   *                           ED = EDIT FLAG                 *
130  REM   *                      LASTDAY = LAST DAY THAT DATA WAS ENTERED *
140  REM   *                                                          *
150  REM   ************************************************************
160   DIM HIG(100),LOW(100),CLOS(100),RSI(100),ARRY(100)
170  REM
180  REM
190  REM   ***************************INPUT****************************
200   GOSUB 360
210  REM
220  REM
230  REM   ***********************COMPUTATIONS*************************
240   GOSUB 740
250  REM
260  REM
270  REM   ***************************OUTPUT***************************
280   GOTO 1010
290  REM
300  REM
310  REM   *************************PROGRAM END************************
320  REM
330  REM
340  REM
350  REM
360  REM   ************************************************************
370  REM   *                 SUBROUTINE TO ENTER DATA                *
380  REM   ************************************************************
390  REM
400   CLS : REM CLEARS SCREEN AND HOMES CURSOR
410  PRINT "ENTER '999' TO END DATA ENTRY"
420   I = 1 : REM INITIALIZE COUNTER FOR DATA ENTRY
430  PRINT "ENTER CLOSING PRICE FOR DAY #";I; : INPUT CLOS(I)
440   IF CLOS(I) = 999 THEN GOTO 470
450   I = I + 1 : REM INCREMENT COUNTER
460   GOTO 430
470  REM COMES HERE IF I = 999
480   I = I - 1 : REM DECREMENTS COUNTER ON LAST ENTRY
490   LASTDAY = I
500   START = 1 : REM INITIALIZE DAYS COUNTER
510   CLS
520  PRINT "DAY      CLOSE"
530  PRINT "---      --------"
540   FOR I = START TO START + 19
```

```
550 PRINT TAB(1)I;TAB(9)CLOS(I)
560    IF I = LASTDAY THEN GOTO 580
570    NEXT I
580 INPUT "ENTER DAY TO CHANGE OR '0' TO CONTINUE";DAY
590   IF DAY = 0 AND I < LASTDAY THEN START = I : GOTO 510
600   IF DAY = 0 THEN GOTO 660
610   I = DAY
620 PRINT "CURRENT VALUE IS";CLOS(I);"ENTER NEW VALUE";:INPUT CLOS(I)
630 PRINT
640   GOTO 510
650 REM
660 REM ASKS FOR PARAMETERS TO RUN RSI
670 REM
680 INPUT "HOW MANY DAYS IN THE RSI";J1
690   IF J1 <= LASTDAY THEN GOTO 730
700 PRINT : PRINT "ERROR -- THERE IS ONLY DATA FOR";LASTDAY;"DAYS"
710 PRINT
720   GOTO 660
730   RETURN
740 REM ****************************************************************
750 REM *                   SUBROUTINE TO DO COMPUTATIONS             *
760 REM ****************************************************************
770   SUMUP = 0
780   SUMDN = 0
790   RSI(1) = 0
800   FOR I = 2 TO J1 + 1
810    RSI(I) = 0
820    IF CLOS(I) > CLOS(I-1) THEN SUMUP = SUMUP + CLOS(I) - CLOS(I-1)
830    IF CLOS(I) < CLOS(I-1) THEN SUMDN = SUMDN + CLOS(I-1) - CLOS(I)
840   NEXT I
850   AVEUP = SUMUP / J1
860   AVEDN = SUMDN / J1
870   IF SUMDN = 0 THEN RSI(J1+1) = 100 : GOTO 890
880   RSI(J1+1) = 100 - (100/(1+(SUMUP/SUMDN)))
890   FOR I = J1 + 2 TO LASTDAY
900    SUMUP = AVEUP * (J1 - 1)
910    IF CLOS(I) > CLOS(I-1) THEN SUMUP = SUMUP + CLOS(I) - CLOS(I-1)
920    AVEUP = SUMUP / J1
930    SUMDN = AVEDN * (J1-1)
940    IF CLOS(I) < CLOS(I-1) THEN SUMDN = SUMDN + (CLOS(I-1) - CLOS(I))
950    AVEDN = SUMDN / J1
960    IF SUMDN = 0 THEN RSI(I) = 100 : GOTO 990
970   RS = AVEUP/AVEDN
980    RSI(I) = 100 - (100/(1 + RS))
990   NEXT I
1000   RETURN
1010 REM ****************************************************************
1020 REM *                   SUBROUTINE TO OUTPUT RESULTS             *
1030 REM ****************************************************************
1040   CLS
1050 PRINT "DAY        CLOSE          RSI"
1060 PRINT "---        --------        --------"
1070   FOR I = 1 TO LASTDAY
1080 PRINT TAB(1)I;TAB(9)CLOS(I);TAB(22)RSI(I)
```

```
1090   NEXT I
1100 REM
1110 REM *********** WILL RERUN PROGRAM WITH DIFFERENT PARAMETERS ***********
1120 REM
1130 INPUT "WOULD YOU LIKE TO REPEAT THIS PROCESS";Q$
1140 IF Q$ <> "Y" THEN END
1150 GOSUB 660
1160 GOTO 230
```

19
A Trend Measurement System

All of the technical systems we have discussed so far in this section are trend-following systems. They work well if there are large, distinct trends, and work poorly if prices have choppy, sideways movement. The obvious requirement in using these systems, then, is somehow to measure the tendency for trends to develop in the market. The system we will present in this chapter fulfills that need. It can be used to rank the directional movement, or trend, of any futures contract or stock.

The end product of this chapter is the trend movement index, or TMI. This index is intended to be used in conjunction with other technical systems. It is applied to see which markets are the most attractive for a trend-following system. Those markets with the highest index value are the most promising targets for the technical methods of this section.

The index can also be used to measure the stability of important market characteristics. If a market has wide variations in the TMI over time, it is a riskier candidate for technical trading than one with a stable TMI.

This is especially true when a technical system with optimized parameters is being used. As we will see in Chapter 20, the profitability of any technical system can be greatly enhanced by applying it with the correct, optimized parameter values. But these values can only be determined by looking at the performance of the technical system over historical data. The applicability of the system to the future course of the market then depends on

248

how stable the market characteristics are; on how well the past market behavior reflects the near future. If the market continues to follow the same amplitude and magnitude of trends, then the optimization will carry forward to yield large profits in future trading. However, if the market is not stable, and periods of cyclical trends turn unpredictably into periods of flat sideways movement or nondirectional volatility, then the systems cannot be used reliably, whether they are optimized or not. It is possible to get an accurate and valuable measure of the stability of the market by looking at variations in the TMI over the past and comparing the index over the past with its current value.

The measurement of trend is not only useful for the technical systems. It also provides valuable information for option trading strategies. As we will see in the next section, the success of many option trading strategies depends on an accurate prediction of the likelihood of swings in the price of the underlying security. The volatility of price movements is used to measure this. The trend movement index provides a second measure of the likelihood of large directional swings.

The techniques leading to the trend movement index also generate a technical trading system of their own. This system, which is a generalized version of the directional movement system of J. Welles Wilder, can be used independently, or it can provide a backup to the other trading systems that have been proposed in Section III.

MEASURING TREND MOVEMENT

The trend movement index and trend movement trading system start by defining a bandwidth for nondirectional price movement. The bandwidth is specified by the investor, but should represent the range of price movement that characterizes nontrending or nondirection price changes. In the simplest case where day-to-day movements are being monitored, the bandwidth is simply the range of price movement from one day's close to the following day's close. For price movements over longer time periods, the bandwidth is defined around the midpoint of the high and low over that time period.

Figure 19-1 shows the calculation of a 10-day bandwidth. The bandwidth for day A is calculated by looking back for 10 days, and setting the channel for the bandwidth at the mid-point of the highest and lowest price over that

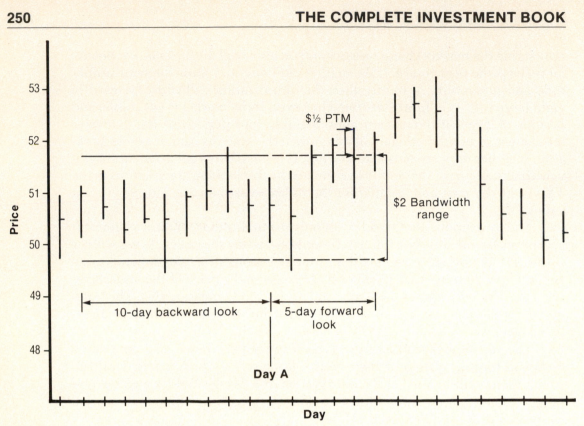

Figure 19-1. Calculating a 10-day bandwidth.

10-day period. The number of days used in determining the bandwidth is called the *backward look*. The solid line in Figure 19-1 shows the bandwidth for a 10-day backward look for a $2 range. The high price over the 10-day backward look is 51 7/8, and the low is 49 1/2. A two-point bandwidth will then be centered at 50 11/16, and range from a low of 49 11/16 to a high of 51 11/16.

This bandwidth is then brought forward a given number of days—the number of days specified as the *forward look* in the computer program—to determine the trend movement for day A. The *trend movement* is defined as the largest price movement outside of the bandwidth over the time period specified in the forward look. If the price over the forward period breaks out to attain a higher level above the bandwidth than it does below the bandwidth, then the price movement for that period is called a *positive trend movement*. If the price breaks out of the bandwidth to attain a lower level below the bandwidth than it does above the bandwidth, then the price movement for that period is called a *negative trend movement*. If the price stays within the bandwidth throughout the forward look, the trend movement is set equal to zero.

For Figure 19-1, the dotted line shows the bandwidth being moved forward five days, the amount of the forward look in this particular example. The price over the five-day period breaks out both above and below the bandwidth. The largest breakout is a \$.50 move above the bandwidth, so for day A there is a positive trend movement of one half a point.

This trend movement is the basis of the trend movement index. The positive trend movements (PTM) and negative trend movements (NTM) are summed up over a specified number of past days. The positive trend movement is then subtracted from the negative trend movement, and this difference is divided by the sum of the positive and negative trend movements over that time period. The value of this calculation is the trend movement index. For example, a 10-period trend movement index for period K would be calculated as

$$TMI_K = \frac{\displaystyle\sum_{i=K-10}^{K} PTM_i - \sum_{i=K-10}^{K} NTM_i}{\displaystyle\sum_{i=K-10}^{K} (PTM_i + NTM_i)}.$$

The construction of this index assures the resulting index value will be between –1 and 1. If all of the price movement is in the positive direction, the index value will equal one. If all the price movement is in the negative direction (i.e., if there is an uncorrected drop in the price), the index value will equal minus one. If the price movement has been equally above and below the bandwidth, or if it has not broken out of the bandwidth, the index will equal zero. This means the further TMI is from zero, the stronger the signal of a trend.

TRADING STRATEGIES BASED ON THE TREND MOVEMENT INDEX

The trend movement index is a useful diagnostic tool in evaluating the attractiveness of a market for trend-following systems. Trend movement can also be applied by using the positive trend movement and negative trend movement to generate trading signals directly. The PTM is a measure of positive breakouts from the bandwidth, and the NTM is a measure of negative breakouts from the bandwidth. Intuitively, we would think that if the PTM is greater than the NTM, a positive trend is developing, and similarly, if the NTM is greater than the PTM, a downard trend is developing.

This is in fact the case. However, it is clear the size of the trend movements will be directly related to the size of the bandwidth we use. To improve the strength of this rule, we first adjust the PTM and NTM for the size of the bandwidth being used. We divide the PTM and NTM by the bandwidth size to form the positive trend indicator (PTI) and the negative trend indicator (NTI):

$$PTI = \Sigma \ (PTM_i/BW_i)$$

and

$$NTI = \Sigma \ (NTM_i/BW_i),$$

where BW_i is the bandwidth for period i.

Getting to the PTI and NTI is a multistage process, but once armed with these indicators, the trading rule is straightforward:

- Buy when the PTI goes above the NTI (when the PTI crosses the NTI from below).
- Sell when the NTI goes above the PTI (when the NTI crosses the PTI from below).

This trading system has a great deal of flexibility. There are a number of important parameters that can be user-specified. These include the size of the bandwidth, the number of days in the backward look and the forward look, and the number of days used in the moving average for the trend index and trend indicator. Furthermore, the stops can be set according to the high, low, or closing price.

The bandwidth is meant to reflect the range of nondirectional price variability. This will obviously vary from one commodity to another. But the proper size for the bandwidth can be related to the number of days in the backward look and the forward look. In particular, the more days used, the larger the bandwidth will tend to be. The minimum range for the bandwidth is the average daily high-low range of the commodity. The ideal bandwidth will display only positive or negative trend movements, depending on whether an upward or downward trend is developing, so the nondirectional volatility will not "spill over" the bandwidth range.

TREND MEASUREMENT: THE TREND MOVEMENT INDEX

Computational Procedure

P_i = price in day i
N_B = number of days in backward look
N_F = number of days in forward look
N_I = number of days in trend moving average
BW = price range of the bandwidth
BWH = price at the top of the bandwidth
BWL = price at the bottom of the bandwidth

1. Computation of the trend movement (TM) the positive trend movement (PTM) and the negative trend movement (NTM).

   The trend movement is the largest of:

   a. The difference between the highest price over the past N_B days and the top of the bandwidth.

   b. The difference between the bottom of the bandwidth and the lowest price over the past N_B days.

      or

   c. zero

   That is, the trend movement for day K is

$$TM_K = \text{Max } \{P_i - BWH_i, BWL_i - P_i, 0\}.$$
$$i = K, ..., K - N_B$$

If $TM_i = P_i - BWH_i$, then $PTM_i = TM_i$
and $NTM_i = 0;$

If $TM_i = BWL_i - P_i$, then $NTM_i = TM_i$
and $PTM_i = 0;$

If $TM_i = 0$, then $PTM_i = NTM_i = 0.$

2. Computation of the positive trend indicator (PTI) and negative trend indicator (NTI).

$$PTI_K = \sum_{i=K-N_I}^{K} (PTM_i/BW_i),$$

$$NTI_K = \sum_{i=K-N_I}^{K} (NTM_i/BW_i).$$

3. Computation of trend movement index (TMI).

$$TMI_K = \frac{\sum\limits_{i=K-N_B}^{K} PTM_i - \sum\limits_{i=K-N_B}^{K} NTM_i}{\sum\limits_{i=K-N_B}^{K} (PTM_i + NTM_i)}.$$

Trading Rule

- Buy when the PTI crosses above NTI.
- Sell when the NTI crosses above PTI.

Use a trend following system on those futures and stocks with the highest TMI.

```
10   REM  ***********************************************************************
20   REM  *                      TREND MOVEMENT SYSTEM                          *
30   REM  *                                                                     *
40   REM  *  THE TREND MOVEMENT SYSTEM COMPUTES THE TREND MOVEMENT INDEX.       *
50   REM  *  IT ALSO GENERATES TRADING SIGNALS BASED ON THE VALUE OF THE        *
60   REM  *  POSITIVE AND NEGATIVE TREND INDICATORS.                            *
70   REM  *                                                                     *
80   REM  *  VARIABLES USED:                                                    *
90   REM  *                                                                     *
100  REM  *                  HIG( )  = ARRAY OF DAILY HIGH PRICES               *
110  REM  *                  LOW( )  = ARRAY OF DAILY LOW PRICES                *
120  REM  *                 CLOS( )  = ARRAY OF DAILY CLOSING PRICES            *
130  REM  *                ARRY$( )  = ARRAY OF SHORT OR LONG POSITIONS         *
140  REM  *                   BW( )  = ARRAY OF BANDWIDTHS                      *
150  REM  *                  BWH( )  = ARRAY OF BANDWIDTH UPPER LIMITS          *
160  REM  *                  BWL( )  = ARRAY OF BANDWIDTH LOWER LIMITS          *
170  REM  *                 MEAN( )  = ARRAY OF BANDWIDTH MIDPOINTS             *
180  REM  *                  HPF( )  = HIGHEST PRICE LOOKING FORWARD            *
190  REM  *                  LPF( )  = LOWEST PRICE LOOKING FORWARD             *
200  REM  *                  HPB( )  = HIGHEST PRICE LOOKING BACKWARD           *
210  REM  *                  LPB( )  = LOWEST PRICE LOOKING BACKWARD            *
220  REM  *                  PTM( )  = DAILY POSITIVE TREND MOVEMENT            *
230  REM  *                  NTM( )  = DAILY NEGATIVE TREND MOVEMENT            *
240  REM  *                 PTMI( )  = PTM OVER RANGE OF DAYS (ND)              *
250  REM  *                 NTMI( )  = NTM OVER RANGE OF DAYS (ND)              *
260  REM  *                  TMI( )  = TREND MOVEMENT INDEX                     *
270  REM  *                     ND = NUMBER OF DAYS IN TREND INDEX AVERAGE      *
280  REM  *                     NI = NUMBER OF DAYS IN TREND MOVEMENT IND.      *
290  REM  *                     NB = NUMBER OF DAYS IN BACKWARD LOOK            *
300  REM  *                     NF = NUMBER OF DAYS IN FORWARD LOOK             *
310  REM  *               TTLPROFIT = TOTAL PROFITS                             *
320  REM  *               CURPROFIT = CURRENT PROFITS                           *
330  REM  *               DAYPROFIT = THE DAY PROFIT                            *
340  REM  *                   XLAST = CLOSING PRICE OF PREVIOUS DAY             *
350  REM  *                                                                     *
360  REM  *                                                                     *
370  REM  *                                                                     *
380  REM      ***********************************************************************
390    DIM HIG(100),LOW(100),CLOS(100),ARRY$(100),BWH(100),BWL(100),MEAN(100)
400    DIM HPF(100),LPF(100),HPB(100),LPB(100),PTM(100),NTM(100),TMI(100)
410    DIM PTMI(100),NTMI(100),BW(100),SPTM(100),SNTM(100),SPN(100)
420  REM
430  REM  **************************ENTER PRICES*********************************
440  REM
450    GOSUB 640
460  REM
470  REM  *********************USER-SPECIFIED PARAMETERS************************
480  REM
490    GOSUB 1340
500  REM
510  REM  ***********************COMPUTATIONS***********************************
520  REM
530    GOSUB 1530
540  REM
```

```
550 REM   **********PRINTS THE RESULTS, STOPS, POSITIONS, AND PROFIT**********
560 REM
570   GOSUB 2360
580 REM
590 REM   *********WILL ALLOW USER TO REPEAT PROCESS WITH NEW PARAMETERS*******
600 REM
610 REM
620 REM
630 REM
640 REM   ****************************************************************
650 REM *                    SUBROUTINE TO INPUT DATA                   *
660 REM   ****************************************************************
670   CLS : REM CLEAR SCREEN AND HOME CURSOR
680 PRINT "ARE YOU GOING TO TYPE IN:"
690 PRINT "1) THE HIGH AND LOW PRICES"
700 PRINT "2) OR ONLY THE CLOSING PRICES"
710 INPUT D
720   ON D GOTO 750,1090
730   GOTO 640
740 REM
750 REM ENTER DATA:  HIGH-LOW
760 REM
770   CLS : REM CLEAR SCREEN AND HOME CURSOR
780   I = 1
790 PRINT "ENTER HIGH  PRICE FOR DAY #";I; : INPUT HIG(I)
800   IF HIG(I) = 999 THEN GOTO 870
810 PRINT "ENTER LOW    PRICE FOR DAY #";I; : INPUT LOW(I)
820   IF LOW(I) = 999 THEN GOTO 870
830 PRINT : REM PRINTS BLANK LINE BETWEEN DAYS
840   IF ED = 1 THEN ED = 0 : RETURN
850   I = I + 1 : REM INCREMENT DAY COUNTER
860   GOTO 790
870   I = I - 1
880   LASTDAY = I : N = I :START = 1
890   CLS : REM CLEAR SCREEN AND HOME CURSOR
900 PRINT "DAY        HIGH        LOW"
910 PRINT "---        --------  --------"
920   FOR I = START TO START + 19
930 PRINT TAB(1)I;TAB(9)HIG(I);TAB(19)LOW(I)
940     IF I = LASTDAY THEN GOTO 960
950   NEXT I
960 INPUT "ENTER DAY TO CHANGE OR `0' TO CONTINUE";DAY
970   IF DAY = 0 AND I < LASTDAY THEN START = I : GOTO 890
980   IF DAY = 0 THEN RETURN
990   I = DAY
1000 PRINT "CURRENT VALUES ARE:"
1010 PRINT "DAY        HIGH        LOW"
1020 PRINT "---        --------  --------"
1030 PRINT TAB(1)DAY;TAB(9)HIG(I);TAB(19)LOW(I)
1040 PRINT "ENTER NEW DATA:" :PRINT
1050   ED = 1 : REM GO INTO EDIT MODE
1060   GOSUB 790
1070   GOTO 890
1080 REM
```

```
1090 REM ENTER DATA:  CLOSING PRICE ONLY
1100 REM
1110  CLS : REM CLEAR SCREEN AND HOME CURSOR
1120  I = 1 : REM INITIALIZE DAY COUNTER
1130 PRINT "ENTER `999' AS CLOSING PRICE TO END DATA ENTRY"
1140 PRINT "ENTER CLOSING PRICE FOR DAY";I; : INPUT CLOS(I)
1150  IF CLOS(I) = 999 THEN GOTO 1180
1160  I = I + 1
1170  GOTO 1140
1180  I = I - 1 : REM DECREMENTS COUNTER ON LAST ENTRY
1190  LASTDAY = I : N = I :START = 1
1200  CLS : REM CLEAR SCREEN AND HOME CURSOR
1210 PRINT " DAY        CLOSING PRICE"
1220 PRINT " ---        -------------"
1230  FOR I = START TO START + 19
1240 PRINT TAB(2)I;TAB(15)CLOS(I)
1250   IF I = LASTDAY THEN GOTO 1270
1260  NEXT I
1270 INPUT "ENTER DAY TO CHANGE OR `0' TO CONTINUE";DAY
1280  IF DAY = 0 AND I < LASTDAY THEN START = I : GOTO 1200
1290  IF DAY = 0 THEN RETURN
1300 PRINT "THE CLOSING PRICE FOR DAY";DAY;" IS";CLOS(DAY);
1310 INPUT "NEW PRICE";CLOS(DAY)
1320  GOTO 1200
1330 REM ***********************************************************************
1340 REM *                      USER SPECIFIED DATA                            *
1350 REM ***********************************************************************
1360  CLS
1370 INPUT "      NUMBER OF DAYS IN TREND INDEX AVERAGE: ",ND
1380 INPUT "NUMBER OF DAYS IN TREND MOVEMENT INDICATOR: ",NI
1390 INPUT "           NUMBER OF DAYS IN BACKWARD LOOK: ",NB
1400 INPUT "            NUMBER OF DAYS IN FORWARD LOOK: ",NF
1410  IF NB+1>=N-NF THEN GOTO 1450
1420  IF NB+ND+1>=N-NF THEN GOTO 1440
1430  GOTO 1460
1440 PRINT "TOO LITTLE DATA FOR SIZE OF TREND INDEX AVERAGE" :GOTO 1370
1450 PRINT "TOO LITTLE DATA FOR SIZE OF BACKWARD AND FORWARD LOOK":GOTO 1390
1460  IF D=2 THEN GOTO 1650
1470 PRINT:PRINT "SET BANDWIDTH"
1480 PRINT "     1. TO TRADING RANGE (HIGH-LOW) OF PREVIOUS DAY"
1490 PRINT "     2. CONSTANT WIDTH"
1500 INPUT "PLEASE ENTER '1' OR'2'      ",B
1510  ON B GOTO 1560, 1650
1520 REM ***********************************************************************
1530 REM *                        COMPUTATIONS                                 *
1540 REM ***********************************************************************
1550 REM
1560 REM TRADING RANGE OPTION
1570 REM
1580  FOR I = 1 TO N
1590   BWH(I) = HIG(I-1)
1600   BWL(I) = LOW(I-1)
1610   BW(I) = BWH(I)-BWL(I)+1
1620   NEXT I
```

```
1630   GOTO 1850
1640 REM
1650 REM CONSTANT WIDTH OPTION
1660 REM
1670 PRINT
1680 INPUT "BANDWIDTH ($): ",BW
1690   FOR I=1 TO N
1700     BW(I)=BW
1710   NEXT I
1720   FOR I=NB+1 TO N
1730     HPB(I)=0 :LPB(I)=0
1740     FOR J=I-NB TO I-1
1750       IF HIG(J) > HPB(I) THEN HPB(I)=HIG(J)
1760       IF LOW(J) < LPB(I) THEN LPB(I)=LOW(J)
1770       IF CLOS(J) > HPB(I) THEN HPB(I)=CLOS(J)
1780       IF CLOS(J) < LPB(I) THEN LPB(I)=CLOS(J)
1790     NEXT J
1800     MEAN(I)=(HPB(I)+LPB(I))/2
1810     BWH(I)=MEAN(I)+BW/2
1820     BWL(I)=MEAN(I)-BW/2
1830   NEXT I
1840 REM
1850 REM COMPUTATION OF TREND MOVEMENT
1860 REM
1870   FOR I=NB+1 TO N-NF
1880     HPF(I)=0 :LPF(I)=0
1890     FOR J=I TO I+NF
1900       IF HIG(J) > HPF(I) THEN HPF(I) = HIG(J)
1910       IF LOW(J) < LPF(I) THEN LPF(I) = LOW(J)
1920       IF CLOS(J) > HPF(I) THEN HPF(I) = CLOS(J)
1930       IF CLOS(J) < LPF(I) THEN LPF(I) = CLOS(J)
1940     NEXT J
1950     PTM(I)=HPF(I)-BWH(I)
1960     NTM(I)=BWL(I)-LPF(I)
1970     IF PTM(I)>NTM(I) AND PTM(I)>0 THEN NTM(I)=0
1980     IF NTM(I)=>PTM(I) AND NTM(I)>0 THEN PTM(I)=0
1990     IF PTM(I)<=0 AND NTM(I)<=0 THEN PTM(I)=0 AND NTM(I)=0
2000   NEXT I
2010 REM
2020 REM COMPUTE TREND MOVEMENT OVER A RANGE OF DAYS
2030 REM
2040   FOR I=NB+ND+1 TO N-NF
2050     PTMI(I)=0 :NTMI(I)=0
2060     FOR K=I-ND TO I
2070       PTMI(I)=PTMI(I)+(PTM(K)/BW(K))
2080       NTMI(I)=NTMI(I)+(NTM(K)/BW(K))
2090     NEXT K
2100     PTMI(I)=PTMI(I)/ND
2110     NTMI(I)=NTMI(I)/ND
2120     PTMI(I)=INT((PTMI(I)+.0005)*1000)/1000
2130     NTMI(I)=INT((NTMI(I)+.0005)*1000)/1000
2140   NEXT I
2150 REM
2160 REM TRADING RULE
```

```
2170 REM
2180  FOR I=NB+2 TO N-NF-1
2190   IF PTMI(I-1)<=NTMI(I-1) AND PTMI(I)>NTMI(I) THEN ARRY$(I)="L"
2200   IF NTMI(I-1)<=PTMI(I-1) AND NTMI(I)>PTMI(I) THEN ARRY$(I)="S"
2210   IF ARRY$(I)<>"L" AND ARRY$(I)<>"S" THEN ARRY$(I)=" "
2220  NEXT I
2230 REM
2240 REM COMPUTE TREND MOVEMENT INDEX
2250 REM
2260  FOR I=NB+NI+1 TO N-NF
2270   FOR K=I-NI TO I
2280    SPTM(I)=SPTM(I)+PTM(K)
2290    SNTM(I)=SNTM(I)+NTM(K)
2300    SPN(I)=SPN(I)+(PTM(K)+NTM(K))
2310   NEXT K
2320   TMI(I)=(SPTM(I)-SNTM(I))/SPN(I)
2330   TMI(I)=INT((TMI(I)+.0005)*1000)/1000
2340  NEXT I
2350 REM ****************************************************************
2360 REM *          SUBROUTINE TO PRINT RESULTS, POSITIONS, AND PROFITS          *
2370 REM ****************************************************************
2380  CLS : REM CLEAR SCREEN AND HOME CURSOR
2390 PRINT "                         POS.      NEG.      TREND      POS.      TOTAL"

2400 PRINT "DAY  HIGH    LOW    CLOSE  T.I.      T.I.      M.I.      S/L  PROFIT"

2410 PRINT "---  -----  -----  -----  -----    -----    -----    ----  ------"

2420   SL$ = " "
2430   IF D=1 THEN XLAST=((HIG(1)+LOW(1))/2)
2440   ELSE XLAST = CLOS(1)
2450   TTLPROFIT = 0 :CURPROFIT = 0 :DAYPROFIT = 0
2460   FOR I = NB+ND+1 TO N-NF
2470    PROFIT = 0
2480    IF ARRY$(I) = " " THEN GOTO 2530
2490    IF SL$ = "S" THEN PROFIT = XLAST - CLOS(I)
2500    IF SL$ = "L" THEN PROFIT = CLOS(I) - XLAST
2510    XLAST = CLOS(I)
2520    SL$ = ARRY$(I)
2530    IF SL$ = "S" THEN CURPROFIT = XLAST - CLOS(I)
2540    IF SL$ = "L" THEN CURPROFIT = CLOS(I) - XLAST
2550    TTLPROFIT = TTLPROFIT + PROFIT
2560    DAYPROFIT = TTLPROFIT + CURPROFIT
2570    DAYPROFIT = INT((DAYPROFIT+.0005)*1000)/1000
2580 PRINT TAB(1)I;TAB(6)HIG(I);TAB(12)LOW(I);TAB(19)CLOS(I);TAB(26)PTMI(I);
2590 PRINT TAB(35)NTMI(I);TAB(45)TMI(I);TAB(54)ARRY$(I);TAB(60)DAYPROFIT
2600   NEXT I
2610   TTLPROFIT = TTLPROFIT + CURPROFIT
2620 PRINT
2630 PRINT TAB(30) "TOTAL PROFIT";TTLPROFIT
2640 INPUT "WOULD YOU LIKE TO REPEAT THIS PROCESS? (Y/N)",A$
2650  IF A$ = "Y" THEN GOTO 1340
2660 END
```

20
Optimizing Technical Systems to Maximize Profit Potential

Throughout Section III of the book, we have repeatedly emphasized that the profitable use of technical systems depends on the proper choice of parameter values. Any technical system can make money or can lose money. The deciding factor in how well the system does is the parameter values that are used. The relevant parameters differ from one system to the other. For the moving average system, the important parameters are the lengths of the short- and long-term moving averages. For the volatility system it is the time period used for the volatility measure, and the value given to the volatility constant.

It is the many values that can be given to these parameters, more than the number of different technical systems, that leads to such a wide divergence in the success of those who use these systems. Two traders can take the same technical system from this book; one can make money while the other can lose money. The difficulty in arriving at the correct parameter values is really of more importance than the selection of the system itself.

There are a number of important aspects to parameter selection. First, the parameters will vary from one commodity to another, and from one time period to another. Second, the success of the trading system for any given parameter value is very much dependent on the criterion used for measuring success. In futures trading, total profit is not always the best measure of success. Short-term swings are magnified so much by the margining of the contract that a system may be able to win the war, but be beaten in the small skirmishes along the way. For this reason, we will propose several methods of measuring trading success.

USING SIMULATIONS TO FIND THE OPTIMAL PARAMETER VALUE

The optimization method that we use is to simulate a trading strategy over the time series of past commodity prices for a range of parameter values, and see which value leads to the most success. For example, Table 20-1 presents the output of the moving average optimization program. This program was run over two hundred days of past daily closing prices, with a number of long-term and short-term moving averages. The short-term moving averages, shown in the lefthand column of the table, ran from one day to six days, while the long-term moving averages, shown in the second column to the left in the table, ran from eight days to twenty-two days, in steps of two days.

Measured on the basis of total profit over the trading period, the shortest term combination of the one-day short and the eight-day long moving average did the best. It gave a total profit of $26. This moving average amounts to running an eight-day moving average on the commodity price itself, since a one-day moving average is nothing more than the commodity price for that one day. By contrast, the longer term combinations did poorly. The four-day short and eighteen-day long combination gave a $17 loss.

Table 20-2 lists some of the data from Table 20-1 in a matrix form. The pattern of profits that arise from the various moving average combinations is clearer here. Notice that the profitability changes gradually as the moving average lengths change. While the 1–8 combination gives the highest profit, the neighboring combinations also do fairly well. And while the 4–18 and 5–18 combinations do the worst, the other long-term combinations also lead to losses.

The point of Table 20-2 is an important one. While there may be a best set of parameters, slight errors in the specification of the parameters will only lead to slight differences in profitability. This feature of the technical systems in this book is important given the underlying assumption behind using optimization over past prices—that the future prices will behave in a way similar to that of the past. If the future price behavior does not change appreciably from what it has been in the past, then the profitability of a trading system will not appreciably change either. A system that was the best in the past, while

TABLE 20-1 Trading Results for the Moving Average Trading System for Various Short-term and Long-term Moving Averages

SHORT MOVING AVERAGE	LONG MOVING AVERAGE	NUMBER OF TRADES	NUMBER OF WINS	NUMBER OF LOSSES	MAXIMUM TOTAL DRAWDOWN	MAXIMUM INTRATRADE DRAWDOWN	PROFIT PER TRADE	TOTAL PROFIT
1	8	7	4	3	0	-4	3.71	26
1	10	5	4	1	0	-4	3.20	16
1	12	5	4	1	-1	-4	1.60	8
1	14	7	4	3	0	-4	1.00	7
1	16	7	3	4	-2	-4	.42	3
1	18	7	3	4	-6	-5	-.15	-1
1	20	7	3	4	-3	-4	.28	2
1	22	7	3	4	-6	-5	-.15	-1
2	8	5	4	1	0	-4	2.40	12
2	10	5	4	1	0	-4	1.60	8
2	12	5	3	2	-1	-4	1.20	6
2	14	5	4	1	0	-4	1.80	9
2	16	5	2	3	-2	-3	1.00	5
2	18	5	1	4	-6	-6	.20	1
2	20	5	1	4	-3	-3	.80	4
2	22	5	2	3	-6	-6	.20	1
3	8	5	4	1	0	-4	2.00	10
3	10	5	2	3	0	-2	2.00	10
3	12	5	2	3	-1	-2	2.00	10
3	14	5	1	4	-1	-2	.60	3
3	16	5	1	4	-3	-2	.20	1
3	18	5	1	4	-7	-6	-.60	-3
3	20	5	1	4	-4	-3	0	0
3	22	5	1	4	-10	-6	-1.00	-5

SHORT MOVING AVERAGE	LONG MOVING AVERAGE	NUMBER OF TRADES	NUMBER OF WINS	NUMBER OF LOSSES	MAXIMUM TOTAL DRAWDOWN	MAXIMUM INTRATRADE DRAWDOWN	PROFIT PER TRADE	TOTAL PROFIT
4	8	5	2	3	0	-3	2.00	10
4	10	5	2	3	0	-2	1.60	8
4	12	5	1	4	-4	-3	0	0
4	14	5	1	4	-3	-3	.20	1
4	16	5	1	4	-10	-3	-1.00	-5
4	18	5	1	4	-19	-7	-3.40	-17
4	20	5	1	4	-16	-4	-2.80	-14
4	22	5	1	4	-19	-7	-3.40	-17
5	8	5	2	3	0	-3	2.00	10
5	10	5	2	3	-2	-3	.40	2
5	12	5	1	4	-9	-3	-.80	-4
5	14	5	1	4	-9	-3	-1.40	-7
5	16	5	1	4	-15	-4	-2.60	-13
5	18	5	1	4	-19	-7	-3.40	-17
5	20	5	0	5	-17	-4	-3.20	-16
5	22	5	0	5	-20	-7	-3.80	-19
6	8	5	2	3	0	-3	1.20	6
6	10	5	1	4	-7	-3	-.40	-2
6	12	5	1	4	-12	-4	-2.00	-10
6	14	5	1	4	-15	-5	-2.60	-13
6	16	5	0	5	-18	-5	-3.40	-17
6	18	5	1	4	-20	-10	-3.80	-19
6	20	5	1	4	-17	-7	-3.20	-16
6	22	5	1	4	-20	-10	-3.80	-19

TABLE 20-2   Total Profit From Moving Average Trading System
for Various Parameter Values

SHORT-TERM MOVING AVERAGE
(In Days)

Long-term Moving Average (In Days)	1	2	3	4	5
8	26	12	10	12	10
10	16	8	10	8	2
12	8	6	10	0	-4
14	7	9	3	1	-7
16	3	5	1	-5	-13
18	-1	1	-3	-17	-17
20	2	4	0	-14	-16

perhaps no longer the best, will still be close to optimal. Saying the price behavior does not change appreciably is not to say that if prices tended to go up in the past, they will continue to go up in the future. Rather, it is that the frequency and speed of trends will be the same; trends will tend to develop in the same way, and will on average have the same amplitude.

Table 20-3 presents a matrix for the parameters arising from the volatility system. Here the moving average employed in the volatility calculation varies from four to twenty days, and the volatility constant varies from 2.7 to 3.3. Here, too, the pattern displayed in Table 20-2 with the moving average system is apparent; the profits cluster about an optimal value, and slight variations in the parameters around that value still do well. The pattern is suggestive of a contour map, where the profit gradually slopes away in all directions from the highest point. The greatest profit is $75, for a volatility constant of 2.95 and volatility averaged over 12, 14, or 15 days. The profit at first drops slowly as the values deviate from the optimum. It then drops more rapidly as the volatility constant moves below 2.8 or above 3.2, and as the averaging of the volatility drops below 9 days or goes above 18 days.

TABLE 20-3   Total Profit From Volatility Trading System for Various Parameter Values

VALUE OF VOLATILITY CONSTANT

Length of Volatility Average (In Days)	2.7	2.75	2.8	2.85	2.90	2.95	3.0	3.05	3.1	3.15	3.2	3.25	3.3
	-27	-26	-26	-21	-4	0	5	-8	-16	-31	-31	-12	-40
5	-13	-12	-5	7	8	8	3	-3	-6	-10	-30	-12	-40
6	0	1	17	-1	9	12	3	6	2	4	6	-8	-30
7	-4	6	10	15	15	22	28	17	22	12	6	4	-25
8	-11	0	12	25	29	37	33	70	30	33	13	12	-17
9	14	20	29	32	34	42	40	32	41	41	40	14	4
10	14	25	34	41	56	59	41	32	40	39	22	6	8
11	22	27	45	60	66	69	48	64	40	42	20	6	-2
12	29	30	43	57	74	75	50	66	48	40	20	18	-2
13	18	30	38	61	69	71	74	66	57	39	30	19	-4
14	21	36	42	40	68	75	72	74	55	31	31	18	10
15	12	40	38	60	70	75	68	73	50	31	31	13	12
16	17	22	35	41	69	70	71	49	39	30	30	13	2
17	4	15	37	51	59	35	61	50	44	28	20	18	14
18	6	27	19	28	32	30	41	20	37	17	14	7	0
19	-5	-8	8	17	22	25	20	16	37	3	2	5	-15
20	-18	-17	-1	3	-12	2	19	17	16	8	1	-9	-3

MEASURING TRADING SUCCESS

While the most obvious measure of trading success is the total profit, in many ways other measures are more useful.

For example, if two strategies give profits of 94 and 45, respectively, over the same set of past prices, but the $95 came after thirty trades, while the $45 required only five trades, the strategy leading to the $45 might be more attractive. Since commissions are not included in the profit calculations, at least as they are presented in the programs in the book, the additional trades might eat up more commission dollars than the incremental profit they deliver. The trade-intensive strategy may also require more "babysitting" of the position, and may take more time in monitoring. The *average profits per trade*, which divides the total profits by the number of trades needed to get those profits, is useful in this regard.

The total number of trades in the third column from the left in Table 20-1 is divided into the number of wins and losses in the following two columns. Looking at these numbers from the perspective of the total profit gives an indication of the trading tempo. For example, if the total profit is high, but the number of losses is greater than the number of wins, then the strategy leads to numerous small losses interspersed with a few big winners.

For the trader who does not have unlimited funds, another important measure of trading success is the drawdown of the strategy. A strategy that leads to a large final profit is not of much use if you run out of funds partway through the course of pursuing the strategy. There are two measures of drawdown given in the optimization programs. The first one is the *maximum total drawdown*. This measures the maximum amount you would have been in the hole if you had pursued the trading strategy over the period of the simulation. For the moving average strategy optimization described in Table 20-1, the maximum total drawdown occurred for the 5-22, 6-18, and 6-22 strategies, with a loss of $20. The optimal strategy, the 1–8 moving average, has a maximum drawdown of 0. That is, there was never a period in following the strategy where there was an overall loss.

The maximum total drawdown will be biased somewhat by the early success of the strategy. If the first trade is good, it may provide enough buffer to keep the total drawdown low even if some of the subsequent trades are less than spectacular successes. So the program uses a second measure of drawdown, the *maximum intratrade drawdown*. This measures how much money was lost in the course of the worst trade. For the 1–8 strategy, the maximum intratrade drawdown is –4, more than the maximum total drawdown for that strategy. Thus, while the first trades did well enough to keep money in the investor's pocket, there was at least one trade that did not give a profit.

TRADING WITH THE OPTIMIZATION PROGRAMS

This chapter contains programs for optimizing the parameters of the moving average system, the volatility system, and the parabolic system. Each of these programs gives the same type of output as is shown in Table 20-1 for the moving average optimization. The critical consideration in the successful use of these programs is the proper selection of the price-time series data for the simulation. The parameter values that are profitable in the simulation will be profitable for trading only if the price behavior of the past is representative of the future. This means a large enough past price history is necessary to give a representative view, while too long a time period may include data that is no longer representative of the commodity, and will thus be counterproductive.

Generally, at least a two-year price history should be used for serious simulations. One check on the stability of the optimal parameters is to take a number of years of past data, optimize over the first two years, and then test the optimal parameter values for those two years on simulated trading for the next two years. This process of optimizing over several years and testing the resulting optimal parameters over the next years can be repeated for the entire time series. This method is obviously time-intensive, and adjustments in the dimension statements of the programs must be made to facilitate this. The optimization programs now only accommodate one hundred observations.

Even before such elaborate steps as a multiperiod simulation are taken, a more qualitative look at the commodity can give insight into the potential of trading by a technical system. A commodity that has undergone recent structural changes or nonrecurring aberrations in pricing behavior will be a poor target for technical trading based on simulations over the past price history. For example, the price behavior of silver during the 1980 run up to $50 was based largely on market manipulation and political influences that are unlikely to be repeated. The change in the Federal Reserve Board policy in targeting the money supply could suggest a different structure to interest rate movements, and might lead to a significant shift in the parameter values of the most successful strategies for Treasury bond futures and other financial futures.

```
10    REM  ******************************************************************
20    REM  *              MOVING AVERAGE OPTIMIZATION PROGRAM              *
30    REM  *                                                              *
40    REM  *    THIS PROGRAM IS A VARIATION OF THE MOVING AVERAGE TECHNICAL *
50    REM  *  SYSTEMS PROGRAM.  IT WILL ALLOW THE USER TO SPECIFY A        *
60    REM  *  RANGE FOR THE SHORT AND LONG MOVING AVERAGES.  THE RESULTS   *
70    REM  *  ARE FORMATTED TO SHOW HOW MANY TIMES A WIN OR LOSS IS        *
80    REM  *  OBSERVED DURING A TRADE, THE MAXIMUM AMOUNT OF MONEY LOST    *
90    REM  *  DURING A TRADE, THE PROFIT PER TRADE, AND THE TOTAL PROFIT.  *
100   REM  *                                                              *
110   REM  *    VARIABLES USED:                                           *
120   REM  *                      CLOS( ) = ARRAY OF DAILY CLOSING PRICES  *
130   REM  *                      ARRY$( ) = ARRAY OF SHORT AND LONG POSITIONS *
140   REM  *                      SMOV( ) = ARRAY OF SHORT MOVING AVERAGE  *
150   REM  *                      LMOV( ) = ARRAY OF LONG MOVING AVERAGE   *
160   REM  *                           JS = STARTING DAY                   *
170   REM  *                           SJ = DAYS IN SHORT MOVING AVERAGE   *
180   REM  *                           LJ = DAYS IN LONG MOVING AVERAGE    *
190   REM  *                            M = NUMBER OF DAYS TYPED IN (DATA) *
200   REM  *                    CURPROFIT = PROFITS FOR CURRENT DAY        *
210   REM  *                    DAYPROFIT = THE PROFITS TO DATE            *
220   REM  *                        XLAST = CLOSING PRICE OF PREVIOUS DAY  *
230   REM  *                           TT = TOTAL NUMBER OF TRADES         *
240   REM  *                          MAX = MAX INTRATRADE DRAWDOWN        *
250   REM  *                   INTRATRADE = PROFIT BETWEEN TRADES          *
260   REM  *                          WIN = NUMBER OF WINNING TRADES       *
270   REM  *                         LOSS = NUMBER OF LOSSING TRADES       *
280   REM  *                                                              *
290   REM  ******************************************************************
300   DIM CLOS(100),ARRY$(100),SMOV(100),LMOV(100)
310   REM
320   REM
330   REM  ********************** INPUT THE DATA ************************
340   GOSUB 500
350   REM
360   REM
370   REM  ********************** GET THE PARAMETERS ********************
380   GOSUB 790
390   REM
400   REM
410   REM  ****************** COMPUTE AND PRINT THE RESULTS *****************
420   GOTO 920
430   REM
440   REM
450   REM  ********************** END OF PROGRAM ************************
460   REM
470   REM
480   REM
490   REM
500   REM  ******************************************************************
510   REM  *                    SUBROUTINE TO ENTER DATA                  *
520   REM  ******************************************************************
530   REM
540   CLS : REM CLEARS SCREEN AND HOMES CURSOR
```

```
550    JS = 1
560    I = 1 : REM INITIALIZE COUNTER FOR DATA ENTRY
570 PRINT "ENTER `999' AS CLOSING PRICE TO END DATA ENTRY"
580 PRINT "ENTER CLOSING PRICE FOR DAY";I; : INPUT CLOS(I)
590    IF CLOS(I) = 999 THEN GOTO 620
600    I = I + 1
610    GOTO 580
620    I = I - 1 : REM DECREMENTS COUNTER ON LAST ENTRY
630    LASTDAY = I :M = I
640    START = 1
650    CLS : REM CLEARS SCREEN AND HOMES CURSOR
660 PRINT " DAY           CLOSING PRICE"
670 PRINT " ---           -------------"
680    FOR I = START TO START + 19
690 PRINT TAB(2)I;TAB(15)CLOS(I)
700    IF I = LASTDAY THEN GOTO 720
710    NEXT I
720 INPUT "ENTER DAY TO CHANGE OR `0' TO CONTINUE";DAY
730    IF DAY = 0 AND I < LASTDAY THEN START = I : GOTO 650
740    IF DAY = 0 THEN RETURN
750 PRINT "THE CLOSING PRICE FOR DAY";DAY;" IS";CLOS(DAY);
760 INPUT "NEW PRICE";CLOS(DAY)
770    GOTO 650
780 REM *********************************************************************
790 REM *        SUBROUTINE TO GET THE PARAMETERS FOR THE MOVING AVERAGE      *
800 REM *********************************************************************
810 REM
820    CLS : REM CLEAR SCREEN AND HOME CURSOR
830 PRINT
840 PRINT
850 INPUT "SPECIFY THE FEWEST DAYS FOR THE SHORT MOVING AVERAGE";FSJ
860 INPUT "SPECIFY THE MOST DAYS FOR THE SHORT MOVING AVERAGE";MSJ
870 INPUT "SPECIFY THE STEP IN DAYS FOR THE SHORT MOVING AVERAGE";SSJ
880 INPUT "SPECIFY THE FEWEST DAYS FOR THE LONG MOVING AVERAGE";FLJ
890 INPUT "SPECIFY THE MOST DAYS FOR THE LONG MOVING AVERAGE";MLJ
900 INPUT "SPECIFY THE STEP IN DAYS FOR THE LONG MOVING AVERAGE";SLJ
910    RETURN
920 REM *********************************************************************
930 REM *                    COMPUTE THE RESULTS AND PRINT                   *
940 REM *********************************************************************
950    CLS : REM CLEAR SCREEN AND HOME CURSOR
960 PRINT "SHORT     LONG       NUMBER   NUMBER   NUMBER   MAX          MAX           PROFIT
    TOTAL"
970 PRINT "MOVING    MOVING     OF       OF       OF       TOTAL        INTRATRADE    PER
    PROFIT"
980 PRINT "AVERAGE AVERAGE TRADES    WINS     LOSSES   DRAWDOWN     DRAWDOWN      TRADE
    "
990 PRINT "-------- -------- --------   ------ ------   --------     ----------    ------
    ------"
1000   FOR SJ = FSJ TO MSJ STEP SSJ
1010     FOR LJ = FLJ TO MLJ STEP SLJ
1020       IF LJ <= SJ THEN LJ = SJ + 1
1030 PRINT TAB(1)SJ;TAB(9)LJ;
1040 REM
```

```
1050 REM COMPUTE SHORT MOVING AVERAGE
1060 REM
1070     SUM = 0
1080     FOR I = 1 TO SJ
1090       SUM = SUM + CLOS(I)
1100       SMOV(I) = 0
1110     NEXT I
1120     SMOV(SJ) = SUM/SJ
1130     FOR I = SJ + 1 TO M
1140       SMOV(I) = (SMOV(I-1) * SJ - CLOS(I-SJ) + CLOS(I)) / SJ
1150     NEXT I
1160 REM
1170 REM COMPUTE LONG MOVING AVERAGE
1180 REM
1190     SUM = 0
1200     FOR I = 1 TO LJ
1210       SUM = SUM + CLOS(I)
1220       LMOV(I) = 0
1230     NEXT I
1240     LMOV(LJ) = SUM/LJ
1250     FOR I = LJ + 1 TO M
1260       LMOV(I) = (LMOV(I-1) * LJ - CLOS(I-LJ) + CLOS(I)) / LJ
1270     NEXT I
1280 REM
1290 REM COMBINE THE TWO MOVING AVERAGES
1300 REM
1310     SL$ = " " : TT = 0
1320     FOR I = 1 TO M
1330       ARRY$(I) = " "
1340 REM
1350 REM TRADING RULE
1360 REM
1370       IF SMOV(I) = 0 OR LMOV(I) = 0 THEN GOTO 1400
1380       IF SMOV(I)>LMOV(I) AND SL$<>"L" THEN SL$="L":ARRY$(I)="L":TT=TT+1
1390       IF SMOV(I)<LMOV(I) AND SL$<>"S" THEN SL$="S":ARRY$(I)="S":TT=TT+1
1400     NEXT I
1410 PRINT TAB(17)TT;
1420 REM
1430 REM COMPUTE PROFITS AND DISPLAY RESULTS
1440 REM
1450     SL$ = " " : LOWDAY = 9999
1460     XLAST = CLOS(1)
1470     CURPROFIT = 0
1480     DAYPROFIT = 0
1490     INTRATRADE = 0 : WIN = 0 : LOSS = 0 : MAX = 0
1500     FOR I = 1 TO M
1510       PROFIT = 0
1520       IF ARRY$(I) = "S" OR ARRY$(I) = "L" THEN GOTO 1540
1530       GOTO 1610
1540       IF INTRATRADE > 0 THEN WIN = WIN + 1
1550       IF INTRATRADE < 0 THEN LOSS = LOSS + 1
1560       INTRATRADE = 0
1570       IF SL$ = "S" THEN PROFIT = XLAST - CLOS(I)
1580       IF SL$ = "L" THEN PROFIT = CLOS(I) - XLAST
```

```
1590      XLAST = CLOS(I)
1600      SL$ = ARRY$(I)
1610      IF SL$ = "S" THEN CURPROFIT = XLAST - CLOS(I)
1620      IF SL$ = "L" THEN CURPROFIT = CLOS(I) - XLAST
1630      XLAST = CLOS(I)
1640      INTRATRADE = INTRATRADE + CURPROFIT
1650      IF MAX > (INTRATRADE + PROFIT) THEN MAX = (INTRATRADE + PROFIT)
1660      IF LOWDAY > DAYPROFIT THEN LOWDAY = DAYPROFIT
1670     NEXT I
1680 PRINT TAB(26)WIN;TAB(33)LOSS;
1690 PRINT TAB(41)LOWDAY;TAB(51)MAX;
1700 PRINT TAB(63) INT(DAYPROFIT * 100/TT) / 100;
1710 PRINT TAB(71) DAYPROFIT
1720    NEXT LJ
1730   NEXT SJ
1740 REM ************************************************************************
1750 REM *          WILL ALLOW USER TO REPEAT PROCESS WITH NEW PARAMETERS      *
1760 REM ************************************************************************
1770 PRINT : PRINT
1780 INPUT "WOULD YOU LIKE TO REPEAT THE PROCESS (Y/N)";AN$
1790  IF AN$ = "Y" THEN GOTO 370
1800 END
```

```
10    REM ***************************************************************
20    REM *                 TECHNICAL VOLATILITY OPTIMIZATION            *
30    REM *                                                              *
40    REM *      THIS IS A VARIATION OF THE VOLATILITY PROGRAM ALLOWING   *
50    REM *    THE USER TO EVALUATE A TECHNICAL SYSTEM OVER A RANGE OF MOVING *
60    REM *    AVERAGES, WITH DIFFERENT CONSTANTS.                        *
70    REM *                                                              *
80    REM *      VARIABLES USED:  HIG( ) = ARRAY OF DAILY HIGH PRICES     *
90    REM *                       LOW( ) = ARRAY OF DAILY LOW PRICES      *
100   REM *                      CLOS( ) = ARRAY OF DAILY CLOSING PRICES  *
110   REM *                     ARRY$( ) = ARRAY OF SHORT OR LONG POSITIONS *
120   REM *                       STP( ) = ARRAY OF DAILY STOPS           *
130   REM *                            M = NUMBER OF OBSERVATIONS IN THE DATA *
140   REM *                    T1,T2,TR = VARIATIONS OF THE TRUE RANGE    *
150   REM *                         AVTR = AVERAGE TRUE RANGE FOR 'X' DAYS *
160   REM *                            C = VOLATILITY CONSTANT            *
170   REM *                          AVC = AVERAGE RANGE TIMES THE CONSTANT *
180   REM *                          SIC = SIGNIFICANT CLOSE              *
190   REM *                          SL$ = SHORT OR LONG SIGNALS          *
200   REM *                     TTLPROFIT = TOTAL PROFITS                 *
210   REM *                     CURPROFIT = CURRENT PROFITS               *
220   REM *                     DAYPROFIT = THE PROFIT TO DATE            *
230   REM *                    INTRATRADE = PROFIT FROM CURRENT TRADING POSITION *
240   REM *                        XLAST = CLOSING PRICE OF PREVIOUS DAY  *
250   REM *                       LOWDAY = MAX TOTAL DRAWDOWN             *
260   REM *                          MAX = MAX INTRA-TRADE DRAWDOWN       *
270   REM *                          WIN = THE NUMBER OF WINNING TRADES   *
280   REM *                         LOSS = THE NUMBER OF LOSING TRADES    *
290   REM *                    AVEPROFIT = THE AVERAGE PROFIT PER TRADE   *
300   REM *                     TTLTRADES = THE TOTAL NUMBER OF TRADES    *
310   REM *                                                              *
320   REM ***************************************************************
330   DIM HIG(100),LOW(100),CLOS(100),STP(100),ARRY$(100)
340   REM
350   REM
360   REM ********************** INPUT THE DATA ***************************
370   GOSUB 490
380   REM
390   REM
400   REM ********************** DO COMPUTATIONS **************************
410   GOTO 1550
420   REM
430   REM
440   REM ********************** END OF PROGRAM ***************************
450   REM
460   REM
470   REM
480   REM
490   REM ***************************************************************
500   REM *-                 SUBROUTINE TO INPUT DATA                    *
510   REM ***************************************************************
520   REM
530   JS = 1
540   CLS : REM CLEAR SCREEN AND HOME CURSOR
```

```
550 PRINT "ARE YOU GOING TO TYPE IN:"
560 PRINT "1) THE HIGH, LOW, AND CLOSING PRICES"
570 PRINT "2) OR ONLY THE CLOSING PRICES"
580 INPUT ISERIES
590   ON ISERIES GOTO 640,1110
600   GOTO 540
610 REM
620 REM ********** INPUT DATA FOR HIGH, LOW, AND CLOSING PRICES ************
630 REM
640   CLS : REM CLEAR SCREEN AND HOME CURSOR
650 PRINT "ENTER '999' TO END DATA ENTRY"
660   I = 1
670 PRINT "ENTER HIGH  PRICE FOR DAY #";I; : INPUT HIG(I)
680   IF HIG(I) = 999 THEN GOTO 770
690 PRINT "ENTER LOW   PRICE FOR DAY #";I; : INPUT LOW(I)
700   IF LOW(I) = 999 THEN GOTO 770
710 PRINT "ENTER CLOSE PRICE FOR DAY #";I; : INPUT CLOS(I)
720   IF CLOS(I) = 999 THEN GOTO 770
730 PRINT TAB(40) "ENTER '999' TO END DATA ENTRY"
740   IF ED = 1 THEN ED = 0 : RETURN
750   I = I + 1 : REM INCREMENT DAY COUNTER
760   GOTO 670
770   I = I - 1 : REM DECREMENT DAY COUNTER WHEN DATA = 999 (LAST TIME)
780   LASTDAY = I : M = I
790   START = 1
800   CLS : REM CLEAR SCREEN AND HOME CURSOR
810 PRINT "DAY        HIGH        LOW         CLOSE"
820 PRINT "---       --------    --------    --------"
830   FOR I = START TO START + 19
840 PRINT TAB(1)I;TAB(9)HIG(I);TAB(19)LOW(I);TAB(29)CLOS(I)
850    IF I = LASTDAY THEN GOTO 870
860   NEXT I
870 INPUT "ENTER DAY TO CHANGE OR '0' TO CONTINUE";DAY
880   IF DAY = 0 AND I < LASTDAY THEN START = I : GOTO 800
890   IF DAY = 0 THEN GOTO 1010
900   I = DAY
910 PRINT "CURRENT VALUES ARE:"
920 PRINT "DAY        HIGH        LOW         CLOSE"
930 PRINT "---       --------    --------    --------"
940 PRINT TAB(1)DAY;TAB(9) HIG(I);TAB(19)LOW(I);TAB(29)CLOS(I)
950 PRINT "ENTER NEW DATA:"
960 PRINT : REM SEPARATE WORDS ON SCREEN
970   ED = 1 : REM GO INTO EDIT MODE
980   GOSUB 670
990   GOTO 800
1000 REM
1010 REM SET PARAMETERS
1020 REM
1030 INPUT "SPECIFY LOW VALUE FOR MOVING AVERAGE:";LMOVAVE
1040 INPUT "SPECIFY HIGH VALUE FOR MOVING AVERAGE:";HMOVAVE
1050 INPUT "SPECIFY STEP SIZE:";SMOVAVE
1060 INPUT "SPECIFY LOW VALUE OF THE CONSTANT:";LCONST
1070 INPUT "SPECIFY HIGH VALUE OF THE CONSTANT:";HCONST
1080 INPUT "SPECIFY STEP SIZE:";SCONST
```

```
1090   RETURN
1100 REM
1110 REM ********** LOAD DATA FOR CLOSING PRICE ONLY ***********************
1120 REM
1130   CLS : REM CLEAR SCREEN AND HOME CURSOR
1140   I = 1 : REM INITIALIZE DAY COUNTER
1150 PRINT "ENTER ' 999' AS CLOSING PRICE TO END DATA ENTRY"
1160 PRINT "ENTER CLOSING PRICE FOR DAY";I; : INPUT CLOS(I)
1170   IF CLOS(I) = 999 THEN GOTO 1200
1180   I = I + 1
1190   GOTO 1160
1200   I = I - 1 : REM DECREMENTS COUNTER ON LAST ENTRY
1210   LASTDAY = I : M = I
1220   START = 1
1230   CLS : REM CLEAR SCREEN AND HOME CURSOR
1240 PRINT " DAY        CLOSING PRICE"
1250 PRINT " ---        -------------"
1260   FOR I = START TO START + 19
1270 PRINT TAB(2)I;TAB(15)CLOS(I)
1280    IF I = LASTDAY THEN GOTO 1300
1290   NEXT I
1300 INPUT "ENTER DAY TO CHANGE OR '0' TO CONTINUE";DAY
1310   IF DAY = 0 AND I < LASTDAY THEN START = I : GOTO 1230
1320   IF DAY = 0 THEN GOTO 1370
1330 PRINT "THE CLOSING PRICE FOR DAY";DAY;" IS";CLOS(DAY);
1340 INPUT "NEW PRICE";CLOS(DAY)
1350   GOTO 1230
1360 REM
1370 REM ********** FIND HIGH AND LOW LOOKING BACK 'X' DAYS *****************
1380 REM
1390 INPUT "HOW MANY DAYS IN THE BACKWARD LOOK";JS
1400   FOR I = JS TO M
1410    XLOW = 9999
1420    XHIG = -9999
1430    FOR K = I - JS + 1 TO I
1440     IF XLOW > CLOS(K) THEN XLOW = CLOS(K)
1450     IF XHIG < CLOS(K) THEN XHIG = CLOS(K)
1460    NEXT K
1470    LOW(I) = XLOW
1480    HIG(I) = XHIG
1490   NEXT I
1500   GOSUB 1010
1510   RETURN
1520 REM
1530 REM ********** PRINT HEADING AND COMPUTE THE RESULTS ******************
1540 REM
1550   CLS : REM CLEAR SCREEN AND HOME CURSOR
1560 PRINT "MOVING        TOTAL    # OF  # OF   MAX TOTAL   MAX INTRA  AVE PROFIT
TOTAL"
1570 PRINT " AVE    CONST   TRADES WINS LOSSES DRAWDOWN    TRADE DD   PER TRADE
   PROFIT"
1580   PRINT "------  -----  ------ ---- ------ ---------  ---------  -----------
------"
1590   FOR J1 = LMOVAVE TO HMOVAVE STEP SMOVAVE
```

```
1600    FOR C = LCONST TO HCONST STEP SCONST
1610 PRINT TAB(2)J1;TAB(8)C;
1620    TR = 0 : TTLTRADES = 0 : T1 = 0 : T2 = 0 : SUMTR = 0 : AVTR = 0
1630    WIN=0 : LOSS=0 : SL$="L": INTRALOW=9999: INTRATRADE=0: MAX=0
1640    SIC = CLOS(1)
1650    FOR I = 1 TO J1
1660      IF CLOS(I) > SIC THEN SIC = CLOS(I)
1670    NEXT I
1680    IF CLOS(J1+3) > SIC THEN SL$ = "S"
1690    FOR I = 3 TO M
1700      STP(I) = 0
1710      ARRY$(I) = " "
1720      J = I - 1
1730      TR = HIG(J) - LOW(J)
1740      T1 = HIG(J) - CLOS(J-1)
1750      T2 = CLOS(J-1) - LOW(J)
1760      IF TR < T1 THEN TR = T1
1770      IF TR < T2 THEN TR = T2
1780      IF I > J1 + 3 THEN GOTO 1830
1790      SUMTR = SUMTR + TR
1800      AVTR = SUMTR/J1
1810      IF SIC < CLOS(I) THEN SIC = CLOS(I)
1820      IF I <= J1 + 3 THEN GOTO 2060
1830      X = J1
1840      AVTR = (AVTR * (X-1) + TR)/X
1850      ARC = AVTR * C
1860      IF SL$ = "L" THEN GOTO 1880
1870      GOTO 1960
1880      STP(I) = SIC - ARC
1890      IF LOW(I) < STP(I) THEN GOTO 1910
1900      GOTO 1960
1910      SL$ = "S"
1920      ARRY$(I) = "S"
1930      TTLTRADES = TTLTRADES + 1
1940      SIC = CLOS(I)
1950      GOTO 2060
1960      IF SL$ <> "S" THEN GOTO 2040
1970      STP(I) = SIC + ARC
1980      IF HIG(I) <= STP(I) THEN GOTO 2040
1990      SL$ = "L"
2000      ARRY$(I) = "L"
2010      TTLTRADES = TTLTRADES + 1
2020      SIC = CLOS(I)
2030      GOTO 2060 : REM NEXT I
2040      IF CLOS(I) < SIC AND SL$ = "S" THEN SIC = CLOS(I)
2050      IF CLOS(I) > SIC AND SL$ = "L" THEN SIC = CLOS(I)
2060    NEXT I
2070 PRINT TAB(15) TTLTRADES;
2080 REM
2090 REM COMPUTE PROFITS AND DISPLAY RESULTS
2100 REM
2110    SL$ = " " : LOWDAY = 9999
2120    XLAST = CLOS(1)
2130    CURPROFIT = 0
```

```
2140      DAYPROFIT = 0
2150      INTRATRADE = 0 : WIN = 0: LOSS = 0 : MAX = 0
2160      FOR I = 1 TO M
2170       PROFIT  = 0
2180       IF ARRY$(I) = "S" OR ARRY$(I) = "L" THEN GOTO 2200
2190       GOTO 2270
2200       IF INTRATRADE > 0 THEN WIN = WIN + 1
2210       IF INTRATRADE < 0 THEN LOSS = LOSS + 1
2220       INTRATRADE = 0
2230       IF SL$ = "S" THEN PROFIT = XLAST - CLOS(I)
2240       IF SL$ = "L" THEN PROFIT = CLOS(I) - XLAST
2250       XLAST = CLOS(I)
2260       SL$ = ARRY$(I)
2270       IF SL$ = "S" THEN CURPROFIT = XLAST - CLOS(I)
2280       IF SL$ = "L" THEN CURPROFIT = CLOS(I) - XLAST
2290       DAYPROFIT = DAYPROFIT + CURPROFIT + PROFIT
2300       XLAST = CLOS(I)
2310       INTRATRADE = INTRATRADE + CURPROFIT
2320       IF MAX > (INTRATRADE + PROFIT) THEN MAX = (INTRATRADE + PROFIT)
2330       IF LOWDAY > DAYPROFIT THEN LOWDAY = DAYPROFIT
2340      NEXT I
2350 PRINT TAB(26)WIN;TAB(33)LOSS;
2360 PRINT TAB(41)LOWDAY;TAB(51)MAX;
2370 PRINT TAB(63) INT(DAYPROFIT * 100/TTLTRADES)/100;
2380 PRINT TAB(71) DAYPROFIT
2390    NEXT C
2400   NEXT J1
2410 REM
2420 REM ****** WILL ALLOW USER TO REPEAT PROCESS WITH NEW PARAMETERS *******
2430 REM
2440 PRINT
2450 INPUT "WOULD YOU LIKE TO REPEAT THIS PROCESS";AN$
2460  IF AN$ <> "Y" THEN END
2470  ON ISERIES GOSUB 1010,1370
2480  GOTO 400
```

```
10   REM   ****************************************************************
20   REM   *                 PARABOLIC OPTIMIZATION PROGRAM               *
30   REM   *                                                              *
40   REM   *      THIS PROGRAM IS A VARIATION OF THE PARABOLIC PROGRAM.  IT *
50   REM   *   WILL ALLOW THE USER TO USE A RANGE OF PARAMETER VALUES IN   *
60   REM   *   A TRADING SIMULATION, WITH THE RESULTS SHOWING THE NUMBER OF *
70   REM   *   WINS AND LOSSES FROM EACH TRADING STRATEGY, AS WELL AS THE   *
80   REM   *   MAXIMUM TRADING LOSS, PROFIT PER TRADE, AND TOTAL PROFIT.    *
90   REM   *                                                              *
100  REM   *      VARIABLES USED: HIG( ) = ARRAY OF DAILY HIGH PRICES      *
110  REM   *                      LOW( ) = ARRAY OF DAILY LOW PRICES       *
120  REM   *                     CLOS( ) = ARRAY OF DAILY CLOSING PRICES   *
130  REM   *                   ARRY$( ) = ARRAY OF SHORT OR LONG POSITIONS *
140  REM   *                      STP( ) = ARRAY OF DAILY STOPS            *
150  REM   *                           M = NUMBER OF OBSERVATIONS IN THE DATA *
160  REM   *                          AF = ACCELERATING FACTOR FOR THE CONSTANT *
170  REM   *                      ALIMIT = CEILING LIMIT FOR THE CONSTANT  *
180  REM   *                         SL$ = SHORT OR LONG SIGNALS           *
190  REM   *                    TTLPROFIT = TOTAL PROFITS                  *
200  REM   *                    CURPROFIT = CURRENT PROFITS                *
210  REM   *                    DAYPROFIT = THE PROFIT TO DATE             *
220  REM   *                   INTRATRADE = PROFIT ON CURRENT TRADING POSITION *
230  REM   *                       XLAST = CLOSING PRICE OF PREVIOUS DAY   *
240  REM   *                      LOWDAY = MAX TOTAL DRAWDOWN              *
250  REM   *                         MAX = MAX INTRA-TRADE DRAWDOWN        *
260  REM   *                         WIN = NUMBER OF WINS                  *
270  REM   *                        LOSS = NUMBER OF LOSSES                *
280  REM   *                    AVEPROFIT = TOTAL PROFIT / TOTAL TRADES    *
290  REM   *                                                              *
300  REM   ****************************************************************
310  DIM HIG(100),LOW(100),CLOS(100),STP(100),ARRY$(100)
320  REM ************************* INPUT THE DATA ************************
330  GOSUB 410
340  REM ************************* DO COMPUTATIONS ***********************
350  GOTO 1430
360  REM ************************* END OF PROGRAM ************************
370  REM
380  REM
390  REM
400  REM
410  REM   ****************************************************************
420  REM   *              SUBROUTINE TO INPUT DATA                        *
430  REM   ****************************************************************
440  JS = 1
450  CLS : REM CLEAR SCREEN AND HOME CURSOR
460  PRINT "ARE YOU GOING TO TYPE IN:"
470  PRINT "1) THE HIGH, LOW, AND CLOSING PRICES"
480  PRINT "2) OR ONLY THE CLOSING PRICES"
490  INPUT ISERIES
500  ON ISERIES GOTO 550,1020
510  GOTO 450
520  REM
530  REM ***********INPUT DATA FOR HIGH, LOW, AND CLOSING PRICES *************
540  REM
```

```
550   CLS : REM CLEAR SCREEN AND HOME CURSOR
560  PRINT "ENTER `999' TO END DATA ENTRY"
570   I = 1
580  PRINT "ENTER HIGH  PRICE FOR DAY #";I; : INPUT HIG(I)
590   IF HIG(I) = 999 THEN GOTO 680
600  PRINT "ENTER LOW   PRICE FOR DAY #";I; : INPUT LOW(I)
610   IF LOW(I) = 999 THEN GOTO 680
620  PRINT "ENTER CLOSE PRICE FOR DAY #";I; : INPUT CLOS(I)
630   IF CLOS(I) = 999 THEN GOTO 680
640  PRINT : REM PRINTS BLANK LINE BETWEEN DAYS
650   IF ED = 1 THEN ED = 0 : RETURN
660   I = I + 1 : REM INCREMENT DAY COUNTER
670   GOTO 580
680   I = I - 1 : REM COMES HERE WHEN DATA = 999
690   LASTDAY = I : M = I
700   START = 1
710   CLS : REM CLEAR SCREEN AND HOME CURSOR
720  PRINT "DAY       HIGH       LOW        CLOSE"
730  PRINT "---       --------   --------   --------"
740   FOR I = START TO START + 19
750  PRINT TAB(1)I;TAB(9)HIG(I);TAB(19)LOW(I);TAB(29)CLOS(I)
760    IF I = LASTDAY THEN GOTO 780
770   NEXT I
780  INPUT "ENTER DAY TO CHANGE OR `0' TO CONTINUE";DAY
790   IF DAY = 0 AND I < LASTDAY THEN START = I : GOTO 710
800   IF DAY = 0 THEN GOTO 910
810   I = DAY
820  PRINT "CURRENT VALUES ARE:"
830  PRINT "DAY       HIGH       LOW        CLOSE"
840  PRINT "---       --------   --------   --------"
850  PRINT TAB(1)DAY;TAB(9)HIG(I);TAB(19)LOW(I);TAB(29)CLOS(I)
860  PRINT "ENTER NEW DATA:"
870  PRINT : REM SEPARATE WORDS ON SCREEN
880   ED = 1 : REM GO INTO EDIT MODE
890    GOSUB 580
900    GOTO 710
910  REM
920  REM *****************SET PARAMETERS FOR PARABOLIC SYSTEM****************
930  REM
940  INPUT "SPECIFY LOW VALUE FOR ACCELERATING FACTOR";LAF
950  INPUT "SPECIFY HIGH VALUE FOR ACCELERATING FACTOR";HAF
960  INPUT "SPECIFY STEP FOR THE ACCELERATING FACTOR";SAF
970  INPUT "SPECIFY LOW VALUE FOR THE STEPPING FUNCTION";LLIMIT
980  INPUT "SPECIFY HIGH VALUE FOR THE STEPPING FUNCTION";HLIMIT
990  INPUT "SPECIFY THE STEP SIZE FOR THE STEPPING FUNCTION";SLIMIT
1000   RETURN
1010 REM
1020 REM **************** INPUT DATA FOR CLOSING PRICE ONLY ****************
1030 REM
1040   CLS : REM CLEAR SCREEN AND HOME CURSOR
1050   I = 1 : REM INITIALIZE DAY COUNTER
1060 PRINT "ENTER `999' AS CLOSING PRICE TO END DATA ENTRY"
1070 PRINT "ENTER CLOSING PRICE FOR DAY";I; : INPUT CLOS(I)
1080   IF CLOS(I) = 999 THEN GOTO 1110
```

```
1090   I = I + 1
1100   GOTO 1070
1110   I = I - 1 : REM DECREMENTS COUNTER ON LAST ENTRY
1120   LASTDAY = I : M = I
1130   START = 1
1140   CLS : REM CLEAR SCREEN AND HOME CURSOR
1150 PRINT " DAY        CLOSING PRICE"
1160 PRINT " ---        -------------"
1170   FOR I = START TO START + 19
1180 PRINT TAB(2)I;TAB(15)CLOS(I)
1190    IF I = LASTDAY THEN GOTO 1210
1200   NEXT I
1210 INPUT "ENTER DAY TO CHANGE OR `0' TO CONTINUE";DAY
1220   IF DAY = 0 AND I < LASTDAY THEN START = I : GOTO 1140
1230   IF DAY = 0 THEN GOTO 1300
1240 PRINT "THE CLOSING PRICE FOR DAY";DAY;" IS";CLOS(DAY);
1250 INPUT "NEW PRICE";CLOS(DAY)
1260   GOTO 1140
1270 REM
1280 REM ******* SUBROUTINE TO FIND HIGH AND LOW LOOKING BACK `X' DAYS *******
1290 REM
1300 INPUT "HOW MANY DAYS IN THE BACKWARD LOOK";JS
1310   FOR I = JS TO M
1320     XLOW = 9999
1330     XHIG = -9999
1340     FOR K = I - JS + 1 TO I
1350       IF XLOW > CLOS(K) THEN XLOW = CLOS(K)
1360       IF XHIG < CLOS(K) THEN XHIG = CLOS(K)
1370     NEXT K
1380     LOW(I) = XLOW
1390     HIG(I) = XHIG
1400   NEXT I
1410   GOSUB 910
1420   RETURN
1430 REM ***************************************************************************
1440 REM *                 SUBROUTINE TO DO CALCULATIONS                          *
1450 REM ***************************************************************************
1460   CLS: PRINT
1470 PRINT "ACC   STEP   TOTAL   WINS   LOSSES   MAX TOTAL   MAX INTRA-   AVE PROFIT
     TOTAL"
1480 PRINT "FAC   SIZE   TRADES                 DRAWDOWN    TRADE DD     PER TRADE
     PROFIT"
1490 PRINT "---   ----   ------   ----   ------   ---------   ----------   ----------
     ------"
1500   FOR AF = LAF TO HAF STEP SAF
1510     FOR ALIMIT = LLIMIT TO HLIMIT STEP SLIMIT
1520 PRINT AF ;TAB(6)ALIMIT;
1530     ITIME = 0
1540     WIN = 0 : LOSS = 0
1550     ARRY$(1) = " "
1560     ARRY$(2) = " "
1570     SL$ = "L"
1580     LSIP = LOW(1)
1590     EP = LOW(1)
```

```
1600     STP(2) = LOW(1)
1610     TTLTRADES = 0
1620     SSIP = HIG(1)
1630     C = 0
1640     IF CLOS(1) > CLOS (2) THEN GOTO 1660
1650     GOTO 1690
1660     SL$ = "S"
1670     EP = HIG(1)
1680     STP(2) = HIG(1)
1690     FOR I = 3 TO M
1700      ITIME = ITIME + 1
1710      ARRY$(I) = " "
1720      IF C = 0 THEN STP(I) = EP : GOTO 1740
1730      STP(I) = STP(I-1) + C * (EP - STP(I-1))
1740      C = C + AF
1750      IF C > ALIMIT THEN C = ALIMIT
1760      IF SL$ = "L" THEN GOTO 1780
1770      GOTO 1910
1780      IF STP(I) > LOW(I-1) OR STP(I) > LOW(I-2) AND ITIME<>1 THEN GOTO 1800
1790      GOTO 1820
1800      IF LOW(I-1) < LOW(I-2) THEN STP(I) = LOW(I-1) : GOTO 1820
1810      STP(I) = LOW(I-2)
1820      IF STP(I) > LOW(I) THEN GOTO 1840
1830      GOTO 1910
1840      SL$ = "S"
1850      ARRY$(I) = "S" : TTLTRADES = TTLTRADES + 1
1860      SSIP = LOW(I)
1870      EP = LSIP
1880      C = 0
1890      ITIME = 0
1900      GOTO 2100
1910      IF SL$ = "S" THEN GOTO 1930
1920      GOTO 2060
1930      IF STP(I)<HIG(I-1) OR STP(I)<HIG(I-2) AND ITIME<>1 THEN GOTO 1950
1940      GOTO 1970
1950      IF HIG(I-1) > HIG(I-2) THEN STP(I) = HIG(I-1) : GOTO 1970
1960      STP(I) = HIG(I-2)
1970      IF STP(I) < HIG(I) THEN GOTO 1990
1980      GOTO 2060
1990      SL$ = "L"
2000      ARRY$(I) = "L" : TTLTRADES = TTLTRADES + 1
2010      LSIP = HIG(I)
2020      EP = SSIP
2030      C = 0
2040      ITIME = 0
2050      GOTO 2100
2060      IF SSIP > LOW(I) AND SL$ = "S" THEN SSIP = LOW(I)
2070      IF LSIP < HIG(I) AND SL$ = "L" THEN LSIP = HIG(I)
2080      IF SL$ = "S" THEN EP = SSIP
2090      IF SL$ = "L" THEN EP = LSIP
2100     NEXT I
2110 PRINT TAB(12)TTLTRADES;
2120 REM ***********************************************************************
```

```
2130 REM *                        COMPUTE PROFITS AND DISPLAY RESULTS              *
2140 REM *********************************************************************
2150    SL$ = " "  : LOWDAY = 9999
2160    XLAST = CLOS(I)
2170    CURPROFIT = 0
2180    DAYPROFIT = 0
2190    INTRATRADE = 0 : WIN = 0 : LOSS = 0 : MAX = 0
2200    FOR I = 1 TO M
2210     PROFIT = 0
2220     IF ARRY$(I) = "S" OR ARRY$(I) = "L" THEN GOTO 2240
2230     GOTO 2310
2240     IF INTRATRADE > 0 THEN WIN = WIN + 1
2250     IF INTRATRADE < 0 THEN LOSS = LOSS + 1
2260     INTRATRADE = 0
2270     IF SL$ = "S" THEN PROFIT = XLAST - CLOS(I)
2280     IF SL$ = "L" THEN PROFIT = CLOS(I) - XLAST
2290     XLAST = CLOS(I)
2300     SL$ = ARRY$(I)
2310     IF SL$ = "S" THEN CURPROFIT = XLAST - CLOS(I)
2320     IF SL$ = "L" THEN CURPROFIT = CLOS(I) - XLAST
2330     DAYPROFIT = DAYPROFIT + CURPROFIT + PROFIT
2340     XLAST = CLOS(I)
2350     INTRATRADE = INTRATRADE + CURPROFIT
2360     IF MAX > (INTRATRADE + PROFIT) THEN MAX = (INTRATRADE + PROFIT)
2370     IF LOWDAY > DAYPROFIT THEN LOWDAY = DAYPROFIT
2380     NEXT I
2390     AVEPROFIT = INT(DAYPROFIT * 100/TTLTRADES)/100
2400     DAYPROFIT = INT(DAYPROFIT * 100)/100
2410     LOWDAY = INT(LOWDAY * 10)/10
2420     MAX = INT(MAX *10)/10
2430 PRINT TAB(19)WIN;TAB(25)LOSS;
2440 PRINT TAB(33) LOWDAY;TAB(44) MAX;
2450 PRINT TAB(56) AVEPROFIT;
2460 PRINT TAB(68) DAYPROFIT
2470   NEXT ALIMIT
2480  NEXT AF
2490 REM
2500 REM ******** WILL ALLOW USER TO REPEAT PROCESS WITH NEW PARAMETERS ******
2510 REM
2520 PRINT
2530 INPUT "WOULD YOU LIKE TO REPEAT THIS PROCESS";AN$
2540 IF AN$ <> "Y" THEN END
2550 ON ISERIES GOSUB 910,1300
2560 GOTO 340
```

Technical Systems References*

There are literally hundreds of books available that outline the general principles of technical systems. Three of the classics—which, as it happens, do not espouse any of the methods proposed in this section—are by Edwards and Magee (1948), by Elliot (1938), and by Gann (1976b). More recent books with less mystical approaches to the market include Kaufman (1978) and Wilder (1978). The trading methods in this book draw heavily from the techniques discussed in Wilder.

Fosback (1976) describes the use of a broad set of market indicators, ranging from short-sales ratios to money supply data, in predicting stock market movements.

The countervailing efficient market view has its roots in Cootner (1964). Two other influential works on efficient markets and the random walk hypothesis are by Jensen (1969) and by Fama (1970). A review of efficient markets is presented by Vasicek and McQuown (1972).

*Refer to bibliography at the back of this book for complete citations.

IV
OPTION TRADING

21
Introduction to Option Trading Strategies

Organized option trading began in 1973 with the opening of the Chicago Board Option Exchange. Since that time, the number of stocks with traded options has grown from less than two dozen to over 350, and the volume of stock option trading exceeds the volume of shares traded on the American Stock Exchange. Options are now also traded on a wide range of other securities, including Treasury bonds and Treasury notes, debt and commodity futures, and a number of market indexes. The volume of trading on options rivals, and often exceeds, the trading on the underlying securities. First viewed as a market for the speculator, where high leverage was tempered with a bound on losses, options are now used widely by institutional investors to hedge positions and to alter portfolio return characteristics.

The popularity of the options market in the investment community is mirrored by the academic interest in option pricing methods. Many securities, including warrants, convertible bonds, even the equity of a levered firm, can be viewed as options. Option pricing theory has become a powerful tool of analysis for these securities, and has provided a method for understanding and pricing in such disparate areas as equity-linked life insurance and mortgage-banking loan commitments. Options can be priced using elegant yet practical arbitrage pricing methods. These pricing methods are used widely by option traders, both market makers trading on the floor and sophisticated institutional traders. There are a number of popular on-line option pricing services, and many option pricing programs available for the small investor. Many investment houses have their own in-house pricing models. The methods presented in this section are comparable to the methods used by a number of option services and investment houses, and are superior to most microcomputer programs on the market. They are designed to reflect the most recent work in the area of option pricing while maintaining the need for computational efficiency and practical value.

THE OPTION CONTRACT

A *call option* is a contract that gives the holder the right to buy 100 shares of stock at a given price on or before a specific date. The price at which the stock can be bought is called the *exercise price* or the *striking price* of the option. The last date on which the option can be exercised is called the *expiration date* or the *maturity date*. The issuer of the option contract, the person who is obligated to sell the stock at the exercise price, is called the *option writer*.

Call options are also available on a number of securities besides stocks, and the standardization there may differ from the 100-share contract size of stock options. For example, the options on stock index futures specify the option contract as giving the right to buy one futures contract.

Table 21-1 lists some of the option quotes from the Chicago Board Option Exchange, the largest of the four stock option exchanges in the United States. The first column on the left in the table lists the name of the stock, with the closing price of the stock listed below it. For example, Brunswick shows a New York closing price of 34¾. The second column from the left gives the striking price of the option. Brunswick has options with striking prices ranging from 25 to 40, in increments of five. The number of exercise prices listed is governed by the recent range of the stock price—a new exercise price is listed when the stock price passes that exercise price. The more the stock price has varied in the recent past, the more exercise prices will be listed. The exercise

TABLE 21-1 Listed Options Quotations

Chicago Board

Option & NY Close	Strike Price	Calls–Last Sep	Calls–Last Dec	Calls–Last Mar	Puts–Last Sep	Puts–Last Dec	Puts–Last Mar
Apache	..15	1-16	⅜	½	r	r	r
BrisMy	..40	8¾	r	r	r	5-16	½
48⅜	...45	4	5½	r	¼	1	r
48⅜	...50	⅞	2⅜	r	1⅞	2¾	r
Bruns	...25	10	r	r	r	r	r
34¾	...30	5⅛	6¼	r	1-16	r	r
34¾	...35	1⅜	3	3¾	r	2	r
34¾	...40	¼	1 3-16	r	r	r	r
Celan	60	13⅛	r	r	r	r	r
73⅛	...65	8¼	8¾	r	r	r	r
73⅛	...70	r	r	r	¾	r	r
73⅛	...75	r	3⅛	r	r	r	r
73⅛	...80	r	1 15-16	s	r	r	s
Chamin	.15	6	6⅜	7	r	r	r
21	20	1 9-16	2⅜	3¼	⅝	1 5-16	1½
21	25	¼	11-16	1¼	4¼	4½	r
21	30	1-16	¼	s	r	r	s
CompSc	.10	r	3¾	r	r	r	r
13⅜	...15	¼	1⅛	r	r	r	2¾
13⅜	...20	1-16	r	7-16	r	r	r
Dow Ch	.25	r	6½	6¾	r	r	r
31⅛	...30	1¾	2¾	3¾	5-16	1¼	1⅝
31⅛	...35	3-16	13-16	1½	r	r	r
FBost	...45	6⅞	r	r	r	r	r
51	50	2½	4¾	r	r	r	r
Ford	30	r	r	r	r	1-16	3-16
45½	...35	10⅝	11½	12½	r	5-16	⅝
45½	...40	5¾	7⅛	8⅛	3-16	1	1⅝
45½	...45	1⅞	4	5¼	1¼	2⅝	3⅜
45½	...50	7-16	1 15-16	3⅛	r	5⅜	6¼
Gen El	..45	r	r	r	r	3-16	r
58⅛	...50	8⅜	9⅛	10½	1-16	7-16	r
58⅛	...55	3⅝	5⅛	6¼	⅜	1½	r
58⅛	...60	13-16	2⅜	3¾	r	3⅝	4⅜
G M	60	r	r	r	1-16	5-16	⅝
75⅞	...65	11¼	12½	r	1-16	11-16	1 1-16
75⅞	...70	6¾	8¼	9	¼	1⅜	2¼
75⅞	...75	2¾	4¾	6	1 3-16	3¼	4⅛
75⅞	...80	11-16	2 11-16	3⅞	4	6	r
75⅞	...85	⅛	s	s	r	s	s
Glf Wn	..30	1 7-16	2 13-16	4	11-16	1½	1⅞
30⅞	...35	3-16	1	1 11-16	r	r	r
HughTl	..15	⅞	1⅞	2¼	5-16	⅞	r
15⅝	...20	1-16	⅜	⅝	r	r	r
15⅝	...25	r	1-16	s	r	r	s
I T T	20	7¼	8	8½	r	r	7-16
27¼	...25	2⅝	4	4¾	5-16	1 1-16	1⅝
27¼	...30	¼	1½	2 5-16	r	3½	r
27¼	...35	r	½	1⅛	r	7⅞	r
27¼	...40	1-16	r	s	r	r	s
K mart	..30	3⅞	4¾	r	⅛	⅝	1
33¾	...35	⅝	2	2⅝	r	2½	r
33¾	...40	r	11-16	1 1-16	r	r	r
Litton	...65	11½	13½	r	r	r	r
76	70	7¼	9⅛	r	5-16	1½	r
76	75	2⅝	6	8	1 9-16	3½	r
76	80	⅞	3½	r	4⅝	r	r
76	85	¼	r	r	r	r	r
Loews	..85	r	r	r	r	r	3½
89¾	...95	r	5	r	r	r	r
MaryK	..10	1½	2¼	2¾	⅛	⅜	⅝
11⅜	...15	1-16	7-16	11-16	3¼	3⅝	r
Mc Don	.60	r	r	21	r	r	r
78¼	...65	13½	r	16¾	r	r	r
78¼	...70	8⅞	r	r	1-16	r	r
78¼	...75	4⅜	7	r	9-16	1¾	r
78¼	...80	1 7-16	4	6¼	2¾	r	r
78¼	...85	s	2	r	s	r	r
Mid SU	..10	2⅜	2 7-16	2½	r	¼	7-16
12⅜	...15	r	r	¼	r	2¾	2 15-16
N C R	.23¾	3½	r	s	r	r	s
27⅛	.27½	1⅛	2½	s	1½	2½	s
27⅛	...20	7⅛	r	8¼	r	¼	r
27⅛	...25	2 5-16	3½	4¾	7-16	1⅛	1⅝
27⅛	...30	7-16	1 7-16	2¼	3¼	4	r
NorSo	...60	11-16	2	r	r	r	r
NorTel	..35	6¼	r	r	r	r	r
40⅞	...40	1¾	3¾	5	1⅛	r	r
40⅞	...45	⅜	1½	r	r	r	r
Nw Ind	..45	4¼	5⅜	r	⅜	13-16	1¼
48¾	...50	13-16	2⅜	3½	r	2⅞	r
48¾	...55	⅛	⅞	1⅞	r	r	r
Parady	..10	r	r	6¼	1-16	¼	r
15¾	...15	1½	2 5-16	2⅞	½	1 7-16	r
15¾	...20	⅛	⅝	1⅛	r	r	r
R C A	...30	5¾	6⅝	r	⅛	r	r
35½	...35	1⅜	3	r	13-16	1 13-16	r
35½	...40	3-16	1	1¾	r	r	r
RalPur	..25	5	5½	r	r	⅜	r
30	30	⅞	2⅛	2⅞	15-16	1⅝	2
30	35	⅛	r	⅞	r	r	r
Revlon	..30	8⅜	8⅞	s	r	r	s
37⅞	...35	3½	5¼	r	⅜	1⅝	2⅛
37⅞	...40	15-16	2⅞	3⅞	3⅛	4⅛	5
37⅞	...45	5-16	1⅜	2⅛	7¼	r	r

Listed Options Quotations

Friday, August 24, 1984

Closing prices of all options. Sales unit usually is 100 shares. Security description includes exercise price. Stock close is New York or American exchange final price.

Option & NY Close	Strike Price	Calls–Last Oct	Calls–Last Jan	Calls–Last Apr	Puts–Last Oct	Puts–Last Jan	Puts–Last Apr
32⅝	...40	3-16	⅝	s	r	r	s
32⅝	...45	⅛	s	s	r	s	s
Kerr M	..30	1⅜	2⅜	3	1⅜	r	r
29¾	...35	5-16	⅞	r	r	r	r
Loral	...25	4½	r	r	r	r	r
29	30	1⅝	r	r	2	r	r
Merck	..80	5⅞	r	r	¾	r	r
84⅛	...85	3⅛	4¾	6¾	3	r	r
84⅛	...90	1⅛	3	r	6¼	7	r
84⅛	...95	⅜	r	s	r	r	s
84⅛	..100	r	⅝	s	r	r	s
M M M	.70	r	r	r	r	5-16	r
83½	...75	9½	r	r	¼	r	r
83½	...80	5½	r	r	15-16	r	r
83½	...85	2¼	4¼	5¾	2⅞	r	4½
83½	...90	¾	2¼	3⅜	r	r	r
Monsan	47½	3	r	s	r	r	s
48⅞	...45	4¾	6¼	r	½	1⅛	r
48⅞	...50	1¾	3⅜	r	r	r	r
48⅞	...55	½	1⅜	2½	r	r	r
Nw Air	..40	1 9-16	3	r	r	r	r
39	45	½	r	r	r	r	r
PaineW	..25	r	r	r	3-16	r	r
33¾	...30	5	r	r	1	r	r
33¾	...35	2⅜	4	r	3	3¾	r
33¾	...40	15-16	2	3	r	r	r
Pennz	...30	7	6⅞	r	1-16	r	r
36½	...35	2⅛	3	3¼	¾	r	r
36½	...40	⅜	15-16	1¼	r	r	r
Pepsi	...40	4½	r	r	r	r	r
43⅞	...45	1	2⅛	3⅛	r	2¾	r
Polar	...25	6⅞	r	r	⅛	7-16	r
31⅞	...30	2 15-16	3¾	r	⅞	1¾	2
31⅞	...35	¾	1⅝	2¼	r	r	r
Sabine	...15	r	r	r	r	r	7-16
19	20	1 1-16	r	r	r	r	r
Sperry	...30	12¾	r	r	r	r	r
42½	...35	7¾	8¼	r	⅛	½	r
42½	...40	3½	4⅞	r	1	1⅞	r
42½	...45	1 1-16	2½	3¼	r	4⅛	r
42½	...50	⅜	s	s	r	s	s
Squibb	...40	7¾	9¼	r	⅛	r	r
46⅜	...45	3½	5⅜	r	⅞	1¼	r
46⅜	...50	¾	1¾	3¼	3⅛	r	r
StorTec	...5	r	6⅞	7	r	r	r
11⅝	...10	2 1-16	2¾	3½	5-16	11-16	1 1-16
11⅝	...15	⅜	15-16	1 5-16	3½	4	4
Tandy	..30	1 15-16	r	r	r	r	r
Teldyn	.180	r	88	s	r	r	s
265	...190	r	78	s	r	1	s
265	...200	r	r	s	⅜	r	s
265	...210	55	r	s	⅝	r	s
265	...220	47	r	s	⅞	r	s
265	...230	38½	45½	r	1¾	r	r
265	...240	29½	37	40	2⅞	6¾	10½
265	...250	22	r	r	5	10	r
265	...260	15¾	r	28¼	9	13⅞	r
265	...270	10	17¾	24	14¼	r	r
265	...280	6⅝	13½	19	r	r	r
Teldy o	170	96	98	s	r	r	s
Tex In	.110	r	39	r	⅛	1	r
145½	.120	25½	r	r	7-16	1½	r
145½	.130	16¾	22	r	⅞	3½	r
145½	.140	10¼	15	18¼	3¼	r	6½
145½	.150	5	9¾	13¼	8	11	r
Upjohn	..40	r	r	r	r	5-16	r
52⅞	...45	8⅜	r	r	r	r	r
52⅞	...50	4	5¾	7½	1	r	r
52⅞	...55	1⅝	3½	4¼	3½	r	r
52⅞	...60	9-16	r	3	r	r	r
52⅞	...70	r	r	s	16½	r	s
Weyerh	..25	r	r	r	3-16	r	r
29½	...30	1¼	2	3¼	r	2	r
29½	...35	¼	⅝	r	r	r	r
Winnbg	..10	2¾	3¼	r	r	9-16	r
12⅜	...15	9-16	1 1-16	1⅝	r	r	r
Xerox	...35	4⅝	5⅜	r	r	⅞	1¼
39½	...40	1 5-16	2¼	2 15-16	1 15-16	2⅝	3⅜
39½	...45	5-16	¾	1¼	r	r	r
39½	...50	⅛	s	s	r	s	s
		Nov	**Feb**	**May**	**Nov**	**Feb**	**May**
Amdahl	.10	3¼	3⅞	r	⅜	r	r
12¾	...15	11-16	1⅜	1¾	r	r	r

Option & NY Close	Strike Price	Calls–Last Nov	Calls–Last Feb	Calls–Last May	Puts–Last Nov	Puts–Last Feb	Puts–Last May
23¼	...25	1⅛	2	r	r	r	r
23¼	...30	½	r	s	r	r	s
U A L	...30	r	r	s	r	¾	s
38⅝	...35	5⅛	r	r	1¼	2	r
38⅝	...40	2½	r	4½	3¼	r	5½
38⅝	...45	15-16	2⅛	r	r	r	r
U Tech	..30	r	r	s	r	¼	s
39¾	...35	5⅝	6⅛	r	r	r	1½
39¾	...40	2 5-16	3¼	r	1¾	2⅝	3¼
39¾	...45	¾	1⅜	2⅛	6	r	r
J Walt	..25	r	r	r	11-16	r	r
WarnCm	15	6⅛	6⅝	r	3-16	r	r
20⅞	...20	2¼	3¼	4	1	1½	1¾
20⅞	...25	½	1¼	2	4¼	4¾	r
20⅞	...30	⅛	s	s	r	s	s
Willms	..25	3¾	4	r	7-16	13-16	r
28⅛	...30	⅞	1 11-16	2⅛	r	r	r

Total call vol. 160,673 Call open int. 3,358,766
Total put vol. 68,835 Put open int. 1,312,779

American Exchange

Option & NY Close	Strike Price	Calls–Last Sep	Calls–Last Dec	Calls–Last Mar	Puts–Last Sep	Puts–Last Dec	Puts–Last Mar
Alcan	25	r	5½	r	r	r	r
29⅝	...30	1	2¼	3½	1¼	r	r
29⅝	...35	⅛	13-16	1¼	r	r	r
29⅝	...40	r	¼	s	r	r	s
Amax	...15	6½	r	r	r	r	r
21	20	1⅝	r	3⅛	⅝	1	r
21	25	⅛	⅞	1⅜	r	r	r
AmBrnd	.55	r	r	r	⅛	⅜	r
60⅛	...60	1¼	2½	r	1 1-16	r	r
Asarco	...20	3½	4¼	5	3-16	1	1⅜
23⅜	...25	11-16	1¾	2½	2¼	r	r
23⅜	...30	1-16	½	r	r	r	r
Beat F	..25	4	4⅜	4⅝	r	r	r
29	30	7-16	1⅛	2	⅜	2	2⅜
29	35	1-16	3-16	⅝	r	r	r
BwnFer	.30	r	r	8⅞	r	r	r
37⅝	...35	2⅞	r	r	⅜	r	1⅞
37⅝	...40	r	1¾	2⅝	r	r	r
BucyEr	..15	¼	½	¾	r	r	2⅝
Chase	...35	7½	r	r	1-16	r	r
42½	...40	3⅛	r	5	½	1 9-16	2¼
42½	...45	½	1⅝	r	r	3⅞	r
42½	...50	r	9-16	s	r	r	s
42½	...55	r	¼	s	r	r	s
Chevrn	..30	r	6½	r	r	5-16	9-16
36⅛	...35	1½	2½	3	5-16	1⅛	r
36⅛	...40	1-16	½	1	r	r	r
Coastl	27¼	r	r	s	¼	r	s
29⅛	.31⅞	¼	r	s	r	r	s
29⅛	.36⅜	1-16	r	s	r	r	s
29⅛	...25	4¼	5	s	¼	r	s
29⅛	...30	r	1 13-16	s	r	1⅞	s
Deere	...25	2⅜	r	r	r	r	r
26¾	...30	¼	1⅛	1⅞	3⅛	r	3¾
EmrsEl	.65	4⅞	r	r	r	1	r
69½	...70	1 5-16	3⅜	r	1¾	r	r
69½	...75	r	1⅛	2⅛	r	r	r
G Tel	...40	2	r	3⅞	r	r	r
41⅜	...45	3-16	¾	1 5-16	r	r	r
Gillet	45	8	8⅜	r	r	r	r
52¾	...50	3⅛	5	r	7-16	1⅜	r
52¾	...55	13-16	2½	3⅛	r	3⅝	r
GlobMr	...5	1¾	2⅛	2⅜	r	¼	⅜
6⅝	10	r	3-16	7-16	r	3¼	r
Hecla	10	r	r	r	r	⅛	r
16	15	1½	2⅝	3⅛	⅝	1¼	1⅜
16	20	3-16	13-16	1⅜	4¼	4¼	4½
16	25	r	5-16	s	r	r	s
Hercul	...25	9	r	r	r	r	r
33⅞	...30	4	r	5⅜	r	r	r
33⅞	...35	11-16	1⅞	r	r	r	r
33⅞	...40	r	½	r	r	6⅛	r
Kaneb	..10	2¾	3¼	3¾	r	r	½
12⅝	...15	⅜	¾	1 3-16	2⅝	3	2⅞
12⅝	...20	1-16	3-16	¼	r	r	r
L T V	..10	2½	r	3⅜	r	5-16	9-16
12⅜	...15	⅛	11-16	1	2¾	3	r

price goes up in increments of five for prices below 100, and in increments of 10 for prices above 100.

The next three columns from the left in Table 21-1 list the call option prices for each striking price according to the expiration date of the option. The expiration dates are set three months apart, and extend up to nine months out. For Brunswick, the closest expiration date is in September. The following expiration dates are in December and March. Other stocks may have a different set of expiration dates. They may fall in March/June/September/December, like the Brunswick options, in January/April/July/October, or in February/May/August/November. The expiration date of the option falls on the Friday before the third Saturday of the expiration month.

The Brunswick September 35 call has a listed price of 1⅜. This price is multiplied by 100 to get the market price of the option, $137.50. Options are not offered or traded for all exercise prices and times to expiration listed. If a stock moves away from an exercise price, new options will not continue to be listed at that exercise price. Options with exercise prices that are far from the current stock price will not be frequently traded. And it may be advantageous to exercise certain options before expiration. These cases are denoted in the option quotes by an r, meaning the option has not traded, or an s, meaning the option is not listed.

The last three columns of the options quotes list the prices of put options. A *put option* is a contract that gives the owner the right to sell 100 shares of the underlying stock at a given price on or before a given date.

A put option is the same as a call option, except the holder has the right to sell the underlying security to the option writer rather than buy the security from the writer. (One way to think of this is that a call option gives the holder the right to call the stock from the writer, while a put option gives the holder the right to put the stock to the writer.)

CHARACTERISTICS OF OPTION PRICES

The option price is a complex function of a number of variables. Obviously, the stock price and the option's exercise price and time to expiration will be important to the option price, since these enter directly into the terms of the option contract. We will discuss the impact of the variables that are important in determining the option price.

Stock Price

The value of a call option will increase with an increase in the price of the underlying stock. The right to buy a stock at a given price is worth more the higher the price of the stock. For example, if an option has an exercise price of 50 and the stock is at 55, the option must be worth at least $5, since the option holder can exercise the option, buy the stock for 50 and turn around and sell it at the market price of 55. The stock price minus the exercise price of a call option is called the *intrinsic value* of the call option. It is the value of the option if it is exercised. If the stock is at 60, then the intrinsic value will increase to $10. If the stock drops to 45, the intrinsic value of the call will be zero; the option can never be worth less than zero, since the holder has the right, not the obligation, to purchase the stock.

For a put option, the stock price has the opposite effect. The value of a put option will increase with a decrease in the stock price. It is more valuable to have the right to sell a stock at a given price the lower the going market price of the stock. If an option has an exercise price of 50, and the stock is at 45, the option holder can buy the stock in the market and turn around and sell the stock at 50 to the option writer, netting a profit of $5. The intrinsic value of a put option is the exercise price minus the stock price. If the stock drops in value, the intrinsic value of the put option will increase with it. The intrinsic value of a call option and put option are illustrated in Figures 21-1 and 21-2. At the time of expiration of the option, the market value of the option will equal its intrinsic value. Before expiration, however, the option price may be greater than its intrinsic value, since there is also the potential for the stock to move favorably.

Exercise Price

The exercise price affects the price of an option in the opposite way of the stock price. Since the intrinsic value of an option is determined by the difference between the stock price and the exercise price, an increase in one will have the same net effect as a decrease in the other. Call options will increase in value the lower the exercise price, and put options will increase in value the higher the exercise price.

Time to Expiration

Even an option with no intrinsic value will have some market value. If a call option has an exercise price of 50, and the current stock price is 45, the value of that option is zero if it is exercised now. No one will want to exercise the right to buy a stock at 50 when it is available in the market for 45. But there is always the chance the stock will increase in value before expiration, and that chance is greater the longer the time to expiration. This means call options with exercise prices above the current stock price and put options with exercise prices below the current stock price (these options are called out-of-the-money options), will still have some value. The value of any option will increase with

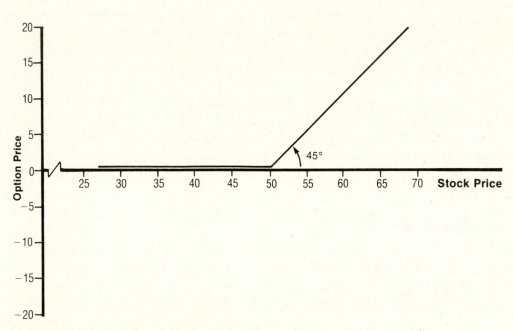

Figure 21-1. Intrinsic value of a call option with exercise price of $50.

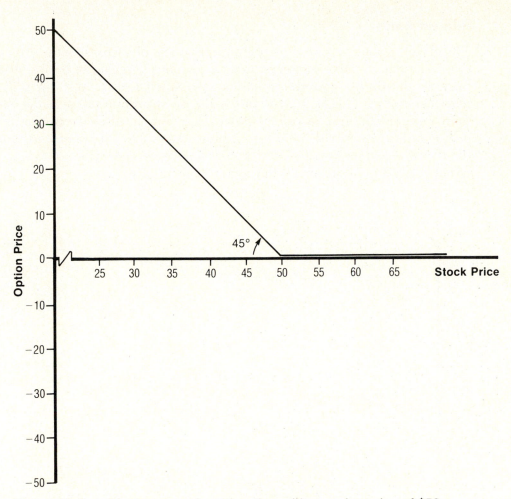

Figure 21-2. Intrinsic value of a put option with exercise price of $50.

the time to expiration of the option. The option price as a function of time to expiration is illustrated in Figures 21-3 and 21-4.

Interest Rates

The effect of interest rates on option prices is less obvious than the effects of the first three variables. Interest rates are a consideration in option pricing because the option contract contains an implicit loan to buy (or sell) the underlying security. The interest rate is also an important factor in the option price because the option price is set to equate a combined position in the option and the stock with the risk-free interest rate. We will discuss this in more detail in the next section. The effect of interest rates on the price of a representative call option is presented in Figures 21-5 and 21-6.

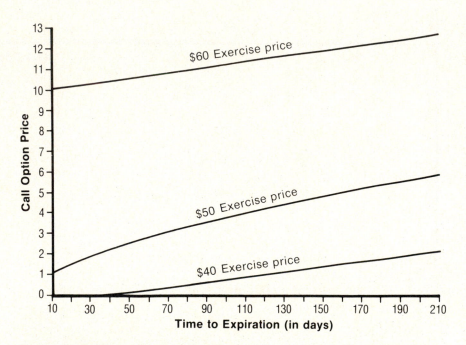

Figure 21-3. The price of call options as time to expiration approaches. The stock is assumed to be at $50 a share.

Stock Volatility

Stock volatility is a measure of how variable the stock price is over time. It is a measure of how likely the stock is to move a given amount up or down. Only the size of the move, not the direction of the price move, is a consideration in volatility.

An option will be more valuable the greater the volatility of the underlying stock. This is because the option is protected against unexpectedly large unfavorable movements—if the call option drops below the exercise price, it does not matter how far below it drops—while the option benefits fully from any favorable price movements. The option feature essentially eliminates the downside risk of the option holder. The holder has nothing to lose from unfavorable stock price movements, but gains from the favorable stock price

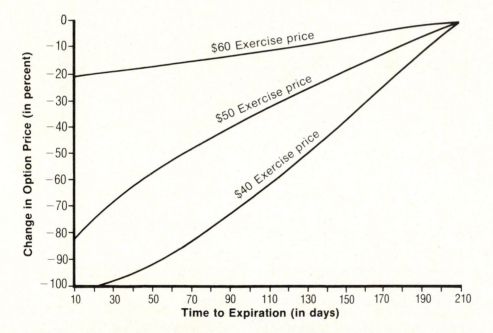

Figure 21-4. The percentage change in the price of call options as the time to expiration approaches. The percentage change is taken using the price with seven months (210 days) as the base.

changes. And the higher the volatility, the more likely large price moves will be.

The stock volatility is a critical determinant of the option price and is more difficult to estimate than the other variables. Chapters 25 and 26 are devoted to techniques for estimating the volatility. There, the relationship between option prices and volatility is discussed in detail.

OPTION PRICING: THE ARBITRAGE ARGUMENT

The key to option pricing is the concept of forming an option position that will be unaffected by changes in the price of the underlying stock. This position

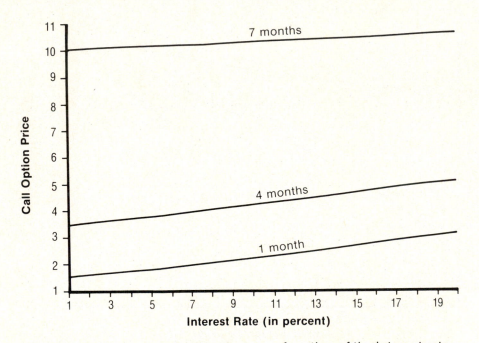

Figure 21-5. The price of call options as a function of the interest rate. Call options with one, four, and seven months to expiration are plotted, with the options assumed to be at the money (i.e., the exercise price is set equal to the current stock price).

may be formed by combining an option with a position in the stock or by hedging one option with another option. Unless the option is correctly priced, this option position will lead to arbitrage profits—sure profits that require no net investment. We illustrate this arbitrage pricing argument with a simple example: Consider a stock with a very simplified return process. Over the next time period, the stock will either go up by 10% or down by 5%. Setting the current stock price at $100, this means next period the stock will either be worth $95 or $110. This sort of a two-pronged process, called a binomial process, is depicted at the left of Figure 21-7. Now suppose there is a call option on the stock with one period to expiration and with an exercise price of $100. If the stock drops in value next period, the option will expire worthless, but, if the stock goes up to $110, the option will be worth $1000. (The stock

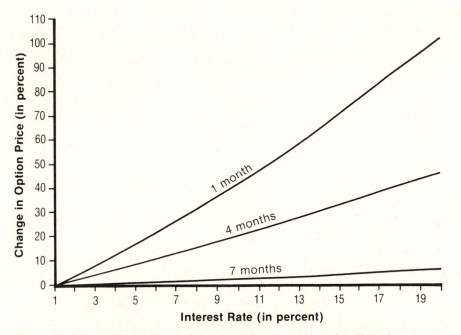

Figure 21-6. The percentage change in the price of call options as a function of the interest rate. The percentage is taken using a one-percent interest rate as the base.

price minus the exercise price times 100.) The possible path of the option price is depicted at the right of Figure 21-7.

Suppose an investor writes (sells) three call options and buys two hundred shares of the underlying stock. What will the return to this investment position be next period when the option expires? If the stock drops to 95, the options will expire worthless, and the two hundred shares of stock will be worth $19,000, so, the total value of the investment will be $19,000. If the stock goes up to 110, the stock position will be worth $22,000, but the investor will be obligated to pay off the option position, which will cost $3000. The total value of the investment if the stock goes up will therefore be $19,000.

The remarkable feature of this investment strategy is that no matter which way the stock moves, the investor's position remains the same, $19,000. The investor has effectively formed a riskless hedge between the stock and the option, a hedge that leaves the position unaffected by movements in the stock price. This is possible because, in this simplified case, the stock and the option values are linearly related, and by combining the two with the proper weighting, the relative movements of the stock and the option will cancel each other out.

What is left, after applying this riskless hedging strategy, is a position that mimics a riskless asset, an asset with a future value that is constant for all states of the world. To avoid arbitrage, where essentially the same asset can be bought and sold at two different prices, it must be the case that this position

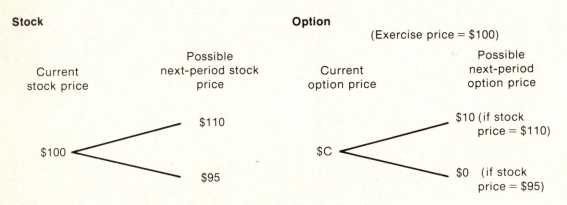

Figure 21-7. A one-period binomial process for stock prices.

gives the same return as the riskless asset prevailing in the market. (Generally, Treasury bills provide the best example of a riskless asset in the marketplace, since they are riskless in terms of default.) Given a market price for the riskless asset and the price of the stock, this arbitrage possibility determines the price the option must have today.

Suppose the riskless interest rate over the period is 6%. At that interest rate, an investment of $17,924 gives a return of $19,000 in one period. As we have already seen, the cost of receiving a certain return of $19,000 with the option-stock strategy just described is the cost of two hundred shares of stock, $20,000, less the proceeds from writing three options. As Table 21-2 illustrates, if the current price of each option is $692, the price of securing a riskless return through the option-stock strategy will be the same as doing so through the riskless asset in the market: 20,000-(3×692)=17,924.

If the price of the option is greater than $692, then it is cheaper to create the riskless asset with the riskless option-stock hedge than through the riskless asset in the market. The investor can obtain an arbitrage profit by simultaneously selling the market asset (i.e., borrowing money) and buying the

---

TABLE 21-2   Trading Strategy When the Option Price is $692

		END-OF-PERIOD POSITION	
Current Position		S = 95	S = 110
Buy 200 shares of stock	(20,000)	19,000	22,000
Write three call options	2,076	0	(3,000)
Net cost of strategy	17,924		
Borrow 17,924 at 6% to cover cost of strategy			
Net return of strategy		19,000	19,000
Cost of borrowed funds at 6% (17,924 × 1.06)		19,000	19,000
Profit		0	0

cheaper synthetic riskless asset through the riskless hedge. The result of this strategy is shown in Table 21-3 for an option price of $750.

If the options sell at $750, as depicted in the example in Table 21-3, then the $17,750 investment from applying the strategy of buying 200 shares of stock and writing three call options leads to a 7% return: the $17,750 grows to $19,000 by the end of the period. But the market return is only 6%. The strategy for securing a profit, then, amounts to borrowing at the 6% market rate and using these funds in the option-stock strategy to generate the 7% return.

Obviously, if the market price of the option is less than $692, the opposite strategy of selling the synthetic riskless asset by buying options and short-selling stock in a three-to-two ratio, and buying the riskless asset (lending money at the riskless rate) would lead to an arbitrage profit.

THE HEDGE RATIO

There are two important steps in this arbitrage trading strategy. The first step is knowing that at $750, the option is overpriced and should be written. The second step is knowing the option transaction should be hedged by the stock in

---

TABLE 21-3   Trading Strategy When the Option Price is $750

		END-OF-PERIOD POSITION	
Current Position		S = 95	S = 110
Buy 200 shares of stock	(20,000)	19,000	22,000
Write three call options	2,250	0	(3,000)
Net cost of strategy	(17,750)		
Borrow 17,750 at 6% to cover cost of strategy			
Net return of strategy		19,000	19,000
Cost of borrowed funds at 6% (17,750 × 1.06)		(18,815)	(18,815)
Profit		185	185

a 2/3 ratio, two hundred shares of stock for every three options on 100 shares of stock. If the hedge is not put on in this ratio, the riskless character of the strategy will be gone, and the arbitrage opportunity will be gone with it. An understanding of the hedge ratio is therefore critical to understanding the arbitrage trading strategy, and the nature of option pricing.

The *hedge ratio* is defined as the ratio of stock to options held to obtain a neutral or riskless hedge. This ratio is simply the negative of the change in the option price with a change in the stock price. That is, the hedge ratio h = $-\Delta C / \Delta S$, where Δ means "change in." This definition leads to the hedge ratio also being referred to as the option's *delta*. The minus sign is used to remind us that the stock and call option must be held in opposite positions. By convention, a positive sign is used to denote a long position, and a minus sign is used to denote a negative or short position. Since the call option is always held opposite the stock, the ratio of the two will always be negative. If the call is written, the stock will be held long. If the call is bought, the stock will be sold short. A put option moves in the opposite direction of the stock, so the hedge ratio for a put option will be positive—if the stock is held long, the put option will also be held long.

In the trading example just presented, the hedge ratio is –2/3, two hundred shares of stock bought for each three options written. Since the hedge ratio is determined by the change in the option price that occurs with a change in the stock price, the hedge ratio of –2/3 means the option price changes by two-thirds of a point for a one-point change in the stock price. In the case of the trading example, a neutral hedge results from holding a ratio of two-thirds a position in stock to every one position in the option. If an investor holds two hundred shares of stock and the stock goes up one point, the stock position will go up by $200. If the investor writes three options, then, since each option goes up by two-thirds of a point with the one-point increase in the stock, the short position in the options will have a total drop of two points, three times the two-thirds-point drop in each option. The net effect of the hedge in the options and the stock will be a change of zero. The option position will exactly counterbalance the stock position.

It is important to note there is nothing magical about the 2/3 ratio used in this example. The hedge ratio for a call option can vary anywhere from zero to minus one. The hedge ratio will vary according to the riskless interest rate, the exercise price and time to expiration of the option, and the volatility of the stock.

The example used in this chapter is too simplistic to be of practical value.

Stock prices can vary over a wide range of values; they do not change according to the simple binomial process used here. Also, options are not traded in a one-period framework. Stock and option prices move continually from the time of a trade until the time of expiration. The simplifications of this example will be relaxed in the pricing formulas presented in this section of the book, but the intuition leading to the option pricing will remain the same: Options are priced to eliminate arbitrage pricing opportunities.

OVERVIEW OF OPTION PROGRAMS

Three types of programs are presented in this section. There are three programs providing option pricing formulas, two programs for estimating the volatility, and one program for evaluating option strategies.

The next chapter, Chapter 22, develops the binomial option formula, and Chapter 23 develops the Black-Scholes formula. Both formulas are adjusted to include dividends, and both calculate the hedge ratio along with the formula option value. While the Black-Scholes formula is the best known option formula, the binomial formula is better at making adjustments for the complexities of the option market. The potential of early exercise is easily included in the numerical procedure of the binomial formula, while it is difficult to do so with the Black-Scholes formula. The binomial formula is also of pedagogical interest, and so we will present it first. Chapter 24 then presents a version of the Black-Scholes formula modified to price options on futures. There are a host of other option formulas developed in the option literature, but the variations in the resulting prices are largely of academic interest. With the exception of options that are way in or out of the money (and are therefore not traded frequently enough to make interesting investment targets), most of these option formulas give prices that are within an eighth of a point of each other.

The critical determinant of trading success after that point passes on to the estimation of volatility. A small change in the volatility estimate can make a significant change in the theoretical option price. And volatility is the one parameter that is not readily available from financial quotes. The two chapters on volatility estimation, Chapters 25 and 26, present the most recent developments in volatility estimation methods. Chapter 25 presents three techniques for using historical stock data to form the volatility estimate and Chapter 26 backs the volatility out of the market option price, arriving at what is called the implied or implicit volatility.

The last program is a tool of sensitivity and strategy analysis. It can be used to generate the effects of stock price, time to expiration, interest rates, and volatility on option prices, much as we have done above in describing the characteristics of option prices. It can also sketch out the profit profile of various option strategies, showing how a position using any combination of options will be affected by changes in the stock price and the other option pricing parameters.

22

The Binomial Option Pricing Formula

The binomial option pricing formula begins with the binomial process for stock prices used in the simple arbitrage pricing example in Chapter 21. But it then extends the binomial model into a multiperiod framework. As we will see, relaxing the one-period assumption makes the use of the binomial process more realistic, and leads to a very practical formula for option trading.

THE ONE-PERIOD BINOMIAL FORMULA

We will start by rephrasing the example in Chapter 21 algebraically. Let the current stock price be S, and assume the stock price next period will either be up to u times its current price or will be down to d times its current price. That is, the stock price next period will either be uS or dS. (In the example in Chapter 21 S=100, uS=110 and dS=95.)

The option expires next period, and will have a price at expiration that is a function of the stock price. The call option price at expiration can be expressed as the maximum of 0 or S^*-E, where S^* denotes the stock price at the time of expiration: $C = Max(0, S^*-E)$. The option price at expiration if the stock price has gone up, C_u, will be $C_u = Max(0, uS-E)$. The option price at expiration if the stock price has gone down, C_d, will be $C_d = Max(0, dS-E)$. The stock and option prices are shown in Figure 22-1. In the case of the introductory example, $C_u = Max(0, 110-100)=10$, and $C_d = Max(0, 95-100) = 0$.

We will now consider forming a riskless hedge between the stock and the option. The riskless hedge requires we hold the stock and the option in a ratio that leaves the overall position the same no matter which way the stock moves. That is, we want to hold a fraction h of stock that will give the same value to the hedged position whether the stock rises to uS or drops to dS; we want

$$huS - C_u = hdS - C_d. \tag{1}$$

Solving for h gives a hedge ratio of

$$h = (C_u - C_d)/((u-d)S). \tag{2}$$

We know that holding the stock and the option according to the hedge ratio h will give a return that is riskless (i.e., that is the same no matter which way the stock price moves). It must be, then, that the return to our investment in forming this position equals the riskless rate. The hedged position involves buying hS shares of stock and writing one option. The return to the position is $huS - C_u$. To avoid arbitrage then, we must have

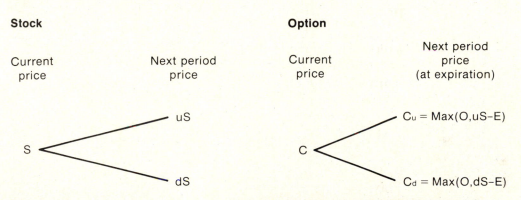

Figure 22-1. Price movement in a one-period binomial model. (Adapted from Bookstaber, R., *Option Pricing and Strategies in Investing*, Fig. 4-1. © 1981 Addison-Wesley, Reading, MA. With permission)

$$huS - C_u = R(hS - C), \tag{3}$$

where R is one plus the risk-free interest rate, $R = (1+r)$. (We could sell short the stock and buy the option and adjust the return accordingly, or we could use $hdS - C_d$ in place of $huS - C_u$ without changing the results.)

Substituting for h, we can solve this equation for the current option price, C,

$$C = (pC_u + (1-p)C_d)/R, \tag{4}$$

where $p = (R-d)/(u-d)$.

This gives the one-period binomial option formula price. The formula price is a function of the current stock price, S, the exercise price of the option as expressed in the equations for C_u and C_d, the riskless interest rate, r, and the volatility as measured by the amount the stock may move up or down, u and d.

Perhaps more significant than what the formula depends on is what it does not depend on. The formula does not require any knowledge of the expected return of the stock. There is no need for a measure of the likelihood the stock will go up or down. There is no need for a measure of market expectations for the stock price. This is significant, because such expectations are subjective and highly variable.

We will illustrate this one-period formula with the numbers from the example in Chapter 21. Let S=100, E=100, u=1.1, d=.95, R=1.06. The value of p = (1.06−.95)/(1.1−.95) = 11/15. The option price then is

$$C = ((11/15)10 + (4/15)0)/1.06 = 6.92.$$

Multiplying this by 100 to reflect the fact that the option is a contract on 100 shares of stock gives the price of 692 obtained in Chapter 21. The hedge ratio can also be computed,

$$h = (10-0)/((1.1-.95)100) = 2/3.$$

We can gain some valuable insight into the option pricing formula by thinking of the variable p as a probability. If we think of p as the probability the stock will go up and (1–p) as the probability the stock will go down, the current option price in Equation (4) simply equals the expected future option price discounted by the riskless interest rate. Keep in mind we did not obtain the value of p as a probability of the stock price going up or down. In fact, the point was just made that one of the attractive features of the option pricing formula is that the probability of the stock price moving up or down is not needed as an input. But it turns out that p is the probability of the stock going up *if* the expected return to the stock is set equal to the return to the risk-free rate. That is, if we let q equal the probability of the stock going up to uS, and if we set the expected return of the stock equal to the risk-free return, then

$$q(uS) + (1-q)(dS) = RS.$$

Solving for q, we find $q = (R-d)/(u-d) = p$. For the purposes of option pricing, the riskless hedging argument allows us to act *as if* the expected return of the stock equals the riskless rate of return. This is because the hedge eliminates any risk from the stock price, and so we can approach the option pricing problem from a risk-neutral perspective. This means we can calculate the price of an option as the present value of its expected return given the expected return to the stock equals the risk-free rate.

BINOMIAL PRICING OVER MANY TIME PERIODS

We have already mentioned that the one-period assumption is unrealistic. The stock moves many times over the life of an option. By repeated application of the one-period option pricing formula, we can determine the option price under the more realistic assumptions of many time periods to expiration and of a stock price that can take on any number of values over the life of the option contract. We will first illustrate the procedure for doing this with a two-period case.

THE TWO-PERIOD OPTION PRICING FORMULA

To price an option with two periods to expiration, we first must trace out the possible stock price paths over the two time periods. Continuing with the assumption of a binomial process, the stock movement next period will either be uS, if the stock goes up, or dS, if the stock goes down. Two periods from now, the stock may again go either up or down. We assume the amount the stock can go up or down is the same each period. This means two periods from now the stock can take on any of three values. If the stock goes up both periods, its value two periods from now will be uuS. If it goes down one period and up the other, its value will be udS. If the stock goes down both periods, its value will be ddS. These price paths are illustrated in Figure 22-2.

The next step in determining the current option price is to calculate the value of the option at expiration as a function of the stock price. Recall this value will be $Max(0, S^*-E)$, where S^* is the stock price at expiration. The three possible option prices that correspond to the three stock prices are $C_{uu} = Max(0, uuS-E)$, if the stock goes up both periods; $C_{ud} = Max(0, udS-E)$, if the

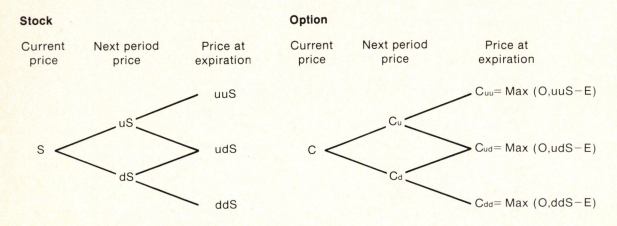

Figure 22-2. Price movements in a two-period binomial model. (Adapted from Bookstaber, R., *Option Pricing and Strategies in Investing,* Figs. A-1 and A-3. © 1981, Addison-Wesley, Reading, MA. With permission)

stock goes up one period and goes down the other period; and $C_{dd} = \text{Max}(0, ddS-E)$, if the stock goes down both periods. Given the option prices at expiration, we can apply the one period option formula to obtain the option prices one period before expiration:

and

$$C_u = (pC_{uu}+(1-p)C_{ud})/R, \tag{5}$$

$$C_d = (pC_{ud}+(1-p)C_{dd})/R. \tag{6}$$

Given these option prices one period before expiration, we can proceed backwards with another application of the one period formula to obtain the current option price, two periods before expiration:

$$C = (pC_u+(1-p)C_d)/R. \tag{7}$$

where C_u and C_d are the values computed from above.

We can determine the current option price directly by substituting for C_u and C_d in Equation (7), but from a computational standpoint, this substitution is unnecessary and, in more complex settings, may even be undesirable. The following numerical procedure is more important:

---

1. Generate the possible stock prices for the time of expiration of the option.
2. Use these prices to compute the possible option values at expiration as given by the terms of the option contract.
3. Use the one-period option pricing formula to solve backward one period at a time from the time of expiration until the current option price is calculated.

THE MANY-PERIOD FORMULA

These same steps are applied in computing the price over many time periods. In an n period model, the stock prices at the time of expiration of the option can be represented by $u^j d^{n-j}S$, for $j=0,...,n$. Here j represents the number of up moves in the stock over the life of the option contract. The option prices at expiration can then be expressed by the array of values Max(0, $u^j d^{n-j} S$) for j=0,...,n. These option prices are taken into the one-period option pricing formula two at a time to get the prices for the next period back, and the process is repeated period by period until the current option price emerges. This general numerical solution method is outlined in Figure 22-3.

As with the two-period option pricing formula, the many-period formula can be solved by recursive substitution to obtain a closed form expression. However, as we will now see, when some of the important institutional realities of the market are included in the option pricing procedure, no closed form expression of this sort is possible, and accurate option pricing employs modifications of the step-by-step numerical approach.

OPTION PRICING WHEN THERE MAY BE EARLY EXERCISE: THE PRICING OF PUT OPTIONS AND OPTIONS ON STOCKS PAYING DIVIDENDS

The options listed on the Chicago Board Option Exchange and other U.S. exchanges are called *American options.* An American option is an option that may be exercised any time *on or before* the expiration date. In contrast, a European option is an option that can only be exercised *on* the expiration date. For pricing call options on stocks that do not pay dividends over the life of the option, it turns out that the price of an American option will equal the price of a European option. This is because under those circumstances it is never optimal to exercise an American option early.

But if dividends are paid over the life of an option, it may be optimal to exercise the option just before the stock goes exdividend. This is because if the option is exercised the option holder will capture the value of the dividend, while if the option is not exercised, the stock price will drop after the dividend payment by roughly the value of that payment, and the option on the stock will also drop.

For example, consider an option with an exercise price of 50 on a stock that is currently priced at 55. Say the stock will pay a dividend of $4 in one day. The stock price will drop by about $4 after it goes exdividend. If the option holder exercises the option now, he will get a stock worth 55. If he does not exercise the option, the value of the option after the exdividend date will drop

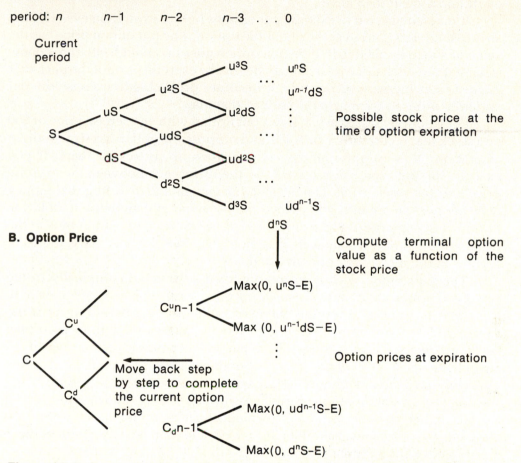

A. Stock Price Movement

B. Option Price

Figure 22-3. Computing the call option price using the binomial pricing model. (Adapted from Bookstaber, R. and Clarke, R. *Option Strategies for Institutional Investment Management,* Fig. 2-2. © 1983, Addison-Wesley, Reading, MA. With permission)

proportionately with the $4 loss in the stock value. The value of the option if left unexercised may drop well below the $5 value the investor will get if he exercises the option before the exdividend date. As can be seen, the option is worth more dead than alive.

It may be optimal to exercise put options before expiration even if there are no dividends paid over the life of the option. The put option price has the value of a loan implicit in it. If the put option goes far enough into the money, (that is, if the stock price is far enough below the exercise price of the put), or if interest rates increase sufficiently, it becomes profitable to exercise the put option in order to terminate the costs of that loan.

For example, suppose you buy a put option with an exercise price of $50 on a stock that is currently worth $50, and suppose the option has six months to expiration. Now, suppose next week the stock drops to $5 a share. If you exercise the put, you will receive $45—the difference between the exercise price and the stock price. The interest you can gain in investing that money over the next six months will exceed the potential in continuing to hold the option until expiration, and so it will be best to exercise the put. A look at the listed option quotes will indicate that such early exercise is a reality; there are few far in the money put options listed.

The possibility of early exercise adds a substantial complexity to the pricing of options. Rather than evaluating the exercise value of the option only at expiration, a check must now be made at every time period to see if the option will be worth more exercised than not, and the option price must take on the greater of these two values. Fortunately, the numerical procedure of the binomial pricing method provides a natural way for making this check, since the solution already involves a pricing calculation at every time period. When the one-period option pricing formula is applied at every time period, all we need is to include a second check to compare the resulting option price with the value the option will have if it is exercised, and then use the greater of these values as the option price.

COMPUTATIONAL CONSIDERATIONS

The binomial formula approximates reality better as more time periods are used. That is, rather than splitting six months into six periods of one month each, we might split six months into twenty-six periods of one week each.

The objections to having the stock follow a simplistic binomial price change are reduced with further time periods, since then over those time periods the stock can take on a wide range of values. The most important question for application then is how many time periods are necessary to get a good approximation of reality. Table 22-1 answers this by comparing the binomial model for various volatilities, times to expiration, and exercise prices. It also compares the price from the binomial formula with the price of its continuous time counterpart, the Black-Scholes formula. The table looks at the binomial approximation with only five periods and with 25 periods.

In the limit, as each time period becomes smaller and smaller, and the number of time periods used in the binomial formula approaches infinity, the binomial formula approaches the Black-Scholes formula. (The Black-Scholes formula has the drawback, however, of not considering the possibility of early exercise.) But from Table 22-1, it is clear that the number of time periods does

TABLE 22-1 Comparison of the Binomial and Black-Scholes Models

		(Stock price=50; Risk-free interest rate=10%)					
	DAYS TO EXPIRATION	$\sigma = .2$ EXERCISE PRICE			$\sigma = .4$ EXERCISE PRICE		
Model		45	50	55	45	50	55
Binomial	30	5.38	1.40	.07	5.87	2.60	.83
with	120	6.74	3.21	1.12	8.03	5.53	3.06
N=5	210	7.95	4.59	2.14	10.00	7.58	5.15
Binomial	30	5.37	1.36	.08	5.82	2.50	.78
with	120	6.70	3.13	1.08	8.23	5.35	3.29
N=25	210	7.93	4.49	2.14	10.07	7.35	5.21
Black-Scholes	30	5.39	1.36	.08	5.83	2.49	.77
Binomial	120	6.75	3.15	1.09	8.25	5.35	3.27
with N=∞	210	8.02	4.54	2.21	10.11	7.36	5.22

not need to get too large for the formula values to closely coincide. For 25 periods, the two formulas are often within a few pennies of each other. Thus for practical purposes, as few as 25 periods will generally be sufficient.

TRADING WITH THE BINOMIAL OPTION PRICING FORMULA

The purpose of the binomial option formula is to pinpoint mispriced options. The hedge ratio of the formula will indicate the proper ratio of stock to hold for each option in order to form an arbitrage hedge position. The trading rules for the binomial option pricing formula are:

1. Take a position in a mispriced option: If the option is overpriced (if the market price of the option is greater than the formula price), write it. If the option is underpriced (if the market price of the option is less than the formula price), buy it.

2. Hedge the mispriced option with the stock according to hedge ratio. For a call option, hold the stock position opposite that in the option: If the call is held long, short the stock. If the call is written, hold the stock long. For a put option, hold the stock position in the same direction as that in the option: If the put is held long, hold the stock long. If the put is written, short the stock.

3. When the market price of the option returns to the formula price, close out the position.

As we will see in Chapter 27 on option strategy, the hedge position can also be formed using another option as the hedging vehicle rather than using the stock. There will often be advantages to doing this. The commissions may be lower when another option is used, and if the one mispriced option can be hedged with another option that is also mispriced appropriately, the profit potential can be doubled.

   For option positions that are held over long periods of time or during large changes in the stock price, another step must be added to the trading strategy. The hedge ratio will vary with time to expiration and with the stock price, and as these variables change, the hedge ratio will change as well. The hedge ratio must therefore be recalculated periodically, and the hedge position readjusted if the hedge ratio has changed. The adjustment can be made by changing either side of the hedge. The rule to follow is to make the adjustment in the way that is consistent with the mispricing. Buy more of the mispriced option if it is underpriced, write more of the mispriced option if it is overpriced. If this is not possible, then make the adjustment by changing the size of the position in the stock. Generally, a readjustment of the hedge will only be necessary for positions held for more than three weeks or for a stock price change of 5% or more.

BINOMIAL OPTION PRICING FORMULA

Computational Procedure

    S = current stock price
    R = one plus the riskless interest rate
    u = possible up movement in the stock price each period
    d = possible down movement in the stock price each period
    i = counter for periods, $i = 0,...,n$, with n the current time period, 0 the time period of option expiration
    j = counter for number of up moves of the stock
    δ = dividend as a percent of stock price; $\delta = D/S$, where D is dollar dividend payment
$M(i)$ = number of exdividend dates occurring by period i

1. Compute the option prices at expiration, given there have been j up moves in the stock (and therefore $n-j$ down moves in the stock). Letting $C(0,j)$ be the option price in period 0, the period of option expiration, the price of call option with j up moves is

$$C(0,j) = \text{MAX } [0, u^j d^{n-j}(1-\delta)^{M(0)}S-E],$$

$$j = 1,...,n.$$

The term $(1-\delta)^{M(0)}$ reduces the stock price for the number of exdividend dates that have occurred by the last period, $M(0)$.

2. Apply the one-period option formula to compute the option price one period from expiration, in period 1,

$$(pC(0,j+1) + (1-p)C(0,j))/R,$$

where $p = (R-d)/(u-d)$, and then set the option price in period 1 to equal the greater of this value or the value of the option if exercised:

$$C(1,j) = MAX\ [u^j d^{n-1-j}(1-\delta)^{M(1)}S-E,\ (pC(0,j+1) + (1-p)C(0,j))/R],$$
$$j = 0,...,n-1.$$

3. Continue back period by period, solving the general equation

$$C(i,j) = MAX\ [u^j d^{n-i-j}(1-\delta)^{M(i)}S-E\ (pC(i-1,j+1) + (1-p)C(i-1,j))/R]$$
$$\text{for } j = 0,...,n-i.$$

for each period i in turn, until the current option price of period n is determined.

4. Compute the hedge ratio as $h = \dfrac{C(n,1) - C(n,0)}{(u-d)S}$.

Put option pricing is done in an analogous manner, except the contract specification of the put option requires reversing the sign of S and E. For example, the value of the put option at expiration will be

$$P(0,j) = MAX\ [0, E-u^j d^{n-j}(1-\delta)^{M(0)}S].$$

The u and d, and the per-period interest rate, R, can be computed as follows:

$$u = \exp(\sigma\sqrt{t/n}\,)$$
$$d = 1/u$$
$$R = (1 + r)^{t/n}$$

where t is the time to expiration as a fraction of a year, n is the number of periods used, σ is the stock volatility, r is the riskless interest rate as a decimal value.

Trading Strategy

- Buy the option if the market price is less than the formula price. Write the option if the market price is greater than the formula price.

- Hedge the option against the stock according to the hedge ratio, h.

```
10    REM  ********************************************************************
20    REM  *                   BINOMIAL OPTION PRICING MODEL                  *
30    REM  *                                                                  *
40    REM  * THIS PROGRAM CALCULATES THE VALUE OF A CALL OR PUT WHEN DIVIDENDS *
50    REM  * MAY MAKE EXERCISE DESIRABLE BEFORE EXPIRATION.                    *
60    REM  *                                                                  *
70    REM  * VARIABLES USED: S=CURRENT STOCK PRICE IN DOLLARS                  *
80    REM  *                 E=EXERCISE PRICE IN DOLLARS                       *
90    REM  *                 R=ANNUAL RISK FREE RATE OF INTEREST IN PERCENT    *
100   REM  *                 D=DIVIDEND PAID PER QUARTER IN DOLLARS            *
110   REM  *                 T=TIME TO EXPIRATION IN DAYS                      *
120   REM  *                 V=MEASURE OF VOLATILITY                           *
130   REM  *                 C=OPTION PRICE                                    *
140   REM  *                 H=HEDGE RATIO                                     *
150   REM  *                 T1=TIME TO FIRST DIVIDEND IN DAYS                 *
160   REM  *                                                                  *
170   REM  * THE USER MUST SPECIFY WHETHER COMPUTATION OF A PUT OR CALL IS     *
180   REM  * DESIRED.                                                          *
190   REM  *                                                                  *
200   REM  *                                                                  *
210   REM  *                                                                  *
220   REM  *                                                                  *
230   REM  ********************************************************************
240   Y1=0
250   DIM SE(25),NU(25),CP(25,25)
260   PN=25
270 REM
280 REM
290   GOSUB 1020:REM**********************INPUT DATA**************************
300 REM
310 REM
320   GOSUB 470:REM*********************DO COMPUTATIONS***********************
330 REM
340 REM
350   GOSUB 1450:REM**********************OUTPUT DATA*************************
360 REM
370 REM
380   END:REM*****************************STOP PROGRAM***********************
390 REM
400 REM
410 REM*********************************************************************
420 REM                         SUBROUTINE TO DO COMPUTATIONS
430 REM*********************************************************************
440 REM
450 REM INITIALIZE VALUES
460 REM
470   PL=T/PN
480   D=1-D/S
490   T=T/365/PN
500   RH=(R/100+1)^T
510   UP=EXP(V*SQR(T))
520   DN=1/UP
530   P=(RH-DN)/(UP-DN)
540 REM
```

```
550 REM DETERMINE NUMBER OF EX-DIVIDEND DATES OCCURING DURING NEXT N-I PERIODS
560 REM
570  N=0
580  FOR I=0 TO PN
590   IF CINT(T1/PL)=I THEN NU(I)=N+1:N=N+1:T1=T1+90 ELSE NU(I)=N
600  NEXT I
610 REM
620 REM DETERMINE STOCK PRICES IN LAST PERIOD
630 REM
640  FOR I=0 TO PN
650   SE(I)=S*(DN^(PN-I))*(UP^I)*(D^NU(PN))
660  NEXT I
670 REM
680 REM DETERMINE CALL/PUT VALUES IN LAST PERIOD
690 REM
700  FOR J=0 TO PN
710   C1=SE(J)-E
720   IF A1=2 THEN C1=-C1
730   IF C1>0 THEN CP(PN,J)=C1 ELSE CP(PN,J)=0
740  NEXT J
750 REM
760 REM WORKING BACKWARD, DETERMINE CALL/PUT VALUES IN PRECEDING PERIODS
770 REM
780  FOR I=PN-1 TO 0 STEP -1
790   FOR J=0 TO I
800    C1=(DN^(I-J))*(UP^J)*(D^NU(I))*S-E
810    IF PC$="P" THEN C1=-C1
820    C2=(P*CP(I+1,J+1)+(1-P)*CP(I+1,J))/RH
830    IF C1>=C2 THEN CP(I,J)=C1 ELSE CP(I,J)=C2
840 REM COUNTER TO MONITOR THE TIME IN THE LOOP
850    IF I=PN-1 AND J=0 THEN PRINT "CURRENTLY ON ITERATION 1"
860    IF I=20 AND J=0 THEN PRINT "CURRENTLY ON ITERATION";(PN-20)
870    IF I=10 AND J=0 THEN PRINT "CURRENTLY ON ITERATION";(PN-10)
880   NEXT J
890  NEXT I
900 REM
910 REM DETERMINE HEDGE RATIO AND CALL/PUT VALUE IN CURRENT PERIOD
920 REM
930  H=-(CP(1,1)-CP(1,0))/((UP-DN)*S)
940  C=CP(0,0)
950 RETURN
960 REM
970 REM************************************************************************
980 REM                         SUBROUTINE TO INPUT DATA
990 REM************************************************************************
1000 REM
1010 PRINT "YOU MAY ENTER THE FOLLOWING VARIABLES:"
1020 PRINT TAB(10);"CURRENT STOCK PRICE ($)";TAB(55):INPUT ;S
1030  IF Y1=1 THEN RETURN
1040 PRINT TAB(10);"EXERCISE PRICE ($)";TAB(55):INPUT ;E
1050  IF Y1=2 THEN RETURN
1060 PRINT TAB(10);"ANNUAL INTEREST RATE (%)";TAB(55):INPUT ;R
1070  IF Y1=3 THEN RETURN
1080 PRINT TAB(10);"QUARTERLY DIVIDEND ($)";TAB(55):INPUT ;D
```

```
1090   IF Y1=4 THEN RETURN
1100 PRINT TAB(10);"TIME TO EXPIRATION (DAYS)";TAB(55):INPUT ;T
1110   IF Y1=5 THEN RETURN
1120 PRINT TAB(10);"VOLATILITY";TAB(55):INPUT ;V
1130   IF Y1=6 THEN RETURN
1140 PRINT TAB(10);"TIME TO FIRST DIVIDEND (DAYS)";TAB(55):INPUT ;T1
1150   IF Y1=7 THEN RETURN
1160 PRINT TAB(10);"OPTION SPECIFIED (C=CALL, P=PUT)";TAB(55):INPUT ;PC$
1170   IF Y1=8 THEN RETURN
1180 PRINT:PRINT
1190 PRINT "YOU MAY CHANGE ANY OF THE VALUES ENTERED ABOVE AS FOLLOWS:"
1200 PRINT TAB(10);"CHOICE";TAB(20);"ITEM TO CHANGE";TAB(55);"CURRENT VALUE"
1210 PRINT TAB(10);"------";TAB(20);"--------------";TAB(55);"-------------"
1220 PRINT TAB(10);"0";TAB(20);"PRINT HEDGE RATIO AND";
1230   IF A1=1 THEN PRINT " CALL VALUE" ELSE PRINT " PUT VALUE"
1240 PRINT TAB(10);"1";TAB(20);"CURRENT STOCK PRICE ($)";TAB(55);S
1250 PRINT TAB(10);"2";TAB(20);"EXERCISE PRICE ($)";TAB(55);E
1260 PRINT TAB(10);"3";TAB(20);"ANNUAL INTEREST RATE (%)";TAB(55);R
1270 PRINT TAB(10);"4";TAB(20);"QUARTERLY DIVIDEND ($)";TAB(55);D
1280 PRINT TAB(10);"5";TAB(20);"TIME TO EXPIRATION (DAYS)";TAB(55);T
1290 PRINT TAB(10);"6";TAB(20);"VOLATILITY";TAB(55);V
1300 PRINT TAB(10);"7";TAB(20);"TIME TO FIRST DIVIDEND (DAYS)";TAB(55);T1
1310 PRINT TAB(10);"8";TAB(20);"OPTION SPECIFIED (C=CALL, P=PUT)";TAB(56);PC$
1320 PRINT
1330 PRINT
1340 INPUT "WHICH CHOICE DO YOU DESIRE (0-8)";Y1
1350   ON Y1 GOSUB 1020,1040,1060,1080,1100,1120,1140,1160
1360   IF Y1=0 THEN RETURN
1370 PRINT
1380 PRINT
1390   GOTO 1190
1400 REM
1410 REM*********************************************************************
1420 REM                    SUBROUTINE TO OUTPUT DATA
1430 REM*********************************************************************
1440 REM
1450 PRINT:PRINT
1460 PRINT TAB(10);"THE HEDGE RATIO=";TAB(41);:PRINT USING "###.###";H
1470 IF PC$="C" THEN PRINT TAB(10);"THE CALL VALUE=";TAB(42);:PRINT USING "###.#
     ##";C
1480 IF PC$="P" THEN PRINT TAB(10);"THE PUT VALUE=";TAB(42);:PRINT USING "###.##
     #";C
1490 PRINT:PRINT
1500 REM
1510 REM RETURN T, T1, AND D TO ORIGINAL VALUES
1520 REM
1530   T=T*365*PN
1540   D=S-S*D
1550   T1=T1-90*NU(PN)
1560 INPUT "DO YOU WISH TO GO AGAIN WITH MODIFIED DATA (1=YES, 2=NO)";A3
1570   IF A3=1 THEN GOSUB 1180:GOTO 310
1580 RETURN
```

23

The Black-Scholes Option Pricing Formula

The best known and most widely used option pricing formula was developed by Fisher Black and Myron Scholes in 1973. Other option formulas preceded theirs, and indeed the Black-Scholes formula bears a striking resemblance to a number of the earlier formulas.

The contribution of the Black-Scholes formula, and the feature of this formula that revolutionized option pricing, is that it depends only on observable variables. The formula does not require knowledge of investors' attitudes toward risk or their expectations of future market performance. By recognizing the possibility of creating a riskfree hedge, and then, following a suggestion by their MIT colleague Robert Merton, by giving that riskfree hedge a riskless rate of return, Black and Scholes could express the option price strictly as a function of the terms of the option contract—the exercise price and time to expiration—and the stock price, interest rate, and stock price volatility.

Interest in option pricing, and in the Black-Scholes formula in particular, was fueled by the opening of listed option trading the same year the option formula was published. Firms emerged to provide the theoretical option price based on a straightforward application of the Black-Scholes formula, and market makers and traders used the formula price in making trading decisions. Now more sophisticated formulas have been developed, still based on the same riskless hedging argument, but adjusted to take dividends and other complexities of stock prices into account. However, the Black-Scholes formula provides an adequate pricing and hedging benchmark for many option trading strategies.

The Black-Scholes formula for call options is:

$$C(S, T, E, r, \sigma) = SN(d_1) - Ee^{-rT}N(d_2) \tag{1}$$

where

$$d_1 = [\ln 1/2 + (r + (S/E)\,\sigma^2)T]/\sigma\sqrt{T}$$

and

$$d_2 = d_1 - \sigma\sqrt{T}.$$

In this formula, ln is the natural logarithm, e is the exponential (e = 2.7183), and σ is the standard deviation of stock price movements, commonly called the stock volatility. The other variables are current stock price, S, option exercise price, E, time to expiration of the option, T, and riskless interest rate, r. The function N( ) is the cumulative normal distribution function.

UNDERSTANDING THE BLACK-SCHOLES FORMULA

The Black-Scholes formula is the limiting case of the binomial formula presented in Chapter 22. While the binomial formula assumes the stock price moves in discrete jumps period by period, the Black-Scholes formula assumes the stock price moves continuously, with a very small price change at each instant. We can derive the Black-Scholes formula using the same argument we used to derive the binomial formula. Indeed, the Black-Scholes formula follows from the binomial formula when the time to the expiration of the option is divided up into an infinite number of time periods and the price change per time period approaches zero. Unfortunately, going from the discrete framework of the binomial formula to the continuous time framework of the Black-Scholes formula requires advanced mathematics. Here we will only try to get an intuitive feel for the formula, so that we can look at it as more than a mass of algebra.

There is no way around the fact that this formula is complicated. To get a feel for the formula, first let us develop the option formula under the assumption that it is certain the stock price will be above the exercise price at the time of expiration (i.e., it is certain the option will be exercised at expiration). In that case, the option holder knows he will receive stock at time T in exchange for the payment of the exercise price E. The present value of the stock the option holder will receive at time T is simply the value of the stock now, S. At the time of expiration you need to pay the exercise price E to get the stock. The present value of this payment is $e^{-rT}E$.

The value of this option, then, is simply the current stock price minus the discounted value of the exercise price, or

$$C = S - e^{-rT}E. \tag{2}$$

Now assume there is some chance the option will expire out-of-the-money (i.e., there is some chance the stock price at the time of expiration will be less than the exercise price), and the option will not be exercised. In this case, we must adjust the option price for the probability it will not be exercised. That is, we will get the stock if and only if the stock price at expiration is greater than the exercise price, and similarly, we will pay E if and only if the stock price at expiration is greater than the exercise price. In this case, we must weight the terms in the option price by the probability the option will end up in the money. This is the purpose of the $N(d_1)$ and $N(d_2)$ terms in the Black-Scholes formula. The first term, $SN(d_1)$, is the present value of the stock price at expiration, given the probability that value is above the exercise price, and the second part, $Ee^{-rT}N(d_2)$ is the present value of the payment of the exercise price times the probability that payment will be made.

We can see the relationship between the Black-Scholes formula and the simple option formula of Equation (2) by considering the limit of the Black-Scholes formula as the volatility of the stock price goes to zero (i.e., as the stock price movement becomes certain). As the volatility goes to zero, both d_1 and d_2 become very large. The normal distribution terms, $N(d_1)$ and $N(d_2)$ will then approach one, and the Black-Scholes formula will approach Equation (2).

We have already noted that the Black-Scholes formula does not depend on investor preferences in any way. The investors' attitudes toward risk do not enter into the formula because the riskless hedging opportunity eliminates any risk inherent in the stock. Since attitudes toward risk can be ignored, the option can be priced acting as if investors are risk neutral, that is, acting as if investors care only about the expected return of investments, and do not care about the uncertainty of that return. In this risk-neutral world, the price of the option now will equal the present value of the expected option price at expiration. That is, the option price will equal

$$C = e^{-rT}E[\text{Max}(0, S-E)], \tag{3}$$

where E denotes the expected value. When the distribution of the stock price is given, the expectation can be taken to get an expression for the option price. The assumption of the Black-Scholes formula is that the stock price is lognormally distributed. Evaluating the expected value of Equation (3) with this distribution leads to the Black-Scholes formula.

PRICING PUT OPTIONS

The Black-Scholes formula is a call option formula. It can also be applied to the pricing of put options since put and call prices are related by the put-call parity equation,

$$P = C - S + e^{-rT}E.$$

Using the call price, C, from the option formula, subtracting the current stock price, and adding the present value of the exercise price, leads to the price of a put with the same exercise price and time to expiration.

ADJUSTMENTS FOR DIVIDENDS

The Black-Scholes formula was developed under the assumption the option could not be exercised before expiration. Strictly speaking, then, the Black-Scholes formula is a pricing formula for European options. Listed options in the United States are American options; the holder has the right to exercise on or before the expiration date. As discussed in Chapter 22, for a dividend-paying stock, such early exercise may be optimal. A stock paying a dividend will usually drop by approximately the amount of the dividend payment. If the option is not exercised before the exdividend date, the value of the option will drop, reflecting this stock price decline. The option holder can capture the dividend by exercising the option and taking ownership of the stock before the stock goes exdividend. For put options, early exercise may also be optimal even for nondividend-paying stocks. If the option formula does not take the features of early exercise into account, it will tend to underprice options when the feature of early exercise may be attractive.

The Black-Scholes formula cannot be directly modified to adjust for the value of early exercise of put options. It can, however, be modified to approximate the value of early exercise for dividend payments. We will present two methods for doing so. It should be stressed that both methods are only approximations. The numerical approach of the binomial formula must be used to take the early exercise feature of American call options fully into account.

Adjustments for Continuous Dividend Payments

The simplest adjustment for dividends is to assume the dividend payments are paid out continuously, like an interest rate. Let the dividend yield be δ. For example, if the annual dividend paid out on a $50 stock is $2.50, then δ will equal .05. To modify the Black-Scholes formula to include this dividend rate, we discount S to reflect the drop in the stock price caused by the continuous dividend payout, multiplying the stock price at the start of the formula by $e^{-\delta T}$, and we subtract δ from r in the $N(d_1)$ and $N(d_2)$ terms so the mean return to the capital appreciation in the stock price plus the return to the stock due to dividend payments is equal to the riskfree rate.

A Pseudo-American Call Option Formula

Since dividends are actually paid quarterly, not continuously, the assumption of continuous dividend payments will obviously be inexact. The adjustment will be more accurate in between dividend payments, and least accurate right before the stock goes exdividend. The continuous dividend payment adjustment also skirts the issue of the possibility of early exercise. When dividends are assumed to be paid out continuously rather than in discrete lumps, it is never optimal to exercise the option early to capture the dividend payment.

A second method for adjusting the Black-Scholes formula for dividend payments takes the possibility of early exercise into account. The only time we need to worry about early exercise is immediately before the stock goes exdividend. Since options have a time to maturity of less than nine months, this means there are at most two quarterly dividends and therefore two possible times it may be optimal to exercise early. The pseudo-American call option replaces the European call option with a set of three European call options—one expiring at the first exdividend date, one expiring at the second exdividend date, and one expiring at the actual expiration date of the option. The option price is set to equal the largest of these three option prices.

The value of the option at the time of expiration is simply the Black-Scholes value adjusted for the present value of the dividend payments that will be made before expiration. Letting t_1 be the time of the nearest exdividend date, and d_1 be the dividend payment at that time, and letting t_2 be the time of the following exdividend date, and d_2 be the dividend payment at that time, the option value if it is not exercised before T, C_T, is

$$C_T = C(S - d_1 e^{-rt_1} - d_2 e^{-rt_2}, T, E, r, \sigma),$$

where the values in the function $C(\cdot)$ are entered into the Black-Scholes formula, in Equation (1).

The value of the option expiring at the time of the second exdividend date, t_2, has the stock price adjusted for the present value of the dividend payments, and also has the exercise price reduced by the present value of the dividend at the time of the time, t_1. This adjustment is done because if the option is exercised before the second dividend payment, the option holder will capture the value of value of that dividend. The price of this option, then, is

$$C_{t_2} + C(S - d_1 e^{-rt_1} - d_2 e^{-rt_2}, T, E-d_2, r, \sigma).$$

The value of the option expiring at the time of the nearest exdividend date, t_1, has the stock price adjusted for the present value of the dividend payments, and also has the exercise price reduced by the present value of both the dividend at time t_1 and the dividend at time t_2, since if the option is exercised at t_1, both of these dividends will be captured in the stock price. The formula price for this option is

$$C_{t_1} = C(S - d_1 e^{-rt_1} - d_2 e^{-rt_2}, \ T, \ E - d_1 - d_2 e^{-r(t_2 - t_1)}, \ r, \ \sigma).$$

Since the American option gives the option holder the choice of exercising at the expiration date of any of these options, the value of the Pseudo-American call option is equal to the largest of these three European option values:

$$C = Max[C_T, \ C_{t_2}, \ C_{t_1}].$$

THE EFFECTIVENESS OF THE BLACK-SCHOLES FORMULA IN TRADING STRATEGIES

The prices of traded options conform surprisingly well to the values predicted by the Black-Scholes formula. The option pricing formula has an empirical accuracy rarely approached by theoretical models in economics or finance. This is particularly impressive given the complexity of both the option contract and the formula.

Empirical tests have found some systematic biases in the formula. The most notable is that the model systematically underprices deep out-of-the-money options and near-maturity options while it overprices deep in-the-money options. This bias has been found to occasionally reverse itself. Recent work suggests the bias is in part due to the limitations of the Black-Scholes formula in taking dividends and early exercise into account. But even stocks that do not pay dividends display these biases, so other factors, most probably related to the distributional assumption of the model and transaction costs in the market, also cause persistent biases in the Black-Scholes formula. The consensus is that the Black-Scholes formula works well for near-the-money or at-the-money options that are not too close to maturity, and does not work as well for those options that are either very close to expiration or are far in or out of the money. More sophisticated option formulas have been developed to overcome these biases. These formulas rely on the same hedging argument that underlies the Black-Scholes formula, but attempt to make more realistic assumptions about the process driving the stock price.

BLACK-SCHOLES OPTION PRICING FORMULA

Computational Procedure

S = current stock price
T = time to expiration in fraction of years
E = option exercise price
r = riskless interest rate as a decimal
σ = stock volatility
δ = dividend yield, $\delta = D/S$ where D is the annual dollar dividend

$$C = e^{-\delta T} S\, N(d_1) - E e^{-rT} N(d_2)$$

where

$$d_1 = [\ln(S/E) + (r - \delta + 1/2\ \sigma^2)T]/\sigma \sqrt{T}$$

and

$$d_2 = d_1 - \sigma \sqrt{T}.$$

$N(\ )$ is the cumulative normal distribution function.

The hedge ratio h is calculated directly from the first term of the option formula,

$$h = -e^{-\delta T} N(d_1)$$

The put-call parity equation can be used to give the price of a put option in terms of a call option, with the same exercise price and time to expiration,

$$P = C - S + E\, e^{-rT}.$$

Trading Strategy

- Buy the option if the market price is less than the formula price.
- Write the option if the market price is greater than the formula price.
- Hedge the option against the stock according to the hedge ratio h.

```
10   REM *****************************************************************************
20   REM *                    BLACK-SCHOLES OPTION PRICING MODEL                     *
30   REM *                                                                           *
40   REM *                                                                           *
50   REM *                                                                           *
60   REM * THE BLACK-SCHOLES MODEL PRICES CALL AND PUT OPTIONS.  THE USER MAY        *
70   REM * SPECIFY A DIVIDEND RATE, WHICH THE MODEL ASSUMES IS PAID OUT              *
80   REM * CONTINUOUSLY.                                                             *
90   REM *                                                                           *
100  REM * VARIABLES USED:                                                           *
110  REM *              R=ANNUAL RISK FREE RATE OF INTEREST IN PERCENT               *
120  REM *              D=ANNUAL CONTINUOUS DIVIDEND RATE IN PERCENT                 *
130  REM *              T=TIME TO EXPIRATION IN DAYS                                 *
140  REM *              V=MEASURE OF VOLATILITY                                      *
150  REM *              C=OPTION PRICE                                               *
160  REM *              H=HEDGE RATIO                                                *
170  REM *         THE USER MUST SPECIFY WHETHER COMPUTATION OF A PUT OR CALL IS     *
180  REM *         IS DESIRED.                                                       *
190  REM *                                                                           *
200  REM *                                                                           *
210  REM *                                                                           *
220  REM *****************************************************************************
230   Y1=0
240  REM
250  REM
260   GOSUB 920:REM************************INPUT DATA****************************
270  REM
280  REM
290   GOSUB 410:REM********************DO COMPUTATIONS**************************
300  REM
310  REM
320   GOSUB 1360:REM********************OUTPUT DATA**************************
330  REM
340  REM
350  REM *****************************************************************************
360  REM                     SUBROUTINE TO DO CALCULATIONS
370  REM *****************************************************************************
380  REM
390  REM INITIALIZE VALUES.
400  REM
410   R=R/100
420   D=D/100
430   T=T/365
440   A2$="N"
450  REM
460  REM TEST FOR SMALL VALUES OF T.
470  REM
480   IF T>=.001 THEN GOTO 580
490   A2$="Y"
500   IF PC$= "P" THEN GOTO 540
510   IF S <= E THEN C=0 : H=0
520   IF S > E THEN C=S-E : H=-1
530   GOTO 1360
540   IF  S >= E THEN C=0 : H=0
```

```
550   IF S < E THEN C=E-S : H=1
560   GOTO 1360
570 REM
580 REM COMPUTE D1 AND D2.
590 REM
600   N2=V*SQR(T)
610   D1=(LOG(S/E)+(R-D+V*V/2)*T)/N2
620   D2=D1-N2
630 REM
640 REM COMPUTE H AND C
650 REM
660   Z=D1
670   GOSUB 800:REM***************COMPUTE NORMAL VALUE FOR D1***************
680   H=-N
690   Z=D2
700   GOSUB 800:REM***************COMPUTE NORMAL VALUE FOR D2***************
710   C=S*(-H)*EXP(-D*T)-E*N*EXP(-R*T)
720   IF PC$="P" THEN C=C-S+E*EXP(-R*T):H=H+1
730   RETURN
740 REM
750 REM *********************************************************************
760 REM *                  SUBROUTINE TO COMPUTE NORMAL VALUES             *
770 REM *                  USING POLYNOMIAL APPROXIMATION                  *
780 REM *********************************************************************
790 REM
800   A6=ABS(Z)
810   T3=1/(1+.2316419*A6)
820   B1=.3989423*EXP(-Z*Z/2)
830   N=(((((1.330274*T3-1.821256)*T3+1.781478)*T3-.3565638)*T3+.3193815)
840   N=1-B1*T3*N
850   IF Z<O THEN N=1-N : RETURN
860   RETURN
870 REM
880 REM *********************************************************************
890 REM *                      SUBROUTINE TO INPUT DATA                    *
900 REM *********************************************************************
910 REM
920 PRINT "YOU MAY ENTER THE FOLLOWING VARIABLES:"
930 PRINT TAB(10);"CURRENT STOCK PRICE ($)";TAB(55):INPUT ;S
940   IF Y1=1 THEN RETURN
950 PRINT TAB(10);"EXERCISE PRICE ($)";TAB(55):INPUT ;E
960   IF Y1=2 THEN RETURN
970 PRINT TAB(10);"ANNUAL INTEREST RATE (%)";TAB(55):INPUT ;R
980   IF Y1=3 THEN RETURN
990 PRINT TAB(10);"ANNUAL DIVIDEND RATE (%)";TAB(55):INPUT ;D
1000   IF Y1=4 THEN RETURN
1010 PRINT TAB(10);"TIME TO EXPIRATION (DAYS)";TAB(55):INPUT ;T
1020   IF Y1=5 THEN RETURN
1030 PRINT TAB(10);"VOLATILITY";TAB(55):INPUT ;V
1040   IF Y1=6 THEN RETURN
1050 PRINT TAB(10);"OPTION SPECIFIED (C=CALL, P=PUT)";TAB(55):INPUT ;PC$
1060   IF Y1=7 THEN RETURN
1070 PRINT
1080 PRINT
```

```
1090 PRINT "YOU MAY CHANGE ANY OF THE VALUES ENTERED ABOVE AS FOLLOWS:"
1100 PRINT TAB(10);"CHOICE";TAB(20);"ITEM TO CHANGE";TAB(55);"CURRENT VALUE"
1110 PRINT TAB(10);"------";TAB(20);"--------------";TAB(55);"-------------"
1120 PRINT TAB(10);"0";TAB(20);"PRINT HEDGE RATIO AND";
1130  IF PC$="C" THEN PRINT " CALL VALUE"
1140  IF PC$="P" THEN PRINT "  PUT VALUE"
1150 PRINT TAB(10);"1";TAB(20);"CURRENT STOCK PRICE ($)";TAB(55);S
1160 PRINT TAB(10);"2";TAB(20);"EXERCISE PRICE ($)";TAB(55);E
1170 PRINT TAB(10);"3";TAB(20);"ANNUAL  INTEREST RATE (%)";TAB(55);R
1180 PRINT TAB(10);"4";TAB(20);"ANNUAL DIVIDEND RATE (%)";TAB(55);D
1190 PRINT TAB(10);"5";TAB(20);"TIME TO EXPIRATION (DAYS)";TAB(55);T
1200 PRINT TAB(10);"6";TAB(20);"VOLATILITY";TAB(55);V
1210 PRINT TAB(10);"7";TAB(20);"OPTION SPECIFIED (C=CALL, P=PUT)";TAB(55);PC$
1220 PRINT
1230 PRINT
1240 INPUT "WHICH CHOICE DO YOU DESIRE (0-7)";Y1
1250  ON Y1 GOSUB 930,950,970,990,1010,1030,1050
1260  IF Y1=0 THEN RETURN
1270 PRINT
1280 PRINT
1290  GOTO 1090
1300 REM
1310 REM
1320 REM ********************************************************************
1330 REM *                      SUBROUTINE TO OUTPUT DATA                   *
1340 REM ********************************************************************
1350 REM
1360 PRINT
1370 PRINT
1375  IF A2$="N" THEN GOTO 1390
1380 PRINT TAB(10);"THESE COMPUTATIONS ARE BASED ON THE";
1382 PRINT TAB(10);"TERMINAL CONDITIONS OF THE OPTION VALUE BECAUSE"
1385 PRINT TAB(10);"TIME TO MATURITY IS TOO CLOSE TO ZERO"
1390 PRINT TAB(10);"THE HEDGE RATIO=";TAB(41);H
1400  IF PC$="C" THEN PRINT TAB(10);"THE CALL VALUE=";TAB(42);C
1410  IF PC$="P" THEN PRINT TAB(10);"THE PUT VALUE=";TAB(42);C
1420 PRINT
1430 PRINT
1440 REM
1450 REM
1460 REM RETURN R AND D TO PERCENT; T TO DAYS.
1470 REM
1480 REM
1490  R=R*100
1500  D=D*100
1510  T=T*365
1520  A2$="N"
1530 INPUT "DO YOU WISH TO GO AGAIN WITH MODIFIED DATA (1=YES, 2=NO)";A3
1540  IF A3=1 THEN GOSUB 1070:GOTO 290
1550  IF A3=2 THEN END
```

24
A Pricing Model for Options on Futures

The market for options on stocks, large though it is, is dwarfed by the market for options on futures and related commodity and financial instrument options. There are options traded on financial futures, there are options traded on index futures, and there are options traded on foreign exchange and commodity futures.

Options are traded on the spot instruments as well as the futures. For example, besides the Standard and Poor's 500 futures and the New York Stock Exchange composite futures, which both have listed options, the Chicago Board Options Exchange trades options based on the value of the spot index of current stock price. Other spot and futures index options are traded on the complex of indexes traded on the American Stock Exchange and the Chicago Board of Trade. The dollar investment represented by the daily trading volume on these stock index instruments is two to three times that of the New York Stock Exchange stocks themselves.

Although options are often listed on both the spot and the futures, with the exception of the incredibly popular Standard and Poor's 100 index options traded on the Chicago Board Option Exchange—a contract that regularly has a daily trading volume near the one hundred thousand contract range—options on futures are usually more popular than are the options on the spot instruments. This is because the futures contracts are generally more liquid than their spot counterparts. The prices of the futures are easily quoted and trades can be quickly executed with low bid-asked spreads.

THE OPTION PRICING FORMULA FOR OPTIONS ON FUTURES

The Black-Scholes formula presented in Chapter 23 cannot be used to price options on futures without some modifications. There is a fundamental difference between options on spot instruments such as stocks and options on futures contracts. The difference lies in the funding requirements for hedging the option against the underlying instrument.

Recall that options on stocks are priced so that a riskless hedge position between the option and the stock will give a return equal to the risk-free rate. In creating the hedge, a position must be taken in the stock; the stock might be purchased or it might be sold short. In either case, this position leads to a net investment of funds in the stock. The opportunity cost of these funds must be reflected in the pricing of the hedge. The return to the funds invested is set equal to the risk-free interest rate in the Black-Scholes formula to take care of this.

By contrast, no investment is necessary to take a position in a futures contract. (While there is a margin requirement, this can usually be satisfied by putting Treasury bills or other interest bearing securities in the margin account. There is then no opportunity cost to the money being used for margin.) This means that, unlike the stock position which gives a return equal to the risk-free rate, the return to the futures position will be zero. So in the option pricing formula for options on futures, there is no term to reflect a cost for funds invested.

The formula for pricing options on futures is:

$$C(F,T,E,r,\sigma) = e^{-rT}FN(d_1) - Ee^{-rT}N(d_2)$$

where

$$d_1 = [1n(F/E) + 1/2\,\sigma^2\,T]/\sigma\sqrt{T}$$

and

$$d_2 = d_1 - \sigma\sqrt{T}.$$

The terms in this formula are defined in the same way as those in the Black-Scholes formula discussed in Chapter 23, except that we have replaced the stock price S with the future price F. T is the time to expiration of the option, measured in fractions of a year; E is the exercise price of the option; r is the risk-free rate of interest; and σ is the price volatility for the underlying futures contract.

This formula differs from the Black-Scholes formula by replacing the price of the stock, S, with the *discounted* price of the futures contract, $e^{-rT}F$. Substituting $e^{-rT}F$ for S throughout the formula eliminates the riskless interest rate in the $N(d_1)$ and $N(d_2)$ terms. This will set the expected return of the strategy at zero rather than at the risk-free rate. The interest rate term still appears in the discount factor e^{-rT} in the second term of the formula. This is because the payment for the option still occurs at the time of expiration, and so this payment must be discounted back to the present time.

This small change from the specifications of the Black-Scholes formula can lead to significant changes in the model value of options. Table 24-1 compares the prices that arise from the two formulas for different interest rates. As would be expected, the difference increases with an increase in the interest rate. The difference also increases with the time to expiration, since then the interest effect is greater.

The binomial formula can also be easily adjusted to price options on futures. For the binomial formula, the interest rate drops out of the one-period pricing formula, leaving $p = (1-d)/(u-d)$, rather than having $p = (r-d)/(u-d)$. (The interest rate here is set to one rather than to zero because the interest rate term used in the binomial formula is actually equal to one plus the interest rate. That is, if the interest rate is .15, the interest rate term in the binomial formula will equal 1.15.)

The value of a put option can be determined directly from the price of a call option that has the same exercise price and time to expiration. This relationship will be similar to the put-call parity equation presented in Chapter 23, but with the price of the futures contract discounted along with the exercise price, since the payment for the futures need not be made until the time the option expires. The put value will then be

$$P = C + e^{-rT}(E-F).$$

Note that if the option is at the money (i.e., if the futures price equals the exercise price), the put and call will be worth the same amount. By contrast, as the put-call parity equation for options on stocks shows, the call option on a stock will always be worth more than the put option when the option is at the money.

TABLE 24-1 A Comparison of the Black-Scholes and the Futures Option Pricing Models for Alternative Interest Rates*

INTEREST RATE (In Percent)	TWO MONTHS TO EXPIRATION CALL OPTION VALUES		FIVE MONTHS TO EXPIRATION CALL OPTION VALUES		EIGHT MONTHS TO EXPIRATION CALL OPTION VALUES	
	Black-Scholes	Futures	Black-Scholes	Futures	Black-Scholes	Futures
4	1.78	1.60	2.96	2.51	3.88	3.14
5	1.82	1.60	3.07	2.50	4.05	3.12
6	1.86	1.60	3.17	2.49	4.22	3.10
7	1.90	1.59	3.29	2.48	4.40	3.08
8	1.95	1.59	3.40	2.47	4.59	3.06
9	1.99	1.59	3.52	2.46	4.78	3.04
10	2.04	1.59	3.63	2.45	4.97	3.02
11	2.09	1.58	3.75	2.44	5.16	3.00
12	2.13	1.58	3.87	2.43	5.36	2.98
13	2.18	1.58	4.00	2.42	5.56	2.96
14	2.23	1.58	4.12	2.41	5.77	2.94
15	2.27	1.57	4.25	2.40	5.97	2.92
16	2.32	1.57	4.38	2.39	6.18	2.90
17	2.37	1.57	4.51	2.38	6.40	2.88
18	2.42	1.56	4.64	2.37	6.61	2.87
19	2.47	1.56	4.77	2.36	6.83	2.85
20	2.52	1.56	4.91	2.35	7.05	2.83

*The stock price = $50, exercise price = $50, and volatility = .2

USING THE FUTURES PRICING FORMULA IN TRADING STRATEGIES

We saw in the last two chapters that some adjustments are necessary to bring the theoretical construction of the option pricing formula into the reality of real-world trading. For stock options, the greatest concerns are the possibility of early exercise, and the effect of dividend payments on stock prices. For options on futures contracts, there are these and other concerns.

Options on stock indexes will have to adjust for stock prices dropping at the exdividend date. Since many stocks go exdividend within a few weeks of each other, the underlying stock index will have significant drops over the course of each quarter, and these must be built into both the futures and the option prices. There is also the possibility of early exercise, since all exchange traded options are American options that allow for early exercise. As we have already seen, the option pricing formulas can be adjusted to take these problems into account.

A more difficult problem in dealing with options on futures has to do with the seemingly esoteric subject of the assumptions underlying the return distribution of the futures contract. The Black-Scholes formula assumes the returns to the underlying asset are lognormally distributed. The binomial formula also assumes lognormality in the limiting case. For stock returns, this assumption is less than completely acceptable, stock returns are actually found to have slightly thicker tails in the distribution than the lognormal has. But the lognormal distribution is close enough to the distributional reality for stocks to provide a workable basis for developing a stock option pricing formula.

Unfortunately, the same cannot be said for options on a number of other instruments. For example, stock indexes are formed as the arithmetic average of stock prices. Even if we go along with the assumption that the returns of each stock in the index are lognormally distributed, the average of these returns will not have a lognormal distribution. The interaction of the returns on each stock is very complex, and it is difficult to say just what the final distribution of the index will be.

This is true for bond futures and other financial instruments as well. Debt instruments will have a very complex distribution. Bond prices cannot be a lognormal process, since they are tied to par value at maturity. Also, they are complex functions of interest rates, so even if we were to make the simplifying assumption that interest rates follow a lognormal process—which is probably worse than the assumption of lognormality for stock returns—it still would not be clear what that would mean for the distribution of the bonds.

This may all seem worlds away from the marketplace, but the implications are important for trading: If the returns to the futures do not follow the distributional assumptions of the option model being used, then the option prices will be wrong. Options will appear to be mispriced when they are not, and some options will appear to be fairly priced when they are not.

All this said, the fact still remains that many traders and institutions dealing full time with these markets use the option model in this chapter for their trading strategies.

FUTURES OPTION PRICING FORMULA

Computational Procedure

F = current futures price
T = time to expiration in fraction of years
E = option exercise price
r = riskless interest rate as a decimal
σ = stock volatility

where

$$C = e^{-rT}F\,N(d_1) - Ee^{-rT}\,N(d_2)$$

and

$$d_1 = [\ln(F/E) + 1/2\ \sigma^2 T]/\sigma\sqrt{T}$$

$$d_2 = d_1 - \sigma\sqrt{T}.$$

$N(\ )$ is the cumulative normal distribution function.

The hedge ratio h is computable directly from the first term of the option formula,

$$h = -e^{-rT}N(d_1).$$

The put-call parity equation can be used to give the price of a put option in terms of a call option, with the same exercise price and time to expiration,

$$P = C + e^{-rT}(E-F).$$

Trading Strategy

- Buy the option if the market price is less than the formula price.
- Write the option if the market price is greater than the formula price.
- Hedge the option against the futures contract according to the hedge ratio h.

```
10   REM  *****************************************************************
20   REM  *                 OPTION PRICING FOR FUTURES OPTIONS            *
30   REM  *                                                               *
40   REM  * THIS PROGRAM CALCULATES THE BLACK-SCHOLES PRICE FOR A CALL OR PUT *
50   REM  * ON A FUTURES CONTRACT.                                        *
60   REM  *                                                               *
70   REM  * VARIABLES USED: F=CURRENT FUTURES PRICE IN DOLLARS            *
80   REM  *                 E=EXERCISE PRICE IN DOLLARS                   *
90   REM  *                 R=ANNUAL RISK FREE RATE OF INTEREST IN PERCENT *
100  REM  *                 T=TIME TO EXPIRATION IN DAYS                  *
110  REM  *                 V=MEASURE OF VOLATILITY                       *
120  REM  *                 C=OPTION PRICE                                *
130  REM  *                 H=HEDGE RATIO                                 *
140  REM  *                                                               *
150  REM  * THE USER MUST SPECIFY WHETHER COMPUTATION OF A PUT OR CALL IS *
160  REM  * DESIRED.                                                      *
170  REM  *                                                               *
180  REM  *                                                               *
190  REM  *                                                               *
200  REM  *                                                               *
210  REM  *****************************************************************
220  Y1=0
230  REM
240  REM
250  GOSUB 930:REM*********************INPUT DATA**************************
260  REM
270  REM
280  GOSUB 430:REM********************DO COMPUTATIONS*********************
290  REM
300  REM
310  GOSUB 1290:REM*********************OUTPUT DATA**************************
320  REM
330  REM
340  END:REM************************STOP PROGRAM**************************
350  REM
360  REM
370  REM  *****************************************************************
380  REM                   SUBROUTINE TO DO CALCULATIONS
390  REM  *****************************************************************
400  REM
410  REM INITIALIZE VALUES.
420  REM
430  R=R/100
440  D=D/100
450  T=T/365
460  A2$="N"
470  REM
480  REM TEST FOR SMALL VALUES OF T.
490  REM
500  IF T>=.001 THEN GOTO 600
510  A2$="Y"
520  IF PC$= "P" THEN GOTO 560
530  IF F <= E THEN C=0 : H=0
540  IF F > E THEN C= F-E : H=-1
```

```
550    GOTO 1290
560    IF F>=E THEN C=0 : H=0
570    IF F<E THEN C= E-F : H=1
580    GOTO 1290
590 REM
600 REM COMPUTE D1 AND D2.
610 REM
620    N2=V*SQR(T)
630    D1=(LOG(F/E)+(V*V/2)*T)/N2
640    D2=D1-N2
650 REM
660 REM COMPUTE H AND C
670 REM
680    Z=D1
690    GOSUB 820:REM****************COMPUTE NORMAL VALUE FOR D1****************
700    H=-N*EXP(-R*T)
710    Z=D2
720    GOSUB 820:REM****************COMPUTE NORMAL VALUE FOR D2****************
730    C=F*(-H)-E*N*EXP(-R*T)
740    IF PC$="P" THEN C=C+(E-F)*EXP(-R*T):H=H+EXP(-R*T)
750 RETURN
760 REM
770 REM ************************************************************************
780 REM                 SUBROUTINE TO COMPUTE NORMAL VALUES
790 REM                   USING POLYNOMIAL APPROXIMATION
800 REM ************************************************************************
810 REM
820    A6=ABS(Z)
830    T3=1/(1+.2316419*A6)
840    B1=.3989423*EXP(-Z*Z/2)
850    N=(((((1.330274*T3-1.821256)*T3+1.781478)*T3-.3565638)*T3+.3193815)
860    N=1-B1*T3*N
870    IF Z<0 THEN N=1-N : RETURN ELSE RETURN
880 REM
890 REM ************************************************************************
900 REM                      SUBROUTINE TO INPUT DATA
910 REM ************************************************************************
920 REM
930 PRINT "YOU MAY ENTER THE FOLLOWING VARIABLES:"
940 PRINT TAB(10);"CURRENT FUTURES PRICE ($)";TAB(55):INPUT ;F
950    IF Y1=1 THEN RETURN
960 PRINT TAB(10);"EXERCISE PRICE ($)";TAB(55):INPUT ;E
970    IF Y1=2 THEN RETURN
980 PRINT TAB(10);"ANNUAL INTEREST RATE (%)";TAB(55):INPUT ;R
990    IF Y1=3 THEN RETURN
1000 PRINT TAB(10);"TIME TO EXPIRATION (DAYS)";TAB(55):INPUT ;T
1010   IF Y1=4 THEN RETURN
1020 PRINT TAB(10);"VOLATILITY";TAB(55):INPUT ;V
1030   IF Y1=5 THEN RETURN
1040 PRINT TAB(10);"OPTION SPECIFIED (C=CALL, P=PUT)";TAB(55):INPUT ;PC$
1050   IF Y1=6 THEN RETURN
1060 PRINT:PRINT
1070 PRINT "YOU MAY CHANGE ANY OF THE VALUES ENTERED ABOVE AS FOLLOWS:"
1080 PRINT TAB(10);"CHOICE";TAB(20);"ITEM TO CHANGE";TAB(55);"CURRENT VALUE"
```

```
1090 PRINT TAB(10);"------";TAB(20);"--------------";TAB(55);"--------------"
1100 PRINT TAB(10);"0";TAB(20);"PRINT HEDGE RATIO AND";
1110   IF A1=1 THEN PRINT " CALL VALUE" ELSE PRINT " PUT VALUE"
1120 PRINT TAB(10);"1";TAB(20);"CURRENT FUTURES PRICE ($)";TAB(55);F
1130 PRINT TAB(10);"2";TAB(20);"EXERCISE PRICE ($)";TAB(55);E
1140 PRINT TAB(10);"3";TAB(20);"ANNUAL INTEREST RATE (%)";TAB(55);R
1150 PRINT TAB(10);"4";TAB(20);"TIME TO EXPIRATION (DAYS)";TAB(55);T
1160 PRINT TAB(10);"5";TAB(20);"VOLATILITY";TAB(55);V
1170 PRINT TAB(10);"6";TAB(20);"OPTION SPECIFIED (C=CALL, P=PUT)";TAB(55);PC$
1180 PRINT:PRINT
1190 INPUT "WHICH CHOICE DO YOU DESIRE (0-6)";Y1
1200   ON Y1 GOSUB 940,960,980,1000,1020,1040
1210   IF Y1=0 THEN RETURN
1220 PRINT:PRINT
1230   GOTO 1070
1240 REM
1250 REM ******************************************************************
1260 REM                      SUBROUTINE TO OUTPUT DATA
1270 REM ******************************************************************
1280 REM
1290 PRINT
1300 PRINT
1310 IF A2$="Y" THEN PRINT TAB(10);"THESE COMPUTATIONS ARE BASED ON THE";:
     PRINT TAB(10); "TERMINAL CONDITIONS OF THE OPTION VALUE BECAUSE";:
     PRINT TAB(10)"'TIME TO MATURITY' IS TOO CLOSE TO 0"
1320 PRINT TAB(10);"THE HEDGE RATIO=";TAB(41);H
1330   IF PC$="C" THEN PRINT TAB(10);"THE CALL VALUE=";TAB(42);C
1340   IF PC$="P" THEN PRINT TAB(10);"THE PUT VALUE=";TAB(42);C
1350 PRINT
1360 PRINT
1370 REM
1380 REM RETURN R AND D TO PERCENT; T TO DAYS.
1390 REM
1400   R=R*100
1410   D=D*100
1420   T=T*365
1430 INPUT "DO YOU WISH TO GO AGAIN WITH MODIFIED DATA (1=YES, 2=NO)";A3
1440   IF A3=1 THEN GOSUB 1060:GOTO 280
1450   IF A3=2 GOTO 340
1460 PRINT "PLEASE ENTER '1' OR '2' " :GOTO 1430
```

25
Volatility Estimation Using Historical Data

The five principle inputs into the option pricing formula are the stock price, the exercise price of the option, the time to expiration of the option, the risk-free interest rate, and the stock price volatility. The first three of these inputs are listed in published option quotes. The risk-free interest rate can be proxied by the Treasury bill rate or the certificate-of-deposit rate prevailing for the time until the expiration of the option. The interest rate may vary slightly depending on what instrument is used for the measurement, but the option price will not be particularly sensitive to these small differences in the interest rate.

The critical input for the successful use of the option pricing formula is the stock volatility. Annualized volatilities for stocks with traded options generally range between .1 and .6. That is, the annual standard deviation of stock returns is between 10% and 60%. Occasionally a stock may have a volatility significantly above this range for a short time period. The volatility for any particular stock may vary by as much as .1 over the course of several months. Such variations translate into significant changes in the theoretical price of options on the stock. Figures 25-1 and 25-2 illustrate the effect of volatility on the price of in-the-money, at-the-money, and out-of-the-money options. As is clear from these figures, even a movement of volatility of .02 is enough to make a fairly priced option appear significantly mispriced.

In theory, there is little problem in getting an adequate volatility estimate.

Unlike attempts to estimate the direction of the stock price, the estimation of the volatility of the stock price does not require any divination into the future direction of the price of the stock or into the mind set of the other investors in the market. Volatility estimators are simply a reflection of how variable one expects the stock price movement to be—irrespective of the direction of that movement. The investor does not need to know which direction the stock is likely to move, only the degree to which the stock tends to move.

But in practice, volatility estimation is complicated by a number of factors. The most significant problem is the instability of volatility over time. Figure 25-3 traces the volatility for Bank of America, a relatively stable stock, over a six-year period. Each of the estimates in this figure was made using data over 60 trading days. The volatility has a mean of approximately .4, but there are times when the stock heats up, and the volatility takes sudden jumps—at

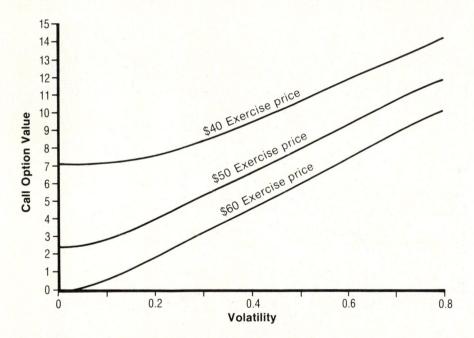

Figure 25-1. The price of call options as a function of the stock volatility. The prices of call options with 40, 50, and 60 exercise prices are plotted, with the stock assumed to be $50 a share.

two points the volatility went above .6. This instability exacerbates volatility estimation methods that rely on past data. If the volatility shifts about erratically, there is no reason to expect the volatility estimated over past stock prices to reflect the volatility of the current stock price.

A second, less serious difficulty in volatility estimation arises from inadequacies in the stock price data. The stock price is only observed when a trade takes place. There is no way to know what the stock price is doing in between trades. For stocks with low transaction volume, this means the estimated volatility will tend to underestimate the true stock volatility; that is, the volatility estimate will be downward biased.

To illustrate this, suppose a stock trades at 2:00 p.m. and then again at 2:30 p.m., and both trades are at a price of 55. It appears from these two trades the stock has very low volatility. But what we do not know from these two trades,

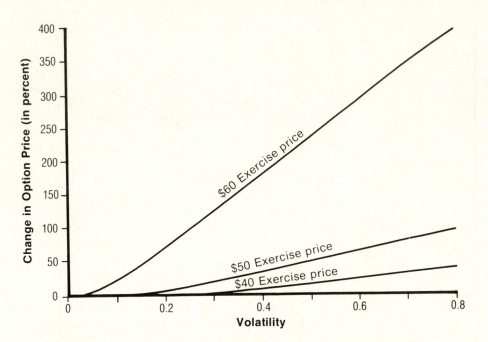

Figure 25-2. The percentage change in the price of call options as a function of stock volatility. The percentage is taken using the option price with a .01 volatility as the base.

and what we must know to get a complete picture of the volatility, is what the stock price of a trade would have been had a trade occurred any time between 2:00 and 2:30. It may well be that the unobserved stock price path over this half-hour period was extremely erratic; perhaps a trade at 2:15 would have cleared at a price of 57, while a trade at 2:20 would have dropped the price to

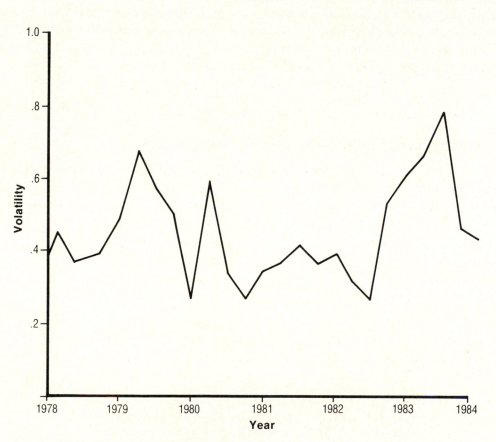

Figure 25-3. Price volatility of Bank of America stock.

53. These fluctuations go unobserved, because the two snapshots of the price path we have happen to be at the same price. This problem is less severe for stocks with a large number of transactions a day, and some estimation methods are less sensitive to it than others.

VOLATILITY ESTIMATION USING PAST PRICES

Volatility is a measure of the standard deviation of stock returns. The estimators for volatility therefore are essentially variance estimators. Indeed, the most straightforward volatility estimator, which uses closing stock prices, is simply the maximum likelihood variance estimator from elementary statistics. But estimating volatility with only closing stock prices ignores other valuable information in the stock price summary data. The open, high, and low stock price also contain information about the variability of stock prices, and after we discuss the close-to-close estimator, we will discuss two of these more powerful volatility estimators.

Estimation Using Close-to-Close Price Changes

Letting C_t be the closing price of the stock for period t, we define the stock return R_t as the price relative between period t–1 and period t, $R_t = C_t/C_{t-1}$. To approximate the continuously compounded returns we use the natural log of R_t in the computations. Denoting the mean return over n time periods by m,

$$m = \frac{1}{n} \sum_{t=1}^{n} \ln R_t,$$

the variance can be computed using the standard maximum likelihood variance estimator:

$$\sigma^2 = \frac{1}{n-1} \sum_{t=1}^{n} (\ln R_t - m)^2.$$

The volatility is obtained as the square root of σ^2. Note that we divide the sum by (n–1) rather than n. This is necessary to obtain an unbiased estimate of the variance.

From this we see the volatility is simply the square root of the variance. The volatility should be adjusted to give an annualized value. If weekly closing prices are used in the variance calculation, then the resulting volatility is multiplied by the square root of 52. If daily closing prices are used, the daily volatility must be multiplied by the square root of the number of trading days (not the total number of days) in the year. While this will vary from year to year, it is approximately 250 days.

A natural question arises as to what time period to use for the volatility estimation, and how many past data points to use to get a good estimate of the volatility.

In theory, using more past data will lead to a better estimate, and the estimate will be better when smaller time periods, daily rather than monthly prices, are used. Unfortunately, while a long past time period will give a tight estimate of the volatility over that time period, it may not reflect the present volatility as well as an estimator based only on the more recent past. Given the wide variability in volatility over time, it would be sensible to restrict the data set to more recent time periods. These will have more in common with the current stock return characteristics. This would suggest taking daily closing prices over the past twenty trading days rather than using monthly closing prices over the past two years. Difficulties may arise when daily closes are used on stocks with infrequent transactions, as nonuniform time periods may result. For example, say the closing trade for a stock on Tuesday occurs at 4:00, on Wednesday at 2:30, and on Thursday at 4:00. The price relative for the return between Tuesday and Wednesday will actually reflect the price change over a smaller time period than will the price relative for the return between Wednesday and Thursday. Returns based on time periods of differing lengths may result in serious errors for the volatility estimate.

A precise estimate of the volatility over any time period is possible with only a moderate number of observations. The variance of the volatility estimate decreases proportional to the fourth power of the volatility as the number of observations increases. Taking a volatility in the .1 to .6 range to the fourth power leads to a very small number, and thus to a very tight estimate. The accuracy of the estimate of past volatility is therefore not the critical problem. The critical problem is whether that volatility estimate, based as it is on past prices, reflects the current volatility. A good rule of thumb is to use the past twenty trading days for short-term volatility estimates, and the last twenty weeks of data (possibly using weekly closes), for longer term volatility.

The Extreme Value Method: Using High and Low Prices

Intuitively, we would think high and low prices encompass important information about the volatility of a stock that closing prices do not. This is indeed the case; the extreme value method, based on high and low prices, is roughly five times as precise an estimator as the close-to-close estimator previously discussed. The high and low prices over the past n days will give as good an estimate of the volatility over that time period as will using the closing prices over the past 5n days. This is because the closing prices are simply a sample of prices drawn from an arbitrary time, while the high and the low prices are drawn selectively to give an indication of the range of price movements. As we already discussed, it is conceivable two closing prices will be equal while the actual stock price between the closes involves a great deal of variation. The closing prices will misrepresent the actual volatility of the stock in this case, while the extreme value volatility estimator based on high and low prices will pick up this variation.

As with the close-to-close volatility estimator, the extreme value estimator uses the natural log of price relatives, but substitutes the high and the low price for time interval t, H_t and L_t, for the closing prices of the periods C_t and C_{t-1}. It turns out that this value must then be normalized by multiplying it by .601. The resulting volatility estimator is:

$$\sigma_t = .601 \cdot \ln(H_t/L_t).$$

If more than one period is used, the values for the periods are simply averaged together:

$$\frac{1}{n} \sum_{t=1}^{n} \sigma_t.$$

The resulting volatility is annualized in the same way the close-to-close estimator is. If one-week periods are used the volatility is multiplied by the square root of 52, while if daily prices are used the estimate is multiplied by the square root of the number of trading days in the year.

We have already mentioned that the close-to-close estimator will be biased downward if the stock does not trade sufficiently. This bias is even more marked for the extreme value estimator. In addition, we would expect bad trade data to show up more readily in the high and low quotations, as it is likely data errors will be outside the actual trading range of the stock. These problems can be reduced if weekly periods are used rather than daily periods. And empirical tests indicate that these difficulties do not eliminate the advantage the extreme value method has over the close-to-close estimator.

The High-Low-Close Estimator

We developed the extreme value estimator by arguing that the high and low prices contain information that the closing prices do not. But that estimator ignores any potentially valuable information contained in the closing prices. It should be possible to construct an even more efficient estimator for the volatility by combining the close-to-close prices with the high and low prices. Doing so leads to the high-low-close estimator:

$$\sigma_t^2 = .5 \ln(H_t/L_t)^2 - .39 \ln(C_t/C_{t-1})^2.$$

The high-low-close volatility estimator for period t is the square root of σ_t^2. The volatility over a number of time periods can be estimated by taking the mean of the individual volatility terms, as was done for the extreme value estimator:

$$\frac{1}{n} \sum_{n=1}^{t} \sigma_t^2.$$

This estimator is over seven times as efficient as the simple close-to-close estimator and retains the feature of using only readily available summary stock price data. Since this method combines both of the previous methods, the reservations and points of application for those two methods will apply for this estimator as well.

These estimates of volatility may fail to conform closely to the actual volatility because of unpredictable shifts in the volatility, not because of inaccuracies in the estimator itself. The estimator only estimates the volatility over the period of the data used in the estimate. In other words, the three methods are good estimators of the past but less than ideal forecasters of the future course of volatility. Obviously, for the purposes of option pricing, the next step after developing a good estimator of volatility is to develop a method for predicting what the volatility will be over the current and possibly future time periods.

USING VOLATILITY IN OPTION TRADING STRATEGIES

The close-to-close volatility estimator will follow a Chi-square distribution. For any estimate of the volatility, the actual volatility that will be realized for the current period can be set within the error bounds defined by this distribution. A similar procedure can also be used for the other two volatility estimators. These error bounds can be useful in screening option prices to find those prices that appear to depart from their theoretical level even after the variations in volatility are taken into account. A trading strategy may consider an option underpriced only when the market price is below the formula price with the lower bound volatility used, and similarly, an option may be considered to be overpriced only when its value is greater than the formula value with the upper bound volatility used. The confidence bounds are largely judgmental. The bounds should be set to screen out significantly mispriced options, while not making too many options appear mispriced. If many options on a stock continually appear mispriced, it is likely the bounds for the volatility should be widened.

VOLATILITY ESTIMATION

Computational Procedure

C_t = closing price for period t
H_t = high price for period t
L_t = low price for period t
σ_t = volatility estimate for period t

Close-to-close estimator

Let

$$\sigma_t^2 = \frac{1}{n-1} \sum_{i=1}^{n} (\ln R_{t-i} - m)^2$$

where

$R_t = C_t / C_{t-1}$, and

$$m = \frac{1}{n} \sum_{i=1}^{n} \ln R_{t-i}.$$

Then the volatility estimate for period t is $\sqrt{\sigma_t^2}$.

High-low estimator

$$\sigma_t = \frac{.601}{n} \sum_{i=1}^{n} \ln(H_{t-i}/L_{t-i}).$$

High-low-close estimator

Let

$S_t^2 = .5 \ln(H_t/L_t)^2 - .39 \ln(C_t/C_{t-1})^2$, and

$$\sigma_t^2 = \frac{1}{n} \sum_{i=1}^{n} S_{t-i}^2.$$

Then the volatility estimate for period t is $\sqrt{\sigma_t^2}$.

```
10  REM ***************************************************************
20  REM *                     STOCK VOLATILITY                       *
30  REM *                                                            *
40  REM * THIS PROGRAM CALCULATES THE VOLATILITY OF A STOCK USING PAST PRICE *
50  REM * DATA.  THIS VOLATILITY IS AN INPUT FOR THE OPTION PRICING MODELS,  *
60  REM * AND FOR THE PRICING MODEL FOR CONVERTIBLE BONDS.            *
70  REM * THE VOLATILITY MAY BE CALCULATED IN ANY OF THE FOLLOWING THREE WAYS:*
80  REM *    1.) CLOSE TO CLOSE (ENTER CLOSING PRICE FOR EACH DAY)    *
90  REM *    2.) HIGH-LOW (ENTER HIGH AND LOW PRICE FOR EACH DAY)     *
100 REM *    3.) HIGH-LOW CLOSE (ENTER HIGH,LOW AND CLOSING PRICE FOR EACH DAY)*
110 REM *                                                            *
120 REM *     THE FOLLOWING VARIABLES ARE USED:                      *
130 REM *                     V = THE CALCULATED VOLATILITY          *
140 REM *            SPRICE(H,L,C) = ARRAY OF STOCK PRICES FOR EACH DAY *
150 REM *                     H=HIGH PRICE                           *
160 REM *                     L=LOW PRICE                            *
170 REM *                     C=CLOSING PRICE                        *
180 REM *                                                            *
190 REM *    THE USER MUST ENTER THE STOCK PRICES ACCORDING TO THE METHOD USED *
200 REM ***************************************************************
210 REM
220 REM
230  GOSUB 360 :REM************MAIN MENU***************************************
240 REM
250 REM
260  GOSUB 670 :REM*****COMPUTE VOLATILITY USING CLOSING PRICES****************
270 REM
280 REM
290  GOSUB 1130 :REM*****COMPUTE VOLATILITY USING HIGH AND LOW PRICES**********
300 REM
310 REM
320  GOSUB 1610 :REM***COMPUTE VOLATILITY USING HIGH, LOW AND CLOSING PRICES**
330 REM
340 REM
350  GOSUB 2140 :REM************EDIT DATA FOR DISPLAY ON SCREEN**************
360 REM *********************** MAIN MENU ****************************
370 REM
380  DIM SPRICE(100,3),R(100),S(100):REM DIMENSION ARRAYS
390  CLS:REM CLEAR THE SCREEN AND MOVE CURSOR TO TOP OF SCREEN
400 PRINT:PRINT:PRINT
410 PRINT TAB(10) "THIS PROGRAM CALCULATES THE VOLATILITY OF A STOCK"
420 PRINT TAB(10) "USING ONE OF THREE METHODS.  CHOOSE THE METHOD YOU"
430 PRINT TAB(10) "WISH TO USE. (1-3)
440 PRINT
450 PRINT TAB(10)"1.) CLOSE-CLOSE  (REQUIRES THE CLOSING PRICE FOR EACH DAY)"
460 PRINT
470 PRINT TAB(10)"2.) HIGH-LOW  (REQUIRES THE HIGH AND LOW PRICE FOR EACH DAY)
480 PRINT
490 PRINT TAB(10)"3.) HIGH-LOW-CLOSE (REQUIRES THE HIGH, LOW AND CLOSING PRICE"
500 PRINT TAB(30) "FOR EACH DAY)"
510 PRINT
520 INPUT A1$
530  IF A1$ <>"1" AND A1$<>"2" AND A1$ <> "3" THEN GOTO 390
540 PRINT
```

```
550 PRINT TAB(10)"PLEASE SPECIFY TYPE OF DATA"
560 PRINT TAB(10)"1.) DAILY"
570 PRINT TAB(10)"2.) WEEKLY"
580 INPUT A2$
590  IF A2$ <> "1" AND A2$ <> "2" THEN GOTO 550
600  IF A2$ = "1" THEN MULT = 250
610  IF A2$ = "2" THEN MULT = 52
620  CLS: REM CLEAR SCREEN
630  ON VAL(A1$) GOTO 680,1130,1610
640 REM ************************* END MAIN MENU ***************************
650 REM
660 REM
670 REM ***************************************************************
680 REM *                        CLOSE-CLOSE                          *
690 REM ***************************************************************
700 REM
710 REM ************************* ENTER DATA ***************************
720  COUNT=1 :REM INITIALIZE COUNTER FOR CLOSE-CLOSE
730 PRINT:PRINT "ENTER '999' TO QUIT":PRINT
740 PRINT "ENTER CLOSING STOCK PRICE ";COUNT;": ";:INPUT SPRICE(COUNT,3)
750 IF SPRICE(COUNT,3)=999 THEN GOTO 800
760  COUNT=COUNT+1
770  GOTO 740
780 REM
790 REM ************************* DISPLAY DATA ***************************
800  CLS :REM CLEAR SCREEN AND MOVE CURSOR TO TOP OF SCREEN
810  SCROLL = 1
820  FOR I = SCROLL TO COUNT-1
830 PRINT TAB(10)"CLOSING PRICE ";I;"= ";SPRICE(I,3)
840  IF I = 20 OR I = 40 OR I = 60 OR I = 80 THEN GOSUB 2190
850  NEXT I
860  GOSUB 2190
870  IF A2$ = "Y" THEN GOTO 820
880 REM
890 REM ************************* COMPUTE R(I) ***************************
900 REM
910  FOR I=2 TO COUNT-1
920   R(I)=LOG(SPRICE(I,3)/SPRICE(I-1,3))
930  NEXT I
940 REM
950 REM ************************* COMPUTE MEAN ***************************
960  SUM =0
970  FOR I=2 TO COUNT -1
980   SUM = SUM + R(I)
990  NEXT I
1000  MEAN = SUM/(COUNT-2)
1010 REM
1020 REM ************************* COMPUTE THE VARIANCE *****************
1030  SVAR=0
1040  FOR I=2 TO COUNT-1
1050   SVAR = SVAR +(R(I)-MEAN)^2
1060  NEXT I
1070 REM
1080 REM ************************* COMPUTE THE VOLATILITY ****************
```

```
1090   V = SQR(MULT*(1/(COUNT-3))*SVAR)
1100   GOTO 2630 :REM END ROUTINE
1110 REM
1120 REM
1130 REM ***********************************************************************
1140 REM *                          HIGH-LOW                                   *
1150 REM ***********************************************************************
1160 REM
1170 REM
1180 REM ********************** ENTER DATA ******************************
1190 REM
1200   COUNT = 1 :REM     INITIALIZE COUNTER
1210 PRINT:PRINT "ENTER '999' TO QUIT":PRINT
1220 PRINT TAB(10) "ENTER HIGH STOCK PRICE ";COUNT;": ";:INPUT SPRICE(COUNT,1)
1230   IF SPRICE(COUNT,1)=999 THEN GOTO 1300
1240 PRINT TAB(10)"ENTER LOW   STOCK PRICE ";COUNT;": ";:INPUT SPRICE(COUNT,2)
1250   IF SPRICE(COUNT,2) = 999 THEN GOTO 1300
1260   COUNT = COUNT + 1
1270   GOTO 1220
1280 REM
1290 REM
1300 REM ********************** DISPLAY DATA ****************************
1310   CLS :REM CLEAR SCREEN AND MOVE CURSOR TO TOP OF SCREEN
1320   SCROLL = 1
1330   FOR I = SCROLL TO COUNT - 1
1340 PRINT I;TAB(10)"HIGH PRICE = ";SPRICE(I,1);TAB(40)"LOW PRICE = ";
1350 PRINT SPRICE(I,2)
1360   IF I = 20 OR I = 40 OR I = 60 OR I = 80 THEN GOSUB 2310
1370   NEXT I
1380   GOSUB 2310
1390   IF A2$ = "Y" THEN GOTO 1330
1400 REM
1410 REM ********************** COMPUTE HIGH/LOW ************************
1420   FOR I = 1 TO COUNT -1
1430     S(I)=LOG(SPRICE(I,1)/SPRICE(I,2))
1440   NEXT I
1450 REM
1460 REM ********************** COMPUTE SUMMATION **********************
1470   SUM = 0
1480   FOR I = 1 TO COUNT-1
1490     SUM = SUM + S(I)^2
1500   NEXT I
1510 REM
1520 REM ********************** COMPUTE VARIANCE ***********************
1530   SVAR = (.3606739/COUNT-1)*SUM
1540   SVAR = ABS(MULT * SVAR)
1550 REM
1560 REM ********************** COMPUTE VOLATILITY *********************
1570   V = SQR(ABS(SVAR))
1580   GOTO 2630
1590 REM
1600 REM
1610 REM ***********************************************************************
1620 REM *                       HIGH-LOW-CLOSE                                *
```

```
1630 REM ************************************************************
1640 REM
1650 REM
1660 REM ************************* ENTER DATA *************************
1670 REM
1680   COUNT = 1 :REM INITIALIZE COUNTER FOR HIGH-LOW-CLOSE
1690 PRINT:PRINT "ENTER '999' TO QUIT":PRINT
1700 PRINT TAB(10) "ENTER HIGH STOCK PRICE ";COUNT;": ";:INPUT SPRICE(COUNT,1)
1710   IF SPRICE(COUNT,1) = 999 THEN GOTO 1780
1720 PRINT TAB(10) "ENTER LOW  STOCK PRICE ";COUNT;": ";:INPUT SPRICE(COUNT,2)
1730   IF SPRICE(COUNT,2) = 999 THEN GOTO 1780
1740 PRINT TAB(10) "ENTER CLOSING PRICE    ";COUNT;": ";:INPUT SPRICE(COUNT,3)
1750   IF SPRICE(COUNT,3) = 999 THEN GOTO 1780
1760   COUNT = COUNT + 1
1770   GOTO 1700
1780 REM
1790 REM ************************ DISPLAY DATA ************************
1800 REM
1810   CLS : REM CLEAR SCREEN AND MOVE CURSOR TO TOP OF SCREEN
1820   SCROLL = 1
1830   FOR I = SCROLL TO COUNT - 1
1840 PRINT I;" HIGH PRICE =";SPRICE(I,1);TAB(29)"LOW PRICE =";
1850 PRINT SPRICE(I,2);TAB(52)"CLOSING PRICE =";SPRICE(I,3)
1860   IF I = 20 OR I = 40 OR I = 60 OR I = 80 THEN GOSUB 2450
1870   NEXT I
1880   GOSUB 2450
1890   IF A2$ = "Y" THEN GOTO 1830
1900 REM
1910 REM
1920 REM ************************* COMPUTE R(I) AND S(I) *********************
1930   SUM = 0
1940   FOR I = 2 TO COUNT -1
1950   S(I) = LOG(SPRICE(I,1)/SPRICE(I,2))
1960   R(I) = LOG(SPRICE(I,3)/SPRICE(I-1,3))
1970   SUM = SUM + R(I)
1980   NEXT I
1990   MEAN = SUM/(COUNT-2)
2000 REM
2010 REM ************************* COMPUTE THE VARIANCE ********************
2020   SVAR = 0
2030   FOR I = 2 TO COUNT - 1
2040   SVAR = SVAR + ((.5 * S(I)^2) - (.39 * R(I)^2))
2050   NEXT I
2060   SVAR = SVAR/(COUNT - 1)
2070   SVAR = ABS(MULT * SVAR)
2080 REM
2090 REM ************************* COMPUTE THE VOLATILITY *******************
2100 REM
2110   V = SQR(SVAR)
2120   GOTO 2630
2130 REM
2140 REM ************************************************************
2150 REM *         SUBROUTINE TO EDIT DATA..DISPLAY IN GROUPS OF 20         *
2160 REM ************************************************************
```

```
2170 REM
2180 REM ************************* CLOSE-CLOSE *****************************
2190 INPUT "DO YOU WISH TO CHANGE A NUMBER? (Y/N) ";A2$
2200  IF A2$= "Y" THEN 2220
2210  RETURN
2220  SCROLL = I
2230 INPUT "SPECIFY THE NUMBER OF THE ENTRY TO CHANGE :";I
2240  IF I=999 THEN I=0 :RETURN
2250 PRINT "CURRENT VALUE OF ENTRY NUMBER ";I;"=";SPRICE(I,3);" NEW VALUE=";
2260 INPUT SPRICE(I,3)
2270  I=SCROLL - 20
2280  IF I<0 THEN I=0
2290  RETURN
2300 REM ************************* HIGH-LOW ********************************
2310 INPUT "DO YOU WISH TO CHANGE A NUMBER? (Y/N) ";A2$
2320  IF A2$ = "Y" THEN 2340
2330  RETURN
2340  SCROLL = I
2350 INPUT "SPECIFY THE NUMBER OF THE ENTRY TO CHANGE :";I
2360  IF I= 999 THEN I = 0:RETURN
2370 PRINT "CURRENT HIGH PRICE OF ENTRY NUMBER ";I;" = ";SPRICE(I,1);
2380 PRINT " NEW VALUE = ";:INPUT SPRICE(I,1)
2390 PRINT "CURRENT LOW PRICE OF ENTRY NUMBER ";I;" = ";SPRICE(I,2);
2400 PRINT " NEW VALUE = ";:INPUT SPRICE(I,2)
2410  I = SCROLL -20
2420  IF I<0 THEN I=0
2430  RETURN
2440 REM ************************* HIGH-LOW-CLOSE **************************
2450 INPUT "DO YOU WISH TO CHANGE A NUMBER? (Y/N) ";A2$
2460  IF A2$ = "Y" THEN GOTO 2490
2470  RETURN
2480  SCROLL = I
2490 INPUT "SPECIFY THE NUMBER OF THE ENTRY TO CHANGE :";I
2500  IF I = 999 THEN I = SCROLL:RETURN
2510 PRINT "CURRENT HIGH PRICE OF ENTRY #";I;" = ";SPRICE(I,1);
2520 INPUT "NEW VALUE = ";SPRICE(I,1)
2530 PRINT "CURRENT LOW  PRICE OF ENTRY #";I;" = ";SPRICE(I,2);
2540 INPUT "NEW VALUE = ";SPRICE(I,2)
2550 PRINT "CURRENT CLOSING PRICE OF ENTRY #";I;" = ";SPRICE(I,3);
2560 INPUT "NEW VALUE = ";SPRICE(I,3)
2570  I = SCROLL - 20
2580  IF I<0 THEN I=0
2590  RETURN
2600 REM ***************************************************************
2610 REM *                       END ROUTINE                         *
2620 REM ***************************************************************
2630  CLS :PRINT :PRINT :PRINT :PRINT :PRINT
2640 PRINT "VOLATILITY = ";V
2650 PRINT :PRINT :PRINT
2660 INPUT "DO YOU WISH TO CALCULATE ANOTHER? ";A1$
2670  IF A1$="Y" THEN GOTO 390
2680  END
```

26
Volatility Estimation Using the Volatilities Implied in Option Prices

For investors who have a high regard for the wisdom of the market, the ideal estimate of volatility would come from polling those who are trading in the market. The volatility estimates of the traders might be averaged together, perhaps with more weight given to the larger and assumably better informed traders. Unfortunately, no such poll is taken, and in any event, the larger and more successful traders probably would not be forthcoming with their estimates. But the end result of the poll, the weighted average of the volatility estimates held by those in the market, is readily available; it is implicit in the market price of every option.

We have already seen the fair option value is a function of the stock price, the time to expiration and exercise price of the option, the riskless interest rate, and the stock price volatility. Given the values of the other parameters and the market price of the option, we can solve for a unique volatility that will lead to the market option price. If the market price of the option is taken to be the correct price, the volatility we back out of the formula will be the best estimate of the correct volatility. Put another way, since in the aggregate the market takes the market price to be correct, the volatility implied by the market price is the market's opinion of what the stock volatility should be.

This volatility estimate is called the *implicit volatility* or the *implied volatility*. We can derive the implied volatility using an option formula. If we denote the option formula by $C(S,T,E,r,\sigma)$, and denote the current market option price by C_m, then the implied volatility is that volatility σ^* that sets the formula value equal to the market value; the implied volatility is the value σ^* that solves the equation

$$C_m = C(S,T,E,r,\sigma^*).$$

Any option formula can be used. Although not included in this expression, the formula can include dividend payments, and it may allow for the possibility of early exercise. Just as each formula leads to different values for the option price, the resulting volatility estimate will vary according to the formula used.

The implied volatility is an attractive shortcut to volatility estimation. It lets the market do the work, leaving the final calculation to depend only on the current stock and option quotes, and the choice of the model. But there are obvious problems in using the implied volatility as presented here for finding mispriced options. Putting the implied volatility into the option pricing formula will always show the option to be correctly priced, since the implied volatility came from setting the formula price equal to the market price in the first place. But as we will see, this identity between the market option price and the formula price can be avoided by using the average of the implied volatilities of a number of options on the same stock. Also, the implied volatility can be used directly in pinpointing mispriced options without re-entering the implied volatility into the option pricing formula.

THE USE OF WEIGHTED IMPLIED VOLATILITIES

Table 26-1 lists the implied volatilities for the options on National Semiconductor. The implied volatilities vary from a low of .41 to a high of .49. Taking the average of these would give a volatility for the stock. But using the mean as the volatility estimate does not combine the information of the implied volatilities most efficiently because not all option prices are equally sensitive to the value of the volatility. Some options will hardly change value at all with a large change in the volatility, while for other options a slight change in the volatility will significantly alter the option price. In particular, in-the-money options have little sensitivity to volatility, especially when they are close to expiration, whereas near-the-money options, options with an exercise price near the current stock price, are the most sensitive to the volatility specification.

To get the best estimate of the volatility, the implied volatilities should be weighted to take into account their relative sensitivity to the option price, with those that are the most sensitive given the most weight. One way to do this is to weight each option according to the change in the option price induced by a change in the volatility, or according to the elasticity of the option price with respect to the stock volatility. A simpler alternative is to use only the implied volatilities from those options that are the most sensitive to the exact specification of the volatility, the at-the-money or near-the-money options. This method is justified by the argument that all the available information should be reflected in these options, and the less sensitive options have too much noise to give any added information. While empirical work on the accuracy of weighted implied volatilities is limited, the work that has been done indicates that this simpler method gives more accurate volatility estimates than other weighting schemes.

TABLE 26-1   Implied Volatilities for Options on National Semiconductor

CURRENT STOCK PRICE = $50
TIME TO JULY EXPIRATION = 65 DAYS
INTEREST RATE = 9%

Exercise Price	July T=65	October T=155	January T=245
40			
Option Price	7-1/8	9	11
Implied Volatility	.45	.41	.43
50			
Option Price	4-3/8	6-1/4	8
Implied Volatility	.48	.41	.41
55			
Option Price	2-1/2	4-1/8	6
Implied Volatility	.49	.41	.41

Just as important as the weighting scheme is the sample of option prices used in calculating the implied volatilities. Opening and closing option prices tend to be "dirty" samples. Trading at these times is not representative of the trading during the day. Many traders are interested in closing out their positions, either to avoid the risks of holding a position overnight or to avoid carrying costs. Closing trades will be thus priced to reflect the risks in holding positions overnight. Since these risks are different from the risks in the intraday trading period, the prices at closing may differ from the intraday prices. The volatility estimates should be taken from a trade during the day rather than from the opening or closing price.

The implied volatility estimate from low-volume options may also be inaccurate, even if it is taken during the course of the trading day. The posted market price of an infrequently traded option may not give a timely representation of the current option price. For example, say the last trade for a particular call option occurred one hour ago, and the stock price at the time of that trade was 49. Suppose over the last hour the stock price has risen to 50. There is no way to know, looking at the posted option price, that the option trade corresponds to a stock price of 49, and not to a stock price of 50. The true implied volatility will be misestimated if the current stock price and the posted option price are used to compute the implied volatility. In this particular example, the resulting volatility estimate will be too high. But there is no way to tell from the quotes that the stock price of 49 should be used in the volatility estimate rather than the current stock price of 50.

There are two ways to avoid this nonsimultaneity problem. Generally, the higher the volume of an option, the more frequently it will be traded. Therefore, the problems of nonsimultaneity can be minimized by using only the higher volume options. Fortunately, the options that are the best for volatility estimation, the at-the-money options, have the highest volume and are the most frequently traded. These problems can also be reduced by computing the implied volatility immediately after a trade occurs.

TRADING STRATEGIES USING IMPLIED VOLATILITY

There is only one volatility for each stock. If the implied volatility for one option is .49, and the implied volatility for another option is .41, both volatilities cannot be correct. There is no way to know which of the two volatilities is closest to the truth without further investigation, but for some option trading strategies, it is enough to know that the two volatilities differ significantly. Since a higher option price will lead to a higher implied volatility, it is clear the option with the .49 volatility is overpriced relative to the option with the .41 volatility, and a profitable spread may be executed by buying the underpriced option and writing the overpriced option against it.

The implied volatility already has all the information necessary to find relatively mispriced options. If two options have a wide spread in their implied volatilities, a profit opportunity may exist. If the implied volatility on one option is far out of line with the volatilities on the other options, that alone is enough to indicate a mispricing. It must be kept in mind that the implied volatility is only as correct as the option formula that was used to find it. If the option formula does not allow for early exercise or does not include dividends, the implied volatility will reflect that misspecification. But in some cases, these misspecifications will affect all of the option prices in the same way, and the variations in the implied volatilities of the options may still reflect relative mispricing. If the magnitude of the specification errors does not vary greatly from option to option, the spreads in the implied volatilities will still lead to the discovery of profit opportunities.

IMPLIED VOLATILITIES

Computational Procedure

Let $C(S,T,E,r,\sigma)$ be the option pricing formula. The implied volatility, σ^*, is the σ that solves the equation.

$$C_m = C(S,T,E,r,\sigma^*)$$

C_m is the market price of the option. Because of the complexity of the option formula, this equation cannot be solved directly. The program solves for σ^* using the Newton-Raphson numerical method.

Trading Strategy

- Buy options with low implied volatilities and write options with high implied volatilities. Hedge the low and high volatility options against each other.

```
10   REM ***********************************************************************
20   REM *                        IMPLICIT VOLATILITY                         *
30   REM *                                                                    *
40   REM * THIS PROGRAM CALCULATES THE IMPLICIT VOLATILITY OF A CALL OR PUT    *
50   REM * OPTION.                                                            *
60   REM *                                                                    *
70   REM * VARIABLES USED: S=CURRENT STOCK PRICE                              *
80   REM *                 E=EXERCISE PRICE IN DOLLARS                        *
90   REM *                 R=ANNUAL RISKFREE INTEREST RATE IN PERCENT         *
100  REM *                 D=ANNUAL CONTINUOUS DIVIDEND RATE IN PERCENT       *
110  REM *                 T=TIME TO EXPIRATION IN DAYS                       *
120  REM *                CP=FORMULA OPTION PRICE                             *
130  REM *              CMKT=CURRENT MARKET PRICE OF OPTION                   *
140  REM *                 V=VOLATILITY                                       *
150  REM *                                                                    *
160  REM * THE USER MUST SPECIFY WHETHER COMPUTATION OF A PUT OR CALL IS       *
170  REM * DESIRED. THE PROGRAM SOLVES FOR THE IMPLICIT VOLATILITY USING       *
180  REM * THE NEWTON-RAPHSON ITERATIVE METHOD.                               *
190  REM *                                                                    *
200  REM *                                                                    *
210  REM *                                                                    *
220  REM *                                                                    *
230  REM ***********************************************************************
240  Y1=0
250  ITMAX=20
260  KMIN=.001
270  REM
280  GOSUB 1010:REM*****************INPUT DATA********************************
290  REM
300  REM
310  GOSUB 470:REM***************DO COMPUTATIONS******************************
320  REM
330  REM
340  GOSUB 1360:REM***************OUTPUT RESULTS******************************
350  REM
360  REM
370  END:REM*********************PROGRAM END**********************************
380  REM
390  REM***********************************************************************
400  REM*                    SUBROUTINE TO CALCULATE FORMULA                 *
410  REM*              OPTION PRICE AND OTHER CRITICAL VARIABLES             *
420  REM***********************************************************************
430  REM
440  REM INITIALIZE VALUES
450  REM
460  REM
470  R=R/100
480  V=.25
490  D=D/100
500  T=T/365
510  REM TEST FOR SMALL VALUES OF T
520  IF T<=.001 THEN A2$="Y" ELSE A2$="N":GOTO 550
530  IF S<=E THEN CP=0 ELSE CP=S-E
540  GOTO 1360
```

```
550  REM TEST FOR BOUND ON MARKET PRICE OF OPTION
560   IF CMKT<=S-E*EXP((-R)*T) THEN A3$="Y" ELSE A3$="N":GOTO 820
570   GOTO 1360
580  REM COMPUTE D1 AND D2
590   N2=V*SQR(T)
600   D1=(LOG(S/E)+(R-D+V*V/2)*T)/N2
610   D2=D1-N2
620  REM COMPUTE H AND CP
630   Z=D1
640   GOSUB 740:REM COMPUTE NORMAL VALUE FOR D1
650   H=-N
660   Z=D2
670   GOSUB 740:REM COMPUTE NORMAL VALUE FOR D2
680   CP=S*(-H)*EXP(-D*T)-E*N*EXP(-R*T)
690   IF PC$="P" THEN CP=CP-S+E*EXP(-R*T): H=H+1
700  REM COMPUTE THE DERIVATIVE OF CP WITH RESPECT TO V
710   DCALPR=S*SQR(T)*((EXP((-.5)*H*H))/SQR(2*3.141592654#))
720  RETURN
730  REM
740  REM***********SUBROUTINE TO COMPUTE NORMAL VALUES***************
750  REM
760   A6=ABS(Z)
770   T3=1/(1+.2316419*A6)
780   B1=.3989423*EXP(-Z*Z/2)
790   N=(((((1.330274*T3-1.821256)*T3+1.781478)*T3-.3565638)*T3+.3193815)
800   N=1-B1*T3*N
810   IF Z<0 THEN N=1-N : RETURN ELSE RETURN
820  REM
830  REM******************DETERMINATION OF  IMPLICIT VOLATILITY*******
840  REM
850   FOR I=1 TO ITMAX
860    GOSUB 580
870    INCREMENT=(CP-CMKT)/DCALPR
880    V2=V-INCREMENT
890    IF ABS(V2-V)<KMIN GOTO 340
900    IF V2<.01 THEN A4$="Y" ELSE A4$="N":GOTO 920
910    GOTO 1360
920    V=V+(V2-V)/2
930   NEXT I
940   IF ABS(V2-V)>.01 THEN A5$="Y" ELSE A5$="N"
950  RETURN
960  REM
970  REM*******************************************************************
980  REM                  SUBROUTINE TO INPUT DATA
990  REM*******************************************************************
1000 REM
1010 PRINT "YOU MAY ENTER THE FOLLOWING VARIABLES:"
1020 PRINT TAB(10);"CURRENT STOCK PRICE ($)";TAB(55):INPUT ;S
1030  IF Y1=1 THEN RETURN
1040 PRINT TAB(10);"EXERCISE PRICE ($)";TAB(55):INPUT ;E
1050  IF Y1=2 THEN RETURN
1060 PRINT TAB(10);"ANNUAL INTEREST RATE (%)";TAB(55):INPUT ;R
1070  IF Y1=3 THEN RETURN
1080 PRINT TAB(10);"ANNUAL DIVIDEND RATE (%)";TAB(55):INPUT ;D
```

```
1090   IF Y1=4 THEN RETURN
1100 PRINT TAB(10);"TIME TO EXPIRATION (DAYS)";TAB(55):INPUT ;T
1110   IF Y1=5 THEN RETURN
1120 PRINT TAB(10);"MARKET PRICE OF OPTION";TAB(55):INPUT ;CMKT
1130   IF Y1=6 THEN RETURN
1140 PRINT TAB(10);"OPTION SPECIFIED (C=CALL, P=PUT)";TAB(55):INPUT ;PC$
1150   IF Y1=7 THEN RETURN
1160 PRINT:PRINT
1170 PRINT "YOU MAY CHANGE ANY OF THE VALUES ENTERED ABOVE AS FOLLOWS:"
1180 PRINT TAB(10);"CHOICE";TAB(20);"ITEM TO CHANGE";TAB(55);"CURRENT VALUE"
1190 PRINT TAB(10);"------";TAB(20);"--------------";TAB(55);"-------------"
1200 PRINT TAB(10);"0";TAB(20);"PRINT IMPLIED VOLATILITY"
1210 PRINT TAB(10);"1";TAB(20);"CURRENT STOCK PRICE ($)";TAB(55);S
1220 PRINT TAB(10);"2";TAB(20);"EXERCISE PRICE ($)";TAB(55);E
1230 PRINT TAB(10);"3";TAB(20);"ANNUAL INTEREST RATE (%)";TAB(55);R
1240 PRINT TAB(10);"4";TAB(20);"ANNUAL DIVIDEND RATE (%)";TAB(55);D
1250 PRINT TAB(10);"5";TAB(20);"TIME TO EXPIRATION (DAYS)";TAB(55);T
1260 PRINT TAB(10);"6";TAB(20);"MARKET PRICE OF OPTION";TAB(55);CMKT
1270 PRINT TAB(10);"7";TAB(20);"OPTION (C=CALL, P=PUT)";TAB(55);PC$
1280 PRINT
1290 INPUT "WHICH CHOICE DO YOU DESIRE (0-7)";Y1
1300   ON Y1 GOSUB 1020,1040,1060,1080,1100,1120,1140
1310   IF Y1=0 THEN RETURN
1320 PRINT:PRINT
1330   GOTO 1160
1340 REM
1350 REM*************************************************************
1360 REM                  SUBROUTINE TO OUTPUT RESULTS
1370 REM*************************************************************
1380 REM
1390 PRINT:PRINT
1400   IF A2$="N" THEN GOTO 1430
1410   IF A2$="Y" THEN PRINT TAB(10);"COMPUTATION IS NOT DONE BECAUSE";:
1420       PRINT TAB(10)"TIME TO MATURITY IS TOO CLOSE TO 0"
1430   IF A3$="N" THEN GOTO 1460
1440   IF A3$="Y" THEN PRINT TAB(10);"COMPUTATION IS NOT DONE BECAUSE";:
1450       PRINT TAB(10)"THE OPTION PRICE IS TOO LOW-- V IS UNDEFINED"
1460   IF A4$="N" THEN GOTO 1490
1470   IF A4$="Y" THEN PRINT TAB(10);"COMPUTATION IS NOT DONE BECAUSE";:
1480       PRINT TAB(10)"THE IMPLICIT V IS TOO LOW TO GIVE AN ACCURATE RESULT"
1490   IF A5$="N" THEN GOTO 1510
1500   IF A5$="Y" THEN PRINT TAB(10);"DID NOT CONVERGE AFTER MAXIMUM ITERATIONS"
1510   IF A2$="Y" OR A3$="Y" OR A4$="Y" OR A5$="Y"  THEN GOTO 1540
1520 PRINT TAB(10);"THE IMPLICIT VOLATILITY =";TAB(42);V
1530 PRINT:PRINT
1540 REM RETURN R AND D TO PERCENT; T TO DAYS
1550   R=R*100
1560   D=D*100
1570   T=T*365
1580 INPUT "DO YOU WISH TO GO AGAIN WITH MODIFIED DATA (1=YES, 2=NO)";A7
1590   IF A7=1 THEN GOSUB 1170:GOTO 310
1600   RETURN
```

27
Option Strategy Analysis

The first step in forming a profitable option trading strategy is to find an option that is mispriced. The option formula and the volatility estimation methods presented in the previous chapters are valuable tools in doing this. After a mispriced option is pinpointed, a successful option strategy requires the proper hedge of that option to eliminate the risk of unfavorable stock price movements. Even the clearest profit opportunity can turn against an investor who is not correctly hedged. The option can be hedged against the stock or against another option. The investor may choose a hedge that will completely insulate against stock price changes—the neutral hedge will do this—or one that will leave the position exposed to profits or losses depending on the direction the stock moves. There are many popular option strategies, each leading to different exposure to the stock price, and each profiting from a different mispricing. The option strategies used in traditional option trading are actually just a small subset of the possible option positions, and indeed all the traditional option strategies can be analyzed in a very simple, yet general option analysis framework.

We will first summarize some of the widely used option strategies and then discuss the general techniques of option strategy formation and analysis.

TRADITIONAL OPTION STRATEGIES

An option strategy involves a position taken in one or more options, and possibly in the underlying stock.

The simplest strategy is to buy a call or buy a put. If both a put and a call are purchased, each with the same exercise price, the resulting position is called a straddle. A straddle will be most profitable if the stock moves far from the exercise price in either direction. If the stock increases in price, the call option will go up in value, while if the stock declines, the put will go up. Of course, while the stock price will increase the value of one side of the straddle, it will decrease the value of the other side of the straddle; if the stock goes up, the put option will drop in value, but this will not totally counterbalance the gains to the call option. This is because the loss on the one option is limited to its purchase price, but there are no limits on the gains to the other option.

Figure 27-1 plots the profit of the straddle as a function of the stock price.

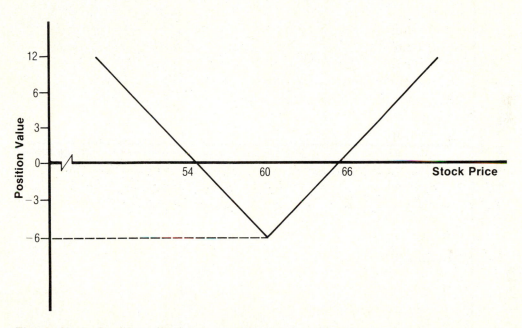

Figure 27-1. Profit profile for a straddle. A put and call are both purchased, each with an exercise price of $60.

The exercise price of the options is $60. The plot shows the position price at the time of the expiration of the options. At expiration, the value of the call option will be the difference between the stock price and the exercise price or zero, whichever is greater, while the value of the put option will be the greater of the difference between the exercise price and the stock price or zero.

This type of plot, which we call a profit profile, shows the profit of the straddle is the lowest when the stock price is equal to the exercise price of the options—the time when both options expire worthless—and increases as the stock price moves away from the exercise price. The greatest loss is at a stock price equal to the exercise price of 60. At that price, the total cost to the position, assumed here to be $6, is lost. A movement of the stock $6 either way

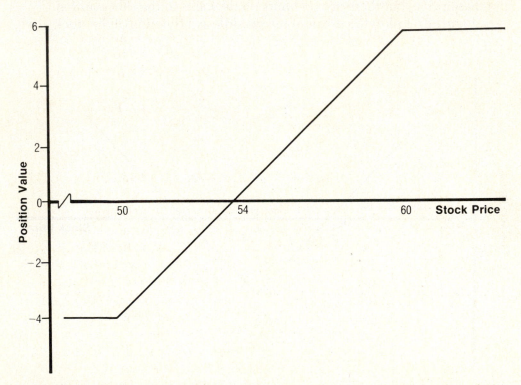

Figure 27-2. Profit profile for a bull spread. A call with an exercise price of 50 is purchased, and a call with an exercise price of 60 is written.

from 60 leads the investor to break even. The further the stock moves from the 60 exercise price, the greater the profit to this position.

Another popular strategy is called the spread. A spread is constructed by buying one option and writing another option of the same type on the same stock. That is, if a call is bought, another call on the stock is written. The options may differ in exercise price or in time to expiration. If a longer term option is bought and an option with a shorter time to expiration is written, the resulting strategy is called a *time spread*. If a call option with a lower exercise price is bought and a call with a higher exercise price (but the same time to expiration) is written, the resulting strategy is called a *bull spread*. The opposite of this strategy, buying a call with an exercise price that is higher than the exercise price of the call that is written is called a *bear spread*. Figures 27-2 and 27-3 sketch out the profit profile for the bull and bear spreads. These strategies use call options with exercise prices of 50 and 60. As the name of the strategy suggests, the bull spread increases in value with an increase in the stock price, while the bear spread increases in value with a decrease in the stock price. These two spreads are not the only ones that are sensitive to the stock price. Any spread that does not involve a neutral hedge will be affected by stock price changes.

These are only a few of the possible option strategies. Table 27-1 gives a fuller but still less than comprehensive list.

OPTION STRATEGY ANALYSIS: A GENERAL APPROACH

The sheer number of option strategies listed in Table 27-1 suggests categorizing option strategies type by type is not a very fruitful or enlightening approach. And these strategies are nowhere near exhaustive. For example, what about a spread involving buying one call option and writing a second call that has a longer time to expiration and a higher exercise price. Instead of forming strategies by name, the strategy analysis program for this chapter will employ a more general approach for describing a strategy. This approach involves describing the strategy in terms of the number of each option held.

Consider two call options, C_1 and C_2. A strategy that is formed by holding n_1 of the first option and n_2 of the second options would have a value $n_1 C_1 + n_2 C_2$. If an option is bought, n is positive, while if it is written, n is negative. For example, if C_1 is the IBM October 120 call and C_2 is the IBM July

120 call, a time spread formed by buying the longer term option and writing the shorter term option would be represented by $C_1 - C_2$. There is a minus sign because C_2 is being written, and so $n_2 = -1$. A back spread would be $-C_1 + C_2$. Now the minus sign precedes the longer term option, since in a back spread the longer term option is the one that is written.

This same approach can be used for the other strategies. For example, if we denote the IBM October 120 put option by P_1, a straddle would be represented by $P_1 + C_1$. If we were to write a straddle, we would place a minus sign before both options to indicate they have been written rather than bought, and have $-(P_1 + C_1)$.

The stock can also be used in positions. For example, a synthetic put,

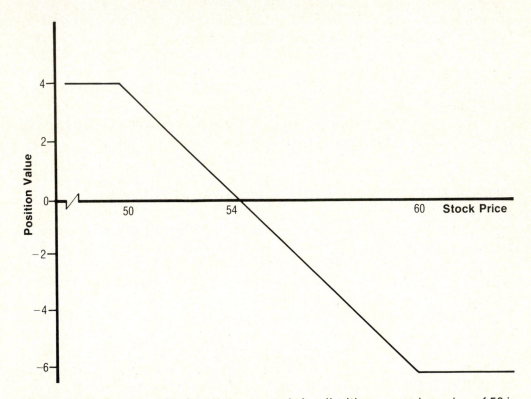

Figure 27-3. Profit profile for a bear spread. A call with an exercise price of 50 is written, and a call with an exercise price of 60 is purchased.

composed of a short position in 100 shares of stock and a long position in a call would be C – 100S, where S is the stock price.

This method of describing the option strategy has considerable flexibility. If we were to hold ten time spreads rather than the one time spread, the position would involve setting n_1 and n_2 equal to 10 and –10, respectively; the strategy would have a value of $10C_1 – 10C_2$. Any strategy could be represented in this way. A strategy consisting of buying five of the IBM October 120 calls and writing three of the July 120 calls would be $5C_1 – 3C_2$. Thus, besides allowing you to evaluate the traditional option strategies such as those listed in Table 27-1, the option strategy program allows you to tailor-make an option

---

TABLE 27-1 Traditional Option Strategies

Covered Write—Buy 100 shares of stock, write one call option.

Straddle—Buy a call and a put with the same exercise price.

Short Straddle—Write a call and a put with the same exercise price.

Strangle—Buy a call with an exercise price above the stock price, and buy a put with an exercise price an equal distance below the stock price.

Time Spread—Buy an option with a longer time to expiration, write an option with a shorter time to expiration.

Back Spread—Buy an option with a shorter time to expiration, write an option with a longer time to expiration.

Bull Spread—Buy a call with a lower exercise price, write a call with a higher exercise price.

Bear Spread—Buy a call with a higher exercise price, write a call with a lower exercise price.

Forward Conversion—Buy 100 shares of stock, write a call and buy a put with the same exercise price and time to expiration.

Reverse Conversion—Short 100 shares of stock, buy a call and write a put with the same exercise price and time to expiration.

Synthetic Call—Buy 100 shares of stock, buy a put option.

Synthetic Put.—Short 100 shares of stock, buy a call option.

Butterfly Spread—Buy a call with a high exercise price, buy a call with a low exercise price, and write two calls with an exercise price in between the high and low exercise prices, with all options having the same expiration date.

Strap—Buy two calls and one put, all with the same exercise price and time to expiration.

Strip—Buy two puts and one call, all with the same exercise price and time to expiration.

---

position by specifying the options to be used in the strategy, and the number of each option to be held, with a minus sign indicating the option or stock is being held short (i.e., writing the option), and a plus sign indicating the position is held long.

OPTION STRATEGY ANALYSIS

Once an option strategy is selected, you will undoubtedly be faced with a number of questions: How will my position be affected by changes in the stock price? What will happen to the position as the options approach expiration? How sensitive is my profit to misspecifications in the volatility estimate? What is the maximum profit I can expect? What is the range of my potential losses?

The option strategy program allows you to see how the important variables in the market will affect the value of the option position. You can trace out the effects of stock price, time to expiration, or volatility changes on the position value. The effects of these variables on the option position are computed by using the Black-Scholes pricing formula.

Analyzing the Effects of Stock Price Changes on Position Value

Suppose with 70 days left to July expiration, an investor forms a time spread by writing 10 July 75 Kodak options, priced at 4¼ and buying 10 of the 75 October Kodak option with a price of 6. The current value of this position is ten times the 4¼ received for each of the July options less ten times the $6 paid for the October options, for a net outflow of $17.50. What will the value of this position be if the stock rises from its current price of 74⅛ to 75?

We need to know how both options will be priced if the stock price is 75. This can be determined using the option pricing formula. Assuming a volatility for Kodak of .3, and a riskless interest rate of 8%, the Black-Scholes value of the July option, with 70 days to expiration, will be 4.496, while the value of the October option, with 160 days remaining until expiration, will be 7.214. The overall position value will then be

$$V = 10 \times 7.214 - 10 \times 4.496 = 27.18.$$

A similar exercise could be done for other possible stock prices. Table 27-2 computes the position value and the position profit when the stock price takes on a range of values between $65 and $80. This table is in the same form

---

TABLE 27-2   The Value of an Option Strategy for Various Stock Prices, With 70 Days to Expiration[a,b]

STOCK PRICE	POSITION VALUE	NET POSITION VALUE[c]	OPTION 1 70 DAYS TO EXPIRATION	OPTION 2 160 DAYS TO EXPIRATION
65	17.10	-.39	.79	2.50
66	18.55	1.05	.99	2.85
67	19.94	2.44	1.22	3.22
68	21.25	3.75	1.49	3.62
69	22.48	4.98	1.80	4.05
70	23.59	6.09	2.14	4.50
71	24.58	7.08	2.53	4.99
72	25.44	7.94	2.96	5.50
73	26.16	8.66	3.43	6.04
74	26.74	9.24	3.94	6.61
75	27.18	9.67	4.50	7.21
76	27.47	9.97	5.08	7.83
77	27.63	10.13	5.71	8.48
78	27.66	10.16	6.38	9.15
79	27.58	10.08	7.08	9.84
80	27.39	9.89	7.82	10.56
81	27.11	9.61	8.58	11.29
82	26.74	9.24	9.37	12.05
83	26.31	8.81	10.19	12.82
84	25.83	8.33	11.03	13.62

[a]The current price of Option 1 is 4¼, and of Option 2 is 6. Both have an exercise price of 75. Volatility is .3, and the interest rate is 8%. The strategy consists of writing 10 of Option 1 and buying 10 of Option 2.

[b]The values in this table are subject to rounding error.

[c]Calculated as the position value minus the initial position cost of $17.50.

as the program output. The first column on the left in the table gives the values of the independent variable, in this case the stock price (although the program can also show the effect of volatility, interest rates, and time to expiration). The next column gives the value of the position formed by holding the specified number of each option as a function of the stock price and the other parameters of the model. This is called the position value. The third column gives the net position value; it is the position value minus the cost of taking on the position. In this case, the cost of the position is $17.50. Following the overall position value, each of the options values is tabulated separately for each of the various stock prices. These values are the number of options held multiplied by the Black-Scholes option price.

The resulting profit values are plotted in the profit profile of Figure 27-4. The profit profile is a valuable diagnostic tool for strategy analysis. The height

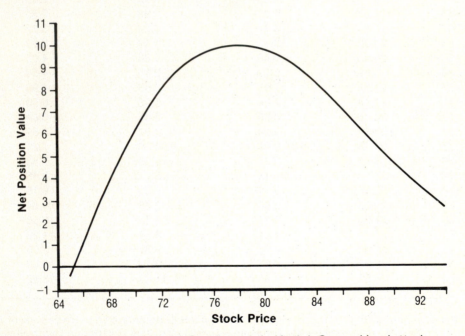

Figure 27-4. The net value of a October–July Kodak Spread is plotted as a function of the stock price. This profit profile gives a visual representation of the profit potential and risk of the spread.

of the profit profile indicates the profit of the position for various stock prices. The slope of the profit profile indicates the exposure of the position to the stock price; a positive slope indicates a bullish position, a negative slope a bearish position. The inflection point of the slope, where the slope levels off, indicates the stock price at which the option position will give a neutral hedge. This plot indicates that the time spread in question will have positive exposure to the stock price for stock prices below 78, and the exposure will turn negative for stock prices above this point. The peak of the plot, at a stock price of 78, represents the stock price for which this particular time spread will be a neutral hedge. At that price, slight changes in the stock price will not noticeably affect the position value.

The profit profile can be plotted for various times to expiration. Figures 27-1, 27-2, and 27-3 plotted the profit profile of various option strategies at the time of expiration. The strategy analysis of Table 27-1 can be redone for other times to expiration as well. For example, Table 27-3 lists the results of the same strategy as Table 27-2, but for 30 rather than 70 days to the July option expiration.

Analyzing the Effects of Volatility on Strategy Profitability

The volatility estimate is the weak point in successfully executing a profitable option strategy. An incorrect volatility estimate will make correctly priced options appear mispriced, and will lead the investor to form unprofitable option strategies. The obvious first step in overcoming this problem is to get the most accurate possible estimate of volatility (this step is discussed in Chapters 25 and 26). The second step is to analyze how much margin for error there is in the volatility estimate by seeing how far off the volatility estimate can be while still giving a profit.

This sensitivity analysis can be performed by tracing out the position value for a range of volatilities. In the previous Kodak example, a volatility estimate of .3 was used. With this volatility, the July option is mispriced. Its market price is 4¼, while the formula price is 4.00. The October option is also slightly mispriced, with a market price of 6.00 and a formula price of 6.69. The theoretically correct price of the time spread is therefore, $26.90, 9.40 points higher than the actual cost of putting on the spread. But how sensitive is this mispricing of the position to the volatility estimate being used?

This can be answered by using the strategy analysis program to trace out the position value for a range of volatilities. The position value for volatilities ranging from .20 to .40 is given in Table 27-4 in the same form as it appears in the program output.

TABLE 27-3 The Value of an Option Strategy for Various Stock Prices, With 30 Days to Expiration[a,b]

STOCK PRICE	POSITION VALUE	NET POSITION VALUE	OPTION 1 30 DAYS TO EXPIRATION	OPTION 2 120 DAYS TO EXPIRATION
65	16.07	−1.42	.14	1.75
66	18.26	.76	.21	2.04
67	20.48	2.98	.31	2.36
68	22.68	5.18	.45	2.71
69	24.79	7.29	.62	3.10
70	26.76	9.26	.84	3.52
71	28.54	11.04	1.12	3.97
72	30.07	12.57	1.45	4.46
73	31.31	13.81	1.84	4.97
74	32.26	14.76	2.30	5.52
75	32.88	15.38	2.81	6.10
76	33.20	15.70	3.39	6.71
77	33.21	15.71	4.03	7.35
78	32.96	15.46	4.72	8.01
79	32.47	14.97	5.46	8.71
80	31.78	14.28	6.25	9.43
81	30.94	13.44	7.07	10.17
82	29.98	12.48	7.93	10.93
83	28.94	11.44	8.83	11.72
84	27.85	10.35	9.74	12.52

[a]The current price of Option 1 is 4¼, and of Option 2 is 6. Both have an exercise price of 75. Volatility is .3, and the interest rate is 8%. The strategy consists of writing 10 of Option 1 and buying 10 of Option 2.

[b]The values in this table are subject to rounding error.

Analyzing the Effects of Time to Expiration on Position Value

The value of any option will drop as the time to expiration approaches. The premium of an option, the value of the option above its intrinsic value, is a reflection of the combined effect of volatility and time to expiration. The

TABLE 27-4 The Value of a Time Spread for Various Volatilities[a]

| | | | OPTION PRICES | |
Volatility	POSITION VALUE	NET POSITION VALUE	OPTION 1 70 DAYS TO EXPIRATION	OPTION 2 160 DAYS TO EXPIRATION
.20	20.62	3.12	2.72	4.78
.21	21.23	3.73	2.85	4.97
.22	21.85	4.35	2.98	5.16
.23	22.46	4.96	3.11	5.35
.24	23.08	5.58	3.24	5.54
.25	23.70	6.20	3.37	5.74
.26	24.32	6.82	3.49	5.93
.27	24.94	7.44	3.62	6.12
.28	25.56	8.06	3.75	6.31
.29	26.18	8.68	3.88	6.50
.30	26.81	9.31	4.01	6.69
.31	27.43	9.93	4.14	6.88
.32	28.05	10.55	4.27	7.07
.33	28.68	11.18	4.40	7.26
.34	29.30	11.80	4.53	7.46
.35	29.93	12.43	4.65	7.65
.36	30.55	13.05	4.78	7.84
.37	31.17	13.67	4.91	8.03
.38	31.80	14.30	5.04	8.22
.39	32.42	14.92	5.17	8.41

[a]The current price of Option 1 is 4¼, and of Option 2 is 6. Both have an exercise price of 75. Volatility is .3, the interest rate is 8%, and the stock price is 74⅛. The strategy consists of writing 10 of Option 1 and buying 10 of Option 2.

more time there is before the option expires, the more likely the option is to appreciate in value.

The deterioration of the time premium may work for or against the investor, depending on the investor's option position. Obviously, a long position in the option will be hurt by the deterioration of the time premium, while a short position will be helped.

For the popular time spread, the rate of deterioration in the time premium is the name of the game. The time spread involves writing options that are close to expiration, and hedging the short position in those options with a long position in another option that has longer to expiration. The strategy

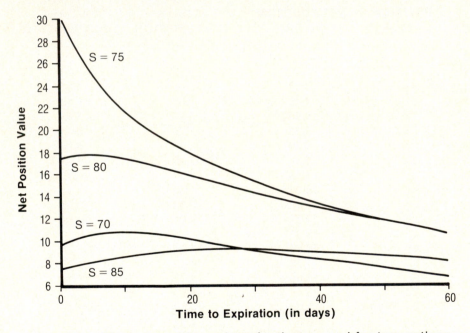

Figure 27-5. The net position value of a time spread for two options with a $75 exercise price is plotted as a function of the time left to the expiration of the option nearest maturity. The plot is made assuming various stock prices are maintained throughout the time period. The further the stock price moves from $75, the lower the profit from this time spread.

objective is for the premium on the option that is written to drop in value faster than the premium on the longer term option that is used to hedge it. The end result is that the investor can pocket the premium from the option that is written while the value of the position in the longer term option remains essentially unchanged.

The option strategy analysis program allows you to see how the position value will change as time to expiration approaches. Figure 27-5 shows the effect of the passage of time on a time spread for each of a number of stock

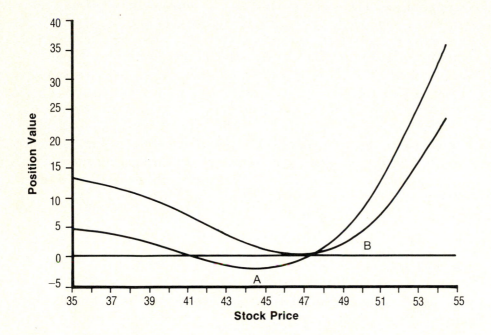

Figure 27-6. The profit profiles for two neutral hedging strategies are plotted. Curve A is the profile for the strategy designed to give a neutral hedge at a stock price of $45. Note that the profile flattens out at the $45 range, leading to small changes in position value for stock price movements around the $45 value. Curve B is the neutral hedge profile for a stock price of $48. The curve flattens out slightly to the left of the $48 mark. This is a result of rounding the neutral hedge to integer contract amounts.

prices. The position we look at here is the same one that was used in looking at the effect of stock price changes and volatility changes. The position is established by writing ten options with an exercise price of $75, while buying ten options with the same $75 exercise price, but with three more months to expiration. As before, we assume the premium received from each of the shorter term options is 4¼ dollars, while the longer term options cost $6 each. Thus the initial cost of the position is $17.50.

In this figure, the time to expiration for the shorter term option goes from sixty to zero days, and the stock prices considered are $70, $75, $80, $85. The stock price of $75 gives the greatest value to the position as the time to expiration approaches. This is as we would expect, since at a stock price of $75, the shorter term option that has been written drops to zero while allowing the longer term option to retain the greatest amount of its premium. In contrast, while a stock price of 70 leaves the shorter term option worthless, it also drops the value of the long option, and thereby drops the overall position value.

A higher stock price also reduces the value of the position. For a stock price of $85, the position value peaks at just over $9 when there are thirty days remaining to expiration, and then drops to below $8 at the time of expiration. For high stock prices, the prices of the shorter and longer term options come close together, the premium above their intrinsic value dropping to zero. For all of the cases presented in Figure 27-5, this time spread leads to a profit. But there will be stock prices, both above and below the range we look at here, that will lead to losses.

THE NEUTRAL HEDGE

The key element of option trading rests in the ability of the investor to form a riskless or neutral hedge by taking the proper position in the option and the stock. The neutral hedge is a hedge that is unaffected by small changes in the stock price. It is the neutral hedge that underlies the ability to price options by arbitrage: Since the neutral hedge is essentially a riskless position, it must be priced to give a return equal to the risk-free rate.

We have already seen in Chapter 21 how the riskless hedge works, and the chapters on the binomial option pricing model and the Black-Scholes model gave the specific form of the riskless hedge when those pricing models are used.

Up to now, we have considered only the hedge between the stock and an option on the stock. However, we can just as easily hedge an option with another option. Since all options on a stock move with the stock price, each option will also move in a specific way with any other option on the stock. The hedge ratio between two options, C_1 and C_2, is the ratio of the number of the first option to the number of the second option needed to obtain a riskless hedge, a hedge that leaves the position value unchanged with a (small) change in the stock price. If we denote the hedge ratio of the first option by h_1, and the hedge ratio of the second option by h_2, then the neutral hedge ratio between the two options will equal

$$n_1/n_2 = -h_2/h_1.$$

That is, the ratio of the first option held to the second option held must equal the negative of the inverse of their hedge ratios. If $h_1 = -.5$, so that 50 shares of stock must be held in a position opposite the first option to form a neutral hedge, and $h_2 = -.75$, so that 75 shares of stock must be held opposite each of the second options to form a neutral hedge, then if the first option is combined directly with the second option to form a neutral hedge, the proportion of the first option to the second option, n_1/n_2, will be $-h_2/h_1 = -.5/.75 = -2/3$. That is, if two of the first option are held long, then a riskless hedge will require holding three of the second option short (i.e., three of the second option will need to be written).

Figure 27-6 shows the position value of two neutral hedges, one giving a neutral position for a stock price of $45, and the other giving a neutral position for a stock price of $48. The inflection point of the figure, where the position value flattens out, is the neutral point. At that point, small changes in the stock price will have little effect on the overall position value. For Curve A, a position that is neutral at a stock price of 45 is formed by holding 20 of the first option long and nine of the second option short. With this hedge, a stock price change from $45 to $46 leads to a change in position value of only three-quarters of a dollar. In contrast, a change in the stock price from $50 to $51 on the same curve will result in the position value changing by over $5.

A different hedge ratio is needed to give a neutral hedge for a stock price of $48. The strategy depicted in Curve B uses 20 of the first option held long to 11 options held short.

The neutral hedge computation in the option strategy program will automatically calculate the position hedge for the two options. Holding the two options according to this ratio will lead to a position which, for small stock price changes and over short periods of time, will be unaffected by the stock price. If either of the two options in the position is not priced according to the option pricing model, this hedge will lead to arbitrage profits. The reservations regarding small stock price changes and short time periods must be emphasized. The hedge ratio, and therefore the proper position for achieving a riskless hedge, will change with changes in the stock price or the time to expiration. The hedging strategy for option trading is a dynamic hedging strategy—the proper hedge ratio must be continually evaluated, and occasionally adjusted over time and with stock price changes. A general rule of thumb is that the hedge will rarely be affected by stock price changes of less than a point, and changes in the time to expiration of less than two weeks. However, the precise effect of changes in the time to expiration or the stock price on the position hedge can be evaluated using the strategy program in this chapter.

```
10   REM   ****************************************************************
20   REM   *                      OPTION STRATEGY ANALYSIS                *
30   REM   *                                                              *
40   REM   *  THIS PROGRAM CAN BE USED TO DETERMINE THE EFFECT OF IMPORTANT *
50   REM   *  VARIABLES ON THE VALUE OF AN OPTION POSITION.   THE NUMBER OF *
60   REM   *  OPTIONS, AND THE SPECIFICATIONS OF THE OPTION ARE SELECTED BY *
70   REM   *  THE USER.   THE  VARIABLE  FOR  WHICH  THE SENSITIVITY OF THE *
80   REM   *  POSITION VALUE WILL BE ANALYZED IS ALSO USER-SPECIFIED.   THE *
90   REM   *  POSITION VALUE CAN BE MADE TO VARY AS A FUNCTION OF THE STOCK *
100  REM   *  PRICE, TIME TO EXPIRATION, INTEREST RATE, OR VOLATILITY.     *
110  REM   *                                                              *
120  REM   *  VARIABLES USED:S = STOCK PRICE                              *
130  REM   *                 E = EXERCISE PRICE                           *
140  REM   *                 T = TIME TO EXPIRATION                       *
150  REM   *                 V = VOLATILITY                               *
160  REM   *                 N = NUMBER OF OPTIONS HELD                   *
170  REM   *                 R = INTEREST RATE                            *
180  REM   *                 C = THE RESULTS OF THE BLACK-SCHOLES FORMULA *
190  REM   *                PV = THE POSITION VALUE                       *
200  REM   *               PVN = THE NET POSITION VALUE                   *
210  REM   *               NH$ = THE NEUTRAL HEDGE INDICATOR              *
220  REM   *                                                              *
230  REM   *                                                              *
240  REM   *                                                              *
250  REM   *                                                              *
260  REM   ****************************************************************
270  REM
280  REM
290  DIM TT(5,21),C(5,21),S(21),E(21),T(21),N(21),PV(21),PVN(21),R(21),V(21)
300  DIM D(21)
310  REM
320  REM
330  REM
340  REM   *****************NEUTRAL HEDGE OPTION **********************
350    GOSUB 600
360  REM
370  REM   *****************SELECTION OF OPTIONS **********************
380    GOSUB 940
390  REM
400  REM   *****************VARIATION ON STOCK PRICE *******************
410    GOSUB 1200
420  REM
430  REM   *****************VARIATION ON TIME TO EXPIRATION ************
440    GOSUB 1760
450  REM
460  REM   *****************VARIATION ON INTEREST RATES ***************
470    GOSUB 2300
480  REM
490  REM   *****************VARIATION ON VOLATILITY ********************
500    GOSUB 2770
510  REM
520  REM   *****************CALUCULATIONS FOR BLACK-SCHOLES FORMULA ****
530    GOSUB 3250
540  REM
```

```
550 REM  ********************** END OF PROGRAM ****************************
560 END
570 REM
580 REM
590 REM
600 REM  ******************** NEUTRAL HEDGE OPTION *************************
610 REM
620 CLS
630 INPUT"DO YOU WISH TO COMPUTE A NEUTRAL HEDGE (Y/N)? (2 OPTIONS ONLY) ",NH$
640   IF NH$ = "Y"   THEN GOTO 670
650   GOTO 940
660 CLS
670 PRINT TAB(23)"FOR THE COMPUTATION OF THE NEUTRAL HEDGE:"
680 PRINT TAB(23) "ENTER STOCK PRICE";:INPUT S
690 PRINT TAB(23) "ENTER INTEREST RATE (IN PERCENT)";:INPUT R
700 PRINT TAB(23) "ENTER THE VOLATILITY";:INPUT V
710   FOR I = 1 TO 2
720 PRINT "FOR OPTION";I;", SPECIFY:"
730 PRINT TAB(23)"EXERCISE PRICE:"; : INPUT E(I)
740 PRINT TAB(23)"TIME TO EXPIRATION IN DAYS:"; : INPUT T(I)
750 PRINT TAB(23)"PUT OR CALL (P OR C):"; : INPUT PC$(I)
760   IF I = 2 THEN GOTO 780
770 PRINT TAB(23)"NUMBER OF OPTIONS HELD:"; : INPUT N(I)
780 PRINT TAB(23)"OPTION MARKET PRICE (OPTIONAL):"; : INPUT CMKT(I)
790   E = E(I) : T = T(I) : PC$ = PC$(I)
800   GOSUB 3240 :REM DO OPTION MODEL CALCULATIONS
810   H(I) = H
820  NEXT I
830 REM
840 REM COMPUTE HEDGE RATIO, AND THEN ROUND OFF
850 REM
860   N(2) = -(N(1)*(H(1)/H(2)))
870   N(2) = INT((N(2) + .005)*100)/100
880 CLS
890 PRINT : PRINT "FOR A NEUTRAL HEDGE, ";N(2);"OF OPTION 2 MUST BE HELD"
900 PRINT
910   K=2
920   GOTO 1090
930 REM
940 REM *************** SELECTION OF OPTIONS *****************************
950 REM
960 CLS
970 INPUT "SPECIFY THE NUMBER OF OPTIONS IN THIS STRATEGY (5 MAX):";K
980   IF K > 5 THEN K = 5
990   FOR I = 1 TO K
1000 PRINT "FOR OPTION ";I;",SPECIFY:"
1010 PRINT TAB(23)"EXERCISE PRICE:"; : INPUT E(I)
1020 PRINT TAB(23)"TIME TO EXPIRATION IN DAYS:"; : INPUT T(I)
1030 PRINT TAB(23)"PUT OR CALL (P OR C):"; : INPUT PC$(I)
1040 PRINT TAB(23)"POSITIVE NUMBER IF BOUGHT, NEGATIVE IF WRITTEN"
1050 PRINT TAB(23)"NUMBER OF OPTIONS HELD:"; : INPUT N(I)
1060 PRINT TAB(23)"OPTION MARKET PRICE (IF DESIRED):"; : INPUT CMKT(I)
1070  NEXT I
1080 CLS
```

```
1090 PRINT"SPECIFY THE VARIABLE FOR WHICH THE POSITION VALUE WILL BE ANALYZED:"
1100 PRINT
1110 PRINT TAB(20)"(1)   STOCK PRICE   S"
1120 PRINT TAB(20)"(2)   TIME TO EXPIRATION   T"
1130 PRINT TAB(20)"(3)   INTEREST RATE   r"
1140 PRINT TAB(20)"(4)   VOLATILITY   v"
1150 PRINT
1160 INPUT "                       =>",OPT
1170  ON OPT GOTO 1200,1760,2300,2770
1180   GOTO 1080
1190 REM
1200 REM ********************** STOCK PRICE ********************************
1210 REM
1220 CLS
1230 INPUT "SPECIFY LOW STOCK PRICE ",LSP
1240 INPUT "SPECIFY HIGH STOCK PRICE ",HSP
1250  IF NH$ = "Y" THEN GOTO 1280
1260 INPUT "SPECIFY VOLATILITY ",V
1270 INPUT "SPECIFY INTEREST RATE (IN PERCENT) ",R
1280  COST = 0
1290  FOR I = 1 TO K
1300   COST = COST + (CMKT(I)*N(I))
1310  NEXT I
1320 REM
1330 REM INCREMENT STOCK PRICE RANGE INTO TWENTY INTERVALS
1340 REM
1350  RANGE = (HSP-LSP)/20
1360  FOR J = 1 TO 20
1370   S(J) = LSP + (J-1) * RANGE
1380   S(J) = INT((S(J) + .005)*100)/100
1390   FOR I = 1 TO K
1400    S = S(J) : E = E(I) : T = T(I) : PC$ = PC$(I)
1410    GOSUB 3240 :REM DO OPTION MODEL CALCULATIONS
1420    C(I,J) = C
1430   NEXT I
1440  NEXT J
1450  FOR J = 1 TO 20
1460   PV(J) = 0 : PVN(J) = 0
1470   FOR I = 1 TO K
1480 REM
1490 REM CALCULATE POSITION VALUE AND NET POSITION VALUE
1500 REM
1510    PV(J) = PV(J) + (C(I,J) * N(I))
1520    PVN(J) = PV(J) - COST
1530   NEXT I
1540 REM
1550 REM ROUND OFF POSITION VALUE AND NET POSITION VALUE
1560 REM
1570   PV(J) = INT((PV(J)+.005)*100)/100
1580   PVN(J) = INT ((PVN(J) + .005)*100)/100
1590  NEXT J
1600 CLS
1610 PRINT "STOCK    POSITION    NET POSITION    INDIVIDUAL OPTION PRICES"
1620 PRINT "PRICE       VALUE        VALUE        OPT 1   OPT 2   OPT 3
     OPT 4    OPT 5"
```

```
1630 PRINT "-----   --------   ------------   -----   -----   -----   -----
     -----"
1640  FOR J = 1 TO 20
1650 PRINT S(J);TAB(9)PV(J);TAB(20);PVN(J);
1660   FOR I = 1 TO 5
1670    OPT = INT((C(I,J)+.005)*100)/100 :REM ROUND OFF OPTION PRICE
1680 PRINT TAB(32 + I*8)OPT;
1690   NEXT I
1700 PRINT
1710   NEXT J
1720 INPUT "DO YOU WISH TO ANALYZE ANOTHER STRATEGY (Y/N)";ANS$
1730  IF ANS$ = "Y" THEN GOTO 620
1740 END
1750 REM
1760 REM ********************** TIME TO EXPIRATION **************************
1770 REM
1780 CLS
1790 PRINT "SPECIFY STARTING TIME (IN NUMBER OF DAYS BEFORE THE EXPIRATION"
1800 PRINT "                       OF THE OPTION CLOSEST TO EXPIRATION.) ";
1810 INPUT ST
1820 PRINT "SPECIFY ENDING TIME   (IN NUMBER OF DAYS BEFORE THE EXPIRATION"
1830 PRINT "                       OF THE OPTION CLOSEST TO EXPIRATION.) ";
1840 INPUT ET
1850  IF NH$ = "Y" THEN GOTO 1890
1860 INPUT "SPECIFY STOCK PRICE ",S
1870 INPUT "SPECIFY THE VOLATILITY ",V
1880 INPUT "SPECIFY THE INTEREST RATE (IN PERCENT) ",R
1890  TS = T(1)
1900  COST = 0
1910 FOR I = 1 TO K
1920   IF T(I) < TS THEN TS = T(I)
1930   COST = COST + (CMKT(I) * N(I))
1940 NEXT I
1950  RANGE = (ST-ET)/20
1960 FOR J = 1 TO 20
1970  FOR I = 1 TO K
1980    TT(I,J) = T(I) - ((TS-ST) + RANGE * (J-1))
1990    D(J) = INT(ST - RANGE * (J-1))
2000    PC$ = PC$(I) : E = E(I) : T = TT(I,J)
2010    GOSUB 3240
2020    C(I,J) = C
2030   NEXT I
2040  NEXT J
2050 FOR J = 1 TO 20
2060  PV(J) = 0 : PVN(J) = 0
2070  FOR I = 1 TO K
2080   PV(J) = PV(J) + (C(I,J) * N(I))
2090   PVN(J) = PV(J) - COST
2100   NEXT I
2110  PV(J) = INT((PV(J)+.005)*100)/100
2120  PVN(J) = INT ((PVN(J) + .005)*100)/100
2130  NEXT J
2140 CLS
2150 PRINT " DAYS TO   POSITION   NET POSITION   INDIVIDUAL OPTION PRICES"
```

```
2160 PRINT "EXPIRATION      VALUE         VALUE          OPT 1    OPT 2    OPT 3
     OPT 4     OPT 5"
2170 PRINT "----------     --------     ------------     -----    -----    -----
     -----     -----"
2180  FOR J = 1 TO 20
2190 PRINT D(J);TAB(14)PV(J);TAB(25);PVN(J);
2200    FOR I = 1 TO 5
2210     OPT = INT((C(I,J)+.005)*100)/100
2220 PRINT TAB(32 + I*8)OPT;
2230    NEXT I
2240 PRINT
2250    NEXT J
2260 INPUT "DO YOU WISH TO ANALYZE ANOTHER STRATEGY (Y/N)";ANS$
2270   IF ANS$ = "Y" THEN GOTO 620
2280 END
2290 REM
2300 REM ********************* INTEREST RATES ******************************
2310 REM
2320 CLS
2330 INPUT "SPECIFY LOW INTEREST RATE (IN PERCENT) ",LIR
2340 INPUT "SPECIFY HIGH INTEREST RATE (IN PERCENT) ",HIR
2350   IF NH$ = "Y" THEN GOTO 2380
2360 INPUT "SPECIFY VOLATILITY ",V
2370 INPUT "SPECIFY STOCK PRICE ",S
2380  COST = 0
2390  FOR I = 1 TO K
2400   COST = COST + (CMKT(I)*N(I))
2410   NEXT I
2420  RANGE = (HIR-LIR)/20
2430  FOR J = 1 TO 20
2440   R(J) = LIR + (J-1) * RANGE
2450   R(J) = INT((R(J) + .005)*100)/100
2460   FOR I = 1 TO K
2470    R = R(J) : E = E(I) : T = T(I) : PC$ = PC$(I)
2480     GOSUB 3240
2490     C(I,J) = C
2500    NEXT I
2510   NEXT J
2520  FOR J = 1 TO 20
2530   PV(J) = 0 : PVN(J) = 0
2540    FOR I = 1 TO K
2550     PV(J) = PV(J) + (C(I,J) * N(I))
2560     PVN(J) = PV(J) - COST
2570    NEXT I
2580   PV(J) = INT((PV(J)+.005)*100)/100
2590   PVN(J) = INT ((PVN(J) + .005)*100)/100
2600   NEXT J
2610 CLS
2620 PRINT "INTEREST     POSITION     NET POSITION    INDIVIDUAL OPTION PRICES"
2630 PRINT "  RATE        VALUE          VALUE          OPT 1    OPT 2    OPT 3
     OPT 4     OPT 5"
2640 PRINT "--------     --------     ------------     -----    -----    -----
     -----     -----"
2650   FOR J = 1 TO 20
```

```
2660     PRINT R(J);TAB(12)PV(J);TAB(23);PVN(J);
2670     FOR I = 1 TO 5
2680      OPT = INT((C(I,J)+.005)*100)/100
2690      PRINT TAB(32 + I*8)OPT;
2700     NEXT I
2710  PRINT
2720     NEXT J
2730  INPUT "DO YOU WISH TO ANALYZE ANOTHER STRATEGY (Y/N)";ANS$
2740   IF ANS$ = "Y" THEN GOTO 620
2750  END
2760  REM
2770  REM ********************* VOLATILITY ********************************
2780  REM
2790  CLS
2800  INPUT "SPECIFY LOW VOLATILITY ",LV
2810  INPUT "SPECIFY HIGH VOLATILITY ",HV
2820   IF NH$ = "Y" THEN GOTO 2850
2830  INPUT "SPECIFY STOCK PRICE ",S
2840  INPUT "SPECIFY INTEREST RATE (IN PERCENT) ",R
2850   COST = 0
2860   FOR I = 1 TO K
2870    COST = COST + (CMKT(I)*N(I))
2880   NEXT I
2890   RANGE = (HV-LV)/20
2900   FOR J = 1 TO 20
2910    V(J) = LV + (J-1) * RANGE
2920    V(J) = INT((V(J) + .005)*100)/100
2930    FOR I = 1 TO K
2940     V = V(J) : E = E(I) : T = T(I) : PC$ = PC$(I)
2950      GOSUB 3240
2960      C(I,J) = C
2970     NEXT I
2980    NEXT J
2990    FOR J = 1 TO 20
3000    PV(J) = 0 : PVN(J) = 0
3010     FOR I = 1 TO K
3020      PV(J) = PV(J) + (C(I,J) * N(I))
3030      PVN(J) = PV(J) - COST
3040     NEXT I
3050    PV(J) = INT((PV(J)+.005)*100)/100
3060    PVN(J) = INT((PVN(J) + .005)*100)/100
3070     NEXT J
3080  CLS
3090  PRINT "VOLATILITY    POSITION    NET POSITION    INDIVIDUAL OPTION PRICES"
3100  PRINT "              VALUE       VALUE        OPT 1   OPT 2   OPT 3
      OPT 4   OPT 5"
3110  PRINT "----------    --------    ------------    -----   -----   -----
      -----   -----"
3120   FOR J = 1 TO 20
3130  PRINT V(J);TAB(14)PV(J);TAB(25);PVN(J);
3140    FOR I = 1 TO 5
3150     OPT =INT((C(I,J)+.005)*100)/100
3160  PRINT TAB(32 + I*8)OPT;
3170    NEXT I
```

```
3180  PRINT
3190   NEXT J
3200  INPUT "DO YOU WISH TO ANALYZE ANOTHER STRATEGY (Y/N)";ANS$
3210   IF ANS$ = "Y" THEN GOTO 620
3220  END
3230  REM
3240  REM ****************************************************************
3250  REM                        SUBROUTINE TO DO CALCULATIONS
3260  REM ****************************************************************
3270  REM
3280  REM INITIALIZE VALUES.
3290   R=R/100
3300   D=D/100
3310   T=T/365
3320  REM TEST FOR SMALL VALUES OF T.
3330   IF T >= .001 THEN GOTO 3410
3340   IF PC$ = "P" THEN GOTO 3380
3350   IF S <= E THEN C = 0 : H = 0
3360   IF S > E THEN C = S - E : H = -1
3370   GOTO 3550
3380   IF S >= E THEN C = 0 : H = 0
3390   IF S < E THEN C = E - S : H = 1
3400   GOTO 3550
3410  REM COMPUTE D1 AND D2.
3420   N2=V*SQR(T)
3430   D1=(LOG(S/E)+(R+V*V/2)*T)/N2
3440   D2=D1-N2
3450  REM
3460  REM COMPUTE H AND C
3470  REM
3480   Z=D1
3490   GOSUB 3630:REM************ COMPUTE NORMAL VALUE FOR D1 **************
3500   H=-N
3510   Z=D2
3520   GOSUB 3630:REM************ COMPUTE NORMAL VALUE FOR D2 **************
3530   C=S*(-H)-E*N*EXP(-R*T)
3540   IF PC$ = "P" THEN C=C-S+E*EXP(-R*T):H=H+1
3550   R=R*100 :REM RETURN R TO PERCENT
3560  RETURN
3570  REM
3580  REM ****************************************************************
3590  REM               SUBROUTINE TO COMPUTE NORMAL VALUES
3600  REM                  USING POLYNOMIAL APPROXIMATION
3610  REM ****************************************************************
3620  REM
3630   A6=ABS(Z)
3640   T3=1/(1+.2316419*A6)
3650   B1=.3989423*EXP(-Z*Z/2)
3660   N=(((((1.330274*T3-1.821256)*T3+1.781478)*T3-.3565638)*T3+.3193815)
3670   N=1-B1*T3*N
3680   IF Z<O THEN N=1-N : RETURN ELSE RETURN
3690  RETURN
```

Option Trading References*

Bookstaber (1981) is a professional guide to option pricing and strategies. Other general books on options include Gastineau (1979) and McMillan (1980).

The Black-Scholes option pricing model was first developed by Black and Scholes (1973). Merton (1973) derives the model under less restrictive assumptions, and extends the model for dividend-paying stocks and other complexities. A general survey of the development of the Black-Scholes formula is in Smith (1976). Adjustments in the formula to take discrete dividends into account are developed by Roll (1977) and Whaley (1981). Modifications in the Black-Scholes formula to better fit the return characteristics of stocks may be found in Jarrow and Rudd (1982) and Rubinstein (1983).

Empirical tests of the Black-Scholes formula include Galai (1977), Chiras and Manaster (1978), MacBeth and Merville (1979), and Geske and Roll (1983).

The binomial approach was first suggested by Sharpe (1978), and was developed by Rendleman and Bartter (1979) and Cox, Ross, and Rubinstein (1979). Other discrete-time approaches based on numerical procedures include Parkinson (1977) and Brennan and Schwartz (1977).

The extreme value method of estimating volatility from past price is developed by Parkinson (1980). The extension of the extreme point method to the high-low-close estimator is in Garman and Klass (1980). An econometric approach to the optimal weighting of close-to-close and high-low volatility estimators is presented by Beckers (1983).

The use of implied volatilities was first applied in empirical work by Latane and Rendleman (1976). Further work on the use of implicit volatilities is presented by Beckers (1981).

*Complete citations can be found in the bibliography at the back of this book.

Glossary

Accretion—The increase in bond value resulting from the movement of the bond toward par value at maturity.

Accrued interest—The interest due from the issue date or from the last coupon payment to the present on an interest-bearing security. The buyer of a bond pays the accrued interest to the seller.

American option—A put or call option that can be exercised any time on or before the expiration date. Options listed on the option exchanges are American options. See also European option.

Arbitrage—Buying a security in one market while simultaneously selling it in another market at a higher price. Arbitrage leads to a profit with no risk and with no net investment. Popular usage of the term includes transactions where the position in one security is hedged by taking a position in a set of other securities that closely match the returns of the first. Such transactions may involve some risk, and so, strictly speaking, are not arbitrage transactions. Examples of such an arbitrage transaction include the cash-and-carry transaction in the bond market, covered interest arbitrage in the foreign exchange market, as well as a number of option strategies.

Asked price—The quoted price at which a security is offered for sale.

At the money—An option with an exercise price equal to the current market price of the underlying security.

Bankers discount—A discount calculated by subtracting the percentage discount from the face value of the bond. For example, a Treasury bill with a face value of one million dollars, one year to maturity, and selling at a discount of 10.5% will have a price of $1,000,000(1 − .105) = $895,000.

Basis—The price difference between a cash and futures instrument. Also used as the difference between the price of two securities used in creating a spread (i.e., the net value of a spread).

Basis point—One one-hundredth of a percent.

Bearish—A belief that prices are going to decline.

Beta—A measure of the risk of a stock relative to the risk of the overall market. The beta of a stock shows how much the stock will move, on average, with a given movement in the market. For example, a beta of 1.5 means that if the market return is 10%, the stock will on average be expected to have a return of 15%.

Bid price—The quoted price for buying a security.

Bullish—A belief that prices are going to rise.

Callable bond—A bond that can be redeemed prior to maturity upon payment of a specified call price.

Call option—An option that gives the buyer the right to purchase the underlying asset at a specified price (called the exercise price or the striking price), on or before a given date (called the expiration date). In the case of a call option on a stock, the holder has the right to buy 100 shares of the underlying stock. The exact features of the purchase right differ for options on other securities. See also American option, European option.

Carry—The interest cost in financing a position in a security.

Cash-and-carry transaction—A strategy involving taking a position in the cash security and taking the opposite position in the futures contract. The cash security is either purchased, leading to a positive carrying cost because of the cost of financing the position, or the cash security is shorted, leading to a negative carrying cost because of the return that can be generated by lending out the proceeds of the short sale. The cash position is then closed out at a later date by using the futures contract.

Cash market—The market in which securities are traded for immediate delivery. This is in contrast to the futures market, where a contract is made for deferred delivery. The cash market is also called the spot market. In practice, the actual delivery in the spot market may be delayed several days from the time of the order.

Collateral—An obligation or security used to secure performance. For example, an investor with a short position may deposit securities as a guarantee for meeting the payment required of that short position.

Convertible bond—A bond that includes a provision that allows the holder to convert the bond into a fixed number of shares of stock.

Coupon—A periodic interest payment the bond issuer promises to pay the bondholder. The coupon is a fixed amount, usually paid semi-annually, and is expressed as a percentage of the bond's face value. A bond with a face value of $1000 with coupon payments amounting to $70 annually would have a 7% coupon rate.

Covered—Taking a position that assures the obligation generated from an investment strategy can be met. For example, an option writer can be covered by holding the underlying stock, since he will then have the stock available to deliver if the option is exercised.

Current yield—The yield of a bond calculated by taking the annual coupon payment as a percentage of the current market bond price.

Default—The failure to make payments of interest or principal on a bond. The bond indenture agreement usually specifies that default gives the bond holders claim to the assets of the firm.

Delta—The net exposure of an option position, measured by the change in the value of the position that will result from a change in the price of the underlying security. If an option will change by half a point with a one-point change in the stock, then the option has a delta of .5.

Dilution—The reduction in the value of the equity of a firm that results by the firm issuing additional shares of stock. For example, if a firm with one million shares outstanding issues another million shares of stock without receiving any proceeds from the issue, the value of each share of stock will be reduced by 50%. A shareholder who initially had a claim to one-one millionth of the firm will now have a claim to one-two millionth of the firm. Dilution can result from the exercise of warrants or convertible bonds.

Discount bond—A bond that is selling below par value. A pure discount bond is a bond that pays par value at maturity, with no interest or coupon payments made before maturity. Treasury bills are an example of a short-term pure discount instrument.

Diversification—Reducing risk by spreading investments out among a number of securities that do not move closely with each other.

Efficient markets hypothesis—The hypothesis that all information is fully reflected by the current market price, and that therefore unusually high profits cannot be generated by speculative trading.

European option—A put or a call option that can only be exercised on the expiration date. Options listed on the option exchanges are American options, not European options. However, the European option, by restricting the possible time of exercise, provides a useful construct for developing option pricing models. See also American option.

Exdividend date—The date on which the ownership of a dividend on stock is determined. Owners of the stock at the time of the exdividend date receive the dividend payment. As a result, other things equal, the stock price drops on the exdividend date by approximately the amount of the dividend payment, since those purchasing the stock after that date do not receive the payment.

Exercise price—The price at which an option can be exercised. For a call option, it is the price at which the security underlying the option can be purchased. For a put option, it is the price at which the underlying security can be sold.

Expiration date—The date after which the option is void.

Face value—See Par value.

Foreign exchange rate—The rate at which one currency trades for another currency. If a British Pound Sterling (denoted by the symbol £) costs $2.00, then the dollar/pound exchange rate would be $2.00/£.

Forward contract—A contract that gives the buyer the obligation to deliver the underlying security or asset at a specified price on a specified future date. Similarly, the seller of a forward contract has the obligation to sell the underlying security or asset under the terms of the contract. Unlike a futures contract, there is no margin requirement or marking to the market. Cash settlement for any changes in the asset value are made only on the maturity date.

Fundamental system—A trading system that relies on firm-related information, such as earnings reports, the debt/equity ratio, and other accounting data. It also uses general economic information, such as Federal Reserve data and interest rate levels.

Futures contract—A contract that gives the buyer the obligation to deliver the underlying security or asset at a specified price (the futures price), on a specified future date (the maturity date). Similarly, the seller of a futures contract has the obligation to sell the underlying security or asset under the terms of the contract. A futures contract has a margin requirement to assure performance, and also has daily marking to the market to settle for variations in the futures price. See also Forward contract.

Hedge—Taking an investment position to reduce the risk of another position. For example, a short position in one futures contract may be hedged by taking a long position in another futures contract that moves closely with the first contract, or by buying the spot asset that underlies the futures contract. Or, an option position may be hedged by taking an opposing position in another option that moves closely with the first option, or by holding the underlying security according to the neutral hedge ratio.

Implied volatility—The stock volatility that would equate the option price arising from an option pricing formula with the market price.

In the money—An option with intrinsic value. For a call option, an option with an exercise price that is below the current stock price. For a put option, an option with an exercise price that is above the current stock price.

Intrinsic value of an option—For a call option, the intrinsic value is the current price of the underlying security minus the exercise price of the option. For a put option, the exercise price of the option minus the current price of the underlying security. For example, a call option with an exercise price of $50 will have an intrinsic value of $5 if the current stock price is $55. The intrinsic value of an option cannot be less than zero.

Long—Having a net positive position, or having ownership, of a security.

Margin—The deposit required to collateralize an investment position. Margin is required for futures contracts and for the writing of options. The margin requirement may usually be met by the deposit of stock or interest-bearing securities.

Mark to the market—If a futures or option position requiring margin moves against the investor, additional margin is required to mark the investor's account to the market.

Naked option writing—See Option writing.

Neutral hedge—A hedge position that eliminates any profit or loss from small price changes in the underlying security. For example, if a call option moves half a point for a one-point movement in the stock (so the call option has a delta of .5), then a hedge position consisting of buying 50 shares of stock and writing one call option will be unaffected by small changes in the price of the stock. With this position, the price movement in the option position will exactly counteract the price movement of the stock. The option in this case will have a *neutral hedge ratio* of −.5.

Offer price—See Asked price.

Open interest—The number of listed futures contracts or option contracts outstanding at a particular time.

Option writing—Issuing an option contract, and thereby taking on the obligation to buy the underlying security (in the case of a put option) or sell the underlying security (in the case of a call option) at the specified exercise price at the option of the option buyer. The option writer receives the option premium for writing the contract. A covered writer holds the security underlying the option contract as a hedge for his position, while a naked writer does not hold the underlying security as a hedge.

Out of the money—An option with no intrinsic value. For a call option, an option with an exercise price that is above the current stock price. For a put option, an option with an exercise price that is below the current stock price.

Par value—The principal amount the issuer of a bond agrees to pay when redeeming the bond at maturity.

Portfolio—A set of securities held by an investor.

Premium—For a bond, the amount by which the market price of the bond exceeds the bond's par value. For an option, the premium is the current market price of the option. It is also occasionally used to refer to the difference between the market price of an option and its intrinsic value.

Random walk hypothesis—See Efficient markets hypothesis.

Repurchase rate—The rate of return generated when the holder of securities sells the securities with an agreement to repurchase the securities at a fixed price on a fixed date. In effect, the holder is lending the securities, and the difference between the price paid for the securities and the price at which the securities will be repurchased generates a return for the loan.

Repo Rate—See Repurchase rate.

Risk-free asset—An hypothetical asset that gives a known and certain interest payment with no risk of default. The riskless asset is used extensively in pricing securities and in constructing investment strategies. The best counterpart to the riskless asset in the marketplace is the Treasury bill.

Short—Having a net negative position in a security, a position that requires the purchase of the security in order to be closed. See also Short sale.

Short sale—The sale of a security that the investor does not own. A short sale will be profitable if the security price declines, since the investor can then cover the short sale by buying the security at a lower price than the price at which it was initially sold.

Spot market—See Cash market.

Spread—A position consisting of counteracting positions in related securities. For example, an option spread may consist of a long position in one option and a short position in another option on the same stock but with a different time to expiration or a different exercise price. A futures spread may consist of a long position in one futures and a short position in another futures with a different time to maturity.

Striking price—See Exercise price.

Swap—Selling one security issue while simultaneously buying another issue. Swaps are generally done in the bond and the foreign exchange market.

Technical system—A trading system that relies on market-generated data, such as security prices, short-sales information, and trading volume.

Transaction costs—The costs associated with executing a trade. These include the commissions charged by the broker, as well as the costs reflected in the bid-asked spread.

Treasury bill—A discount bond issued by the U.S. Treasury. Treasury bills are issued with maturities of three months, six months, and one year. They are pure discount instruments, making no interest payments. Treasury bills are priced according to a bankers discount. See also Bankers discount.

Treasury bond—A coupon-paying, long-term bond issued by the U.S. Treasury. Treasury bonds have ten or more years to maturity at the time of issue. Coupon payments are made semi-annually.

Warrant—A call option issued by a firm. A warrant generally has over one year to expiration at the time of issue, and often is issued in conjunction with other securities. Upon the exercise of a warrant, the number of shares of stock in the firm is increased to meet the obligation. This generally results in a dilution of the value of the stock. This is in contrast to listed call options, where no additional shares are issued upon exercise.

Writing—See Option writing.

Yield to maturity—The rate of return of a bond when the bond is held to maturity, and when both interest payments and capital gains or losses are taken into account.

Bibliography

Appel, G. and M. E. Zweig. *New Directions in Technical Analysis.* Great Neck, N.Y.: Signalert, 1976.

Beckers, S. "Standard Deviations Implied in Option Prices as Predictors of Future Stock Price Variability." *Journal of Banking and Finance 5* (September 1981): 363–382.

Beckers, S. "Variances of Security Price Returns Based on High, Low, and Closing Prices." *Journal of Business 56* (January 1983): 97–112.

Bierwag, G. O. "Immunization, Duration and the Term Structure of Interest Rates." *Journal of Financial and Quantitative Analysis 12* (December 1977): 725–742.

Bierwag, G. O., G. Kaufman, and A. Toeus. "Duration: Its Development and Use in Bond Portfolio Management." *Financial Analysts Journal* (July–August 1983): 15–35.

Bierwag, G. O., and C. Khang. "An Immunization Strategy is a Minimax Strategy." *Journal of Finance 34* (May 1979): 389–399.

Black, F., and M. Scholes. "The Pricing of Options and Corporate Liabilities." *Journal of Political Economy 81* (May 1973): 637–654.

Bookstaber, R. *Option Pricing and Strategies in Investing.* Reading, Mass.: Addison-Wesley, 1981.

Bookstaber, R., and R. Clarke. "Options Can Alter Portfolio Distributions." *Journal of Portfolio Management. 7* (Spring 1981): 63–70.

Bookstaber, R., and R. Clarke. "An Algorithm to Calculate the Return Distribution of Portfolios with Option Positions." *Management Science* (April 1983a): 419–429.

Bookstaber, R., and R. Clarke. *Option Strategies for Institutional Investment Management.* Reading, Mass.: Addison-Wesley, 1983b.

Brennan, M., and E. Schwartz. "The Valuation of American Put Options." *Journal of Finance 32* (May 1977): 449–462.

Chiras, D., and S. Manaster. "The Information Content of Option Prices and a Test of Market Efficiency." *Jounal of Financial Economics 6* (March 1978): 213–234.

Christensen, P., S. Feldstein, and F. Fabozzi. "Bond Portfolio Immunization." In *The Handbook of Fixed Income Securities,* F. Fabozzi and I. Pollack, eds. Homewood, Ill.: Dow Jones-Irwin, 1983, pp. 801–817.

Clews, H. *Fifty Years in Wall Street.* New York: Irving Publishing, 1908.

Cootner, P. *The Random Character of Stock Market Prices.* Cambridge, Mass.: MIT Press, 1964.

Cox, J. C., S. A. Ross, and M. Rubinstein. "Option Pricing: A Simplified Approach." *Journal of Financial Economics 7* (1979): 229–263.

Edwards, R. D., and J. Magee. *Technical Analysis of Stock Trends.* Springfield, Mass.: John Magee, 1948.

Elliot, R. N. *The Wave Principle.* New York: Elliot, 1938.

Elton, E. J., and M. J. Gruber. *Modern Portfolio Theory and Investment Analysis,* 2nd Edition. New York: John Wiley & Sons, 1984.

Fama, E. F. "Efficient Capital Markets: A Review of Theory and Empirical Work." *Journal of Finance* (May 1970): 383–417.

Farrell, J. L., Jr. *Guide to Portfolio Management.* New York: McGraw-Hill, 1983.

Fisher, L. and R. L. Weil. "Coping With the Risk of Interest-Rate Fluctuations: Returns to Bond Holders From Naive and Optimal Strategies." *Journal of Business 44* (October 1971): 408–431.

Fosback, N. G. *Stock Market Logic.* Fort Lauderdale, Fl.: Institute for Econometric Research, 1976.

Fowler, W. W. *Ten Years in Wall Street.* Hartford: Worthington, Dustin & Co., 1870.

Francis, J. G. *Investments.* New York: McGraw-Hill, 1984.

Frenkel, J. A. and R. M. Levich. "Transaction Costs and Interest Arbitrage: Tranquil versus Turbulent Periods." *Journal of Political Economy* (December 1977): 1209–1226.

Galai, D. "Tests of Market Efficiency of the Chicago Board Options Exchange." *Journal of Business* (April 1977): 167–197.

Gann, W. D. *The Basis of My Forecasting Method for Grain.* Pomeroy, WA: Lambert-Gann, 1976a.

Gann, W. D. *How to Make Profits in Commodities.* Pomeroy, WA: Lambert-Gann, 1976b.

Garbade, K. *Securities Markets.* New York: McGraw-Hill, 1982.

Garman, M., and M. Klass. "On the Estimation of Security Price Volatilities from Historical Data. *Journal of Business 53* (January 1980): 67–78.

Gastineau, G. *The Stock Options Manual.* New York: McGraw-Hill, 1979.

Geske, R. and R. Roll. "On Valving American Call Options with the Black-Scholes European Formula," *Journal of Finance 39* (June 1984): 443–456.

Gordon, M. *The Investment, Financing, and Valuation of the Corporation.* Homewood, Ill.: Richard D. Irwin, 1962.

Graham, B., D. Dodd, and S. Cottle. *Security Analysis Principles and Techniques*, 4th edition. New York: McGraw Hill, 1962.

Holley, J. L., C. Beidleman, and J. Greenleaf. "Does Covered Interest Arbitrage Dominate in Foreign Exchange Markets?" *Columbia Journal of World Business.* (Winter 1979): 99–107.

Homer, S., and M. Leibowitz. *Inside the Yield Book.* Englewood Cliffs, N.J.: Prentice-Hall, 1972.

Ibbotson, R., and R. Sinquefield. "Stocks, Bonds, Bills, and Inflation: Year-by-Year Historical Returns (1926–1974)." *Journal of Business 49* (January 1976): 11–47.

Ingersoll, J. "A Contingent-Claims Valuation of Convertible Securities." *Journal of Financial Economics 4* (May 1977a): 289–322.

Ingersoll, J. "An Examination of Corporate Call Policies on Convertible Securities." *Journal of Finance 32* (May 1977b): 463–478.

Jarrow, R., and A. Rudd. "Approximate Option Valuation for Arbitrary Stochastic Processes." *Journal of Financial Economics 10* (1982): 347–369.

Jensen, M. C. "Risk, the Pricing of Capital Assets and the Evaluation of Investment Portfolios." *Journal of Business* (April 1969): 167–247.

Jensen, M. C. "Capital Markets: Theory and Evidence." *Bell Journal of Economics and Management Science.* (Autumn 1972): 357–398.

Kaufman, P. J. *Commodity Trading Systems and Methods.* New York: John Wiley & Sons, 1978.

Kidder Reports: A Research Publication, New York: William Kidder.

Klemkosky, R., and B. Resnick. "Put-Call Parity and Market Efficiency." *Journal of Finance 34* (December 1979): 1141–1156.

Latane, H., and R. Rendleman. "Standard Deviations of Stock Price Ratios Implied in Option Prices." *Journal of Finance 31* (May 1976): 369–381.

Lefevre, E. *Reminiscences of a Stock Operator.* New York: George H. Doran, 1923.

Leibowitz, M., and A. Weinberger. "Contingent Immunization: Part I." *Financial Analysts Journal* (November–December 1982): 2–16.

Lintner, J. "Security Prices, Risk, and Maximal Gains from Diversification." *Journal of Finance* (December, 1965): 587–615.

Lorie, J. H., and M. T. Hamilton. *The Stock Market: Theories and Evidence.* Homewood, Ill.: Richard D. Irwin, 1974.

Macaulay, F. R. *Some Theoretical Problems Suggested by the Movements of Interest Rates, Bond Yields, and Stock Prices in the U.S. Since 1856.* New York: National Bureau of Economic Research, 1938.

MacBeth, J., and L. Merville. "An Empirical Examination of the Black-Scholes Call Option Pricing Model." *Journal of Finance 34* (December 1979): 1173–1186.

McMillan, L. G. *Options as A Strategic Investment.* New York: New York Institute of Finance, 1980.

Markowitz, H. "Portfolio Selection." *Journal of Finance*. (March 1952): 77–91.

Markowitz, H. *Portfolio Selection: Efficient Diversification of Investments*. New York: John Wiley & Sons, 1959.

Merton, R. "Theory of Rational Option Pricing." *Bell Journal of Economics and Management Science 4* (Spring 1973): 141–183.

Merton, R., M. Scholes, and M. Gladstein. "The Return and Risk of Alternative Call Option Portfolio Investment Strategies." *Journal of Business 51* (1978): 183–242.

Merton, R., M. Scholes, and M. Gladstein. "The Returns and Risks of Alternative Put Option Portfolio Investment Strategies." *Journal of Business 55* (January 1982): 1–55.

Modigliani, F. and G. Pogue. "An Introduction to Risk and Return." *Financial Analysts Journal* (March–April 1974): 68–86.

Molodovsky, N., C. May, and S. Chottiner. "Common Stock Valuation: Theory and Tables." *Financial Analysts Journal* (March–April 1965): 104–123.

Mossin, J. "Equilibrium in a Capital Asset Market." *Econometrica 34* (October 1966): 768–783.

Parkinson, M. "Option Pricing: The American Put." *Journal of Business 50* (January 1977): 21–36.

Parkinson, M. "The Extreme Value Method for Estimating the Variance of the Rate of Return." *Journal of Business 53* (January 1980): 61–65.

Platt, R., and G. Latainer. "Risk-Return Tradeoffs of Contingent Insurance Strategies for Active Bond Portfolios." *Financial Analysts Journal* (May–June 1984): 34–39.

Rendleman, R., and B. Bartter. "Two-State Option Pricing." *Journal of Finance 34* (December 1979): 1093–1110.

Roll, R. "A Critique of the Asset Pricing Theory's Tests." *Journal of Financial Economics* (March 1977): 129–176.

Ross, S. "Options and Efficiency." *Quarterly Journal of Economics 90* (February 1976): 75–89.

Rubinstein, M. "Displaced Diffusion Option Pricing." *Journal of Finance 38* (March 1983): 213–217.

Rubinstein, M. and L. Hayne. "Replicating Options with Positions in Stock and Cash." *Financial Analysts Journal* (July–August 1981): 63–72.

Seix, C. "Bond Swaps." In *The Handbook of Fixed Income Securities*, F. Fabozzi and I. Pollack, eds. Homewood, Ill.: Dow & Jones-Irwin, 1983, pp. 735–742.

Sharpe, W. F. "A Simplified Model for Portfolio Analysis." *Management Science* (January 1963): 277–293.

Sharpe, W. F. "Capital Asset Prices: A Theory of Market Equilibrium Under Conditions of Risk." *Journal of Finance* (September 1964): 425–442.

Sharpe, W. F. *Investments*. Englewood Cliffs, N.J.: Prentice-Hall, 1978.

Smith, C. "Option Pricing: A Review." *Journal of Financial Economics 3* (March 1976): 3–51.

Stigum, M. *The Money Market: Myth, Reality, and Practice*. Homewood, Ill.: Dow Jones-Irwin, 1978.

Stigum, M. *Money Market Calculations: Yields, Break-Evens, and Arbitrage*. Homewood, Ill.: Dow Jones-Irwin, 1981.

Stoll, H. R. "The Relationship Between Put and Call Option Prices." *Journal of Finance 24* (1969): 802–824.

Treynor, J., and F. Black. "How to Use Security Analysis to Improve Portfolio Selection." *Journal of Business* (January 1973): 66–86.

Vasicek, O. A., and J. A. McQuown. "The Efficient Market Model." *Financial Analysts Journal* (September–October 1972): 71–84.

Waters, J. J., and L. Williams. "Measuring Market Momentum." *Commodities Magazine* (October 1972): 92–103.

Whaley, R. "On The Valuation of American Call Options on Stocks with Known Dividends." *Journal of Financial Economics 9* (1981): 207–211.

Wilder, J. W., Jr. *New Concepts in Technical Trading Systems* Greensboro, N.C.: Trend Research, 1978.

Williams. J. B. *The Theory of Investment Value.* Amsterdam: North-Holland Publishing, 1958.

Williams, L. R. *How I Made One Million Dollars . . . Last Year . . . Trading Commodities.* Carmel Valley, Calif.: Conceptual Management, 1973.

Index